D0411625

Soft Power

By Robert Winder

Bloody Foreigners:
The Story of Immigration to Britain

The Final Act of Mr Shakespeare

Open Secrets:
The Extraordinary Battle for the 2009 Open

The Last Wolf:
The Hidden Springs of Englishness

Soft Power:
The New Great Game

Soft Power

The New Great Game

ROBERT WINDER

Little, Brown

LITTLE, BROWN

First published in Great Britain in 2020 by Little, Brown

1 3 5 7 9 10 8 6 4 2

A CIP catalogue record for this book
is available from the British Library.

Hardback ISBN 978-1-4087-1146-0

Typeset in Bembo by M Rules
Printed and bound in Great Britain by Clays Ltd, Elcograf S.p.A.

Papers used by Little, Brown are from well-managed forests
and other responsible sources.

Little, Brown
An imprint of
Little, Brown Book Group
Carmelite House
50 Victoria Embankment
London EC4Y 0DZ

An Hachette UK Company
www.hachette.co.uk

www.littlebrown.co.uk

To Hermione, Luke & Kit

Contents

Introduction

The New Great Game

On Monday 2 July 2018, in the sunny Russian port of Rostov-on-Don, a group of Japanese footballers demonstrated that it really was possible to turn the worst of times into the best of times. A few moments earlier they had been pounding the turf after losing their World Cup quarter-final against Belgium. In the final minutes of a jittery game (they had snatched a 2–0 lead against much the more fancied team) they tensed up, surrendered their advantage and went out to an agonising last-gasp goal.

It was excruciating. Up in the stands, their supporters wept.

What happened next was unusual. Football is not synonymous with good conduct – players eff and blind as a matter of routine, and the usual reaction of fans at such moments is to smash something. Japan broke with this tradition. First, by way of an apology, the players gave a ceremonious bow to thank their supporters. Then, safe in their dressing room, they showered, rolled up their sleeves and . . . tidied up.

Photographs of their handiwork appeared in the following day's papers, to global acclaim. The dressing room was immaculate. Where was the blood on the wall, the torn curtain, the dent where a stricken player had thumped his fist? Where was the angry graffiti, the hurled boot, the vandalised drinks machine, the spray of beer? Not a hint of such ructions: professional cleaners could not have left it more spotless.

There was even a thank-you card on the white table in the centre of the room, the neat Cyrillic script done with the attention and discipline of a calligrapher.

The footballers may have been inspired by their fans, who a few days earlier had stunned the world in the same way. A tournament braced for fights between hooligans and police was confronted instead by the sight of scrupulous Japanese tourists, some in samurai-style headbands, conscientiously sweeping their leftovers into bin liners. They sparked a trend: Senegal's fans were soon following suit.

It was an object lesson in how to accept defeat. But there was another lesson too. The mopping-up operation was one in the eye for the assumption, common in today's sporting culture, that victory was all that counted, that second place was for wimps. It said that, on the contrary, there could still be victory in defeat. In the era of winning ugly, Japan was reminding the world of a quality that seemed to have been lost or mislaid in the rush to triumph at any cost: the art of losing with good grace.

To anyone who had visited a bookshop in the previous year it was not a complete surprise. Thanks to Marie Kondo, Japan was renowned for its tidiness. In a series of bestsellers, she had urged readers to streamline their homes not by looking for things to discard but by retaining only such objects as delivered a 'spark of joy' – the path of monastic renunciation and self-discipline. Readers everywhere were happy to overlook the risks of taking advice from someone who confessed to having been addicted to household magazines since the age of five: world book sales passed the three million mark. Charity shops took in huge piles of surplus-to-requirements domestic life. For storage reasons, in a nice twist, even *shelves* flew off the shelves.

Kondo's timing was neat, coinciding as it did with a sense that consumer society was drowning in too many possessions. Decluttering became a global fetish (though it made authors anxious, since it seemed to involve managing without books). It inspired a blizzard of newspaper and magazine articles (all of which would have to be thrown away in due course) before becoming a Netflix television series.

Some dismissed the concept as a fad, pointing out that the pleasures of tidying up – the ascetic belief that less could be more – had been a staple of modern design for years (imagine no possessions). So perhaps it wasn't the message so much as the messenger: Kondo herself. She certainly fitted the bill: petite, smiling and clean as a new pin. The personal, it turned out, wasn't just political; it was commercial as well.

But above all she was Japanese. Had her message been a branch of American self-help or Swedish ergonomics it might not have struck so deep a chord, but in Kondo's hands it seemed to draw from some ancient, spiritual well. She had spent five years as an attendant at a Shinto shrine, and while few of her readers could have said exactly what that was, it added profundity to the business of clearing up.

Confirmation that this was not a one-off, but a cultural fact, came when a young Japanese golfer, Hinako Shibuno, won the 2019 Women's British Open, smiling and eating sweets all the way, and when Japanese volunteers touchingly sang the national songs of their visiting guests in the Rugby World Cup later that year.

Shintoism involves a heightened reverence for nature, a transcendent mentality that dovetails well with the eco-friendly *zeitgeist*. Some of that purity seemed to inform even the footballers' dressing room. The match was lost, but something greater was gained. In the era of viral media and instant acclaim, the footballers did more for the national image than a thousand diplomatic initiatives could have achieved. Japan, for years a major presence in global politeness, was now the undisputed world leader.

The incident certainly resonated in Britain, which liked to see itself (despite growing evidence to the contrary) as the motherland of sportsmanship. The *Daily Mail* hailed Japan as 'an example' to us all, while the *Sun* said it 'won the hearts' of the whole world. The world agreed. The Japanese, wrote *Esquire*, were the 'true champions'; ESPN felt that they had handed out 'a lesson in manners'; the *Times of India* called them 'classy'; the *Malaysian Digest* hailed them as the 'true winners'. The whole episode had been 'incredible . . . immaculate . . . a new standard'.

The modern world has a name for this kind of friendly initiative: 'soft power'. It is a common term – almost a modern cliché – and hardly a recent discovery: people have long known that creating goodwill was as important as winning wars. The Greek temples on the shores of Turkey and Sicily remind us that early civilisations planted versions of themselves in foreign lands, while Indonesia's name tells us that people from the Indus Valley had a hand in its early life. Ever since nations began, the quiet or noisy exercise of national charm has been a factor in their calculations.

When Roosevelt advised that great powers should speak softly and carry big sticks, he was not, in other words, saying anything that people didn't already know.[1]

Yet the phrase itself – soft power – is of relatively recent coinage. The American foreign affairs scholar Professor Joseph Nye minted it in a 1990 essay on leadership, and explored it further in a series of articles and books. His argument was simple: at a time when America felt its geopolitical influence to be fading, it should not forget the extent of its cultural projection – its 'soft' power. This, he suggested, was the third great player in international affairs, tucked in behind military and financial prowess.

It was the art of capturing hearts and minds without using the usual weapons: guns or money. It was the magnetic force field of culture, lifestyle, history, heritage and political values, and it was a refreshing advance on the traditional, manly model of diplomacy (which involved missiles) in favour of a more collaborative – might one say more feminine? – approach. It was not be underestimated.

What was it, though? In Nye's view it was nothing less than 'the ability to shape the preferences of others' not through direct pressure or bribery but by subtler means. It was the power of carrots over sticks, of persuasion over force; perhaps even more than that, since carrots were coercive, too. After the wild-eyed era of mutually assured destruction, nations needed to fight fire not with fire but with high-quality soil and with moisture; with charm, not threats. 'You can coerce,' insisted Nye, 'you can induce ... with payments; or you can attract and co-opt.'[2]

Winston Churchill had once called diplomacy the knack of

---

1 Roosevelt once referred to this as a West African proverb, a sign that it was a resonant piece of ancient wisdom – though no one was able to locate its origin.

2 In this he was revisiting the recipe laid down by the historian E. H. Carr in 1939, which identified three sorts of power: military, economic and 'power over opinion'.

persuading people to go to hell in such a way that they would thank you and ask for directions, and perhaps that was soft power's purpose too.[3] Some argued that to be 'colonised' by foreign corporations was as demoralising, in its insidious way, as being subdued by a military machine (witness the profits that flowed from selling cigarettes to emerging countries, or the evasive tax affairs of the digital super-companies), but most, given the choice, preferred to be overwhelmed by a fizzy drink than by an aircraft carrier.

It gave rise to a new notion in human affairs we might call 'feather-bombing'.

The notion caught on fast in the passageways of diplomacy. 'I can think of no more valuable asset to our country,' said Colin Powell, Washington's National Security Advisor, 'than the friendship of future world leaders who have been educated here.' David Petraeus, commander of America's forces in Iraq, agreed: 'I like to go to bed every night with more friends and fewer enemies.' Nearly every global leader said something similar – even if they did not always mean it.

And these were the words of generals, not political scientists. Hadn't Western values toppled the Berlin Wall? Hadn't India and China, the two powers-in-waiting, finally seen the free-market light? The war of ideas seemed to have been won. In the twentieth century the world had been skewered on the conflict between fascism, communism and liberal democracy. Following the collapse of the Soviet Union, and the economic surge of China, it appeared that only the last of these was still standing. All over the world dictatorships were turning to democracy, planned economies were embracing private enterprise, material standards of living were climbing, and both human and environmental rights were gaining traction (although, ironically, they were often quickest to turn their firepower on the political systems that inspired and sustained them). Supranational institutions mushroomed so fast that some pundits went so far as to declare the nation state a dead – or at least a dying – duck. Francis Fukuyama

---

3 He may or may not have said this: hardly anyone is more routinely credited with stray witticisms. And if it wasn't Churchill, it must have been Mark Twain.

referred to this, in a famous essay, as 'the end of history', and
while events such as 9/11, Islamic terrorism and the amazing surge
of China soon made this look like empty rhetoric, it did seem that
the set of ideas behind liberal-minded, market-driven globalism
had indeed won the day. In itself, that was a dramatic enactment
of soft power's ability to change the world.

Once Joseph Nye had put his finger on the idea, allusions to soft
power began to crop up everywhere. In proposing that it was
possible to mould others without attempting to subjugate them,
it was attractive to governments, and they rushed to commission
conferences and papers on how best to make use of it. But there
was a problem. Soft power was complicated, and not entirely a
matter of government policy. It could be made or shaken by spontaneous incidents as much as by official projects. Just as a needless
act of consideration by Japanese footballers could enhance the
national brand, so one violent loner (Anders Breivik) could alter
the world's view of Norway.

Soft power had two different meanings. On the official or
conscious level it was a government project designed to culti-
vate good relations overseas. But it was also something deeper: a
nation's overall glow. Government could take the helm and trim
the canvas, but it was the pilot, not the ship – and certainly not
the ocean.

This led to confusion in the think tanks: people found themselves talking at cross purposes, some taking soft power to be an
urgent policy matter, others feeling that it was out of their hands.
Politicians represented only one part of what a country had to
offer: a nation's standing in the world was no longer measured by
its foreign policy or the size of its fleet. Cheerfulness, politeness
and humour counted, too.

In the end it boiled down to something simple: whether a
country was liked.

Even elevated discussions foundered in this gap between soft
power as a political tool and soft power as part of the national
scenery. As a result, not everyone joined the bandwagon. Some
(*realpoliticians*) deemed it too, well, *soft* to count for much at all: it
was a 'weapon of mass distraction'. They cited Stalin's notorious

quip about the Vatican ('How many divisions has the Pope?') and Mao's equally famous line that power rested only in the barrel of a gun. Undeterred by the fact that these were the maxims of tyrants, many leaders agreed.[4] 'Soft power alone is really no power at all,' said the (Danish) Secretary-General of NATO, Anders Fogh Rasmussen.

That is what one might expect. But non-military voices said the same thing. When Barack Obama entered the White House in 2008, the historian Paul Kennedy (author of *The Rise and Fall of the Great Powers*) cautioned *Guardian* readers that even Obama's fine words might amount to no more than mood music. 'Soft power cannot pay for foreign oil and gas, imported cars, electronic goods, kitchenware and children's toys ... Great nations cannot survive on soft power alone.'

Diplomats were rattled, too. They looked back fondly to the time when, if they wanted to chew the fat with Austria, Kenya or Indonesia, they knew whom to ring: they had (literally) opposite numbers. A dispersed global world of four billion mobile phones was harder to control.

But soft power's advocates never pretended that it could make old-fashioned power obsolete. In the case of imperial Europe it was clearly the camp follower of colonial rule, arriving in its baggage train. The English language crossed the waves in imperial ships; the missionaries who took Anglican values to the tropics were escorted by redcoats; the world hummed with cricket and Shakespeare because they were planted by colonists and settlers. Catholicism sailed to South America with the conquistadores; communism entered Eastern Europe in tanks.

So it swiftly became a major component of international relations. Given the rise of automation and information technology, the value of close, quick connections was obvious.[5] Whether it was multinationals seeking workers, exporters after markets,

---

4 Vladimir Putin may have had Stalin's dismissive sneer in mind when in 2019 his motorcade of armoured cars swept into the Vatican exactly one hour late. When he met the Queen in 2013 he kept her waiting for only thirteen minutes.

5 This was a large subject to sum up in one anecdote, but when Blockbuster Video (85,000 employees) was more or less made obsolete by Netflix (5000 employees) the scale of the challenge became clear.

broadcasters chasing audiences, universities seeking students, churches reaching for converts or football clubs in search of fans, soft power grew more salient every day.

Globalisation had lifted more than a billion people out of poverty and improved their lives in many ways – a heady achievement. But it also looked like a dangerous experiment with the health of the planet, and in some ways appeared to be little more than a get-rich-quick scheme. Within nations there seemed to be more trickle *up* than trickle down. Globalisation had produced a world 'order' that increasingly looked like an exclusive fraternity, preening in five-star luxury while the majority struggled. It was reported that in America the top 0.1 per cent, which a decade earlier had earned a handsome 2 per cent of the national income, now earned a dizzy 5 per cent.

Percentages of this sort were numb beside the anecdotal evidence that supported arguments against inequality around the world. From Chile and Ecuador to Spain and France, these movements were united by economic grievances. A rise in fuel prices here ... a hike in bus fares there ... these were only the surface triggers. Even the student-led protestors of Hong Kong were in part reacting to the fact that they were living four to a broom cupboard with little prospect of a better future. From vantage points like this, globalisation was simply pushing the good life further and further into the distance.

The new levels of super-wealth only added insult to injury. It was reported that the world's second richest man, Bernard Arnault, controller of a luxury goods empire that included LVMH and Christian Dior, was now worth $107 *billion*, while the richest (Amazon's founder Jeff Bezos, with $125 billion) was splashing out on his own trip to the moon and the most expensive house ever seen in Los Angeles.[6] One disgraced British fund manager had special phones created so he could place trades 'out of the office' – that is, riding one of his expensive horses.

The reaction to stories of this sort (and they were legion) was inevitable. So-called 'ordinary' people began to feel that they had

6 Arnault symbolised something else: the commercial value of soft power. He was selling luxurious fashion accessories, fine wine and champagne, expensive luggage and jewellery – and threaded through all those things was ... France.

nothing in common with their wealthier compatriots – they lived different lives. Worse, they could not make themselves heard – it was, above all, their *voices* that had been left behind. A rumble of indignation was inevitable, and while it was not quite synonymous with the nationalism that scarred the twentieth century, it drew from similar wells: anger at the greed of the elites, grief over the fading of traditions, suspicion of foreigners and bafflement over technological change. It all fed into a powerful sense that a golden past had somehow been mislaid.

Whether it was a resurgence of old-fashioned nationalism or its last twitch, perhaps even its death rattle, it felt to many like an old ogre coming back to life. The more determined the effort to create supranational institutions (the United Nations, the European Union, the G7, the IMF and all the others), the more fervent grew the national itch. All over the world, angry populations demanded their old identities back.

As Ivan Krastev and Stephen Holmes pointed out in *The Light That Failed*, when the Berlin Wall fell there were only sixteen military-controlled borders in the world; by 2019 there were sixty-five. Put another way, at the end of the First World War there were sixty nation states; a century later there were 195. It stood to reason there was more nationalism – there were more cauldrons in which it could seethe. An era of convergence had given way to one of fragmentation: those cauldrons were shaking. In many parts of the world the desire to tip over the elite was a more attractive rallying cry than communism, capitalism or democracy.

Analysts queued up to say that the tide of globalisation was turning, that the level of disquiet over inequality, immigration, terrorism and pampered elites was becoming a devouring flame, and that populist politicians had ample material to use as fuel for their own ambitions. Calmer voices tried to remind the public that Americans (for instance) were more likely to be shot by a toddler than by a terrorist – but the raucous tone could not easily be hushed. Trump's America and Brexit Britain confirmed the sense of instability. They were not the fruits of political or economic analysis so much as emotions: mood swings. Beneath the surface agitation about trade arrangements, budget payments and border controls, their central proposition was that nations should turn their clocks back to happier times by treating neighbours and allies as rivals rather than friends.

Many thought it melodramatic to compare minor modern squabbles to the dire events of the 1930s. But there were too many points of comparison to be altogether sanguine. The collapse of the League of Nations ... an unnerving financial crash ... a rising tide of militant nationalism: this was a familiar plot. It resembled not just the period before the Second World War, but, even further back, the great nineteenth-century upheaval that produced the sea changes in science, industry, finance, communications and mass migration that led, eventually, to the First World War.

But nationalism was not by definition disreputable. It had been given a dark and bloody name by the dreadful horrors imposed by twentieth-century tyranny. But it had, by the same token, been the binding agent in an equal number of heroic liberation struggles against imperial oppression. It was a useful (and irrepressible) force when it came to fostering civic belonging and national security, and in sporting arenas could be simple pantomime fun. There were cogent arguments to the effect that nation states might be both the most natural and the most effective mechanisms for managing political and economic aspirations without trampling on local traditions.

However it was interpreted, the fact remained: the collaborative note in international relations did seem to be giving way to the older reflexes of us and them. 'America First' – the slogan trumpeted to keep the US out of foreign entanglements in the 1920s – was making headlines all over again. In this new world order modern nations would once again have to fend for themselves.

General H. R. McMaster, briefly President Trump's National Security Advisor, underscored the change of tack in 2017 when he said: 'The world is not a global community, but an arena where nations engage and compete for advantage.'

The soft-power implication was unavoidable. America was turning away from the very things – openness, friendliness – that had once made it a shining beacon.

The result, expressed in a range of local accents, was anger at the institutions that had appointed themselves globalisation's guardians – in government, finance, law, media, education and culture. People denounced experts and elites of all kinds as if they were no more than a mafia, a self-interested conspiracy.

There was a new 'great game' afoot. In a world jolted by national-populist movements (clearer about what might be torn down than on what might be built) the nineteenth-century concepts of *realpolitik* (defined in 1853 by its founder, Ludwig von Rochau, as meaning that 'the law of the strong is the determining factor in politics') and of the 'sphere of influence' were making a comeback. Fiery movements in all nations were encouraging citizens to rise against their leaders and treat others not as allies but as competing brands.

The original 'great game', the struggle between Britain and Russia for control of Central Asia, was not remotely soft. It was about trade routes, not values, and involved trickery, espionage, feints, bluffs and the occasional burst of red-blooded derring-do. A *Punch* cartoon in 1878 showed a Central Asian figure shivering between the claws of a lion on one side, a bear on the other, with a caption that read: 'Save me from my friends.' It was well understood that the hand of friendship could hold a rod of iron. A generation later, in 1910, Norman Angell swore, in *The Great Illusion*, that the world was far too closely interconnected to contemplate anything as idiotic as war.

There was evidence too that in the short term, at least, soft power could fracture or be overruled. As Edmund Burke wrote: 'Rage and frenzy will pull down more in half an hour than prudence, deliberation and foresight can build in a hundred years.'

Nor was soft power easy to measure. There was no single currency, so it could never be clear exactly how much was required to secure a trade deal, build a military base or create an ounce of GDP. But while it was commonly observed that soft power should be seen as something a nation *had* rather than as something it *did*, that something – a nation's long history – was resilient. It could be beaten into life, like Drake's drum, or summoned up like a genie in a lamp.

To the extent that it was a cultural rather than a material force, soft power mattered in the most obvious way by challenging the ancient reflex to bristle and punch. It was not just another name for pacifism, and no one denied that tyranny sometimes needed to be resisted by force. But the Cold War had shown that the war of ideas could be just as fierce a struggle. Soft power, the world was beginning to realise, was more than placid appeasement. It was an active force that recognised the importance of shared interests, mutual problem-solving and ideas of nationhood that went beyond merely looking out for number one. And it could be more productive than confrontation. If the IRA had not pursued the armed struggle, if Yasser Arafat had chosen peaceful rather than violent dissent, or if America had not invaded Iraq, then Ireland might be united, Palestine might be a state, and the modern Middle East could have been a very different place.

Speculations of that sort could never be proved. But the fact that soft power resisted precise measurement did not prevent it from being momentous, any more than light could be deemed negligible on the trivial grounds that it was weightless.

When Nye addressed a House of Lords Committee in 2013 (a sign that his coinage had taken up residence in the corridors of traditional power), he was at pains to define it as practical – 'getting others to do what you want ... seduction is always more effective than coercion'. He went on to lay out a theory of 'smart' power, urging nations to use all the varieties at their disposal: hard, soft and in-between.

The report that followed ('Persuasion and Power in the Modern World', 2014) was emphatic. 'The days are long gone,' declared the Committee, 'when this nation's or any nation's power could be measured by the size of its military forces ... New, softer methods must now be combined with older approaches.'

It meant that modern governments did need to be more than ever mindful of the messages they sent overseas. Soft power might have seemed to be a branch of public relations, what some called 'nation branding', but actions spoke louder than words. When Germany said yes to a million Syrian refugees it was a stirring break with its own cruel past – indeed it was in part inspired by a sense that the world was not yet ready for pictures of German policemen beating back refugees. By the same token, the Britain that panicked in 2018 at the sight of a few desperadoes crossing the Channel in dinghies, amid cries of a 'national emergency', seemed less confident and open than the Britain that took 10,000 *Kindertransportees* from Central Europe before the Second World War (having welcomed 250,000 displaced Belgians in the First).

The challenge, for governments, was that while they were eager to exploit this interesting new weaponry, there was a developing sense that it derived not *from* government policy but in spite of it. The volunteers who helped refugees or smuggled banned literature across borders were sometimes actually contradicting their own government's official stance. So while official bodies could certainly polish the national halo, funding programmes in education and culture, stimulating free exchange, supporting institutions and enhancing the national image by embodying its finest values (soft power is in large part the power of example), other ingredients were laid down by previous generations, and could not be spun from thin air.

More than anything soft power is, as we will see, a storytelling competition. And what recent times suggest – from the Iraq War to the financial crash to Brexit to Trump to Hong Kong – is that the world has lost track of what the story is. The loss of faith in globalisation is more than just one in the eye for those who believed in it; it is comparable to the loss of religious belief. As G. K. Chesterton once quipped (thinking of the way the religious narrative had dissolved), humankind had not just lost its way – it had lost the map. In the vacuum, a welter of rival narratives have formed, as shrill and insistent as they are contradictory.

Which is why, as the world splinters into competing spheres, states are striving to present their own national stories in the most beguiling and persuasive light. In many cases this involves a quixotic attempt to reduce the complicated lattice of sometimes contradictory stories in their past to one overarching tale – a tempting but impossible task that opens up more wounds than it soothes, not least since it invariably involves discrediting the tales told by others. In olden times it was said that to poison a people you must poison their wells. Today, as the novelist Ben Okri wrote, it is simpler to disparage its myths: 'To poison a nation, poison its stories.'

Which country has the most gripping narrative, the most heroic heroes and heroines, the best ideas?

It may seem mundane to compare the universal power of such stories with the give-and-take of real-life geopolitics, but in the world of soft power it is necessary. As the American professor John Arquilla has said: 'In today's global information age, victory often depends not on whose army wins, but on whose story wins.'

The real quandary facing the world as it considered these national narratives was that most of its member states were locked in bitter internal quarrels about what their story truly was. In nation after nation, arguments about history and identity stretched the body politic on the rack and subjected it to a painful examination.

There are many areas in which soft power is a tangible fact. In tourism, law, science, education, trade, finance, sport and all the other so-called 'invisible' areas of economic life, the appeal of a nation has a palpable effect on its commercial power. Japanese travellers in the Louvre . . . Indian tourists in Bath . . . Americans in Rome . . . Chinese groups on Swiss mountain trains . . . French holidaymakers on the Pyramids . . . Siberians testing the surf in Sydney: all of these are soft power in action.

In 2008 the social scientist Simon Anholt developed an index of national likeability known as the Anholt-Gfk Nation Brands Index. And in 2015 a new global ranking (the 'Soft Power 30') was created by Jonathan McClory for the Portland Consultancy and the University of Southern California. Based on the idea, as McClory put it, that 'power is shifting away from states altogether', it proposed a new way for them to retain their positions of influence, and added a layer of 'objective' data (government spending and educational/digital assets) to Anholt's homely concept of sheer likeability. 'Subjective' factors (the beauty of the physical or cultural scenery) were blended with an evaluation of domestic and foreign policy moves. It has become the leading measurement in the field – 'a soft-power achievement in itself.

Social science of this sort tended to miss out on one of the soft-power engines mentioned above: national history. This is more than a question of cultural heritage commodified as a tourist attraction. The past is a story, and stories are what sway people. They can be more evocative of national character, and thus more 'persuasive', than any number of policy reports. Rankings based on government action often placed small nations above large ones – Singapore ahead of China, Poland above Russia – despite the epic stories created in and about these giant cultures. But the surveys did offer what Nye called 'the clearest picture of global soft power to date', and since governments did not like sliding down such things, it did encourage them to look to their soft-power laurels.

So it does not matter that there is no emphatic answer to the question of soft power's exact value. It is a form of enchantment, working its spell through anecdotes as much as tables: the legacy of long histories that are themselves open to different readings. Yet even at its most insubstantial it can have extraordinary consequences. In June 1945 America's Secretary of War, Henry Stimson, ordered Kyoto to be removed from the list of cities slated to receive the atom bomb, knowing it to be full of irreplaceable culture. Having spent his honeymoon there he knew first-hand how precious it was. Thanks to one fortuitous whim, Kyoto was replaced on the target list by Nagasaki.

Try telling the unbombed citizens of Kyoto that soft power was weightless, or the survivors of Nagasaki that if only they had possessed a larger arsenal of historic shrines and temples they might have been reprieved. Soft power could be godlike.

In the early weeks of 2020 a new disease – Covid-19 or coronavirus – began its lethal journey across the planet, putting paid to ways of life people had come to take for granted. Towns, cities, regions, even nations went into quarantine (the media preferred the term 'lockdown', as if citizens were violent offenders in a TV prison drama). Schools, universities, theatres, shops and restaurants closed; planes, trains and cars ground to a halt. Sport died; borders were raised; markets crashed. The public was ordered to self-isolate at home.

The virus struck a world that was, as we have seen, already churning with nationalist emotion. If anything, it looked, in those innocent days, as if soft power's most urgent duty might be to avert World War III. No one suspected that a tiny microbe, creeping out of the animal kingdom, might be enough to bring the planet to its knees.

Nor could anyone say, when it began, how things might look when the whirlwind passed: the economic and social ramifications were vast. But predictions abounded: less travel, more home-working, lower energy use, busier domestic supply systems, more technology. National governments found they still had awesome powers, and used them to close businesses, empty public spaces and supervise social life. The impact of all that on the world's mentality – and sensibility – has been incalculable.

In short, the complex world created by globalisation – in which, at any one time, a million people were on the move, in a web of global supply chains – was imperilled, and the drift back to national power blocs, with strict control over borders, was given new force. But almost as soon as nations clamped down on their *own* populations, and strove to discourage newcomers, it became clear that this could only be a temporary measure. To defeat this common enemy, nations would have to work in unison.

It was time for soft power to show what it was truly made of.

If past plagues were anything to go by, the world would almost certainly rediscover, in the fullness of time, the pleasures of movement and trade. It could not self-isolate for ever. But hardly anyone thought that the crisis might be merely a chastening jolt after which life could resume its previous course, shifting smoothly back to business-as-usual. On the contrary, the virus looked set to accelerate some compelling social changes already in the pipeline. Economic activity might diminish, and belts might have to tighten; habits would have to change. But there might be silver linings. The new emphasis on hygiene might restrain other viruses, too. The pace of carbon emissions looked set to ease, pointing the way to the cleaner environment for which the world was clamouring. And beauty spots that struggled to cope with the crowd might, for a while at least, have a new worry: *undertourism*.

Some of these novelties would be driven by smart technology, nudging the world into a giant leap forward (cashless commerce, civil surveillance, creative new forms of cultural expression). But the world might also be steered in the direction of simpler pleasures: climbing hills, digging the garden, playing chess, even – perish the thought – reading a book. In this sense it might be poised for a giant leap backwards.

All such thoughts were speculative. But one thing seemed certain. Since traditional or hard power was of no use against such an enemy – the virus could not be beaten back by naval blockades, missile threats, economic sanctions or tirades on Twitter – it would be up to *soft* power – science, education, the cultivation of goodwill, trust and medical cooperation – to limit and repair the damage. It was a world health problem, not a national problem. The world's first reflex (driven both by medical necessity and by the nationalist flavour of the *zeitgeist*) was to pull down the shutters and limit movement – and this had sound medical backing: quarantine was a rational tactic. But it was obviously not feasible for any one nation to lock its doors and try to stay healthy while others suffered. For one to be made safe, *all* had to be deep-cleaned. Because all were equally vulnerable, only a concerted response could quell so hungry and indiscriminate an opponent. If America and Europe wanted to survive, then they would have to help Bangladesh and Eritrea survive too.

Earlier we said that soft power was a storytelling competition, and this implies that it is a form of rivalry that inevitably produces winners and losers. But when the virus closed down a sophisticated global economy that had come to depend on the rapid flow of both people and goods, it became apparent that this was a competition with an unusual twist, since these stories needed to contain a humanitarian strand. The way the nations responded to this new challenge would write a new page in that story. Naturally their own populations came first, but they were also part of a global effort. They had to perform well individually, but also to do their bit for the team. In short, they were competing to show how willing they were to lay down the cudgels of competition, and cooperate. The virus was like a camera flash, exposing in ghoulish detail the flaws and weaknesses (and strengths) of existing structures. National governments, even as they grasped the levers of their astonishing new powers, quaked, knowing that in the fullness of time there would be a medals table for the effectiveness of their choices in this deadly new sport. Almost all had been forced to lock up their citizens, thanks in part to their failure to take the necessary precautions beforehand (for a pandemic that was not unforeseeable – many had predicted it). In due course, the countries that acted wisely would emerge with their credentials burnished; those that acted recklessly, or selfishly, would not soon be forgiven.

Did the strong showing of some countries, for instance (such as Denmark, Iceland, Germany, Finland and New Zealand) prove that women were better governors than men? Or was it simply that sensible countries such as these were more likely to elect women leaders – a correlation rather than a cause-and-effect? Suddenly, soft power's true purpose seemed to take shape, because it was on glimmering questions of governance such as these that the future of the world might hang.

They were especially important in an era that transmits information at a phenomenal speed. When the Indonesian volcano Tambora erupted in 1815, throwing so much ash into the atmosphere that it caused 'the year without a summer', it took six months for the news to reach Britain. Today it would take six seconds. The virus was a perfect storm of rolling news, each hour bringing fresh outbreaks, all magnified in the echo chamber of social media, with its simultaneous power both to inform and to mislead.

In this new setting, the meaning of the national brand was more important than ever.

History is not a reliable guide to the future, but its main lesson is that the world will not end any time soon. Even a catastrophe as appalling as the Black Death, which laid waste one-third of Europe's population, was followed by a dawn that led, in time, to economic renewal, then Renaissance and Reformation. Soft power is about the planting of seeds, and by roving far and wide in search of its manifestations I hope I have, in part at least, traced the story of the force most likely to heal the world.

I

America: Opportunity Knocks

It is not easy – it might be impossible – for a superpower to feel that anything matters more than its military and financial prowess. And the firepower at America's disposal is so stupendous that its gentler qualities might indeed seem irrelevant: it spends up to $700 billion on defence each year, one-third of the world's total military expenditure, more than the seven next-biggest spenders put together. It keeps 1.3 million troops in uniform; three-quarters (760) of the world's attack helicopters are American; it has the largest air force and the largest navy, too; and it operates 800 bases overseas.

Its soft-power assets are just as daunting. It owns the cutting edge of information technology (Amazon, Apple, Facebook, Google, Uber), leads the way in entertainment (Disney, Netflix), has a firm grip on the world's taste buds (Coca-Cola, McDonald's, KFC, Starbucks), and is the driving force in youth culture (Nike, YouTube, MTV). It educates more overseas students than the next two countries (UK and Australia) combined; its writers and artists are known the world over. According to the Portland Soft Power 30: 'Its global culture is ubiquitous.'

The uproars of modern times, as everyone knows, are casting shadows on this bright picture (in the 2019 Soft Power ranking it came fifth – its lowest-ever position). But for most of the twentieth century the story America told was one of infinite aspiration, and it shone like a beacon. As Simon Schama wrote: 'If you want one word to describe the American state of mind it would be: boundless; the beckoning road trip, the shaking loose of fetters.'

Of course, the communist sphere of influence declined to see it that way; but this was the image that took root almost everywhere else – sometimes in unlikely places. Shortly before the collapse of the Berlin Wall, for instance, in the autumn of 1989, unusual images began to appear on Poland's street corners. Like streaks of high cloud signalling a change in the weather – streaks of cirrus over the iron curtain, perhaps – they took the form of posters promoting the cause of the moment: *Solidarnosc* (Solidarity).

Lech Walesa's movement, the first non-communist trade union in Poland, was born in 1980 following a strike in Gdansk's Lenin Shipyard. Within a year it had attracted ten million members – a third of Poland's labour force.[1] It also gripped the West. Thanks to the films of Andrzej Wajda (*Man of Iron* won a prize at Cannes and was nominated at the Oscars), Lech Walesa became a star, and *Solidarnosc* was a global brand. Students across the world pinned Polish insignia to their duffel coats.

The fact that *Solidarnosc* received some $50 million in American aid didn't hurt either.

The work of a graphic designer named Tomasz Sarnecki, the posters that appeared on Poland's streets depicted the famous red lettering of the movement alongside an equally famous image of American freedom-fighting: Sheriff Gary Cooper interrupting his wedding ('Do not forsake me, oh my darling . . .') in favour of a showdown with the hoodlums in Fred Zinnemann's 1952 film *High Noon*.

It took a hero of Polish dissidence and dressed him as an American lawman. Cooper was clutching a ballot paper instead of a gun, and wore the *Solidarnosc* badge above his sheriff's star. No one could miss the message. Poland was marching, loose-limbed but firm of mind, towards a date with destiny. And the clock was ticking.

Film critics had a bone to pick with the notion that a greying fellow some way past his prime might plausibly pass up a honeymoon trip with Grace Kelly (a beauty thirty years his junior)

---

1 The strike flared into life after the sacking of Anna Walentynowicz, a one-time 'Hero of Socialist Labour' who was also a devout Catholic, and who helped form the then-illegal trade union in 1980. She was sacked five months before her retirement, a foolish decision which ignited the entire Baltic uprising. She went on to appear in Andrzej Wajda's 1981 film about the episode, *Man of Iron*, playing herself.

in favour of a shootout with a bunch of unshaven villains. But such thoughts could not harm the soft-power message. Nothing symbolised freedom quite so clearly as a classic Western hero. Cooper's parents may have been English, but the sober decency he brought to the silver screen was clearly and strongly American.

In America itself the Western genre was running out of steam. Its heroes were as anachronistic as medieval knights: audiences preferred an edgier, metropolitan world of cops and private eyes. But in Eastern Europe the genre retained its glamour. A cattle trail in Apache country, a poker game in a mining town, a prospector looking for gold, a lawman with a righteous glint in his eye, the battle between good and evil in a homely world of log cabins and dry goods stores ... these were still gripping archetypes.

Self-help was the order of the day – there was no one else to 'set things right'.

When George Bush declared that Osama bin Laden was 'wanted: dead or alive', he was whipping out a stereotype that was as American as the landscape out of which it grew. Even despots liked it. Hitler's favourite writer was Karl May, a German whose Wild-West stories (*The Desperado Trail*, *The Valley of Death*) sold in their millions. And Khrushchev once revealed that Stalin himself would order a John Wayne movie to watch after dinner, denounce the hero as a capitalist lackey ... then order up another.[2]

The films contained another alluring message. Since their characters were constantly on the move – drifting south, heading west, dreaming of a big strike in the mountains – there was a stirring sense of freedom, and there were few more powerful soft signals than that. But by 1989 this too was double-edged. The astounding trek west was still an epic adventure, but it was no longer possible to forget the fact that it had involved the violent death of 130 million indigenous people, at a time when America's cotton and tobacco harvest was brought in by African slaves

---

2 When Khrushchev visited California in 1959 he made two requests: one was to see Disneyland (Mickey Mouse declined) and the other was to meet John Wayne. It was even said that Stalin sent a pair of KGB agents to California to assassinate Wayne. The Duke was unflustered: 'No goddamn commie's gonna frighten me.'

in conditions of dreadful cruelty. The basic proposition of the
Western no longer held. Conquering new lands fell out of fashion,
and the way the old movies demonised 'hostiles' and 'savages' had
lost whatever charm it had. Those reflexes migrated to the fantasy
world of video gaming, which offered a raucous schooling in us-
and-them violence.

From its earliest days, it now seemed, America had been a
land of both hope *and* violence – two strands locked in an awkward embrace ever since. But even in the enlightened modern
world the old imagery still cast a luminous spell. It was also a
display case for America's amazing topography – its mountains,
plains, rivers and canyons – and its history: the Declaration of
Independence, the Gettysburg Address. It still held out to all the
promise that they might make it big or strike it lucky.

The monument that did most to fix that idea in the imagination
of the world was the Statue of Liberty. And this French gift also
expressed the powerful idea that America was a nation created by
immigrants. Everyone now understands that the New World was
not virgin territory: the migrants came as colonisers, and showed
no mercy. But between 1830 and 1930 some twenty-five million
Europeans crossed the Atlantic, casting off the shackles of their
birthplaces to better themselves with an irresistible mythology
of self-improvement. If they bent their backs, sharpened their
elbows and raised their fists there was no limit to what they might
achieve. Go west, young man.[3] It was everyone's manifest destiny
to pursue the vision of a brighter tomorrow.

And it had sprung from so little – a tiny trickle of pilgrims
from Shakespearian England doing what migrants of all ages have
done: fleeing religious persecution, war and poverty. In 1776,
when British rule was overthrown, America consisted of only
thirteen states (former colonies) and some two million people,
several hundred thousand of whom were African slaves. A hundred years later there were fifty million people, and America
was the world's biggest economy. Today it is an economic giant.

---

3 The phrase is often attributed to the journalist Horace Greeley, who in 1865 (in the
midst of the Civil War) urged readers to flee to the world beyond the Mississippi. But
he himself claimed he was merely the publisher, not the author, of the idea.

Endless migration from everywhere on the planet had swollen the population to 250 million.

Thus ran the founding script. It was not nuanced – it did not tell the whole story, and it skipped over the darker episodes. But it was a clarion call to the world.

There was soft power in the determined tramp of all those footsteps. They brought all the virtues of the Europe they were leaving; and all its vices, too. Europe gave itself a fresh start in a new land. Though the newcomers retained enough of themselves to be recognisable to their ancestors, they acquired accents and manners that were new to all of them, and shared. It was a Jewish Londoner (Israel Zangwill, in a New York play) who coined the phrase 'melting pot', but that is what America became. Unlike all those countries who thought that nationhood was a matter of birthright, blood and soil, America alone stood for the principle that it could be something else: an idea.

Some of America's most iconic brands were created by this process. The blue jeans made famous by all those Hollywood cowboys were designed by a Latvian tailor from Reno, Nevada, who teamed up with a Bavarian-born dry goods merchant named Levi Strauss to make trousers using hard-wearing cloth from Provence (*de Nimes*). They became the uniform not just of the cowboy but of the American outdoors in general.

Another ubiquitous mass-market product, McDonald's, actually became a soft-power case study. Thomas Friedman, the *New York Times* columnist and author of many notable works on globalisation, elevated it into a theory which he called (in *The Lexus and the Olive Tree*) 'The Golden Arches Theory of Conflict Prevention'. It held that 'no two countries that both had McDonald's had ever fought a war against each other'. It was intended as a rough indicator of the spread of the consumer society – and such societies tended to shun war: 'they preferred to wait in line for burgers'.

He did not emphasise that McDonald's had been the brainchild of Ray Kroc, the restless son of a property dealer from the then-Czechoslovakia, who happened upon the idea of fast food in a sales trip to California – but he might have, because the burgers were not just cheap or convenient. A classic migration fable, they carried the essence of America. That no-frills, have-a-nice-day approach, price-conscious and demotic, was a hit in every time zone. Popcorn, cigarettes, fast food, fizzy drinks, gum, posters of Marilyn Monroe ... Even America's detractors could not resist.

Naturally, sceptics pointed out the dangers of Friedman inferring from the fact that war had not happened yet that it never would. So in *The World is Flat* he updated his idea into 'the Dell theory of conflict prevention', and proposed that countries hooked into the same just-in-time global supply chain could not possibly contemplate violence. This too opened the author up to reminders about what had happened to flat-earthers in the past. But beneath the surface it was a stark reminder that migration and communication were powerful soft forces in America's message to the world.

It was not a coincidence that the McDonald's in Prague was installed below the Museum of Communism (and next door to a casino).

The energy of America's immigrant economy lay behind a thousand such stories. And the Statue of Liberty became a monument not only to America's origins as a refuge for migrants, but to the very principle of international movement. At its foot stood Ellis Island, the gate through which so many millions of European migrants passed. The soft-power lesson of these business stories, moreover, is unmistakable: the migration of people is not just a noble abstraction ('Give me your tired, your poor') but an extraordinary strategy for economic success – nothing less than the most successful commercial strategy the world has ever known.

In large parts of the modern world immigration is seen as a problem – at best, as a challenge – and has sparked a political tumult. America reminds us that far from being a burden or a brake on progress, inward migration has been ... rocket fuel.

Nothing else comes close. Astonishing natural resources ... free markets ... a legal system ... scale ... freedom ... variety. But nothing has been as crucial as the dynamism of the incoming population. Alexis de Tocqueville once wrote that America's character resided in this 'restless spirit', the way its people were 'forever brooding over advantages they do not possess'. This is both an immigrant and an *emi*grant mentality, a determined hope that better times must lie around the next bend, across the next river, beyond the next hill . . . and, of course, next year.

It was a demographic experiment without precedent. Bring-me-your-poor was the best business idea the world ever had. The melting pot was a nuclear reactor.

Put bluntly: if migration were a problem, America would not be a superpower.

This simple and ancient process — the movement of people — may be the most important of soft power's many features. It carries a moral message, implying freedom and the quest for safety. But it is also a pushy, ambitious dynamo. In offering itself as a — *the* — land of opportunity, America became the home of innovation, too. Most of the household names the world now associates with American technology have a tangle of migration stories in their backgrounds. The story of how two brainy go-getters, Steve Wozniak and Steve Jobs (the former of Polish ancestry, the latter the adopted son of a Syrian), turned a printed circuit board in a Californian garage into a ground-breaking personal computer — which a few decades later became the world's first trillion-dollar corporation (Apple) — is only the most famous in a very long list.

Of course, there is a dark side to this. People carry not just ideas and ambitions, but cruelty and disease too. The ancient world was riddled with plague, and lethal viruses had always played their part in the evolution of the world. From the Black Death (which also crept from China to Europe via Venice) and the Great Plague of 1665 (during which a quarantined Isaac Newton wrote *Principia Mathematica*) to Spanish Flu (which killed 50 million worldwide), Russian Flu (one million) and SARS (which was predicted to kill quarter of a million, but in fact killed fewer than a thousand), there have been many such outbreaks. In taking 'civilisation' to the New World, European colonists also took smallpox, typhus, cholera and other fatal illnesses.

As a rule, however, innovation has always drawn strength from the meeting of minds.

The frontier spirit was still alive.

*

If soft power is, as we have suggested, a storytelling competition, then America was its de facto leader, thanks to the dream factory it built in Hollywood. Every single one of the hundred highest-grossing films in history was born in the USA. A handful (Harry Potter and *Lord of the Rings*) told British or other stories, sometimes even with British or other actors. But all were American products, infused with American notions.[4]

This itself was a migration story: in no other arena had newcomers made so stirring a mark. Hollywood was created largely by immigrants: the early pictures were written, financed, directed, produced, acted in and scored by refugees: Capra, Chaplin, Cukor, Dietrich, Goldwyn, Hitchcock, Lubitsch, Preminger, Wilder, Wyler and others ... They brought something larger than the sum of their talents: they evolved an idea of 'story' that became the template for an entire industry. To them it seemed only natural that a story was a journey. The Western, in particular, was an allegory of their own careers: had not they themselves run such risks as they battled their way to the New World? Was not life itself a search for pastures new under bigger, freer skies?

A life was a quest. A plot was a pilgrim's progress.

This notion of narrative as 'journey' was powerful. Tolstoy had once said that there were only two stories in the world – a man leaves his home/a stranger arrives in town – and Hollywood engraved this thought on its heart. *All* stories were journeys – even when no one went anywhere, when the voyages were inward-looking.

This soon seemed like revealed truth. A story involved the pursuit of a goal by a hero or heroine who had to slay the various dragons that fate or their own character placed in their way. It was an obstacle course, with the audience cast as 'crowd'.

A lively cottage industry of how-to guides and screenwriting courses rested on this idea that the more intensely audiences rooted for heroes and hissed at villains, the more successful the story was. The fact that it tacitly promoted an us–and–them,

---

4 This is no two-way street; it is (literally) cultural projection. Overseas films do not trouble the American box office. More than half of Hollywood's revenue comes from abroad, yet foreign-language films comprise only 1 per cent of American sales.

goodies-vs.-baddies mentality that hid nuance and stoked enmities (and the possible social and political consequences of this) seemed not to matter at the time. And while Hollywood, like life, doled out endings in a haphazard way (some stories ended happily; some not), on the whole it sold success stories, reinforcing the sense that America was a place – perhaps the only place – where dreams could come true.

This was a powerful soft weapon – almost an ideology: an insistent way of thinking. Even the Western could be revived: though set in the past, it addressed the future by pushing for better times, refusing to take no for an answer . . . and not looking back.

It was not propaganda as such.[5] But it was a strong statement of American values. And while the economic significance spoke for itself – an industry built by immigrants told migrant parables and basked in the proceeds – the cultural impact was greater. When Disney made *Mulan* in 1998 (the story of a Chinese Joan of Arc who takes up arms for her family, her emperor and herself) it was not well received in China, thanks to a self-help message ('Who is that girl I see?') too blatant and individualistic by half. It also erred by making cherry blossom – a Japanese motif – one of its leading motifs. It was given only a limited release – a concession, seeing that China only permitted a limited quota of American films (thirty-six per year) on its screens.[6]

Cinematic stories are soft power in its purest form, winning people over to ideas so artfully they do not even suspect they are being seduced. The *Transformers* series grossed more than $4 billion around the world (despite offending critics) and while it seemed mere playful mayhem, it was also selling an American story of self-realisation. Superhero vehicles like *Black Panther* and *Captain Marvel* slipped on-trend messages about race and gender into action-movie stereotypes, and found box-office glory too.

---

5 Though it could be. When war threatened, Britain was able to pursue a soft-power mission of its own in Hollywood, working hard (in films like *Mrs Miniver*) to plant a rose-tinted vision of dear old Blighty in the American mind: thatched cottages, cream tea, castles and country lanes – surely to God a place worth fighting for.

6 Undeterred, Disney tried again with a live-action version and Chinese actors. When the trailer was released in 2019 there was some talk of historical inaccuracy, but this looked likely to be overwhelmed by enthusiasm for a vivid Chinese heroine – until the lead actress expressed sympathy for the protest movement in Hong Kong.

It had an important soft-power side-effect, too: *glamour,* a commodity in itself. The fame of the Hollywood stars, boosted by mass-market papers and magazines, created a fashionable new currency: celebrity. The world would not look back.

There was a chicken-and-egg question here. Was it America's dominant position in the world – its military and economic bulk – that gave these products their global reach? Or was it the other way round – was it the products that spread American culture? This was the soft-power enigma writ large.

In truth, both played a role, even if the message was sometimes contradictory. The world's enthusiasm for American goods (its drinks sell in hot lands where millions do not even have a tap) has led it to absorb American ideas and habits, and some see that as a form of ideological bullying. The axioms of the Harvard Business School drive corporate strategy on every continent; as do the wheeler-dealer reflexes of Wall Street. There are gleams of America in African shanty towns and Asian back streets, and half the teenage girls in the world, it sometimes seems, want to be Beyoncé.

Of course this is a stereotype. And America casts more than one shadow – it is the land of cowboys and riverboat gamblers, but also the cradle of civil rights, feminism and all forms of political correctness. It is the home of skyscrapers and lunar rockets, but has tramps, gangsters and every other form of huckster too. No single stereotype can catch the range of its flavours. So fans tapping their feet to Bob Dylan or Madonna might not actually be humming 'God Bless America' under their breath; the millions round the world who drink Coke, gobble corn flakes, smoke Winstons and lap up Hollywood blockbusters do not have to wish they had a star-spangled banner to wave. But the air they breathe has an American flavour whether they like it or not. Every time they contact a friend on WhatsApp, crack a joke on Twitter, order a driver through Uber or take a photo of their brunch on an iPhone, they are subscribing to the American way.

It may be that America's soft power peaked in 1945, before the world even knew the term. At that time it stood alone. Its military strength was obvious (the nuclear bombs in Japan left no one in any doubt about its ferocity) but it still had the bright halo of a liberator. In Europe and Asia American troops handed out chocolate, chewing gum, nylon stockings *and* freedom to cheering crowds. Half the world swooned.

America understood. Long before Joseph Nye, Senator William Fulbright gave a concise outline of soft power when he said: 'The age of warrior kings and of warrior presidents has passed ... In the long course of history, having people who understand your thought is of much greater security than having another submarine.'

The feeling was given geopolitical shape by the Marshall Plan, the four-year project in which America funnelled $13 billion (roughly $130 billion today) to help rebuild not just its allies but its opponents, too. Some of the soft-power signals were nuanced: where some saw generosity and goodwill, others saw colonial self-interest. Indeed, it became common to see the Marshall Plan not as an act of generosity but as a 'martial' or imperial plan – one of the causes of the Cold War, no less. Europe and Japan were in ruins, and in saving them for freedom and democracy, America was also securing them for commerce. There was some truth in this. But the desire to keep Europe out of the Soviet orbit had humanitarian motives as well: life under Stalin looked set to be little different from life under Hitler – millions had already died.

Motives aside, the fact was: few victorious powers had ever dealt with defeated enemies so gently. At the end of the First World War, the punitive measures imposed on Germany had led to a renewal of hostilities two decades later (even Churchill, no peacenik, called them 'malignant and silly'). Perhaps a lesson had been learned.

And as Alistair Cooke pointed out in a famous 'Letter from America' in praise of Marshall, it was common for those who had been rescued by burly lifeguards to feel, when they were safe, that they could have made it out on their own.[7] Subsequent generations could assume that the mod cons they took for granted ('supermarkets and frozen food') were facts of life, rather than

---

7 One reason why America fell out of love with France after liberating it was that, according to a 1950 poll, two-thirds of French people believed the Marshall Plan had been bad for their country. This made some Americans want their money back.

gifts from America. He, however, recalled Dean Acheson insisting to US Senators that with respect to the Marshall Plan they could not back away: 'This thing must be done, simply to restore the fabric of European life.'

Serious money backed by the threat of force – in most ways this was hard power, the opposite of our subject. But the Marshall Plan was a glowing moment for American soft power too – and an illustration of how closely the two are entwined. The money may have been 'hard' currency, but the message behind it was gentle. President Harry Truman could invoke 'fundamental principles of righteousness and justice' without being thought duplicitous.

That was the dream captured in those Polish posters of Gary Cooper: America as the special case, the one place founded on the idea of attracting all-comers – risk-takers and idealists, fortune-seekers and ne'er-do-wells. At the height of the Cold War it sent not just films but jazz performers – Louis Armstrong, Duke Ellington, Dizzy Gillespie – behind the Iron Curtain, and what they played was more than music. On a 1958 tour of Poland, the pianist Dave Brubeck was told: 'What you brought wasn't just jazz. It was the Grand Canyon, it was the Empire State Building. It was America.'

2

America: White House Blues

When coronavirus flared in Italy and began to frighten the rest of Europe, Donald Trump's America at first rejected the idea that it was any sort of threat, calling it a minor illness caused by 'one person from China' or a 'hoax'. A few weeks later, hundreds of Americans had died, the stock market had imploded, and while flights into the United States were being banned every day, it was clear that the spread could not be checked *within* the world's largest market. It did not help that the President had long since put the allure of the American project in jeopardy. All that vote-catching talk about draining swamps and building walls told the world an unpleasant truth: in this new crisis it could no longer count on American leadership.

The virus didn't care: it was not on Twitter, and could not be bullied. So the fact that in a single year (2017) the President had made two thousand 'false or misleading statements' was significant: it turned the world's most powerful nation into easy prey. The reason Dracula sailed to Britain, in Bram Stoker's original telling of the tale, was that in liberating itself from peasant superstition it no longer believed in him, and left itself all the more vulnerable. In the long run, it was possible that coronavirus might restore the world's faith in 'experts' by creating a compelling need for honest and well-informed science – but in the short term Trump's urge to denounce, deny and sow the seeds of mistrust could only bruise America's standing in the world.

In June 2017 America walked away from the Paris Agreement – the 2016 accord in which 196 nations had, in an unprecedented fit of togetherness, and after years of dull negotiation, committed to reducing carbon emissions. To green eyes it was not stringent enough – too mild to be worth walking out of. But it was a historic breakthrough: the world was agreeing to cooperate to meet a global challenge. Trump opted out, claiming that it was not good for America.

In 2018 two more treaties were abandoned: the North American Free Trade Agreement and the Trans-Pacific Partnership, on the grounds that they were 'bad' for US jobs, along with three UN arrangements: UNHCR (refugees), UNRWA (Palestinian Relief) and UNESCO (culture and heritage) – the last because it was 'anti-Israel'.

Ironically, it was America's signatory, Archibald MacLeish, who in 1945 had helped compose UNESCO's *raison d'être*. 'Since wars begin in the minds of men,' it ran, 'it is in the minds of men that the defences of peace must be constructed.'

That was soft power in a nutshell.

It was certainly tempting, as the new incumbent conducted geopolitics by tweet, bringing about an era that might one day be known as 'post-credible', to see Donald Trump as the motor or cause of this change. In truth, he may have been the noisy symptom of a deeper rumble. Either way, as befitted a property mogul whose idea of business was that for him to win, someone else must lose, America certainly adopted a confrontational and thin-skinned approach to international diplomacy. In some ways he was reaffirming the superiority of old-school methods, reverting to the with-us-or-against-us world view of the Cold War.

This was delicate. According to David Skidmore (in *Paradoxes of Power,* 2007), America had indeed been seduced by the way the Cold War ended into taking a lofty and negligent attitude to foreign parts. 'Few Americans noticed,' he added, 'that with the advent of the information revolution, soft power was becoming more important.' US-funded radio, for example, at the height of the anti-communist chill, reached three-quarters of people in Eastern Europe. Now, it had died. 'On the eve of the September 11 attacks, a mere 2 per cent of Arabs listened to the Voice of America.'

The consequences of that withdrawal are apparent. In 2016 the United States came top of the Portland 30, but by 2019 it was no longer seen as the guardian of the 'rules-based' international order. In an unusually strong phrase, Portland suggested that it was 'a negligent great power at best, a selfish, malevolent one at worst'.

Even its commercial giants, seemingly immune to the ups and downs of Washington politics, could sense a cooling in the world's enthusiasm for the American way. American energy, American roads, America's diet and the lack of concern for the environment were out of tune with the eco-friendly, healthy-eating spirit of the age. Even the technology titans found themselves berated for shirking tax 'obligations'. Suddenly, Silicon Valley was no longer the world's coolest workplace.

America's immense reserve of traditional soft power was passing behind a cloud. The blazing values it used to transmit – freedom, opportunity, the chance to get ahead – were no longer so radiant. And it had a raucous and divided new personality, each side clinging to a very different story of America's past. Its corporations still bestrode the world, and the tales spun by its movie moguls continued to capture the global imagination. But the scandals surrounding Harvey Weinstein shone a harsh light on corruption in this dream factory, and the old urge to explore seemed to have given way to an urge to circle the wagons and pick up that trusty Winchester.

As a consequence, in poll after poll the world was falling out of love with America. One survey ('Global Attitudes') found that in 2015 fully two-thirds of foreigners had a favourable view; in 2018 only 47 per cent felt the same. In Mexico, only 30 per cent had positive feelings, while 77 per cent of Latin Americans did not trust Donald Trump to 'do the right thing'. A Gallup poll in 134 countries came to a bleak conclusion: less than a third admired America, compared to 50 per cent in the days of Barack Obama.

That was an awful lot of goodwill to squander in so short a time.

These public relations setbacks are surprising in a nation so wedded to the pre-eminent value of marketing. There was little that could have been more bruising to the traditional idea of America than the get-off-our-lawn rhetoric of 'America First'. Openness, as we have seen, was part of its *raison d'être*. So the shift of tone represented a marked revision of its historic message. When the President himself deployed an old slur by urging his non-white fellow politicians to 'go home', the world could see that something had changed, something that went against the grain of America itself.

And it came, ironically, at a time when America was already losing its competitive advantage in the field of migration. Most modern nations now had their own high levels of inward move-ment (not all of it welcome: it was easy to ignore the fact that the clearest sign of national failure, in nations like Syria or Venezuela, was a desperation to leave). America was no longer the only melting pot.

Given that America's attitude to immigrants was intricately bound up with its own origins, this was a serious soft-power gamble. The implication of 'Make America Great Again' was that America was *no longer* great, that it had mislaid itself.

There was a subtler problem. In seeking to advance a new story about America – one showing it to be a tough, take-no-prisoners winner – the government was obscuring the old idea that it was (as the Kennedy administration put it) Camelot. The message of those soundbites and tweets did not match the story told by the country as a whole, creating a dramatic disconnect in the state-ment it broadcast to the world.

Soft power is both more potent and mistier than public rela-tions, but stories this twisted and signals this mixed do not play well in faraway lands.

It would be a mistake to see this as a sudden rupture. America had been changing course for a while: the glow of 1945 soon froze. By 1953 America was fearful, and John Foster Dulles was urging the public to wake up: 'We have enemies who are plotting our destruction ... Any American who isn't awake to that is like a sentry asleep at his post.' The spirit of the old West was sum-moned: hoodlums were gathering in the railroad yard.

There were other factors. The McCarthy era, with its crackdown on 'false' thinking, and the shocking images from Vietnam – the summary execution of a Viet Cong official, the broken father holding up the body of his child, the little girl on the napalmed road – put further cracks in the image. Wars in Korea and Cambodia, plots in Chile, Iran, Nicaragua, Somalia, the Philippines and the Middle East . . . These all pecked holes in the idea of America as the brave guardian of international peace and freedom. If anything, it came to resemble, in many eyes, that same sentry firing blindly at an enemy he could not even see – not a strategy likely to win friends.

In recent times the scandals of Guantanamo Bay, Abu Ghraib, and the so-called 'war' on drugs and terror added new flames to the bonfire.

Something similar was happening to the idea of Soviet righteousness in these years: there was something 'mutually assured' about the new atmosphere. Even true believers began to fall out of love with the communist utopia when the truth about Ukraine and the Siberian gulag trickled out, and when tanks rolled into Hungary.

On the home front, too, America was ceasing to be the promised land. Apart from anything else, it was dangerous. The inalienable right to bear arms was expensive. Some 30,000 civilians were being killed by guns every year, with a further 80,000 injured. In the last fifty years more Americans had been shot in ordinary life than in all of the wars in America's history. And in two particular categories – school murder sprees and recreational killings – America was a world leader. On the twentieth anniversary of Columbine, in 2019, it emerged that in the two decades since that massacre there had been no fewer than sixty-eight similar incidents, a deadly roll-call that inspired heartfelt protest marches against gun laws . . . and little in the way of government action.

Defenders of guns argued that the numbers would be even worse without their reassuring presence, and that the principle – the right to self-defence – was absolute.

All of these things changed the way America was perceived. The world had been more than happy to see the bands of American brothers that clawed their way up the beaches of Normandy in 1944 as heroic saviours; but the army that blew into Iraq in 2004 struck many (including some of America's staunchest allies) as semi-criminal – a sledgehammer squashing a gnat. And Iraq was not even as big as California.

There is a soft-power lesson here. Hard power (military muscle) may be the fastest way to win arguments; but it comes at a cost. Gore Vidal went to his grave holding forth against the 'military-industrial complex' that ran America, and was often felt to have been exaggerating. But more and more commentators subscribed to the view that America, with its awesome military power, really did require the motivating thrill of a common enemy. When the Second World War ended, the Cold War became the spur for space-age defence-industry spending; when the Berlin Wall fell, the 'war on terror' became an urgent patriotic cause; and as the new century wore on a new dragon appeared: China.[1]

Soft power had to take a back seat with beasts this big in the room. Yet in 2001 the fact that America was the world's only military superpower did not deter the pilots who brought down the twin towers. Confronted by US troops in Afghanistan and Iraq, the enemy multiplied. Some modern threats could be vanquished only by soft means: charm, tact, persuasion. In reaching for the gun, America invited the world to notice that it was not only the land of the free, the home of the brave and the friend of the wretched, but an aggressive pioneer in more violent fields as well.

It might even be proposed, as a soft amendment for the modern world, that the greater the military strength, the dimmer the cultural halo.

It may be premature to suggest, however, that the world's foremost power might go down in history as a parable in how swiftly such power can dissolve. America may seem to have injured itself in soft terms, but the richest aspects of a nation's history can outlast the ups and downs of geopolitics.

J. K. Galbraith once called pessimism 'the mark of superior intellect'; it seems more profound than its complacent opposite (optimism). Yet sometimes it only appears to be deep. It may be the case, in the short term, that the more eagerly America forms its wagons into a circle, the weaker its soft-power glow will become. But it would be unwise to assume that the future can be

---

1 It could even be said that when the Berlin Wall collapsed, so too did America's sense of itself as an optimistic nation united around a fervent common cause. It fell, instead, to internal quarrelling. Machiavelli would have smiled.

so easily extrapolated from one trend. One of America's strengths, historically, has been its adaptability: its willingness to change.

As Anatole Kaletsky has written,[2] rejecting the idea that the American business model is broken, free-market capitalism is 'not a static set of institutions but an evolutionary system that reinvigorates itself through crisis'. Tim Harford made the same point (in *Adapt: Why Success Always Starts with Failure*, 2011) when he wrote that success begins with trial and error. 'Ten per cent of American businesses disappear every year,' he wrote – but this was an evolutionary advantage: the survivors all thrived.

Adaptability is not an objective measure. But it is powerful. If the past is anything to go by, whatever the next era brings, it is likely that America will be in the front seat. Driverless cars? Airborne home delivery? Thought-controlled shopping? Self-cleaning houses? Colonies in space? All sound implausible; but so, once, did skyscrapers, moon landings, online shopping and booking holidays on a phone.

As Michael Lewis wrote of Silicon Valley (in *The New New Thing*, 1999): 'For a technology company to succeed, it always needed to be looking to destroy itself. If it didn't, someone else would ... high-tech could not remain high-tech for long.' It was 'the fine art of tearing down and building anew' – a clear American trait.

Creative destruction was one thing; in the face of a health panic, however, *laissez faire* was risky. America's raw, freewheeling nature was certainly a historic strength – even a soft-power resource. But it was not perhaps the best way to mobilise a national and international healthcare effort. This perhaps was what Joseph Nye foresaw when he urged Washington to develop the kind of institutions in which soft power could grow and thrive. Its existing network of embassies housed a Bureau of Educational and Cultural Affairs, but this did not compare to the British Council, Institut Français or Goethe-Institut. Voice of America reached 275 million listeners per week, many fewer than

---

2 In *Capitalism 4.0* (2010) – a spirited defence of capitalism, but not a Panglossian one. It did not argue that all was well, merely predicted that the 'system' was more supple than people imagined, more willing to experiment and change, and that the announcement of its death was therefore premature.

the BBC, with 426 million. America was represented primarily by CNN, which played in 384 million households and almost every hotel in the world.

In the Cold War the government did subsidise culture of the most forthright kind. Radio Free Europe broadcast anti-communist news east of the Iron Curtain, and when that was jammed by the KGB it developed a publishing arm, Free Europe Press, which sent balloons into the Soviet empire to drop leaflets and books. Between 1951 and 1956 some half a million leaflets were distributed in this way, along with copies of George Orwell's *Animal Farm* (which was translated into Ukrainian by refugees).

There has been a similar decline in education. The US is still the top destination in the world for students – a million at any one time – and its range of scholarships and leadership programmes means that more than three hundred future presidents and prime ministers have been schooled in America.[3] But this energetic exchange is vulnerable (especially to tough talk about foreigners and migrants), so between 2016 and 2017 the number of applications to American graduate schools fell by 3 per cent.

This is no trivial matter in an age when, thanks to social media, public opinion is both more volatile than ever and a louder instrument. In the past it was a nation's emigrants that helped shape the way their home country was seen abroad; now, increasingly, that role falls to immigrants. In the age of digital superhighways and social media, a nation's immigrants have become one of the primary means by which a national reputation is spread – by the messages and images they send home.

It follows that the way a country treats its foreign-born needs to be a central part of its soft-power strategy.

The sudden emergence of Barack Obama, though, followed by the equally abrupt rise of Donald Trump, reminded the world that governance itself was subject to surprising squalls and storms. In the febrile new atmosphere, even superficial pronouncements could carry far. Modern politicians were

---

3 An American education did not come cheap. But as Derek Bok, former president of Harvard University said: 'If you think education is expensive . . . try ignorance'.

juggling with gelignite whenever they opened their mouths. When President George Bush let slip that he hated broccoli, sales plummeted; when Barack Obama chose an unusual family pet – a Portuguese Water Dog – enquiries to breeders soared.

The industrial powerhouse, the home of innovation, the farm, the myth factory ... America remained all these things. But affection? If anything there was a backlash against so much size and strength. That have-a-nice-day smile seemed painted on.

In another twist, while it was a clear advantage to America that the world shared its language (roughly a quarter of the world's population spoke English), this too cut both ways. It made it easier to sell American cigarettes in Asia, but also allowed American jobs to slide to Mexico, China and India. In a world of producers and customers, something similar went for the idea of liberty itself. Freedom for the haves did not necessarily lead to freedom for the have-nots.

So much to do with soft power is double-edged in this way. The game of Monopoly was devised as a biting critique of the free market – left to its own devices, one person would end up with all the money – but came to symbolise the exact opposite: the fun of kickass deal-making. The little green light at the end of Scott Fitzgerald's *The Great Gatsby* was a glowing advertisement for the American dream, but also a warning that the dream was a shallow delusion. By the same token, the cameras that spread American glamour so successfully in the first half of the twentieth century, boosting the world's hunger for American products, later proved equally good at undermining it.

Even the toughest nuts flinched. 'The real key is not how many enemies I kill,' mused Newt Gingrich, the conservative former Speaker of the House, but, 'the number of alliances I gain.' And in 2018 Joseph Nye issued a reminder that soft power had only two sources – culture (which made a country liked) and political values (which made it respected). In both fields, he ventured, America was squandering a valuable resource.

Even in the extraordinary uproar of 2020, we should not forget that many of the world's most progressive causes (feminism, identity politics, civil rights, anti-war protest and environmental activism) took root in America first. It was a free market in ideas as well as products. But a radiant image, once gone, can take a while to recover. In 2018, Hal Brands, professor at Johns Hopkins University, wrote: 'It will be a long time before the world ever looks at America in quite the same way again.'

3

Britain: The Soft Footprint

In the long-gone summer of 2018 I was walking through London's Green Park when I saw a stream of people hurrying across the grass ahead of me, some dragging cases like passengers running for a plane. Curious to see what the fuss might be, I followed.

After only a few strides I heard the drumming of a regimental band, glimpsed a flash of scarlet moving through the trees and realised that this was nothing out of the ordinary, but a regular London event: the Changing of the Guard.

Still, I joined the crowd. It struck me that, like many people who have lived in the city for decades, I had long known about this sight but never actually seen it: it is no longer intended for Londoners – it is a ritual maintained for tourists.

There were certainly plenty of those. Several thousand filled the road outside the palace gates, pushed against the barricades and waited patiently on the Victoria Memorial, the monument unveiled in 1911 to commemorate the late Queen.[1]

I went with them, and at once took a step back in time. The memorial is grander than appears from the park; with 2000 tons of white marble, it is the largest monument to any monarch in the country. The queen sits high in her niche below a golden model of the Greek goddess Nike, flanked by stern symbolic representations of TRUTH, JUSTICE and CHARITY, with COURAGE and CONSTANCY in close attendance. Lions guard the steps,

---

1 Kaiser Wilhelm, the late Queen's grandson, attended the ceremony; a youngish Home Secretary named Winston Churchill took charge of the speeches.

along with bronze depictions of PEACE, AGRICULTURE, MANUFACTURE and PROGRESS.

There are nautical touches to suggest Britain's mastery of the sea (the bows of ships, mermaids, dolphins, shells), and her throne is arranged to face up the Mall through lines of lamp-posts topped by black sailing ships. This is Nelson's fleet, parading for inspection before the Admiral himself on his column in Trafalgar Square.

It evokes a Britain that no longer exists: a grandiose and self-confident imperial power. Indeed, the memorial itself was paid for by 'a grateful empire': Australia gave £25,000, and West Africa's tribes sent cargo to be sold for funds. An inscription beneath AGRICULTURE once read: 'Gift of New Zealand'.[2]

Everything about the scene reeked of tradition: the guardsmen in their top-heavy bearskins and scarlet tunics (designed under Henry VII more than five hundred years ago), the police horses, the implacable motion of the troops drilling their unswerving path through the sea of tourist heads, the stamp of feet on gravel. Inevitably, the odd tourist tried to break their sangfroid by pulling a face or taking a point-blank photo; the way the guards ignored such antics was all part of the stiff-upper-lip pantomime.

Many essential aspects of Britishness were present: royal ceremony, military pride, archaic manners, a commitment to doing things properly (i.e. as they have been done in the past) and a haughty keeping up of appearances. Of course, these sentiments are vestigial now – they meant something when London was the heart of a global empire, but now seem not just quaint but foolish. This is what tourists expect, however, and this is exactly the place they expect to see it. Only a small number shuffle through Buckingham Palace itself (50,000 per year – not much more than two busy days for the British Museum) but millions more jostle to witness this four-times-a-week ceremony. It is Royal Britain, an intrinsic part of the British brand.

Just when I was surrendering to the eccentric magic of the scene (enhanced rather than spoiled by the modern touches – plastic traffic cones, high-visibility jackets, announcements warning

---

2 The imperial subscription turned out to be so generous that there was enough left over to build Admiralty Arch, at the other end of the Mall.

of pickpockets), I became aware of a jaunty new thrum in the music. A moment ago it had been one of those plodding regimental marches most of us know but cannot quite pin down – 'Crown Imperial', maybe, or 'Orb and Sceptre'. Now it was something brasher and more light-hearted.

It was hard to place (it was so *out* of place). It was the theme from *Star Wars*.

The Guards playlist is a compendium of such hits – *Dr Who*, *Blackadder*, *Game of Thrones*, *Pirates of the Caribbean*. And while these last may be witty comments on Britain's history, they dramatically change the tone of the event. It is jarring to stand on the Victoria Memorial, waist deep in historical echoes, while military trombones play (ho-ho-ho) 'Dancing Queen'. It felt befuddled, like rabbit ears on the *Mona Lisa*, and betrayed a sheepish lack of confidence in the very traditions people from around the world were flocking to see. It was one thing to see these as antiquarian curiosities; another to reproduce them as easy pastiche. The figures bore this out. A 2013 VisitBritain survey found Buckingham Palace to be one of the top three reasons why people came to London (along with the London Eye and the Shard); but in the TripAdvisor ranking of customer satisfaction it came 121st. It was a proven let-down.

It opened a gap between expectation and reality. The beep-beep-beep of a reversing lorry seemed to be flashing an unmistakable signal: GAME OVER.

But perhaps, in another way, it was fitting. Britain was no longer the land of 'Pomp and Circumstance'. In 2016 it emerged that one-sixth of all the records sold worldwide had been British, but none of these were scored for orchestra or brass – the world was humming to Ed Sheeran and Adele, and becoming fluent in useful phrases such as 'It's so typical of me to talk about myself' or 'I'm stumbling off drunk'.

Just as fans of Bruce Springsteen or Ella Fitzgerald might feel a shiver of America in their music, so these new singers trigger sharp national associations.[3]

---

3 The UK might win only a modest haul of silverware at the Winter Olympics, but there is a good chance of hearing Coldplay or Oasis in the ice rink, as brilliant skaters from elsewhere dance to British tunes.

More to the point, this regal setting was now mainly a venue for street parties, concerts, marathons and other days out. A mish-mash of show tunes and pop anthems, with a wink of self-mockery, was perfectly in keeping with the new national culture. It could act the pompous Edwardian butler, yet poke fun at itself too.

Both Britains were here: one old, one new. In soft-power terms the message, and the metaphor, was clear: Britain itself was undergoing a changing of the guard.

The importance of Royal Britain can hardly be denied. The Queen has been sovereign of thirty-two nations, and is the symbolic head of a fifty-three-state Commonwealth.[4] She has made 260 official visits to 116 different countries, flying the flag for an old-fashioned idea of what Britain means. For various reasons the country takes this for granted (though a sizeable number of Britons would be more than happy to put an end to the royal hoopla if they could). But it is a cultural relations bonanza.

Its popularity and importance have been amply demonstrated by the worldwide success of the television series *The Crown*. Even hardened republicans could not resist – and had to concede the weight of the £2 billion per year the Royal Family was judged to attract to the national purse through tourism and brand loyalty.[5]

It is one of Britain's most successful exports. Though it symbolises contradictory things – class division, inequality and the hereditary principle as well as gracious manners and historical continuity – it carries a striking soft-power message. In the person of the Queen, the voice of the past continues to thrum in the present.

After a gloomy period, the brand was revived by the marriages of William to Kate, and Harry to Meghan. The latter, in the spring of 2019, gave a spectacular television audience (numbering up to two billion) a celebrity-packed gala in the bright Windsor

4 Yet how many of us have any idea when Commonwealth Day falls, let alone mark it in any way (the second Sunday in March, as it happens)?

5 A sizeable sum, even when set against the £292 million a year it costs the British taxpayer. And there are intangible proceeds too, in the way the Queen stands for qualities – decorum, restraint, duty – that feed the wider imagery of Britishness.

sunshine, with horses, castles, expensive dresses and sacred music, a merger of Britain and America, ancient and modern, white and mixed race. There was no way to measure how this might affect anyone's view, but it was a mood-lifting event for a nation embroiled in the seemingly insoluble wrangle over Brexit.

It proved short lived. Before the year was out, Britain's media had changed its tune, and was taking exuberant glee in finding fault with someone far too pretty, and far too foreign, to be granted more than the briefest honeymoon. And two years later the image cracked when the newlyweds decided to withdraw from the royal spotlight.

Just when I was brooding on matters of this sort there was a loud thump and the shocking scream of breaking glass. People glanced nervously, pulled faces, and even stopped taking photographs for a moment. All were thinking the same thing.

A bomb.

But the band played on, imperturbable, and the crowd relaxed: it must have been rubble in a building site – look at the forest of cranes down towards Victoria.

It was a sharp reminder of a dangerous fact of British life, however: it is no longer safe. The old cartoon – a friendly bobby on the beat, keeping the peace with a quiet word here and there – may have been rose-tinted, but now it was a distant memory. So far as the rest of the world was concerned, Britain was no longer orderly.

Terrorism was not new. The IRA bombing campaign had been an attack on the British – a local problem. But the Islamic jihadists did not recognise nationality. The attack on Borough Market in 2017 killed French, Australian, Canadian and Spanish passers-by. The car that ran riot on Westminster Bridge later that year killed an American visiting London for his twenty-fifth wedding anniversary, three French children on a school trip and a Romanian woman who was tipped into the Thames.[6] The bombers of 7 July 2005 were even less discriminate: twenty of the fifty-two casualties were foreign: from Poland, Italy, France, Ghana, Afghanistan,

6 The injured list included people from China, France, Germany, Italy, Poland, Portugal and South Korea.

India, New Zealand, Israel, Mauritius, Romania, Nigeria, Sri Lanka, Turkey, Iran, Grenada, Vietnam and Kenya.

There were outraged headlines in all of these countries, so Britain was not alone in no longer seeming a tranquil place where such things did not happen. And it wasn't just terrorism. The hair-raising increase in stabbings (no less troubling for being euphemistically termed 'knife crime') was also changing perceptions. In London there were 132 murders in 2018 (more than two a week); in 2019 there were seventy-eight in six months. Of course, this was not significant compared to Caracas (3387 dead in 2018), Cape Town (2493) or Tijuana (1897). And yes, London was far safer than it had been in the eighteenth century. But 'violent crime', according to the Office of National Statistics, had risen from 600,000 incidents a year in 2013 to an alarming 1.4 million in 2018. By modern standards this was a new and worrying phenomenon.

Once again, many of the victims were from overseas: a refugee from war in the Congo was stabbed in Gospel Oak; a Romanian working as a bouncer in Mayfair was killed by angry partygoers on New Year's Eve. When Britons die abroad (in Tunisia, Egypt or Thailand), whether by terrorism, thuggery or shark attacks, the media and the Foreign Office urge people not to travel unless their journey is *absolutely necessary*. By the same token, murders on British streets make headlines abroad.

A century on from the Victoria Memorial, a new and more troubling sculpture began to tour the country. A grieving figure made from 100,000 knives harvested by police amnesty boxes, it was called *The Knife Angel* – the blades were feathers on the wings. On the surface it was a heartening instance of swords-into-ploughshares, but the more insistent message was that Britain was a land of lethal weapons.

It was a powerful soft-power product in itself – created in the British Ironworks at Oswestry in Shropshire, near the place where iron began: Coalbrookdale. But in other ways it was a rupture with that past. And while the story it told – that British life had a dangerous new edge – may have had an immediate impact on tourist numbers, the greater harm was done in people's minds. The sense that London was a peaceful city through which a person could stroll home at night grew a fraction less secure.

More important, Britain was ... divided. The home of the Industrial Revolution was riven by rancorous politics; the home of royal pageantry was a backdrop for knife crime. For a nation with the word 'United' in its name, these were troubling signs.

When people ask what governments can best do to boost their soft power, the simplest answer is: govern. Read my lips ... deeds, not words. The soft story sent by mounting crime figures was matched by the messages implicit in other government policies, in all areas where the world encounters Britain for the first time. Whether it is queues at the airport, the migration and refugee system (which needs to be comprehensible, fair and above all quick), the 'customer experience' at overseas embassies, the range of educational openings, the extent of foreign aid and the strength of the helping hand ... in all these fields Britain needs, if it wants to be admired, to be at its best.

We might call this the soft power of first impressions, and it gives rise to a paradox: to impress foreigners, governments need to focus as keenly on domestic matters as they do on international affairs. Soft power, one could say, begins at home.

There could be no greater challenge in this area than the one posed by coronavirus. Britain's vaunted health service was rapidly exposed as lacking the resources to cope smoothly with a surge of this sort – decades of cost-cutting management had turned it into a system that ran at full blast even on a quiet day. It was not alone in that, of course, but it was also flat-footed when it came to equipment – equipment, it became increasingly obvious, that Britain no longer manufactured. Unlike Italy, Britain was given due warning: it could see what was unfolding in Lombardy. But a government elected to deliver Brexit and nothing else dragged its feet to an extent that surprised Europe and the wider world. While other nations were quick to impose quarantines, recognising that this (however grim) was a necessity, Britain appeared to cling to the hope that maybe, if it did less rather than more, this thing might just burn itself out.

Its leaders, reaching automatically into an antiquated toolkit, talked about 'bringing in the army', as if the virus could be cowed by Britain's historic regiments doing their sterling best.

In the long run those early missteps might not be remembered. And Britain soon began to show its other side too, in
a blizzard of initiatives that expressed a high degree of neigh-
bourly solidarity: people volunteered to help the health service
in their thousands; footballers opened their hotels to medical
workers; supermarkets created special hours for nurses; networks
sprang up to deliver food to the elderly; and online groups provided quizzes, games, cookery lessons and drinks parties. People
began to look out for each other in ways they had not done since
the Blitz. There was even talk of a land army to pick the crops.

It was not easy. A Conservative government, ideologically
attached to free markets, found itself nationalising large swathes
of the national economy. Indeed, when the virus began to fill
hospitals to groaning point, Britain, like all Western democracies, seemed to face an existential challenge: what was the role
and purpose of government at this exceptional time?

At a time when social media could magnify such revelations
into global news, the nature of each national response took on
an oversized significance. In the early days, the world admired
the way Japan (with its hygienic culture of bowing rather than
hugging) and South Korea (with its quick-footed faith in new
technology) had reacted, while frowning at the more blustering
American-British approach.

Of course there was nothing new about the need for governments to put themselves in a favourable light overseas. In the old
days, Britain sought to offer foreigners a taste of its charms by
planting oases all over the world. People with long memories
could recall British Council Libraries in unlikely places – I have
fond memories of one in Tehran – which were calm oases of
books, papers and magazines, along with tea, biscuits and other
British essentials. Such places could be dozy clubs for expatriates;
but also the setting for the initial contact, the warm or cool first
impression. They were the corners of a foreign field that were
forever Britain.

V. S. Naipaul fell in love with England when, as a child
in Trinidad, he came across an image of Constable's view of
Salisbury Cathedral in an illustrated guide. Soft power may be
as simple a matter as providing picture books.

And we are all familiar with the national features that would fill those books. The arrows in Britain's soft quiver cannot all be photographed, but they are sharp.

Let us count the ways.

The first is the extraordinary history that led Britain to establish a world-spanning empire. Through language, literature, liturgy and law, it left its footprints all over the world, sometimes simply by stamping its names on faraway places – whether physical wonders (Victoria Falls, Mount Everest, Hudson Bay) or cities (Darwin, Wellington, Kingston, Port Elizabeth). In different circumstances the world's highest mountain might have been named after the Indian mathematician who calculated its height (Radhanath Sikdar) rather than the retired Welsh surveyor (George Everest) who in 1865 was honoured by having 'Peak XV' named after him.[7] But the British name tells an accurate truth about who held power at that time. To rename it Mount Sikdar today would be to subtract an important part of its story.

The British Council has estimated that the 'long-term benefit' of the world adopting English as its second language is worth £405 billion – an unprovable number that is nevertheless a way of saying that it is of tremendous importance (even if it is equally important to the other countries that speak it, in North America, Australasia, Africa and India). It is visible in ways large and small. As Susan Sontag has noted, it is the default setting of aviation: 'An Italian pilot landing in Vienna speaks to the tower in English. An Austrian landing in Palermo does the same.' Even internal flights – Madrid to Barcelona, say – use English during take-off and landing. This became the standard after several disasters (over Tenerife in 1977, where 583 died, or the 1996 mid-air collision near Delhi) were blamed on linguistic confusion.

Inducing a quarter of the world to speak your language? Now *that's* soft power. It may have been earned the hard way, with armies, colonial magistrates, economic threats and gunboat diplomacy, but when those are gone, the overhang remains.

---

7 Everest himself objected to the choice of his name, on the touching grounds that it was hard to say in Hindi (he had once been Surveyor-General of India). But the Royal Geographical Society ignored him. He died the following year.

Britain's history means that Britain is *known*: the first prerequisite of soft power.

The consequences are too numerous to list. Government buildings in Lagos, Lahore and Wellington; mansions in Port of Spain; churches in Hong Kong and Delhi; colonial houses and hill stations in Africa and India, where the cottages by the cricket pitch are called Harrow-on-the-Hill and Lily of the Valley, with St Stephen's up on its ridge ... The stones of Empire shaded these lawns long after Britain itself was sent packing. In New Zealand, South Africa, Singapore and Hong Kong, couples can have English-themed weddings, complete with red telephone boxes, bridge tables, boating scenes, Victorian lamps, wrought-iron lamp-posts and Georgian railings.

The ancient story that winds from Stonehenge to Brexit and from Romans in Britain to the spirit of the Blitz, through medieval wars, maritime roving, political advance and industrial revolution, still grips the world (1.58 million visitors drove down the A303 to see the ring of stones in 2017) not because it is a righteous fable, or the opposite, but because it reveals the dramatic interplay of both. The Foreign Office spokesman Edwin Samuel likes to call this 'soft power with a hard edge'. In his view, soft power alone is not enough; it needs the backing of government. 'You can have as many opera festivals as you like,' he said. 'But you must also *matter*.'

Thanks to Britain's imperial past, this saga is no longer a source of automatic pride; but the hangover from those domineering years is palpable. It manifests itself both in the Commonwealth subjects who now live in Britain, and in Britons who live abroad. On a diplomatic level it works with a formal network of international organisations. But it has an even more telling resonance in the realm known as 'the Anglosphere' – the mostly white former colonies that in different ways speak, think and conduct their affairs in English. It is not a diplomatic bloc – the historian Robert Conquest has called it 'weaker than a federation, but stronger than an alliance' – but it is a nostalgic binding agent, a banner brandished by conservative spirits loyal to what Winston Churchill called 'the special genius of the English-speaking peoples'.

The historian Andrew Roberts and others have pointed out that the wars of the twentieth century were all joint endeavours conducted by this Anglosphere, and this is true. Not all of them were volunteers, however. And though the Anglosphere is not imaginary – it shares military intelligence and other substantive assets along with personal and cultural connections – the modern bonds are more fragile than they were. A shared history, even if nations are on different sides of it (conquerors and conquered), is not the same thing as a shared story: there are opposite sides.

The second string of British influence is the rule of law. Ever since the Magna Carta in 1215 Britain has self-identified as a land where the law is a brake on arbitrary authority; the Crown is subject to its rules; citizens are equal; individual and commercial rights are governed by its principles; and disputes are settled in court.

Eight centuries after Magna Carta, the legal principles it inspired were planted in a surprising new home: Kazakhstan. To most British minds this was terra incognita, but it was a vast new presence in the world, bigger than France, Germany, Spain, Italy, Britain, Portugal, Austria, Switzerland, Holland and Belgium combined, while still leaving room for another Germany. It was more or less as big as Europe. And it was rich: it had palatial oil reserves and a GDP (in 2017) worth $160 billion.

Kazakhstan was also, thanks to its strategic position on the new international trade route with China, a commercial centre of booming importance. In reconnecting with global business after the long Siberian winter of Soviet-era rule, the country needed a reliable legal system to help keep the goods flowing. Free markets required lawyers, and Russia was a cautionary parable, with its special brand of gangster capitalism.

For that rarest of commodities – trust – Kazakhstan turned to . . . Britain. In 2018 it announced that the former Lord Chief Justice Lord Woolf would be leading an eight-judge team to establish and operate a new commercial law court in Astana.

There were similar courts in Singapore, Hong Kong, Dubai and Abu Dhabi, but this would be the first in Central Asia. It would settle any disputes that might arise in the course of trade on the new trade route – the judges would visit five times a year, and preside over cases in robes of sky blue (the colour of the national flag).

In so doing they would serve a soft-power purpose, flying the flag of British fair play in a region that had once been a Soviet gulag. In practice there were hardly any cases, and some saw it as a lapse – trying to turn a hard-won set of principles into an easy commodity: justice for sale. Could impartiality be just another product? But Woolf insisted that the court exemplified the importance of the rule of law, while also having a diplomatic aim: strengthening the status of British justice as a model for others to follow. This was true: more than thirty nations governed themselves according to the 'Westminster System', and while in some cases the system was more honoured in the breach than the observance, it remained a powerful soft imprint.

'Trust' may seem an abstract quality, featuring in few balance sheets of the national interest. But it may be the most precious feature of Britain's soft power, underpinning all others. The Spanish-American philosopher George Santayana once observed that the Anglo-Saxon was the most disliked of men – 'except when you needed someone you could trust'. And while this was by no means the full story – tales of British perfidy were legion: in India it was said that the reason the sun never set on the British empire was because even God could not trust an Englishman in the dark – it was true that a high degree of trust had long supported Britain's legal traditions and everyday habits, from driving to queueing. Relative to many places in the world, it still does. It is no longer a place where you can leave your wallet in a bar and expect to find it later, but by most standards it is extremely law-abiding.

This is how Sir John Major put it to a House of Lords committee in 2013: 'I hope I am not seeing this through tainted British eyes – I do not think I am – but people trust us. They may often disagree with us, but they believe we are to be trusted, and believe we deal honestly with them. The value of that is . . . incalculable.'

This is the basis of Britain's longstanding tradition in banking and finance. The City of London may stand in a lucky junction of the time zones – it can speak to Asia in the morning and

America in the afternoon – but it also has a rare heritage of honouring contracts. The world has known for a long time that the word *credit* means credibility; the fiduciary basis of 'trust' funds is inscribed in their very name; and the motto of the London Stock Exchange states 'My Word is My Bond'. In the history of finance, trustworthiness is both the foundation and the glue – the idea that you can deposit (or lend) money in the knowledge that it will not vanish or be damaged. What is the use of a promissory note if one's word cannot be trusted?

There is a clear commercial advantage in keeping this quality at the front of the world's mind. London's status as a financial centre had long allowed it to be a major employer that contributed a heavy slice of the national income. But that was less important than the ideology of fair dealing it still – even after the 2008 crash – represented.

An even more vivid dramatisation of this principle is expressed through British sport. Cricket's faith in fair play and golf's obligation to play the ball as it lies and accept the rub of the green without complaint are powerful principles – even if, in modern times, they no longer hold. The commercialisation of professional sport, indeed, has subverted the old sporting ideals by replacing the original idea that it was the taking part that counted with the ideology of winner takes all. Football's Premier League champions scoop the pot without playing more games than the team placed last; the best players earn millions more than their slower-footed colleagues, without putting in any more hours. It is no longer about doing one's best and may the best man win . . .

The historical legacy remains potent, even so. And Britain did invent or codify most of the world's favourite games: football, rugby, cricket, golf, mountaineering, hockey, rounders (which begat baseball), badminton, snooker, ping-pong and the country pursuits: hunting, shooting and fishing. It did not lead the way in horse-racing – most of Britain's thoroughbreds are descended from a single stallion in Aleppo, the Great 'Darley Arabian' (a fine symbol of the biological benefits of migration) – but its love of gambling helped turn even that into a spectator sport. It could not match Germany, France and Italy in music or painting, but it did have an uncanny knack for devising pastimes (ways to pass the time) the whole world could enjoy.

The results are evident everywhere, most obviously in the global enthusiasm for Premier League football. It is watched in 643 million homes in 188 of the world's 193 countries, with a regular audience many times that. The closing stretch of the 2018/19 season, in which Manchester City and Liverpool jostled for the title, was (according to the market research agency Nielsen) seen by more than three billion viewers. It is said that China has more Manchester United fans than there are members of the Communist Party.

Cab drivers in the Caribbean wear Chelsea trainers; elephant spotters in Kenya shade their eyes with Spurs caps; construction workers in Abu Dhabi wear Arsenal track suits. In 2017, £442 million of Premier League merchandise was sold overseas. Only a few nostalgists believe that this would be the case if the leading teams were not powered primarily by foreign players, connecting their own fan bases in Africa, Europe and Latin America with the sights and sounds of the English weekend. In a 2018 Populus survey conducted in twenty countries, the Premiership was the number one 'British icon'. As Tom Fletcher wrote in *The Naked Diplomat*, 'A British embassy can never have too many pictures of David Beckham on the wall.'

In 2017 there were only five countries (or 'territories', in TV parlance) in the world that did not screen the Manchester derby: Afghanistan, Cuba, Moldova, North Korea and Turkmenistan. This is not just an extraordinary commercial package: given that the Premiership is full of overseas footballers and managers, it sends an extraordinary snapshot of Britain – the vibrant centre of the sport – around the globe.

Those who complain that it deprives talented English teenagers of their chance to play at the top level miss the point that this is a soft-power coup. Ironically, perhaps, it is financed not so much by England's footballing prowess as by its desire to watch games on television – it is driven by domestic couch potatoes. But enduring values flow through such transmissions: the boisterous sound of an English crowd, the funny (or ugly) chants, the witty (or dumb) banners, the geography of its clubs (people in Botswana know where Norwich and Middlesbrough are), the gobbets of post-match English ('to be fair there was contact, but for me it was never a penalty') and the glimpses of fair play at its best and worst — the ostentatious 'respect' for the officials matched only by the vitriol with which they are constantly besieged.

In imperial times it was cricket that most obviously stood — indeed, was urged — as a demonstration of sporting etiquette: honouring the umpire and shaking hands whatever the outcome. The idea that good conduct ('fair play') mattered more than winning was not just school-song whimsy ('Play up, play up, and play the game!'); it was an allegory of the entire imperial system: a message to the world that it should accept defeat gracefully. It made sense that cricket should have become England's, if not Britain's, emblematic pursuit — its rules and rituals were a perfect fit.

It was a powerful weapon on the home front, too. The philosophy of fair play was promoted in Britain's schools as a means of replacing a young man's allegiance to birthplace and family with loyalty to the institutions he would soon represent. It was a succinct statement of what it meant (in theory) to be British. It implied decorum, obedience to authority, a strict ethic about 'doing one's best', sympathy for the underdog, and generosity in both victory and defeat. Anyone could cite instances where people fell short of such standards, but the ideal remained.

> *For when the One Great Scorer comes*
> *To mark against your name,*
> *He writes — not that you won or lost —*
> *But how you played the game.*

The proposition that manners mattered more than the result, that the means might trump the ends, was original. In 1946, when England sent a team to Australia as an expression of thanks for its contribution to the war effort, and the Prime Minister, Clement Attlee, reminded the players that this was a goodwill mission, he was echoing what a previous manager, Pelham Warner, had said in 1932, when he told reporters that cricket was 'a synonym for all that was true and honest', and that the team had a duty to spread 'the gospel of British fair play'. That was not all. 'To say "that is not cricket" implies something underhand, something not in keeping with the best ideals.'

Those words would soon leave a bitter taste, because this was the 'Bodyline' tour – a classic lesson in *un*sporting behaviour. But at this time the idea still commanded respect. And it cropped up in some surprising places – in Arthur Koestler's novel *Darkness at Noon*, for instance. This icy depiction of Stalinist justice, a critique of revolutionary Russia by a Hungarian exile – is not a place one might expect to find allusions to the thwack of leather on willow. But there it stands.

The character at the centre of the story, Commissar Rubashov, is a leading light of the Revolution. Now he himself faces torture and execution as the Revolution begins – like most revolutions – to devour its own heroes. In his anguish he remains proud of the way he and his kind replaced 'the nineteenth century's liberal ethics of fair play' with a purer faith in 'the revolutionary ethics of the twentieth century'. Fair play, in his view, was a misty notion that had long passed its sell-by date: 'A revolution conducted according to the rules of sport is an absurdity, he said.' The new Russia had to throw aside the bourgeois 'conventions and rules of cricket morality'.

Cricket morality? In Siberia?

It was unlikely, but it made sense. To the radical utopians of Koestler's novel, 'fair play' was an outright heresy, since it held that the end did *not* justify the means, that utopia might *not* be worth the human price. As Lenin himself had cried: 'What, did you think this could be accomplished without firing squads?' In the brave new world, Rubashov had to denounce such talk. How could a solid 13 not out be judged 'finer' than a century; how could there be such a thing as 'not cricket'? Worse: while cricket was evidently a game enjoyed by the English upper crust, with their country-house lawns, cakes and teacups, it was also a rustic pursuit. Farmers and postmen, too, carried it across the world, along with their teapots and deckchairs.

That is why the Revolution's guns had to be trained on cricket etiquette before it was too late. The end needed to justify the means, no matter how heavy the cost.

It often seems fanciful to give sport this amount of credit as a cultural force. Did not George Orwell disparage it as 'war minus the shooting', a school-boyish conflation of games with grown-up affairs of state? Indeed. But Orwell may, for once, have missed the point of his own *bon mot*. In the soft-power sense, the fact that sport really *was* war by other means was surely highly desirable: it urged playful conflict instead of real slaughter, with rules and a handshake afterwards. Who could sneer at that?

Either way, the fact that such a value could worm its way into a novel like *Darkness at Noon* showed how far and wide the gospel of cricket had travelled. Kofi Annan, the Ghanaian Secretary-General of the United Nations, once quipped that everyone in the world could grasp what was 'not cricket', and while this may not have been always true, the same idea has been celebrated both by school prefect types ('There's a breathless hush in the close tonight ...') and by Marxist historians such as the Trinidadian C. L. R. James, who wrote: 'Eton and Harrow had nothing on us.'

In 'Forever Eton', an essay in the *Observer* (1948), George Orwell agreed that the game did express 'a well-marked trait in the English character, the tendency to value "form" or "style" more highly than success'.[8] This was the ethos that lay behind the Olympic ideal – a French concoction informed by British ingredients. The Baron de Coubertin had been so impressed by the sporting spirit he witnessed on a visit to England after France's humiliation at the hands of Prussia in 1870 that he resolved to introduce the same combative zeal in France – and did so through the Olympics. It was another instance of the way British sporting power, regarding victory and defeat as Kipling's two imposters, could infect the world.[9]

Koestler knew Orwell and may have owed his knowledge of cricket to him. Just as *Animal Farm* was flown across the Iron

---

8 In 'Raffles and Miss Blandish' (1946) Orwell noticed that cricket did offend the totalitarian mind. The Nazis went so far as to ban it, he wrote, when they saw it gaining 'a certain footing' in Germany.

9 Kipling himself, an eager and influential imperialist, was even then a controversial figure, but this poem remains the 'nation's favourite', and its message – a plea for composure – continues to greet the competitors on Wimbledon's Centre Court.

Curtain by balloon, as a propaganda move, so *Darkness at Noon*
was backed by the British government, which subsidised a print
run of 50,000 copies when it emerged that French communists
had been buying and destroying it. It may not have been their
plan to boost Koestler's royalties, but that was what their campaign achieved. Koestler himself later said (with pride) that the
French edition of *Darkness at Noon* may have saved France from
communism.

Governments could not have written such books (though they
could suppress them). But they could enlist them as soft-power
weapons when the need arose.

The fourth great element in Britain's soft power is its literature.
Its leading characters are globe-trotting celebrities. From Arthur
and Merlin, through Holmes and Watson to James Bond, Mary
Poppins, Alice in Wonderland and Harry Potter . . . a long list
of such figures have climbed into foreign minds and introduced
them to British dreams.

So too have British authors – most obviously Shakespeare. He
is revered all over the world. Goethe referred to him possessively
as '*unser* Shakespeare' – a great German who happened to have
been born in Stratford. His work exists in ninety languages.
Nelson Mandela read and annotated *Julius Caesar* during his years
on Robben Island,[10] and Shakespearian lines appear in Moscow's
Metro, Verona's amphitheatre, Japanese stages, Indian villages and
Balkan war zones. One is never far from a Shakespeare festival –
there are four hundred in America alone.

There is more to this than mere popularity. Shakespeare's plays
are earthed in the English landscape: he transmitted a vision of
willows growing aslant brooks, bare ruin'd choirs where late
the sweet birds sang, and look where the darling buds of May
peer through the dawn in russet mantle clad. Rural England
formed his mind.

But he did not restrict himself to English stories (and we are
not conflating England and Britain – the latter did not exist in

---

10 In 2012, the Mandela Shakespeare (now in private hands – he gave it away) featured
in a British Museum exhibition on Shakespeare and the World.

Shakespeare's day). Indeed, an extraordinary number of his heroes and heroines were foreign – Hamlet, Othello, Romeo, Juliet, Timon (of Athens), Antony, Cleopatra, Julius Caesar, Shylock, the two gentlemen of Verona and many others. *Measure for Measure* is set in Vienna, *Much Ado About Nothing* in Messina, *Othello* in Cyprus, *Twelfth Night* in 'Illyria'. The fact that Tudor England had a cosmopolitan imagination explains why these plays are so comprehensible to so many. He belonged to the world, not just England.

He also surmounted the barriers of time. In *Measure for Measure*, when a pure lady objects to the advances of a licentious duke, the latter replies: 'Who will believe you, Isabel?' This was Shakespeare anticipating MeToo by four hundred years, and hitting a universal nerve. His plays gleam with insights into the egalitarian basics of human life – princes and peasants, dukes and chambermaids, all will in the end be food for worms. And that life is rarely simple: it is always composed of light and dark, positive and negative. Wise men are fools; kings are knaves. Villains have their sensitive moments; decent men can be cruel. Life is a mingled yarn, all good and ill together. This is not a uniquely English idea, but Shakespeare clothed it in poetry that made it resonate everywhere. And the language he created was widely echoed. When Lincoln spoke about the better angels of our nature, he was channelling a little piece of Elizabethan England.

That is why, in 2011, the Chinese Premier Wen Jiabao insisted, after he had been shown round the MG factory, on being taken to Shakespeare's birthplace in Stratford-upon-Avon. Shakespeare had been banned under Mao, on the grounds that sad stories about the death of kings were 'revisionist, feudalist, capitalist', but he was still widely admired. So in 2016, the four hundredth anniversary of Shakespeare's birth, the Royal Shakespeare Company was invited to China to celebrate a decade-long project to translate the plays into Chinese. Some saw this as a welcome relaxing of constraints; others deemed it a ploy. There was some glee when the RSC bridled at the cutting of a phrase here and there by Chinese officials, since Shakespeare himself had been subject to censorship by the 'Master of the Revels', who wielded his own blue pencil against sedition – easy to find, in stories about the rise and fall of kings.

Soft power is more subtle than propaganda: it faces both ways.

Nor must we think that fictional characters have no weight. In the preface to his *Dictionary*, Dr Johnson observed: 'The chief glory of every people arises from its authors.' This remains the case. The world's most famous railway platform (Platform Nine and Three-Quarters for the train to Hogwarts) does not exist, yet thanks to Harry Potter it draws thousands of visitors to a souvenir shop in London's King's Cross.

The literary tradition is matched by a scientific heritage that includes Newton, Fleming, Darwin, Faraday, Bell and Baird ... and where would the world be without knowledge of gravity, antibiotics, evolution, electricity, telephones and television?

Apart from giving Britain a worldwide reputation as a scientific pathfinder, figures like these have given enormous prestige to Britain's universities, which are thus a forceful soft-power engine. Despite murmurs in some quarters that the UK's education system is 'broken', most global surveys place three British universities in the world's top ten, making it a magnet for the world's most ambitious students. The sector supports a million jobs, generates £26 billion per annum, drives the national ability to innovate and forges connections hard to achieve in any other way.

Few walks of British life shine so brightly. One in seven recent heads of state (fifty-eight of them) spent time studying in Britain.[11] Australia's Malcolm Turnbull, Burma's Aung San Suu Kyi and Pakistan's Imran Khan went to Oxford; the King of Bahrain and the Prime Minister of Singapore went to Cambridge. Others studied in Manchester (Prime Minister of Iceland), London (President of Syria) or the LSE (President of Colombia). Some attended military school: the Sultan of Brunei and the Grand Duke of Luxembourg both learned to be British at Sandhurst.

The King of Belgium, the Queen of Denmark, the Prime Ministers of Hungary and Malaysia, the Presidents of Finland and Portugal ... It is a formidable list. Imagine a world in which that number of world leaders had been educated in South Korea,

---

11 This according to a 2017 study by Britain's Higher Education Policy Institute.

say, or Tanzania – two countries of similar size? One leader, the Gambian President Adam Barrow, once worked as an Argos security guard while studying property management in London, and later said: 'The UK helped me to become the person I am today. Working fifteen hours a day builds a man.' Since the Argos he worked in was in the Holloway Road, it also made him an Arsenal supporter.

4

Britain: London Calling

B ritish culture has circled the world in plainer ways. Imperial
  settlers in New Zealand took with them an entirely new
ecosystem – pigs, sheep and dairy livestock were new species for
this part of the world. And the keen national enthusiasm for gardening, nourished by Britain's varied soil and plentiful rain, also
ranged far and wide.

It was not merely acquisitive: it operated like a pump. Exotic
species were brought home, anglicised, then taken overseas again.
In Sri Lanka's hill country, for instance, an area of tea plantations
known as Nuwara Eliya ('City on the Plain') became a Little
England of cottages and gardens, with a jacket-and-tie hotel, a
golf course that might have hailed from Worplesdon, and a hundred other flavours of English country life: flower shows, fishing,
fox hunting, whist drives. Thrushes and robins chirped in the
hedges; carrots, leeks and strawberries grew in the raised beds.

There was more to this than rose gardens and orange pekoe
tea, of course. These were only the surface marks of a profounder
imposition. Beside the golf course (founded in 1889) stood a
memorial to a harsher truth about British rule. The grave of
Major Thomas Rogers, it recorded that in his time as a government agent he shot 1400 elephants.

But the softest ingredients were camellia bushes. This was tea
country – and little was more English than that. The green slopes
of Nuwara Eliya, along with similar terrains in Assam, Darjeeling
and Malawi, were a powerful reminder that tea (the most notable
British contribution to world cuisine) relied on components that
did not even grow in Britain: leaves from hills like this; sugar

hacked out of Caribbean islands by enslaved West Africans; and delicate 'china' cups and saucers made in the blasting furnaces of British industry, in Stoke-on-Trent.

Much the same could be said for coffee, chocolate, tobacco and the Spanish oranges required for Dundee or Oxford marmalade. The most ordinary British treats, the staple commodities of the nation's daily life . . . were born abroad.

This is all obvious and well known, but it contains an important fact about soft power – namely, that it is not always the opposite of hard power, or an alternative, but its offspring or afterglow. Cultural stalks flower in soil raked by sterner hands. This is especially relevant in Britain's case. Seventy years after the world liberated itself from British rule, its cultural effects continued to appear in unlikely places.

On Italy's Amalfi coast, for instance, where the Villas Rufolo and Cimbrone, in the hilltop town of Ravello, both have gardens created by British expatriates, with box hedges, ivy-clad walls, hydrangea, fuchsia, geranium and roses (Lady Hillingdon, Stanwell Perpetual and Irene Watts). The trellis is coated with wisteria and jasmine, and pots of begonia stand by the ponds. The lawns are dotted with dandelions – even the *weeds* are British – while the gravel drive is freckled with fallen chestnuts.[1]

Ravello was a popular detour for Grand Tourists needing a break from the heat of Pompeii and Naples. The Bloomsbury Group made itself a bird's nest on this hill when a Yorkshire aristocrat, Lord Grimthorpe, bought the Villa Cimbrone and asked Vita Sackville-West to 'do' the garden for him. Anyone who was anyone came to stay: E. M. Forster, Sir Edwin Lutyens, T. S. Eliot, Virginia Woolf, D. H. Lawrence (*Lady Chatterley's Lover* was written in the Rufolo Hotel), Gertrude Jekyll and many other luminaries of Fitzrovia basked in this airy retreat.

These grand footprints (cause leading to effect leading to cause leading to effect) led Villa Cimbrone to become a five-star hotel, with what might be the finest vista in Europe. That at

---

1 It was at the Villa Rufolo that Wagner found inspiration for the magic garden in his opera *Parsifal*, when he visited this dramatic coast in 1880. A Gothic fantasy set in a beaker of the blue south, it struck a powerful chord. So a powerful nugget of German culture also shines out of the British contribution to this warm Mediterranean setting.

least was the opinion of Gore Vidal, who bought the house next door.

In these gardens it is easy to believe that soft power actually resembles botany. A graft here, a cutting there, an airborne seed, fresh soil, sunlight, the jolt of new water ... Who knows what wonderful cultivars might thrive in such conditions?

There are many English gardens around the world – and by 'English' we do mean a style rather than a nationality: an aesthetic, not a place. Victorian plant hunters mixed remote flora with native stock so eagerly that British horticulture was itself a hybrid: the 'English' style flourished in Hertfordshire and Suffolk before being sent back to India, Singapore, North America and South Africa. It drew on ingredients trawled from everywhere, so could flourish anywhere as well.

And it was not only herbaceous gardens. An even more emphatic export was the country park, the Capability Brown vision of lawns, trees and water through which aristocrats could perambulate. The best known of these, the *Englischer Garten* in Munich, was the largest city park in Europe. But similar spaces appeared everywhere: an expanse of grass and gravel, a lake, an Alpine rockery, a neo-classical pattern of footpaths, a Chinese pagoda – all over the world it was possible to pick up a walking cane, put on an imaginary top hat and act the Anglophile.

In the tropics these gardens were permitted to run wild, with loud colours and heavy foliage. But they were kept under control with paths, dripping stone fountains and a sundial. Just as seeds, bulbs and saplings could be transplanted from continent to continent, so the social atmosphere behind them could drift on the wind.

The world tunes in to an echo of just this every April, when a golf event, the US Masters, plays itself out on the glistening fairways of Augusta, Georgia. It is a vision of tall pines, grassy slopes, wind-ruffled water, arched bridges and pink banks of azalea – the spitting image of Wisley. In Tokyo an 'English Court' attempts to recreate the appearance of a classic London park, though the gardeners can't resist clipping the trees with Kondo zeal until they look like bonsai.

Gardening was not the most important means by which Britain inserted itself into foreign climates. But as a metaphor for the subtle way in which national traits seed themselves it is both tenacious and suggestive. The first admirers of English gardens fell in love with their mix of order and naturalness: they seemed at once harmonious and tranquil. But people soon noticed that this was a pose: Victorian England was also a rush of noise and go-getting. Britain, it appeared, was a country that could dress one way, act in another; say one thing and do the opposite. Thus was born 'perfidious Albion' – a well-groomed garden in which snakes and weeds lurked.

Those elegant pleasure grounds, tributes to sobriety and good taste, were built on the proceeds of slavery; those composed vistas carried hints of whip and chain.

Soft power is ambiguous: in proclaiming one message it can express another. Hard truths lie behind the cycle of flowering and decay. Kew was much more than a place to take the air. Beneath its surface beauties – the arboretum and the palm houses – lay the research engine of Britain's empire. It was here that rubber seedlings from Brazil were prepared for new estates in Malaysia, and here that tea varieties gathered in China were hot-housed and interbred for new hillsides in Sri Lanka and Malawi.

There was more, too, to the English garden than a pastoral touch. It cultivated ideas. Between the moss-free lawns and clumps of suburban colour stand assumptions about the governance of wild places. A jungle or rainforest make natural claims that they can look after themselves, that nature is the best gardener. An English garden insisted that 'natural' terrain was unkempt, and must be brought to heel by people who knew better.

It is no coincidence that one of the first English novels (*Robinson Crusoe*) described a wild island that became a farm. When Crusoe first sees waving sugar cane he finds it 'imperfect' for 'want of cultivation', and decides to create a plantation. Possession is all: his 'secret pleasure' when he comes upon a valley full of melons and grapes is the colonial emotion that 'I was king and lord of all this country'.

The English garden is a green representation of such impulses.

It gathers plants from the four corners of the earth, grafts them in new ways, and sends them out again with fragrant messages about the blessings of British estate management.

Messages of that sort linger for a long time.

The impositions of this imperial past have been well documented, its exploitative nature amply described. But within its acquisitive folds lay an evangelical religious impulse that produced significant after-effects. Britain's charitable sector is one of the busiest and most generous in the world, extending a helping hand to victims of war, famine and disaster all around the world. It is not necessary that people know or care about the nationality of the helping hand (some might even resent it as imperial condescension – the so-called 'white saviour complex'). And it is true that modern charitable work can sometimes resemble imperial service, offering the opportunity to do good deeds while enjoying a daring tropical adventure.

But there is a silver lining to that cloud. British charities are prolific, well funded, not part of national government, and thus a clear soft-power instrument.

Secular kindness rose as churchgoing fell. The cracks opened up in the religious story by Darwin's discoveries were filled by an ordinary humanitarian urge to help. In 1919 a young woman named Eglantyne Jebb, daughter of a Shropshire aristocrat, looked at the ruins of post-war Europe and felt an obligation to *do* something. Berlin and Vienna were stricken by malnutrition and rickets: thousands were starving.

She had learned German and French with a governess, was one of the first women to study history at Oxford, and after travelling in the Balkans was moved by the plight of children trapped behind Britain's blockade of the defeated territories. Together with her sister Dorothy, a Suffragette and reformer who married a Labour MP, she acted. Her social connections helped them to launch the project at the Albert Hall, and they quickly raised £35,000. Before long they were delivering aid to twenty-four countries, and celebrities like Thomas Hardy and George Bernard Shaw were endorsing them in letters to *The Times* (which, in those days, simply *everybody* read).

The name they chose for their new charity was Save the Children.

Jebb was arrested in Trafalgar Square for distributing harrowing images of starving German infants, and her pamphlets were deemed subversive; the public mood was not yet sympathetic to the sufferings of Germans, and the message *was* trenchant: 'Our blockade has caused this . . .' But the prosecuting barrister at her trial was so impressed by her eloquence that he himself volunteered to pay the £5 fine.

A few years later Save the Children was sending shiploads of aid to Russia. Soon it could claim to have rescued a quarter of a million children. Today, it raises nearly £2 billion per annum and in 2016 'reached' twenty-two million children.

Jebb had laid the groundwork for what would soon be a universal principle. Her 'Declaration of the Rights of the Child' was adopted by the League of Nations in 1924 and later emerged again as the UN Convention on the Rights of the Child.

Others followed her lead. At the height (or depths) of the next war, in October 1942, a group of clergymen and academics met in the library of Oxford's University Church of St Mary the Virgin to discuss the famine in Greece. Britain had responded to the Nazi occupation of the Balkans with another blockade, this time based on the assumption (no doubt correct) that food supplies would simply sustain Nazi troops. But it was estimated that some 300,000 Greeks had died in the winter of 1941–2. The Oxford group, many of whom had strong feelings about Greece thanks to their classical education, wanted to intervene. One, indeed, was an Australian-born scholar named Gilbert Murray, a well-known translator of ancient Greek tragedy.

The group agreed to do whatever it could. It called itself the Oxford Committee for Famine Relief, and in time became known by its telegraphic address: OXFAM.

The response was historic. In the eight decades following that initial meeting, Oxfam raised and spent nearly £11 billion (in today's money) on overseas projects, through an organisation that employed five thousand people across the world. Many of those who owed their eyesight or life to Oxfam may not have cared about the charity's roots in Classics at Oxford. But that, it so happened, was the case.

We can infer several contradictory things from these stories. Both of these charities were the brainchildren of the well-born elite – *noblesse oblige* still had force in those days. In another example, Peter Scott, founder of the World Wildlife Fund, was a product of Oundle, Cambridge and the Royal Navy and had won bronze at the Berlin Olympics for dinghy sailing. As a well-connected Conservative candidate he was able to persuade the Duke of Edinburgh to become the WWF's patron, and himself drew by hand the black-and-white panda logo that became its trademark.[2] It was inspired by Chi Chi, a recent arrival from Beijing and the only panda in the West.

Second, the charitable sector began as an act of defiance against government policy, rather than in support of it. Political protest (in Oxfam's case, against the use of starvation as a political weapon) was an intrinsic part of its make-up. So while in one way the charitable impulse was part of the establishment, indeed its child, in another way it was its opponent – or at least its conscience.

Soft power of this sort is not always at the government's beck and call. While Britain's charitable sector is indeed a feather in its soft-power cap, it is rarely keen to be part of an overtly political initiative. Just as the founders were often contravening official policy, so employees across the sector tend to see themselves as working against the grain. Far from seeing themselves as servants of the national cause, they pride themselves on being apart from or even superior to it. Their brand depends on their being *more* humanitarian than the nations they represent. They are, after all, *non*-governmental organisations.

Save the Children and Oxfam are only the most prominent in a long list of such charities. The United Kingdom has more than 200,000 in all, and while some are tiny, and others overlap (competing for funds), en masse they are a major industry. And they have one more thing in common: nearly all were born at the end of Britain's imperial story. The British Red Cross was

---

2 According to one witness, Scott knocked it off in 'about twenty minutes'. Today it might require an extensive consultation process, a seven-figure budget and the input of many stakeholders. In a famous case, the Royal Mail spent £1.5 million rebranding itself as 'Consignia' before being mocked, giving up and restoring the original name.

given its Royal Charter in 1908 (as a branch of the Swiss movement launched in 1863), at the apogee of Britain's potency, but Christian Aid was born in 1945, CAFOD, Amnesty International and the World Wildlife Fund in the early 1960s, WaterAid in 1981 and Comic Relief in 1985. Many smaller agencies, involving relief work, children, animal welfare, prisoners of conscience or refugees, have sprung from these giant trees. All of them echo, in a faint and barely detectable way, the memory of sterner imperial projects.

There is a problem, however. Just as charities may want to distance themselves from governments, so governments may not always want to be associated with them. Charities suffer more than most from reputational damage: the sexual scandals that erupted over Oxfam in Central America were estimated, in one report, to have eroded the value of its brand by 'hundreds of millions of pounds'. Some 7000 donors fled, and the charity was forced to announce that its new priority was restoring trust. 'We can't do good,' said the new Chief Executive, Danny Sriskandarajah, 'while colleagues are causing harm.'

That is not to say that governments are impotent in this area. On the contrary, when it comes to creating and maintaining the institutions on which soft power depends, they are irreplaceable. Britain has a broad range of these, supporting conservation in the landscape (through national parks, alongside the National Trust – a private body), making it accessible, through the Ordnance Survey, subsidising theatre and opera (the RSC, the National, the Royal Opera House and the rest, as well as galleries, museums and libraries) and coping with accidents, through the National Health Service, a world-famous brand (there is a branch of Moorfields Eye Hospital in Dubai).

Britain came top in the 2018 Portland Soft Power 30 primarily thanks to its 'globally recognised institutions' – and also thanks to its sport-and-social calendar: Lord's, Ascot, Henley and Wimbledon. 'The nation still commands significant soft power clout,' the report found. As William Hague said, when Foreign Secretary, thanks to its array of former glories it had the luck to be 'a modern-day cultural superpower'.

The BBC is often put forward as Exhibit A in lists of such resources, and rightly so. It is both a torch-bearer and an export. Overseas sales are close to £2 billion per annum, thanks to shows like *Planet Earth*, *Top Gear* and *Doctor Who* and other formats adopted by different territories.

It is not just the BBC: America loves *Midsomer Murders* and Finland loves *Downton Abbey* (both ITV). But New Zealand likes *Mrs Brown's Boys*, Latvia admires *Call the Midwife* and *Father Brown* (all BBC) while *Sherlock* broke records in Russia and China – when Series 3 was launched in the latter, on an online channel, it attracted seventy-two million viewers and earned Benedict Cumberbatch a new nickname: Curly Fu.

There is a theme here. Many – perhaps the majority – of these international success stories portray a Britain that no longer exists: a world in which people wear black tie for dinner or crunch their cars up gravel drives to stately homes. In regretting that this may be an out-of-date vision of Britain it should be noted that if this is what the customer (who is always right) wants, then that is what he and she will continue to get.

Nor were those sales driven only by a respect for British excellence – Peppa Pig became the world's first farmyard billionaire partly as a way of teaching English (in America it was reported that some children were acquiring English accents). Nor did they deliver a uniform message. David Attenborough supports the idea that the British are serious, but *Top Gear* presents them as bantering jokers. Costume drama suggests a country mired in the past, but the modern formats – *Love Island*, *Come Dine with Me*, *The X-Factor*, *Gogglebox* – reveal Britain to be a land of brash exhibitionists.

But the reputation of the BBC rests less on these than on its historic assets. Less showy than the above, these are what carry its voice into remote parts of the earth, broadcasting not just programmes or news but a vocal version of what it stands for.

As with the charities, it was not inevitable: it was an experiment with an ambiguous message – old/staid and brash/new all mixed in together.

At 9.30 a.m. on 18 December 1932, an innovation hummed in the air over London. It was not visible to the human eye – it was only a short-wave pulse – but it carried a signal that would soon girdle the earth. It rippled one way to Canada and the West Indies, another to Africa and India; then on to Australia and New Zealand. Its first purpose was to give colonial Britons a consoling reminder of home.

No fireworks attended its birth. The BBC's Director-General, Sir John (soon to become Lord) Reith, warned listeners not to expect too much: 'The programmes will neither be very interesting nor very good,' he said. If he sounded weary, it may have been because he was due to repeat this twelve-minute introductory speech five times in the next twenty-four hours, to catch the different time zones.

It is a moment to make a modern listener swoon. A chief executive who launched a media portal today in such downbeat terms would not last long. But it was true. The early broadcasts included the Test Match, Wimbledon and light entertainment. They also included the 'pips', the beep-beep-beep created by Sir John to represent Greenwich Mean Time, which would become the unmistakable voice of Britain. That methodical chirp, and the gonging of Big Ben, gave listeners the feeling that London really was calling. It brought a hint of fog and gaslight to the hottest tropics. Colonial expats could sense the hiss of trains and the slap of a muddy river.

A week later the 'Empire Service' carried a Christmas message composed for the King by Rudyard Kipling. It addressed itself to distant subjects – 'men and women so cut off by the snow, the desert or the sea that only voices out of the air could reach them'. This was wise work by the ageing poet, implying that all the Britons in those dominions, from the sleaziest customs officer to the bossiest memsahib, were intrepid spirits like Dr Livingstone, Lawrence of Arabia or Scott of the Antarctic.

This, of course, was a time when it took weeks for a newspaper to arrive.

In words that now seem prophetic, the King sought to boost morale – even in 1932 there was a sense that grim beasts were stirring in the forests of Germany. 'It may be that our future may lay upon us more than one stern test,' he said, his voice boosted by a string of relay stations. 'Our past will have taught us how to meet it unshaken.'

His message was heard by twenty million listeners. An annual institution was born, and with it a powerful new impression of what Britain stood for: unshakeability. A few years later James Bond was boasting of being 'shaken, not stirred', and Britain's national character had a new image, as an earnest and resolute voice.

In a bold departure, just six years later after its launch, the BBC set up its first foreign channel (in Arabic, to serve Britain's interests in Egypt, Palestine and the Arabian Peninsula). Two years after that it added a German broadcast, which was soon sending messages to resistance agents in France through *Radio Londres*. This was Britain speaking to France through France itself.[3]

It was propaganda. But in a happy accident of war, the BBC, seeking to combat the messages of totalitarian Germany and Italy, stumbled on a beguiling new weapon: the truth. Its coded messages were clumsy (*The blue horse walks on the horizon … It is time to pick tomatoe*s *… I do not like Crêpes Suzettes*) but it successfully expressed the idea that the truth was out there, and that the BBC knew where it was.

Audiences loved it, and broadcasters loved audiences. As Penelope Fitzgerald put it, the BBC 'scattered human voices into the darkness of Europe'.[4]

Its measured tones established it as a sane presence in a turbulent world. At the end of the war the Director-General, William Haley, pledged in a New Year message that the BBC would continue to represent the qualities he saw as strikingly British: 'virility, a sense of endeavour, courage' and 'a spirit of striving'. Already, the broadcasting service was seen as a carrier of national values.

Its famous impartiality was in part a pose – few pro-communist items passed over the Iron Curtain, and the Foreign Office took a lively interest in the broadcasts. But when, in the Suez Crisis of

---

3 Charles de Gaulle, marooned in London, used the new platform to rally his people by broadcasting a five-minute message every night for four years. He was a natural. One BBC staffer later observed: 'I do not remember ever hearing him fluff.'

4 In *Human Voices* (1980), a novel set in the early years of the war, when the BBC realised, in Fitzgerald's words, that 'the truth is more important than consolation'.

1956, the BBC refused to applaud the government's Middle East policy, truth-telling gained new glamour. Accused of 'failing to support' the troops, it won platoons of new admirers, renown and – more important – trust.

When 200,000 Hungarians fled their country that year, it emerged that two-thirds of them were eager listeners to the BBC's Hungarian Service, and believed it implicitly.

Truth-telling was powerful. The more firmly the BBC stuck to its guns, the more it was trusted – and the more (ironically) it served the government's long-term interest. As its forthright motto ran: 'Nation shall speak peace unto Nation'.

Probity couldn't be faked, however. The home front was stuffed with propaganda, screening hours of flag-waving war films in which brave fellows said 'Don't worry, old girl' before marching off to escort Atlantic convoys, but the overseas audience received a more varied diet. Domestic listeners were reminded that the territories under the British flag were lucky to have such wise governors. But the world according to the World Service was a good deal more complex than that.

When the Bulgarian dissident Georgi Markov, a radio broadcaster in London, was murdered by a poison-tipped umbrella in 1978, he became a martyr for the principle that news was sacred. And when Mrs Thatcher complained, during the Falklands War, that Britain and Argentina were 'being treated as equal', she only boosted its prestige.

As a result, the World Service never lacked for praise. Hostages in Beirut would declare on their release that the BBC had been their lifeline. Aung San Suu Kyi listened for four hours a day – 'I couldn't afford to miss it.' One British Council executive reported from Myanmar that people were 'climbing up filing cabinets' to catch the news. Richard Dowden, Director of the Royal African Society, called it 'Britain's strongest instrument of soft power'; Professor James Gow said it was 'the easiest form of humanitarian assistance', especially in emergencies, when it 'gives people the best possible shot at truth'. The presenter Zeinab Badawi concurred: 'If you just listen to the BBC World Service and don't even read a newspaper, you are probably one of the best informed people on earth.'

Sir Kofi Annan called it, 'Britain's greatest gift to the world.'

When Britons rejoice that Britannia rules the waves they are not usually thinking of *air* waves. But though the UK could plausibly be called post-naval – demilitarised Japan has twice as many ships[5] – it is still a superpower in radio. A Chatham House survey of overseas opinion-formers in 2013 found that 74 per cent saw the World Service as the most important server of British interests abroad – equal to the armed forces and foreign aid combined. With reason: it has broadcast news around the clock in no fewer than sixty-eight languages (including 'Welsh for Patagonia') in a manner that gave a global audience of 279 million confidence that it was telling the truth.

On its seventieth birthday it announced that seven million Iranians were regular listeners, almost twice the number tuning in three years earlier. During the Arab Spring the number of listeners in the countries in question quadrupled. Few of them were anxious to keep up with the gossip in Westminster. The World Service was telling them about their own countries, when their own national broadcasters were not. More than half the adults in Afghanistan, and 40 per cent of those in Nigeria, tuned in.

But soft power is not smooth: you cannot befriend a whole country. Cosy up to the government and you alienate the dissidents. Side with the rebels, and wave goodbye to the corridors of power. Yet sometimes, in the worst trouble spots, revolutionary militias and government vigilantes alike lay down their machine guns to listen to the World Service. Foreign correspondents testify that those who claim to detest Britain still attend to the BBC when they want to find out what is actually going on.

If the World Service were merely a microphone for British interests, this would dissolve. What gives it currency is its reputation as a voice of reason. This, it turns out, is how best it serves the national cause – not by trumpeting British virtues but by embodying them. It is popular not because it is fun, or trendy, or even well informed about the 'concerns' of younger listeners (the

---

5 Today's Royal Navy has a fleet of just forty-five vessels. In the Second World War it possessed 1400 – and even that was no longer enough to rule the waves.

things that pollsters insist a radio station should be) – but because it finds out what is happening, and passes it on.

As coronavirus tightened its grip on the news, its status as a truth-teller may actually have been enhanced. Social media was buzzing with conspiracy theories (the virus was a Russian or Chinese plot to destabilise the West, or an American plot to desta-bilise Russia and China – or some combination) which meant that the established networks, so often disparaged as 'mainstream', suddenly became voices of reason. In Germany, Angela Merkel begged people to resist misinformation ('I ask you not to believe rumours') as being a disease almost as dangerous as the virus itself. Similarly, in Britain, the BBC was able to recover its place as *the* trusted source of reliable news. As with the NHS itself, the crisis gave Britain a reminder that institutions of this sort were imperfect, but far from ordinary, and not to be taken for granted.

The BBC is not a lone voice. Reuters, *The Economist*, the *Guardian*, the *Financial Times* and the '*Times* of London' – these and other publications also command wide respect. Plenty of individual broadcasters – wildlife presenters, foreign correspon-dents, cricket commentators and historians – have carried British tones into foreign parts. All are dramatic examples of what soft power can do.

Whether this counts for as much as a missile base or a trade agreement is a moot point, but in this case we can make a rough comparison. The BBC World Service receives (or 'costs the tax-payer') £250 million per year (from the Foreign Office). The *Queen Elizabeth*, the aircraft carrier launched in 2017, is part of a two-carrier defence strategy that cost more than £6 billion. We cannot put a price on the nation's security any more than we can measure the impact of the BBC on its reputation. But there is an exchange rate here: one aircraft carrier equals twelve World Services. It is rough – but since the operating costs of the carrier and its 680 employees will be similar to the annual expense of the World Service, it may even be an understatement.

What serves British interests better – one aircraft carrier or a dozen revered radio networks?

The BBC is trusted because it is the voice of Britain, but not the mouthpiece of its government. Christopher Hitchens once wrote, questioning the way political parties could not resist pandering to electorates: 'People don't like you if all you want is to be liked.' This is true: soft power is not a cheerleader but a hallmark. It does not 'boost' the brand; it can only exemplify it.

We might call that the World Service Paradox. The harder you try, the worse you do.

It is asking a lot of any government to pay for an institution such as the BBC World Service while declining to exercise any influence over it – even though that may be the most cost-effective way of spreading the national message. Historically, that was precisely what made the BBC so unusual, and so credible. As Britain's place at the head of world affairs has slipped, so its governments have looked to economise.

Recent politicians have suggested diminishing its place in the national life, for a range of short-term reasons, some of them understandable. But in the ambiguous realm of soft power, this could be a costly mistake.

If the BBC World Service was the best known of the institutions created to spread British values, the British Council was not far behind. Founded at almost the same time (1934), it was designed to 'promote British culture and fight the rise of fascism', by spreading the holy gospel of English education – it was assumed that exposure to Shakespeare, Dickens and the rest would steer people away from Nazi mythology.

Today it receives £155 million per annum from the government (via the Foreign and Commonwealth Office) and generates about four times that amount by running a globe-spanning programme of English-language classes. Operating in 109 countries, it seeks to 'promote a wider knowledge of the UK' not through advertising or by sponsoring British productions abroad,[6] but by fostering cultural relationships.

The 1940 annual report summarised its purpose in words still used today: it is charged 'to create in a country overseas a basis of friendly knowledge and understanding'. According to its chief

---

6 Though this is indeed part of its mission. Its *Love's Labour's Lost* in Afghanistan in 2015 (in a local language) was the first Shakespeare performance there for seventeen years.

executive, Sir Ciaran Devane, its most important job is to identify and support 'possibilities for collaboration'.

Its finest hour, in his view, came in the years before the fall of the Berlin Wall, when the British Council actively nourished the liberation movements in Budapest, Prague and Warsaw. And in the years that followed it became an energetic language teacher, opening the English-speaking world to new populations – a commercial enterprise (two million students a year pay for its courses – with positive side-effects. Thanks to the connections forged before the fall of the Berlin Wall it was able to fill the breach: between 1989 and 1991 Bulgaria, Czech Republic, Estonia, Hungary, Kazakhstan and Poland all dropped Russian as a compulsory 'option' in schools.

Devane holds that there are three types of people in international relations: *realists*, who believe that force is the only relevant language; *institutionalists*, who believe in a 'rules-based' international order (good for lawyers); and *constructivists*, who think that societies are not products of power or rules but are created by experience – which therefore becomes an important commodity in its own right. He places the British Council in this third group: 'We are the constructivist in the room.'

And since each group sees the world through the prism of its own world view ('If you're a hammer, everything looks like a nail'[7]); his role is to press for fresh approaches ('experiences') on all fronts. His target audience is eighteen- to thirty-four-year-olds, and if he could add one line to every political manifesto it would read: 'Every young person should have an international experience in their education.'

The British Council's founding rubric stated that the purpose of cultural relations was to build 'a sympathetic appreciation of British foreign policy, whatever for the moment that policy may be' – a utilitarian ambition. Today it prefers to stress 'the building of trust' through everything from football camps to language teaching. Each year, it helps three million students sit British exams in their own countries.

---

7 Sometimes known as the 'law of the instrument', this notion was spelled out by the American philosopher Abraham Kaplan in 1964: 'Give a small boy a hammer, and he will find that everything he encounters needs pounding.'

Critics say that this emphasis on grassroots initiatives has led it
to neglect the value of symbolic moves: the days when it would
send Peter Brook's *Hamlet* to Moscow as an ambassador for British
culture, for instance. It is even whispered in diplomatic circles
that the British Council could be a *bit* more willing to act as a
national cheerleader, laying on tours for British artists. And it
attracts criticism any time it seeks to reallocate resources: people
tend to object to closures faster than they toast openings. There
was a cry of protest in 2007 when the British Council shut down
two famous libraries in Athens and Jerusalem in order to boost its
activities in the Islamic world, where there was, it noted, a 'wid-
ening gap of trust'.

This was in keeping with its principles – the British
Council was not intended to be a club for the already-literate
Anglophone – but in some quarters was unpopular.

'I hope the Islamic world is grateful,' commented Fay Weldon.
'I doubt it will be.'

Closing libraries sounds uncivilised (even if they are not
well used).

In 2011 the British Council in Kabul was bombed and twelve
people died. Two years later the same thing happened in Tripoli,
and in a famous case, an Iranian woman who worked for the
British Council in London was arrested as a spy. The Council's
offices are a soft target. But ask Sir Ciaran Devane to name his
greatest fear – what wakes him up at night – and his one-word
answer is 'instrumentalisation'. Any attempt by government to
drape the British Council in the national flag would risk having
the opposite effect. Soft power is an important consideration in
modern geopolitics, but it is an unstable substance that needs very
careful handling.

5

Britain: The Sun Also Sets

In any ledger of Britain's soft-power assets the story of migration has to loom large. And while the highly charged subject of inward migration is an older saga than the modern ructions over it suggest – people have been arriving in Britain ever since the ice melted, either as invaders (Celt, Roman, Angle, Saxon, Dane or Norman) or as everyday nomads – the more important thread in this case is . . . emigration.

Britain's imperial mission gave it a taste for foreign climes. Between the battles of Waterloo (1815) and Mons (1914) some fifteen million Britons went overseas, meaning that there are up to 200 million people of British ancestry in the world today.

We have seen the impact of this global adventuring in architecture, literature, horticulture and every other field. Hardly anywhere is it more visible than in India. In the spring of 2017, for instance, construction workers in Mumbai dug up a battered stone pillar with a letter etched on the face: a capital V. It didn't take long for history-inclined experts to understand that this was something they had long been seeking: a mile post installed by British engineers during the Raj. The V showed the distance from the centre or 'zero point' of the colonial city.[1] It stood 5 miles from St Thomas's Cathedral, the oldest British building in what was then Bombay.[2]

Only the pyramid-shaped tip was visible above the cement,

---

1 That should read twice-colonial city. Britain received the settlement and trading post at Bombay as a dowry gift from its previous European overseer, Portugal.

2 The cathedral was named after the apostle who famously 'doubted' the truth of the resurrection, and whose subsequent heartsick wanderings took him as far as India.

but it was still a major find. Of the fifteen original stones this was the eleventh to have been unearthed, so it was a new piece in an evocative chain. The city's heritage body was planning to restore these stones and create a living memorial to olden times.

The British travellers who measured their outings by such posts may have moved faster than is possible in the traffic jam that is modern Mumbai. But anyone following the line of markers back to their source was in for a treat. The white cathedral of St Thomas was a bastion of the British presence for more than three hundred years – it was founded in 1718 – and continues to be a living reminder of those days.

It stood at the heart of what was almost a British city. A short walk from the cathedral stood a Victorian Gothic university and an Indian-Gothic railway station that was still the headquarters of the Indian railway (Chhatrapati Shivaji Maharaj, commonly known as Victoria Terminus). The turrets of the stately national museum (previously the Prince of Wales) brought a hint of South Kensington to a palm-fringed traffic junction, while the Post Office and the Telegraph Office were monuments to British administrative zeal – close your eyes and you could almost see men in linen suits poring over crop reports or sighing at weather news from the tea plantations.

The Gymkhana Club was a mock-Tudor replica of the cricket pavilions of Sussex, looking over its expanse of cricket fields, while next door sat the Horniman Circle, a neat curve of mansions around a park (named after a British editor of the *Bombay Chronicle* who backed India's fight for independence) just like a square in Bath.

There was more to these buildings than colonial showing-off. They also broadcast British values – spiritual, educational, legal, civic and commercial. And they looked in two directions. To the Indian population the edifices were imposing fortresses of imperial rule; to the British they were also a pointed reminder of home.

Something of the same double emotion still rings through their now ageing stones. Each year, for instance, on 14 November, soon after the Remembrance Day services that honour the 1.3 million Indians who took up arms for Britain in the First World War,

a congregation of well-heeled *Mumbaikars* gather in the cathedral to commemorate Founder's Day of the Cathedral and John
Connon School – the college attended by various members of the
famous Tata family and, as it happens, Salman Rushdie. Created
in 1860 to provide choristers, it upholds its Victorian traditions
with relish.

The visitors in its solid wooden pews, admiring the nave, the
altar, the stained-glass windows, the cool stone columns, the
touching memorials, the flagstones, the eagle-shaped lectern and
the oak board listing the hymns, might easily (were it not for the
ceiling fans and the blare of car horns) imagine themselves on the
outskirts of Oxford or Winchester. But then a choir of Indian
boys and girls make a stately procession up the aisle, in red and
white surplices, led by an 'acolyte' bearing a tall brass cross.

The organ plays a nineteenth-century arrangement of the *Te
Deum* by Henry Smart. The congregation rises, sits and kneels as
instructed, listening to a liturgical language a churchgoer from
Durham would know at once. And though few members of this
congregation are Christian, they respectfully mutter the Anglican
responses ('For these and all thy blessings we thank thee, O God'),
mouth along to hymns they do not know ('All people that on
earth do dwell') and bow their heads to the Lord's Prayer ('Give
us this day our daily bread, and forgive us our trespasses . . .').

Then comes the school song.

> *School! School! Play up, School!*
> *Wherever your lot may be cast*
> *School first, house second, self last.*
> *School! School! Play up, School!*

Few establishments in modern Britain could get away with
this. But as the music swirls to the ceiling fans some may hear the
ringing of a faint bell, for this is the Harrow school song. Written
by Edward Ernest Bowen in 1872, it is still sung, with earnest
gusto, in a thunderous city of twenty-two million on the other
side of the world.

The words have changed, but the song remains the same. The
original begins:

Forty years on, when apart and asunder
Parted are those who are singing today.
When you look back, and forgetfully wonder
What you were like in your work and your play.

The Mumbai version runs as follows:

Prima in Indis, Gateway of India
Door of the East with its face to the West,
Here in Bombay we are living and learning,
India, our country, to give you our best.

Performed by a choir of Indian teenagers, it feels as though
time has slipped a cog.[3]

Like many 'typical' Englishmen, Bowen was not English – he
was born in Ireland – but he was exactly the kind of first-rate
fellow the country most admired. A scholar and a sportsman
(classics at Cambridge; cricket for Hampshire), he helped found
the Football Association and played in the first two FA Cup finals
(1872 and 1873) before becoming a teacher at Harrow, through
whose corridors the young Winston Churchill would soon
be running.

In calling him 'typical' we mean only that he represented a
particular strand in British life – the upper-class all-rounder. He
was a teacher, a sportsman, an author (of books on Napoleon)
and a keen amateur musician. 'Forty Years On' has been a part of
Harrow's fabric ever since the day he wrote it, a plangent exercise
in looking back that mournfully celebrates in advance the pang
one day of 'forgetfully wondering'.

It aimed – and still aims – to plant in young minds an affection for the place they will soon be leaving. But that place might
not be north-west London, because the Cathedral and John

---

3 One thing to note about the words of the song is that they refer to 'Bombay', not
'Mumbai'. This is in part to express loyalty to its own history, but it expresses too a lack
of enthusiasm for the name change. Bombay became Mumbai in 1996, after the Hindu
nationalist party Shiv Sena came to power in the region. As part of a wider movement
of name-changing across India, it replaced the echo of British colonialism with a
tribute to the Maratha Goddess Mumbadevi. Not everyone was happy, though. Some
Mumbaikars, seeing it as a nationalist imposition, cling to the old name.

Connon School is far from the only institution to adopt the song. Wellington College in New Zealand, Kandy High in Sri Lanka, Wesley College and Melbourne High in Australia, Starehe in Kenya, St Timothy's in America, Pretoria High in South Africa, Vajiravudh College in Thailand, Queen's College in Hong Kong, Havergal College in Toronto . . . all sing the same stirring anthem.

Power, we might think, does not get much softer than this – a nostalgic tune used to push home a moral ('let us who have received most be ready to give most') which to many Indians once sounded like the hypocritical boast of a cruel Empire and now emerges, in different mouths, as a simple plea to which hardly anyone could object. Thus does culture creep into faraway hearts and minds, not in the glare of headlines but in the small routines and ceremonies of ordinary life.

Something of this sort is visible in the youthful faces of the Founder's Day choir. Thanks to the jarring convulsions of history, their mental furniture has been shaped by the values of a country very unlike their own. The school motto is *Clarum Efficiunt Studia* ('studies makyth fame' – a phrase taken from Bacon) and in a reversal of Joseph Nye's idea that soft power co-opts rather than forces, the students themselves have now adopted the imperial value-system as fuel for their own hopes and dreams.

> *Out on the maidan[4] our thews and our sinews*
> *We'll train and we'll strengthen a'playing the game.*
> *Then when we leave and go forth to our lifework*
> *Win for our race and our school a fair name.*

Again, few British head teachers would dare to conduct assembly in such terms. But here they have a bracing resonance. Some of the students will use their grounding in British culture to propel them to British or American universities. But even those who walk a few blocks west to Mumbai University will find themselves in a stately foreign precinct, with Victorian tracery by George Gilbert Scott (the man behind the Albert Memorial,

---

4 The *maidan* is the open ground used in Mumbai for cricket pitches; but in this case it carries another connotation, as the playing fields where manliness is cultivated.

St Pancras station and the red telephone box). The clock on the tower above the colonnades is an echo of London's Big Ben; its 129-year-old mechanism still ticks.

An alumnus of Charterhouse or Dulwich (a Nigel Farage, for instance) would feel quite at home in these neo-Gothic surroundings. To wander the university quarter is to step back in both time and place. The Oval Maidan hosts a scene calculated to lift the heart of the most nostalgic imperialist. Half a dozen cricket matches play themselves out in front of white marquees, while the turrets of the old Raj rise in the hot sky.

This is not to defend the British occupation of India, or to propose some irrelevant balance sheet of gains and losses deriving from colonial rule. But soft power is not a morality play. Without its bitter history of imperial occupation India would not be the English-speaking, cricket-playing power that it is today. The past can be appraised; it can be lamented; it cannot be undone. The many echoes Britain left of itself – in law, architecture, faith, language, literature and social life – are something more than souvenirs; they are living glimmers of India's *own* soft power, now reborn in the life of a modern state. As Bismarck said: 'Were the British Empire to disappear, its work in India would remain one of its lasting monuments.'

And most of those monuments are full of ambivalence. E. M. Forster did not write *A Passage to India* out of the troubled goodness of his heart. A classics graduate from Cambridge, he was employed as tutor to a well-born Muslim from India, Syed Ross Masood, himself bound for Oxford. One of Forster's aunts, in a well-publicised panic, said that she did hope the visitor 'wouldn't steal the spoons', but in fact all he did was open the young novelist's eyes – 'he woke me up'. In falling in love with *him*, Forster also fell in love with the whole troubled spell cast by the British in India. Properly and pointedly, the novel itself was dedicated to his Indian friend.

This pattern was repeated all round the world, is the foundation of Britain's influence in modern times, and is likely to remain so into the future. But of course migration is a two-way process, and thanks to inward migration Britain has received as much as it has transmitted. Much has been written about this; here two examples must suffice.

The first, Kumar Bhattacharyya, was born in Bangalore and studied engineering in West Bengal before travelling to Britain in 1960. He was an apprentice for Lucas Industries (diesel engines) then an academic at Birmingham University.

The slump of the 1970s was biting hard. 'I quickly realised,' he wrote in his autobiography, 'that the vibrancy that existed for engineering in India, which I had expected to find in Britain, was not there.' In 1980 he moved to the University of Warwick and set up the Warwick Manufacturing Group, a pioneering joint venture between commerce and academia. The university taught engineering and business studies in association with 'local' manufacturers such as British Aerospace and the Rover Group. Bhattacharyya became a government adviser and a fellow of the Royal Society; he was knighted in 2003 and made a life peer in the House of Lords in 2004.

Those who want to depict migrants as scroungers or a burden on society need to take stock of this career; as do those who want to berate Britain for its racist or intolerant nature. Bhattacharyya was remarkable; Britain's doors were open to him.

Most important of all, however, was the marriage he was able to arrange between his two homes. As a friend of the Tata family he was able to broker (in 2008) the sale of Jaguar Land Rover to Tata Motors. The deal was worth £1.5 billion, and he himself drove Ratan Tata (chairman of the firm, who had a hall named after him at Harvard and was later named Knight Grand Cross of the British Empire − the first Indian to win the honour since independence) round the Midlands in search of suitable sites.

The Tata dynasty had an Anglo–Indian background of its own. The founder, Jamsetji Tata, grew up in Bombay in the middle of the nineteenth century, spent time in the opium trade with China, then set up as a textile manufacturer in Nagpur before creating what became, in 1939, the largest steel producer in the British Empire. One of his sons (Sir Dorabji) went to Cambridge in 1877 before entering the family cotton business and branching into iron, steel and hotels; another (Sir Ratan) settled in England as an art-loving philanthropist.

From the beginning the family was Anglophile. In 1906 Sir
Ratan Tata bought a stately home in Twickenham (once owned
by the Governor of Madras) and became a leading figure in
London society, founding departments at the London School of
Economics and the University of London, and acquiring notable
paintings (some of which now form a collection in the national
art gallery of Mumbai). He died in St Ives and was buried at
Brookwood Cemetery, Woking, beside the grave of his father.

The intricacy of these Anglo-Indian threads cannot be easily
unravelled. And at Bhattacharyya's prompting they became even
more tightly knotted. Tata vigorously expanded its presence in
Britain, acquiring nineteen companies, some of them famous –
ICI, Tetley Tea and Corus – and employing 60,000 people. The
Warwick Manufacturing Hub, meanwhile, stayed on the front
edge of innovation in the important new fields of nanotechnol-
ogy, cyber security and 3-D printing.

When Bhattacharyya died in 2019, the Tata Group bought
space in the *Financial Times* to pay tribute to the man it called
'simply a visionary'. Ratan Tata, meanwhile, was hailed in the
Spectator as 'inward investor of the century'.

This was soft power at its most quiet and forceful. Britain's
presence in India may have been in many ways iniquitous, but it
did give rise to webs of connections (this is one example among
thousands) that still reverberate in the present day.

The second example takes us further back in time, and on
an even stranger journey. In 1848 a young boy named Gottlieb
Wilhelm Leitner left his home in the Austro-Hungarian town of
Pest to study in Constantinople. Though only eight years old he
was already a remarkable linguist, proficient in twenty European
languages; soon he was at home in Turkish and Arabic, too. At
the age of sixteen he became senior interpreter for the British
mission in the Crimea. The position carried the rank of colonel
in the British army, and after the war he returned to London to
continue his studies at King's College. By the age of nineteen he
was a lecturer; at twenty-three he became a professor. Not long
after that he became Chancellor of Lahore University, and wrote
scholarly histories of Islam.

When he returned to Britain for the second time he created

an institute of Oriental Studies in Woking, Surrey (a few miles from the cemetery where the Tata founders were buried), and since many of his students were Muslims he built a mosque for them, commissioning an English architect to recreate the Moghul details.

Not many people know or are proud of the fact Britain's first mosque was built by a Hungarian-Jewish immigrant in the heart of the commuter belt, an hour from Waterloo by train. But these are the pathways migration opens up between nations.

Britain's religious, social and political culture grew out of this constant coming and going. Its language was a compound of German, French, Italian and Greek, spiced with stranger notes. In a globalised world, more than ever reliant on connections and networks, a diverse and dispersed population was a crucial resource. Formal power might depend on armies and navies, but one of its installations was a revolving door. The ebb and flow of people from around the world took new ideas both in and out.

Some of those travellers were ordinary – seamen, labourers, teachers, cooks – but others were celebrities. A long list of eminent foreigners – Franklin, Marx, Lenin, Nehru, Gandhi, Peter the Great and many more – spent time in Britain, and most took something of it away with them when they left.

It was not always the same thing: Voltaire was so impressed by English liberty that he vowed to introduce it in France, while Marx was sufficiently outraged by its slums to object to the entire course of human history. Rodin's encounter with Greek marbles in the British Museum became French sculpture; Gandhi's studies in England gave him an admiration for British justice, which he would then use *against* Britain.

Zola, Monet, Pissarro, Freud and many others, fleeing trouble at home, received a dose of Britishness to carry away like migrating birds. A pub in Clerkenwell still boasts of having once hosted Stalin, Lenin and Trotsky in a dim back room, hunched beneath the clock as they set the world to rights over a pint of British ale.

This may be the single most important aspect of migration: the dynamism created by people who come and then leave, whether as business leaders, students, dissidents, jobseekers or displaced people in search of shelter.

Is it a national asset that foreigners have to come to Britain? Yes.

Is it to Britain's advantage that native people have left these shores? Assuredly.

That is the tidal process by which Britain has imported and exported energy, ideas and investment, forging relationships and stamping impressions of itself on foreign minds. Of all the forces likely to determine our future, it might be the most powerful. Yet it has been easy, in the tense atmosphere surrounding the topic in recent years, to overlook it. In the coal-powered steamship bustle of the nineteenth century not a single foreigner was turned away, and in the twentieth the inward migration was spectacular. It has not always been a smooth or friendly process – far from it. But in its imperfect fashion the country has welcomed religious, political and commercial dreamers of every stripe.

Consider something as British as the Edinburgh Festival. It might seem a rousing fiesta of purely Scottish fun – but four million visitors from more than 150 countries swarm through the city each year. It is indeed a grand advertisement for Scotland and Britain: its famous 'fringe' has long been a nursery of British comedy (and was an iconoclastic private party rather than a government initiative). Today's festival sells more tickets to an international audience than anything except the Olympic Games.

Yet even this was not the product of a national impulse. On the contrary, the festival was created by a Viennese refugee from Hitler named Rudolf Bing. He was part of a major diaspora that brought roughly 70,000 Jewish Germans to Britain to join the large Jewish population that had fled Russian pogroms in the nineteenth century. They were a notable fixture of the cultural elite in art (Freud, Auerbach, Gombrich), philosophy (Berlin, Popper), cinema (Pressburger, Reisz), music (the Amadeus Quartet), literature (Canetti, Koestler), economics, publishing, science and architecture. It is estimated that sixteen Nobel Prizes were brought to Britain by this one unhappy migration.

Before he went to America, Bing also helped two Germans, Carl Ebert and Fritz Busch, work with John Christie to found the Glyndebourne Festival – bringing a little touch of Salzburg to Christie's extremely English house in the South Downs.

The uproar around immigration in recent years has done significant harm to this long history of international ties. For instance, in 2013 the government-backed operation that put 'Go Home' vans on London's streets, in a bid to warn illegal migrants that they were being hunted, backfired and lasted only a month. But the images flashed around the world. And it wasn't just the attitude – the 'hostile environment' they created; it was the clumsy inaccuracy of the thing. Large letters warned that '106' people had been arrested in 'your area' last week; it emerged that only eleven had been removed.

This unfriendly message was reinforced by the sorry story of the West Indians wrongly deported for not having the correct paperwork – the so-called 'Windrush scandal'. There were fears, as Brexit clicked into place, that a new generation of European citizens – a special-needs teacher, say, whose father had flown Spitfires in the war – would find themselves casualties of the same bureaucracy. Britain was not merely unwelcoming – it was untruthful, and incompetent.

This mood was strong enough, however, to help swing the 2016 Brexit referendum in favour of leaving. It is clear now that Brexit was not a straightforward vote on the issue in question but a coalition of grievances focused on a topic that until then people had not greatly cared about either way. Making the widespread concern over immigration synonymous with EU interference (a misleading equation, since migration from outside the EU far outweighed the internal traffic) piped oxygen into the fire. That it showed the nation to be 'divided' was not in itself unusual: Britain had long been harshly divided along lines of class, wealth and taste. But it certainly sent a message around the world that it was not united, or steady, or calm, or resolute ... or any of the things it was traditionally supposed to have been.

The UK's showing in the 2019 Portland Soft Power 30 reflected this – it slipped from first to second (behind France). In the Nations Brands Index developed by Simon Anholt it fell to fourth (behind the United States, China and Japan). These might have been 'blips', but they came with a warning: Britain had not yet left the European Union, Portland pointed out, and might be looking at 'a US-style decline'. Its high score in many measures (history, culture, media, tourism, football, music and so on) was offset by a waning of its educational power in a way that rang 'alarm bells'. And the previous year it had benefited from a one-off – a royal wedding – that was not an annual resource. In short, it could not pat itself on the back. Other surveys were ominous, too. The annual ranking published by *Monocle* magazine placed Britain seventh, below Switzerland ('an enduring brand') and only just ahead of Sweden, which had suffered a soft-power knock owing to the sex scandals around its prime asset: the Nobel Prize. The political turmoil thrown up by Brexit was, it reported, leading Britain to be seen as 'antagonistic . . . chaotic'.

Brexit was not a bolt from the blue, though; the country had been simmering for a long while. The 2008 financial crash and its austere aftermath made the public susceptible to populist, down-with-the-establishment politics to an extent that both Britain's major parties were electioneering on a people-versus-the-elite ticket. And there was a deeper coincidence. The migrant 'crisis' in the Mediterranean – in which several million illegal immigrants were risking a dangerous and expensive route to Europe – blended two alarming aspects of globalisation into one unexpected story. While jobs moved from rich countries to poor countries, *people* were moving in the opposite direction, from poverty to affluence. To an extent that no one had quite predicted, this was not good news for poor people in rich countries, and various politicians and opinion-formers were quick to exploit their anger.

Social media fanned that anger into outrage, spreading distrust through a powerful cocktail of truth, conspiracy and satire. It created an atmosphere in which almost all institutions – Church, state, business, schools, universities – seemed tainted.

The London Olympics, in the summer of 2012, offered a momentary respite: an old nation found a new voice. This was not only because the athletes performed well. The happy crowds, smooth logistics, bright sunshine, vibrant opening ceremony and cosmopolitan team (one-third of Team GB was of migrant background) put Britain in an affable new light. The British government immediately launched a soft campaign – the 'Great' initiative – to capitalise on the hoped-for 'golden legacy'.

A VisitBritain survey the following year noticed a detectable lift in the way the UK was seen. A sizeable 73 per cent of respondents in thirteen countries said that the Games had 'changed the image of Britain for the better'; an extraordinary 99 per cent agreed that this might indeed encourage more people to want to see the country for themselves.

The greatest change was in the number of people who thought Britain 'welcoming'. Traditionally it had been seen as stiff and cold; now, thanks to the unaffected smiles of those helpful volunteers, it seemed outgoing, even friendly.[5]

That was good news for the tourist trade – one of those rare moments where it is almost possible to *see* soft power being minted. Led by the Department of Culture, Media and Sport, the 'Great' campaign looked to marshal the resources of the whole country behind a campaign to boost tourism. The stated target was forty million visitors a year. There were partnerships with foreign governments, food and drink fairs, art happenings and sports events. Some of the budget went on some frankly embarrassing banners (slapped on the sides of yachts and pavilions – there was even one at Davos), which showed that Britain had forgotten the understated manners that were once part of its charm, but even this was an upbeat initiative likely to have positive results.

Yet only a year later Dr Robin Niblett, Director of Chatham House, advised a House of Lords committee that even nations as well endowed with soft power as Britain could not afford to rest on their laurels: 'The UK has enjoyed a privileged position in a western-led world order,' he warned, 'that may soon be eclipsed.'

Hard facts, he seemed to be saying, counted for more than soft imagery.

---

5 This was a nice finding, so one doesn't want to spoil things. But the same survey found that while respondents in India ranked Britain fourth in the world for 'natural beauty', those in Turkey ranked it fortieth. And other surveys found that Britain scored highly for both 'friendliness' and 'unfriendliness'. The eye of the beholder . . .

When Britain did vote to leave the European Union it added force to such fears. Its first consequence was political turbulence, its second a sour quarrel about national identity. Was Britain a historic kingdom entitled by its epic past to throw off the 'manacles' of inconvenient friendships and go it alone ('Alone at last!'), or a grandee fallen on hard times that needed all the friends it could get? A rift of this magnitude, once opened, could not be closed by platitudes about 'healing divisions'.

In some quarters (far from Europe, for the most part) Brexit inspired respect: it looked like old-school British dash and pluck. Others saw only the reckless derring-do that led Marshal Soult to call the troops at Waterloo 'the finest cavalry in all Europe . . . and the worst led'.[6] Some struggled to understand why Britain might, at a jittery time in the world's affairs, press for a divorce from one of the world's four great power blocs – America, Europe, India and China – in favour of its own small canoe.

It was a dramatic soft-power signal. For centuries Britain had seemed, if nothing else, a steady ship; stodgy, but stalwart and upstanding. Not any more. A nation once a byword for reliability had suddenly turned fractious and ungovernable.

When Dean Acheson famously described Britain as a country that had lost an empire and not yet found a role (a phrase that was being repeated daily in newspaper columns), few imagined that this new role was to be . . . a joke. But foreign pundits were shaking their heads. 'What in the world has happened to this country?' asked one Swiss paper. A German radio station called Brexit 'the biggest political nonsense since the Roman emperor Caligula decided to appoint his horse Incitatus as consul'.

As the months passed, the judgements grew harsher, and on the day Theresa May's agreement crashed in the British Parliament, in 2019, the pundits went to town. *Le Monde* described Britain as a Rolls-Royce whose brakes had failed. Others saw it as 'a colossal disaster . . . a 'quagmire' . . . or 'complete chaos'.

The language became even hotter when Boris Johnson became Prime Minister in the summer of 2019. Donald Trump was

---

6 Echoing Pierre Bosquet, the French marshal who watched the charge of the Light Brigade and said: '*C'est magnifique, mais ce n'est pas la guerre; c'est de la folie.*'

upbeat ('He'll get it done') but others were less sure. *Time* magazine wrote: 'Boris Johnson may not be the leader Britain needs,' it wrote. 'But he is what Britain deserves.'

Things were little better at home. In the *Financial Times* Martin Wolf thundered: 'What is happening is not worthy of a serious country. The conclusion is that the UK is no longer a serious country.' In column after column, Britain was 'a rudderless ship of state bobbing haplessly in hostile waters'.

These were domestic reviews, but they travelled the world too. And though they made the more ardent Brexiteers even keener to leave the EU – how *dare* all those nobodies say such things? – elsewhere they left a grim taste. Had Britain truly voted to return to the period *before* it joined the Common Market – that unhappy 1970s *smorgasbord* of inflation, business failure, unemployment, fishing disputes, strikes and violence in Northern Ireland? In seeking to 'take back control' of its borders (a quixotic aim in the modern world, and a dangerous one in Ireland), Britain appeared to have *lost* control of itself. In a fit of anger about a range of things (there were many respectable grievances) it seemed to have fallen out of love with . . . itself.

The soft punches kept on falling. By bearing down on overseas students (to get the immigration numbers down – a policy called 'bananas' by the editor of *The Economist*), the government ensured that the leaders of tomorrow would be more likely to attend universities in America, Australia, Europe and China than in Britain. In the last decade the number of foreign students in Britain had increased by just 3 per cent, while in America it grew by 40 per cent and in Australia by 45 per cent. According to Universities UK, the number of students from India had *halved* in the last five years.

In 2018 it emerged that Australia had overtaken the UK as the world's second most-popular destination for foreign students (behind America). Even the small print suggested a nation that, in seeking to take back control, was losing it. At the end of 2018 a set of stamps designed to mark the seventy-fifth anniversary of the Normandy landings made headlines when it emerged that they showed an American landing craft in the Pacific, a blunder that suggested, in line with the times, that Britain had literally lost its way. A year later, power failure plunged airports and railway stations into darkness, the countryside suffered apocalyptic floods, and one busy London bridge was declared unfit and closed down, seemingly for good.

A pub was shutting down every twelve hours; libraries were closing; public parks were going unmown; high streets were dying; temperatures on the London underground in summer were rising above the permitted levels for livestock. If the world continued to support England's football teams, meanwhile, it was only because they included so many foreign players. Thanks to its appetite for watching televised football, Britain's was able to provide the stage for a global game. But even this was in doubt as the currency fell, and many overseas stars preferred to be paid in euros.

Britain's most important ambassador was forced to resign because someone leaked his confidential description of Trump's White House as dysfunctional – a fact that half a dozen books had long since established in embarrassing detail, and which was presumably similar to what the American ambassador was telling *his* superiors about London. The pride of Britain's navy, meanwhile, a £3 billion aircraft carrier named after the Queen, was having to 'limp' (as the papers put it) back to Portsmouth after suffering an entirely literal leak – 200 tonnes of sea water flooded the decks when a steam pipe broke during sea trials.

It was a long way from *Sink the Bismarck*, that was for sure. Most of these were soft signals the government could do little about.

And all of this was before the virus struck, and Brexit vanished from the headline news like a poltergeist in a huff. When it would return to the agenda was anyone's guess. It seemed, to say the least, an interesting time to be betting the national future on new, globe-spanning trade agreements (in place of a long-standing and close relationship with neighbours who shared so much of its history and culture).

It was emerging, meanwhile, that the world's most useful passport was no longer Britain's (which gave the fortunate bearer visa-free access to 183 countries). Japan and Singapore both offered 189.

It was through details like these, as much as the large facts of international trade, that Brexit news trickled round the globe. They struck small but telling pinpricks into the heart of Britain's reputation overseas.

The world was still full of statesmen who had been educated in the UK, knew it well, spoke its language and revered its political culture. Now they could only shake their heads. It was a textbook example of how to lose friends and alienate people.

And a deeper problem began to appear. After Brexit had thrown the pieces of the British jigsaw up in the air, no one could say how they would land. It was more than possible that the United Kingdom might itself be . . . disuniting. There were plenty in Scotland, Wales and Northern Ireland who thought themselves victims of English imperialism rather than fellow perpetrators (it was true that the common people of Glasgow or Belfast had little say in the affairs of empire; though neither did the put-upon of Salford or Preston – let alone the orphaned children of *Oliver Twist* or *Bleak House*).[7] Nonetheless, the fact that Brexit was an unmistakably English idea meant that the British Union could no longer be taken for granted.

From a soft-power point of view, the larger risk was that in bragging about its historic ability to flourish on its own, Britain was inviting the world to re-examine that past – and there was no guarantee they would like what they saw. Soft power often does come down to a conversation about history – and it is a hot, unstable topic.

Membership of the European Union had kept the glare of world attention away from Britain's past. At the Conservative Party conference in 2016, the first such gathering after the Referendum, Boris Johnson, then Foreign Secretary, spoke eagerly about Britain's prominent place in the world. 'Up the creeks and inlets of every continent on earth,' he said, 'go the gentle, kindly gunboats of British soft power . . .' This was a successful sally: it implied that British greatness might still be self-sufficient. He did not add that this happy state had been achieved

---

7 The empire was in most ways a joint venture. In Calcutta the English Church and the Scottish Kirk were in constant competition over which had the taller steeple.

from *within* the EU, and that it had therefore been no handicap, let alone a set of 'manacles'.

In running up the old imperial flag, Britain was like a company putting itself in play for a takeover. No one could say how the bidding would go. And it was a soft-power warning light in that history was pushing into the present, while Brexit trained a torch on the past. The fact that not everything in that past was pretty fuelled new campaigns to topple imperial statues, repatriate 'looted' art, demand reparations for slavery and empire, 'decolonise' the curriculum, and arraign the past for its many cruelties and disgraces.

It was not easy for a nation to boast about liberty and justice when it had, in its time, invaded more than a hundred other lands, most of which meant it no harm.

As Indra Adnan, author and creator of the Soft Power Network, has said: 'Britain's ambivalence about the value of its immigrants allows the default story to arise – that Britain's interest in the globe was singular and selfish.'

Historic grievances inevitably subside over time: England does not seek reparations from Normandy for the invasion of 1066, or from Scandinavia for its Viking rampages. But such feelings can easily be rekindled. In offering up its past for inspection, Britain was risking being seen not (or at least not only) as the cradle of democracy and equal rights, but also as the home of *un*fair play.

Nothing can change the immensity of Britain's past. The way in which one small wet island roused itself to occupy and dominate the largest empire the world had ever seen is a remarkable story. But that 'Great' Britain belongs to the past. As long ago as 1960 a 'future policy study' warned that it risked being a 'small power' bobbing about between the much greater blocs of America and Europe, and two years later Harold Macmillan agreed: 'We have to consider the state of the world as it is today and will be tomorrow, and not in outdated terms of a vanished past.'

In a world of new great powers (China, India, Russia) this may be increasingly true. Indeed, in a report published immediately after Britain's formal exit in February 2020 (*The Sources of Soft Power*), the British Council emphasised that the United Kingdom was in 'a leading but fragile position' with respect to soft power, and noted with concern a survey of young people's attitudes which revealed a damaging slide in public opinion: even though Britain produced *more* highly rated scientific papers than either Germany or Japan, respondents believed it to be lagging behind both.

This was the sort of immaterial fact that had material consequences, and it was not contradicted by statements that the new government was seeking to cherry pick only the 'brightest and best' of would-be immigrants – it was common knowledge that messages of this sort tended to deter, rather than attract, such desirable assets.

The report advised that Britain's government take energetic steps to boost its image overseas on the grounds that this was 'ever more important' to its future prosperity. In the blinding light of coronavirus, which halted global migration in its tracks, this was, in the short term at least, an unlikely hope. The virus was a wrecking ball, and one of its first targets was the easy movement of people. Britain would not soon have an opportunity to repair the dent it had put in its image as a welcoming haven.

It also faced more competition than in the past. The BBC, for instance, is no longer a lone voice on the world's airwaves and television screens. It now has to compete with a number of well-funded rivals. And the World Service (one of its sturdiest engines) has been obliged to pull in its horns. In 1999 it ceased to broadcast in German, and since then it has wound up more than a dozen other foreign-language services, too.

At a time when China, Germany, the Gulf, Japan and Russia have expanded their own broadcasting arms, and twenty-five countries have launched English-language services, this was an unusual approach to winning friends overseas. Yes, the audience was fading. And in 2017 the World Service did announce new services in twelve languages including Gujarati, Igbo, Korean, Punjabi, Telugu and Yoruba – the busiest expansion since the 1940s. But the withdrawal of traditional services made more headlines than the introduction of new ones, and became a powerful metaphor not just for the slide in Britain's stature but for a waning of its ambition: a retreat from its minute-by-minute place in the life of the world.

When the Hong Kong service fell silent in 2017 it was replaced by China's state channel (Chinese Central Television Channel, not to be confused with the ubiquitous CCTV video surveillance cameras around the world) and that was suggestive, too. Rival stations – CNBC, CNN, Deutsche Welle, Al-Jazeera and Russia Today – were already jostling with the BBC for space on international platforms. Sometimes (to the irritation of business travellers looking for the English football scores) they were supplanting it – just as, across Asia, hotels were displaying the dollar and the euro exchange rate without mentioning the pound.

This was not so much a policy mistake by the BBC as the weakening of its political backing. Inevitably, in the competitive marketplace of 'medianomics', there was a point of view that held state-financed broadcasting to be an anachronism, and while this was not, as mentioned above, a disinterested position (a broken BBC would further the commercial ambitions of others, especially if they succeeded in pushing over the BBC's free website, allowing them to charge for news), it was true that the landscape was changing. But when it appeared, in the wake of Brexit, that the British government might smile on such proposals, louder alarm bells began to ring.

Something similar might be said of the British Council. And there are many fields in which Britain no longer sets the pace. What, for instance, connects the following? Harrods, Rolls-Royce, Fortnum & Mason, Cadbury, Lea and Perrins, Boddingtons, Beefeater Gin, Hovis, Branston Pickle, Terry's Chocolate Orange, Tetley Tea, HP Sauce, Tate & Lyle Golden Syrup?

Answer: not one of them is British-owned. In the twenty-first century, even Smarties are manufactured in Poland.

Britishness has strong value as a brand. In China, Clarks sells shoes under the name 'Clarks England'. And whisky goes down the hatch better as 'Scotch'. Other products – Burberry – cling to their British accents, though they are made in Asia.

Is that what Britain has become – an image, a trademark, a look?

Other metaphors abound. In 1969, for instance, an elegant new aircraft roared into the sky above Bristol. It was white and streamlined – a cross between a falcon and a swan. In the year that America put a man on the moon, Britain too was joining the space age by developing a supersonic jet. A joint venture between Britain and France (with a major contribution from German aviation scientists at the Royal Aircraft Establishment in Farnborough)[8] it seemed to herald the dawning of a new age. There was a diplomatic tiff about its name – Harold Macmillan believed that 'Concord' would be more British; Tony Benn insisted on the French spelling. But this was a minor matter. The plane entered service in 1976, and immediately wowed the world.

Concorde gave a cutting edge to a land that had lost its swagger. Soon it was criss-crossing the Atlantic at twice the speed of sound. It was expensive – each seat cost several times the usual first-class fare – but a bravura way to travel. A BBC ranking of design icons put it top, ahead of the Spitfire, the Mini, the red telephone box, the E-type Jaguar and the London tube map. Japan had monorails; Switzerland had tunnels; Manhattan had skyscrapers; but Britain had its very own glamorous white jet.

It did not last. Though it never looked less than futuristic, it aged badly. It was too high priced to be a commercial success; few airports had runways long enough; and though it looked like a rocket it was soon out of date. In 2003 it was retired.

Something more than an aeroplane withdrew at that point. It was an unmistakable soft-power communiqué. Britain was a country that was – literally – slowing down.[9]

Nothing lasts. Even Rome grew world-weary. As Arnold Toynbee observed, there have been twenty-two empires in the history of the world, and nineteen of them are extinct. Britain still beams across the waves it no longer commands, but the power of its message is fading. Since it was based on industrial power, it might be said that it has run out of steam. Its vaunted strengths – rectitude, firmness and fair play – are in doubt.

---

8 Johanna Weber and Dietrich Küchemann (born in Cologne and Gottingen). The latter worked for the German Air Force during the Second World War, emigrated in 1946, became a British citizen in 1953 and settled in Farnham, Surrey, as a specialist on delta wings.

9 Of course, the same could be said for France, the co-author. But France was already polishing its reputation for high-speed travel with the *Train à Grande Vitesse*.

Of course it can revive, sometimes in unexpected ways. When the naval Task Force sailed to the South Atlantic in 1983 to 'liberate' the Falkland Islands, it struck almost everyone as a demonstration of hard power in the classic sense – ships, missiles and Royal Marines all conducting a strong-jawed defence of a distant flag. But it also had rich soft-power undertones. By sending its aircraft carriers and infantry platoons it was defending civilian values: liberty, law, steadiness under fire, a refusal to be cowed and a willingness to stand up for friends. Some thought it a lurid parody of imperialist showboating; others were pleased. A glimmer of the old Britain – tough, brave, unswerving – was visible through the smoke of fighter jets.

But this was an exception on an otherwise downward path. In general, the dominant note was elegiac. Britain was like one of its own great ships slipping into a fog bank. That in itself was not unusual. Elegy was a fine old English tradition: its literature and landscape – those memories, those ruins – spoke mournfully of the glories of bygone days, nowhere more so than in Britain's most revered author, the repository of its deepest instincts. Shakespeare had neither Brexit nor the loss of imperial cachet in mind (unless the break with Rome was in his thoughts) in writing the following, but in *Henry VI Part I* he did foreshadow much through Joan la Pucelle (Joan of Arc):

> *Glory is like a circle in the water,*
> *Which never ceaseth to enlarge itself,*
> *Till by broad spreading it disperse to nought.*

There was another shadow on the scene. The changing political mood in America and Britain was calling into question one of the dominant forces of modern times: the so-called 'Anglo-Saxon model'. This had nothing to do with the Germanic tribes that moved into England when Rome withdrew; it merely described the intense strain of free-market capitalism, developed in Chicago in the 1970s, which urged the virtues of a free-market, shareholder-led economy based on low taxation, private property, minimal government intervention and open competition.

It drew from deep wells. It owed something to Adam Smith's

'invisible hand', and something to Darwin and Hobbes. And though America and Britain were hardly equal partners in the modern world, they were joined in an intimate way by the 'special relationship' born when pilgrims left England in the seventeenth century to build a religious sanctuary in the New World. They fled Boston, Lincolnshire (a land devastated by religious war), to create a new haven in Boston, Massachusetts. In recent times the bond had been reinforced by alliances in two world wars (and a number of lesser conflicts), so the special relationship was more than an economic pact. It implied a shared enthusiasm for military intervention: the first Gulf War over Kuwait and the invasion of Iraq that followed 9/11 were both seen, in many parts of the world, as Anglo-Saxon projects.

In some circles the phrase had long been pejorative: the Anglo-Saxon model was seen as an Anglo-American project, shorthand for a wider ideology that involved light regulation and favoured short-term profits over long-term planning, with obvious and detrimental consequences both for the environment and for social justice.

That helped explain why, following the financial crash of 2008, some were quick to write its obituaries. 'Self-regulation is finished,' said Nicolas Sarkozy. The British philosopher John Gray agreed – 'an entire model . . . has collapsed'. Nouriel Roubini, Professor of Economics at New York University, wrote: 'The Anglo-Saxon model has failed.' Some thought this an over-reaction. Charles Grant, director of the Centre for European Reform, called it 'hyperbolic froth'. But it was a widely echoed view.

Roubini was taking specific aim at the 'Wild-West model' of banking and finance. But all aspects of the system came under fire: even liberal democracy itself, and the market economies it supported. The Anglo-Saxon model may (since China and India succumbed to the lure of free markets) have achieved more than the daily tide of bad news encouraged people to think; as the Swedish economist Hans Rosling never tired of pointing out, the number of people living below the poverty line had *halved* in the last thirty years – in 1990 one-third of the world's population fell into that category; three decades later it was 10 per cent. Average life expectancy was forty-six in 1950, and seventy now;

in 1960 only 42 per cent of the world could read, less than half the ratio (85 per cent) that is literate today. These achievements were sometimes lost beneath the weight of gloomy foreboding. In some surveys a clear majority of people (nearly 60 per cent) actually believed that things were getting worse, guided as they were by feelings rather than facts.[10] There was a broad tendency to believe stories of national decline and injustice, in the hope that national sovereignty and populist emotion could restore the lost golden age.

It was soft power's job to counter this with a more truthful story. And in one way the virus looked set to perform an important civic duty by reminding both governments and their publics that nothing mattered more than accurate facts, honestly gathered.

Some of these facts were chastening: Britain was throwing away 900,000 tons of bread every year – a million loaves a day. And the growing mountain of evidence on climate change and environmental damage was overwhelming too – it was said (among many other things) that China burned more coal in 2019 than Britain, a leading coal power, had managed in the entire twentieth century. As the virus raged across the world it felt at times as if the planet were shuddering in protest at the burden imposed by the human lifestyle, flexing its muscles – and fighting back.

Even before then, there were delicate soft-power points in this tangle. If people were misinformed about something as basic as global poverty, what did it say about the much-vaunted global information system? Could it be that Gresham's Law held here too, that bad information was driving out good, that it was hard to push past the surface noise? It was once said that in war reporting truth was the first casualty; now the whole concept of accurate news was in doubt: all of it could be dismissed as partisan, one-eyed, *fake*.

There were other signs that the Anglo–Saxon world had lost,

---

10 Rosling's most urgent point came when he asked a Swedish audience whether global poverty had doubled in the last thirty years, halved, or stayed about the same. The truth was that it had halved – but only 25 per cent of the audience knew this. In an entertaining aside, he put the same question to the chimpanzees at Stockholm zoo and (with 33 per cent) they performed much better, having no preconceptions to mislead them.

as it were, its own plot. In Britain, divisions over Brexit led to a wider lashing out at imaginary enemies, past and present. In America, meanwhile, it was reported that one-third of adults believed climate change to be a hoax – the same as the number that thought drugs companies were deliberately hiding the cure for cancer. The *Washington Post* was keeping well-publicised track of the President's gaffes, listing one example every morning for his first forty days, while angry vigilantes continued to spray shopping malls with bullets.

It made sense, in this context, that audiences in both Britain and America should be so enthusiastic about 'reality' television, as artificial a genre as could be imagined.

It was important to resist the temptations of 'declinism' – the assumption that a bad ending was inevitable. But the Anglo-Saxon model was clearly fraying at the edges. Publishers raced to put out books with doom-laden titles such as *Is Capitalism Obsolete?*, *How Democracy Dies*, *The Retreat of Western Liberalism* and *How the West Lost It*.

The journal *Foreign Policy* devoted a complete issue to the topic: 'Is Democracy Dying?' Some part of the inflamed anxiety about climate change – 'the house is on fire' – may have been fed by this strain of apocalyptic pessimism in the *zeitgeist*.

And what if it were true? Edward Gibbon, Oswald Spengler, Arnold Toynbee and many others had all insisted that empires die: they were living organisms, growing and withering as naturally as plants. The present turmoil really might be the first groan of a death rattle. The early years of the twentieth century were peak Britain; might the early years of the twenty-first be peak America?

Empires do not perish from the margins. More often it is the centre that cannot hold. As Toynbee put it: 'Civilisations die by suicide, not by murder.' In this he was echoing John Adams, the American Founding Father, who wrote: 'There has never been a democracy yet that did not commit suicide.'

In *The Rise and Fall of the Great Powers*, Paul Kennedy proposed that nations stumbled when their manufacturing base could no longer produce the funds needed to maintain their military strength; in *Why Nations Fail*, Daron Acemoglu and James

Robinson argued that the cause was the weakness of independent institutions, which allowed government itself to be an 'extractive' industry – as when the inaugural winner of Zimbabwe's National Lottery turned out, to no one's surprise, to be the President himself, Robert Mugabe, who pocketed the $100,000 prize.

These may both have been true. Since 2008 there had been talk of a financial crash . . . an industrial crash . . . a political crash. But the real cause may have been a morale crash, a seizure of confidence not in the fringes but at the heart of things.

As Harold Macmillan, Britain's Prime Minister, said, when decolonisation was at its height: 'The will at the centre is gone. The legions are coming home.'

Are Britain and America ready for a time when their combined national glow, once a go-anywhere brand, dwindles down to a faltering flame? Might the 'Anglo-Saxon model' turn out to be last year's toy? In the anti-elite mood of modern times even the people in charge were beginning to wonder. The delegates at the G7 conferences and Davos forums started to tread a little more warily than in times past, and scuttle home a little sooner than they used to. Fearful of new viruses, they even began to stop shaking hands.

6

France: Vaut le Détour

Montargis, a small town an hour south of Paris, not far from the Loire, is a pretty bustle of bridges, canals and ancient buildings. Long centuries of human habitation cling to the chateau and the medieval church. There are gardens and museums, and not far away stands the house where Leonardo da Vinci spent his last few years.

The area is famous for its pralines: caramelised almonds. The chef who invented them (by roasting nuts in sugar for his employer, the Maréchal du Plessis-Praslin) opened a shop in the town which still exists today, in the Place Mirabeau.

It would not strike anyone, at first sight, as the birthplace of a revolution, but in 1922 a young Chinese student-worker arrived here to 'learn knowledge and truth from the West'. He was part of a youth project called 'Diligent Work, Thrifty Study'.

He disembarked in Marseilles after a seven-week voyage on the *André Lyon* from Shanghai (via Hong Kong, Ceylon and Suez). As a sixteen-year-old he at first attended school, but soon gave up 'thrifty study' in favour of 'diligent work'. He worked first at the Le Creuset ironworks in Paris, then went south to Montargis, to a factory that made rubber boots. One of eighty or so young Chinese in the project, he breathed in a lot of glue, stuck it out for a year and then moved back to Paris to work for Renault.

His name was Deng Xiaoping.

He stayed in France until 1926, which gave him time to explore Western values and methods: the commercial power of capitalist industry as well as the social injustice it bred. His French co-workers introduced him to a riveting new idea: communism.

Along with one of his fellow travellers (Zhou Enlai, later to be famous, as China's Prime Minister, for saying that no one could judge whether the French Revolution had been a success – it was too soon to tell), he became a fervent activist. The Chinese Communist Party was born in 1921; Deng Xiaoping signed up in Paris in 1924.

It is a typical soft-power anecdote, proof of the surprising possibilities and connections thrown up by exchange, education and travel.

Back in China, Deng rose through the ranks of the Communist Party to become Secretary-General in 1957. Thanks to his time in France he was, by the standards of the time, a reformer rather than a hardliner: in 1961 he famously said, in a speech that expressed a willingness not to be doctrinaire: 'It doesn't matter if a cat is black or white, so long as it catches mice.' He was referring to the relative merits of free markets and state-run economics, an extremely daring idea at that time. Mao's 'cultural revolution' had no less an aim than 'to change the mental outlook of the whole of society'. In theory *that* was soft power; in practice it was a clampdown.

Deng's son was imprisoned and tortured (thrown from a high window, he became a paraplegic); he himself was arrested by Red Guards and sent to a work camp.

'The more people you kill,' Mao had said, 'the more revolutionary you are.'

Years later, when Deng replaced Mao, he was able to act on his two-cat strategy. On the one hand it meant the birth of a 'socialist market economy ... socialism with Chinese characteristics'. Foreign investment was welcomed; farmers were given the freedom to invigorate state-run agriculture; liberal economics was given house room. He became the first Chinese leader to visit Japan and was twice named *Time*'s 'Man of the Year'. But it also allowed him to be the stony leader who sent troops against the students in Beijing's Tiananmen Square, killing more than a thousand in order to stamp out any idea that economic deregulation might mean diluted political control.

He retained warm memories of his time in France. As China's leader he showed how deeply he valued travel as a form of creative research by visiting Singapore, Bangkok and Kuala Lumpur; in

1992 he sent more than four hundred missions to Singapore to see first-hand what a successful economy looked like; and according to David Goodman's 1994 biography, he nursed a weakness for French food. When he visited Paris, many years after his stay in Montargis, he bought a hundred croissants for his entourage.

This, we might say, was communism with French character-istics.[1]

In 2014, mindful of the tourist potential, Montargis put up a monument to the year Deng spent in its environs. '*A la mémoire de Deng Xiaoping*,' read the inscription, '*ancien grand dirigeant de la République Populaire de Chine (1904–1997)*'.

It was just round the corner from the *Musée historique de l'amitié franco-chinoise*.

There are two important soft-power threads in this story: revolutionary ideas and cuisine. French soft power is a rare and unusual blend of both, and when Deng and Zhou Enlai visited there was another factor: Soviet communism. Paris was bubbling not just with the most up-to-date fashions but with the latest ideas. Marx may have envisioned communist revolt igniting first in Britain, France and Germany, nations where there actually was an industrialised proletariat to set free, but this quirk of migra-tory history meant that it took hold first in the agrarian, peasant worlds of Russia and China. A simple student exchange, one of the most modest and routine expressions of soft power one can imagine, affected the life of half the world.

France is the fourth keenest exporter of armaments in the world, a nuclear power, a pioneer in new technology, a leader in renew-able energy and a major player in the important modern fields of aerospace, pharmaceuticals and high-speed rail. Like Britain it has historic ties rooted in the colonial past – the Francosphere – and a strong diplomatic presence everywhere. In 2017 it came top of the Portland Soft Power 30 and was praised as 'the best-networked

---

1 Deng Xiaoping was not the only world leader to polish his skills in Paris. On 6 October 1978 the Ayatollah Khomeini arrived on a tourist visa after being expelled by Iran, Iraq and Kuwait. For four months he lived in a rented house in Neauphle-le-Château, a village half an hour west of the capital, receiving visitors in a tent and recording long, hostile tirades against the Shah, which were widely distributed in Iran.

state in the world ... a member of more multilateral organisations than any other country'. The Alliance Française and the Institut Français spread its language and culture across the oceans, the latter through bilateral festivals and 'years' (France–Korea, Paris–New York or France–Colombia). In some eyes this is not so much about the fostering of connections as the trumpeting of Frenchness, but it gives France a major presence in almost every country in the world.

Yet these are not the things that come to mind when people think of France. It is the country that taught the world how to overthrow the *ancien régime*, the land of *liberté, égalité* and *fraternité*; and above all else, perhaps, it is home to the *pain au chocolat*. That is a light way of saying that France has a unique tradition in food and wine. It is very fortunate in its topography. It is Europe's largest country by far (twice the size of Germany) and the only one that can boast both a Nordic *and* a Mediterranean climate: to travel from Calais to Corsica is to move between different earth zones – from shade to sun. The east–west journey from the golden sands of Biarritz to the white crown of Mont Blanc is just as dramatic. France contains every European terrain, butter *and* olive oil, beer *and* wine, apples *and* rice. It is all of Europe in one varied dish.

This geographical blessing has given rise to the culinary culture that has colonised the world with a universal vocabulary of eating and drinking – *café, casserole, chef, canapé, champagne, cuisine, restaurant, menu, omelette, pâté, meringue, biscuit* (twice cooked) ... this is a list that could go on and on.

Some have called it 'croissant diplomacy', and patisserie has indeed flown the French flag with *élan*. Everyone mimics French café society – in today's small world we are never far from a *croque monsieur* or a *tarte aux pommes*. But however faithful the imitation (and it is often said that the capital of modern French cuisine is Tokyo), there is always an echo of the beguiling country where it began. Globalisation may have cost France much of its singularity, but five minutes in a small-town *tabac* or a *salon de thé* are enough to remind us that no one does France quite like the French.

This became official in 1900, when a new red booklet appeared. It was the dawn of motoring, and the pioneer tyre manufacturers Edouard and André Michelin wanted to encourage people to wear out their wheels a little faster. Their scarlet handbooks, bright as poppies, included information on fuel stops and mechanical support, and were given away free as publicity gimmicks (*offert gracieusement aux chauffeurs*). More than 30,000 copies were distributed at the 1900 Paris Expo.

In due course the Guide became more famous as a list of recommended places to eat (or stay), especially after 1926, when it introduced its star ratings. Its inspectors were as incorruptible as Robespierre, and when motoring became a mass-market habit after the Second World War, the Michelin Guide was as indispensable as a map or a watch. It had a larger meaning, too. France became not only the home of fine food, but also the arbiter of taste – judge and jury as well as *chef de cuisine*. Its dry and formal way with compliments (a rare masterpiece might be 'worth the detour') gave it a regal air.

When Björn Frantzen became the first chef in Sweden to win three Michelin stars in 2018, it was major news – like being knighted by the gods. Similarly, when Garima Arora became the first Indian woman to win a star (for her restaurant in Bangkok) the *Times of India* ran a fulsome leader in her praise. French praise was a refined sauce.

In time the star system began to strike some as Gallic imperialism, standing guard on a stodgy tradition of truffled pigeons and *foie gras* terrines. It was criticised too for allowing itself to be bought: four of the eight stars in Guangzhou, China, in 2018, were awarded to expensive restaurants in luxury hotels, hardly representative of local cuisine.

But it remains a robust publicity engine for its *pays d'origine*: France has twenty-seven three-star dining rooms compared to five in Britain and two in Switzerland. Japan has fifteen (one Tokyo booth offers only tempura vegetables – the last word in refinement), and, in an attempt to branch out, Michelin does now give ratings to Singaporean street food. But the main message does not change: France itself was *vaut le détour*.

Anything one might say about French food is true of its other great creation: wine. France may no longer be the world's largest

producer: Italy and Spain make more in gallons, and it is only the
world's third largest vineyard by hectare, behind Spain and – to
many people's surprise – China, whose 800,000 hectares of grapes
took it to second place in 2015. But its historic vineyards are more
than merely French: by waylaying palates everywhere they belong
to the world.

This was obvious even on the day when France was forced to
surrender its title as wine's unquestioned champion. On 24 May
1976, in Paris, a British vintner named Steven Spurrier organised
a blind tasting between France and California. American vineyards had long been insisting that their vintages were a match for
the so-called heavyweights; Spurrier put it to the test.

Eleven elite judges sampled a range of wines: Château Haut-
Brion, Château Mouton-Rothschild, Meursault Charmes Roulot,
Puligny-Montrachet Les Pucelles. Then – *incroyable* – they
handed the garland to New World vintages. A Chardonnay and a
Cabernet Sauvignon from California pipped the *crème de la crème*
of France.[2]

The tournament became known as 'The Judgment of Paris',
and if the source of that name, the beauty contest that led to the
Trojan War, had legendary implications, so did this battle of the
spittoons. Wine had *always* been synonymous with France. Oh,
the Germans had their Hock, and the Hungarians their Tokay;
Spain had its Rioja, and retsina could come only from Greece.
But in most eyes wine was ... French. It wasn't a surprise when
an Italian maker chose a French name – Hirondelle – for its
'plonk' (a British contraction of *vin blanc*). And Robert Mondavi,
the eminent Californian, did the same when he called his Napa
Valley bestseller *Fumé Blanc*.

If you wanted your wine to be taken seriously, it had to have
a château in its name. Some Spanish winemakers set up bottling
plants north of the Pyrenees just so they could print '*Mis en bou-
teille en France*' on the label. It was a commercial necessity.

This was soft power in action. However delicious the wine, and
wherever it was made, a soupçon of the credit went back to France.

---

2 It is tempting to think that Spurrier was deliberately tweaking the tail of overcon-
fident French *viticulteurs*, but if anything the opposite was the case. He aimed only to
prove the superiority of French wine, and was as surprised as anyone by the outcome.

If anything, the more avidly the world grows vines, the more we are reminded of those gnarled old acreages of Burgundy and Bordeaux, Loire and Rhône. And the vintages prized by investors are still French. In 2018 a bottle of 1945 Vosne-Romanée sold at Sotheby's, New York, for $588,000 (after 'frenzied' bidding from Asia).

Only six hundred bottles came out of that vineyard in 1945, making it the rarest of all rare wines. It is unlikely ever to be drunk; it is an intoxicating financial instrument.

It is a statement of the obvious that wine and cheese are expressions of the landscape in which they grow. This is *terroir* – the combination of rock, soil, climate and human habits that makes each slope in each valley in each *commune* in each *département* unlike any other. This is what sustains the personality of France's famous regions. It is an article of faith, even now, that each different locale – Gascony, the Auvergne, Savoie, Jura, Provence, Champagne – has a gastronomic culture all its own.[3]

This presents French soft power with its first difficulty. On the one hand it is proudly nationalist: Louis XIV's boast (*'L'état, c'est moi'*) struck a chord with Charles de Gaulle ('France cannot be France without greatness') and messages of that sort drum in French hearts still. The national days are colourful: flags, fireworks and parades.

It takes its annual holiday in the same month, returning on the same day (the last Sunday in August – an occasion celebrated with spectacular traffic jams). It is the home of *dirigisme*, a state in which every sixteen-year-old sits the same maths exam at the same moment as every other sixteen-year-old, whether staring at the drizzle in Rouen or blinking back sweat in Aix-en-Provence.

There is even a standard French form of handwriting – a looping script all children learn from the earliest age. It derives from a Renaissance font named La Ronde, and the non-negotiable way it is taught is a reminder that *liberté* does not mean 'anything goes'. It might strike British teachers as repressive (what, a 'correct' way

---

3 The diplomat and gourmand Talleyrand once observed that France was a land of 360 sauces and only three faiths, whereas Britain was the other way round.

to hold a pen?) but France is confident enough to insist that the equipping of children with uniform handwriting is not a restraint but an act of liberation.

It has a greater reverence for central government than any-where else in Europe.

Yet it is also fiercely and famously regional. Brittany is a rocky coastal sister of Cornwall and Wales, the Pyrenees are half-Catalan, Savoie is part-Swiss, Lorraine is partly German, Corsica is Italian, Gascony is a law unto itself, Marseilles has African connections, and so on. This may be why the central grasp needs to be so firm – the distinctions are so robust. In the famous defi-nition, how can anyone govern a land, in de Gaulle's famous remark, that has four hundred cheeses? France is large enough for its regional centres – Bordeaux, Lyon, Marseilles, Nantes – to feel like capital cities.

Its long tradition in food and wine has made it the capital of other forms of physical pleasure too. Britain may have led the way in male clothing (wool-working made it the home of the tailor-made suit, while its cool weather gave it expertise in coats). But France ruled the roost in women's clothing – *haute couture*. Agnès B, Chanel, Dior, Hermès and the rest ... who else had so many last words in fashion?

It was the bottling centre of perfume, too. The leading houses, like the famous wines, filled the world with extracts of rose, lav-ender, cedar, sandalwood and citrus.

France was not the first civilisation to explore scent: the prac-tice began in the Arabic world as a spicy way to alleviate the impact of the constant sun. And as the name suggests, *eau de cologne* began life as the *kölnisch wasser* created in Germany in 1709 (by an Italian perfumier).[4] But it was the ancient botanical power of France's landscape, in particular the sunny hills of the Alpes-Maritimes, north of Cannes, with its slopes full of scented fruit and flowers, that made France the home of fragrance.

Perfume and fashion, food and wine ... these are not fripperies.

---

4 The inventor, Giovanni Maria Farina, experimented with citrus oils to produce a scent which, he claimed, 'reminds me of an Italian spring morning, of mountain daffo-dils and orange blossom after the rain'. A German chemist, Wilhelm Mühlens, turned it into a commercial hit by exporting it to France in Napoleonic times.

In soft-power terms they have made France stand for almost all the good things in life (*bien-être*). It was almost inevitable that it should also become known as the symbolic home of romantic love. This began early, in the songs strummed by the troubadours of medieval times, and the reputation survives today, with Paris still attracting amorous couples from all over the world to pledge their love in trysts along the Seine.[5]

In the international story competition that is soft power, this is clearly an advantage. But France has managed to make itself a world leader in cerebral as well as physical pleasures, with a golden heritage in the products of the mind: art, sculpture, music, architecture, philosophy − everything to do with aesthetic and intellectual life.

After the decline of Greece and Rome, a sizeable part of 'Western civilisation' grew in French soil − from monastic scholarship and Gothic buttresses to existentialism and cubism. The world's galleries are filled with its paintings, and the monuments in its countryside have few rivals. It trembles with great literature, philosophy and cinema.

This is the second great ingredient of France's soft inheritance. Braque, Cézanne, Delacroix, Gauguin, Monet, Picasso, Renoir and the rest . . . these are extraordinary advertisements for the land they lived in.

If France's prestige in food and wine is rooted in its landscape, its intellectual and artistic *éclat* rests on its most famous historical episode: the Revolution. That is where France came to be associated with the overturning of tradition, with . . . the new. Even though it came two decades after America's revolution, and echoed the egalitarian ideals laid down by the Founding Fathers, its great moment of national liberation is still the one to which posterity turns as the archetype of such uprisings.

Perhaps this is because France was tearing down a monarchy rather than a colonial power − it was a revolution, not a war. Or maybe it is the fact that revolution gave it so memorable a slogan

---

5 On the Pont des Arts, couples still pledge undying love by clipping padlocks on to the railings, then throwing the key into the river. The fact that workmen occasionally remove the overburdened railings (65 tons have been moved in recent years) has done nothing to dent what has become a significant tourist ritual.

(*Liberté, Egalité, Fraternité*).[6] The symbolic weight of these words is
undimmed. It is embedded in the colours of the national flag and
on town halls, schools, universities, government offices, libraries,
coins and parking tickets.[7] It illuminates many a protest march. In
the *gilets jaunes* uprising of 2018, activists lit flares on the statue of
Marianne (the goddess of liberty, who symbolised the Republic in
1792 and whose bust adorns most of France's town halls and post-
age stamps) in Paris's Place de la République. A strike about the
tax on diesel dressed itself as an assertion of revolutionary liberty.

It was a tribute to the power of the French brand that this still
felt French. As Deng Xiaoping learned, it was, and always would
be, the home of the *coup d'état*.

The French Revolution was a physical upheaval, and the
Napoleonic empire that followed was militarised. But Napoleon
himself acknowledged the importance of soft power by observing
that 'four hostile newspapers are more to be feared than a thousand bayonets'. He knew that he himself had been unleashed by
the projectile force of the revolutionary idea more than by all the
artillery at his command.

Liberté, Egalité, Fraternité . . . the motto still blazes in the world's
political vocabulary, just as it did when Thomas Jefferson wrote:
'All men have two countries – their own, and France.'[8]

As time passes, its meaning grows ambiguous. In the cosmopolitan modern world, *fraternité* can mean a universal sort of
fellow-feeling, but also mean sticking together to repel outsiders.
Liberté can suggest the freedom to assert individual identities,
but also the state's freedom to clamp down. Does *égalité* imply
a redistribution of wealth, or equal opportunities in a diverse

---

6 This has kept sub-editors in jokes for centuries. A plan to cut spending can be *liberté,
égalité, frugalité*; mothers seeking better work–life arrangements can appeal to *liberté, égalité,
maternité*; forbidden love is *liberté, égalité, infidelité*.

7 One of the things guaranteed to bring a smile to the face of foreign tennis fans is the
sound, each summer, at the French Open in Roland Garros, of umpires giving the score
as '*égalité*', meaning deuce – as if each game were an idealistic *cri de coeur*.

8 The provenance is obscure: the phrase does not appear in Jefferson's own writings,
though he expressed a similar sentiment in his *Autobiography*. The line appears in an
1875 play about Charlemagne by Henri de Bornier (*Tout homme a deux pays, le sien et
puis la France*) – which may have been a translation of Jefferson's original. But Jefferson's
Autobiography was not published until 1821, long after the Revolution.

society? All European states are wrestling with such questions, but France has this clear trio of revolutionary ideals to fall back on. When gunmen killed twelve people working for the satirical magazine *Charlie Hebdo*, nearly six million French people took to the streets to demonstrate their support not only for freedom of speech (and the freedom to make bad jokes) but for the idea of *laïcité* – the emancipation of civic life from state power – which grew out of 1789.

This heritage is an important part of France's self-confidence: it is what lies behind both the famous 'Gallic shrug' and the feeling that it is a force of destiny: the light of the world. *Rayonnement* – France holds the torch for all mankind. General de Gaulle himself, undeterred by the fact that his country had twice been rescued by the US and UK, called it *la lumière du monde* – the light of the world – and it did not seem fanciful. Had not Louis XIV been 'the Sun King'? Had not all those painters invented a magical new language of light and colour? Was not Paris the city of light?

Flaubert mocked this grandiosity in his *Dictionary of Received Ideas*, which defined 'The French' as 'the greatest people in the universe'. But it was resilient. Like the Britons who grew weak-kneed at the thought of their own vast empire, France clung to a persistent belief that it was exceptional. It led France to develop a distinctive attitude to its colonies and dominions: they were (and still are) French. The Union Flag no longer flies over St Lucia, but Martinique, a short boat ride away, is a fully fledged *département*: it has the euro, sends deputies to Paris, boasts a pharmacy every 50 yards and has rows of municipal tennis courts. In a famous remark, a French dignitary in London was once asked why, if nuclear testing was so safe, his country conducted them in the Pacific rather than in France. He replied: But Tahiti *is* France.

The French language was learned and used all over the world, but it was hard to shake the conviction that only in *la patrie* could you hope to hear the real thing.

The light was not figurative, in other words, but a literal fact. Among its other gifts to the world, France could include its pioneering work in motion pictures – the work of Georges Méliès and the Lumière brothers. The latter astounded audiences in 1895 with images of workers leaving a factory, or a train arriving at a station, only to declare that cinema was 'an invention without any future'.[9]

The idea of France as a beacon of enlightenment proved powerful. In time the entire concept of intellectual and artistic creativity would come to seem distinctively French, a matter of style as much as thought. The tradition that ran from Montaigne to Sartre broke new ground by invoking old patterns.

It also put forward the *act* of heroic resistance as a French characteristic. From Joan of Arc and the storming of the Bastille to the martyrs of Verdun, from Charlemagne to the French Resistance, France was the home of the freedom fighter. In Britain people might 'down tools' or 'work to rule'; in France they would man barricades. The *gilets jaunes* of recent times do not feel it is a protest unless something is set on fire (they have seen *Liberty Leading the People* by Delacroix). The revolts of 1832 (as depicted in *Les Misérables*), 1871 (the Paris *commune*) and 1968 (student riots) all had echoes of 1789. With due sense of theatre, France called them all *événements*.

Even today, a French strike has a touch of the carnival or battlefield re-enactment about it, even when it is only a blockade of angry lorries.

The most famous depiction of this rebellious streak is fictional: René Goscinny's pesky comic-book hero Asterix thumbed his nose at the over-mighty Romans in a way designed to appeal to France's sense of itself as a pint-sized rebel (rather than the largest country in Europe). As so often, it took outsiders to nail this notion. Though born in Paris, Goscinny was the child of Polish Jews and grew up in Argentina; his collaborator, the illustrator Albert Uderzo, was the son of Italian immigrants.

In 1959 Asterix was launched as a cartoon character, but he soon became a thirty-seven-book empire, selling 325 million copies in a hundred languages. The world, it seemed, agreed.

---

9 George Méliès' film – a lunar voyage in a home-made rocket – was echoed by Wallace and Gromit, the Yorkshire astronauts who went on a cheese-finding trip to the moon; in 2016 Martin Scorsese paid homage by having Ben Kingsley play him in *Hugo*, capturing the man in old age, running a toy shop in Montparnasse station.

Since then there have been films, games, pyjamas, even crisps. And of course there is a theme park near Paris named after the uppity Gaul. It made perfect sense when France's first satellite was called Asterix – the man himself was named after a star.

In 1991, when *Time* magazine devoted an issue to France, who could it put on the cover but ... Asterix? A modern invention, he draws power from the ancient past.

That is how soft power spreads – through adventures and jokes.

But it also works through news stories. When a policeman named Arnaud Beltrame, in Trèbes, near Carcassonne, took the place of a hostage in a supermarket hold-up and was killed, he became a tragic emblem of France's most sacred qualities. No one could say enough about 'his heroism, his bravery, his sacrifice'.

Similarly, when a migrant from Mali shinned up several balconies of a Paris apartment block to rescue a dangling child, it was not only the onlookers who cheered – he was invited to the Elysée Palace by President Macron, thanked for his 'courage and devotion' and granted honorary citizenship. He may not have known it, but he was following in the footsteps of another Malian immigrant, Lassana Bathily, who became a national hero during the Bataclan shootings in 2015, when he sheltered customers in a freezer in a Jewish supermarket from marauding Islamic gunmen.

England could keep Robin Hood. France had plenty of its own plucky heroes.

There was Jean Moulin, the lawyer-leader of the French Resistance, or Berthe Fraser, the clothier from Arras who, when her British husband was interned by the Germans, helped scores of downed airmen escape back across the Channel. Her reward was arrest and torture by the Gestapo, a fate that also befell Madeleine Riffaud, who in July 1944, as a twenty-year-old girl, supported the Allied invasion by shooting a German officer from a bridge over the Seine.

Simone Segouin, an eighteen-year-old heroine who took up with the Partisans in 1944 and helped – among other things – to liberate Chartres, was more fortunate. A smiling girl with a machine gun in one hand and a Croix de Guerre in the other, she became a pin-up for resistance fighters everywhere, not just in France.

It is certainly possible (and often alleged) that the extent of France's resistance has been exaggerated to obscure the humiliating scale of collaboration in the Vichy era.[10] But a larger reason why these heroic episodes are so eagerly remembered is that they fit neatly into an existing tradition: they offer continuity with a glorious past.

In 1999, in Millau, in the south of France, a real-life Asterix emerged in the person of a French farmer named José Bové. With a typical French sense of theatre, he wrapped the idea of protest in the local landscape and its food.

Millau is a long way south: closer to the Pyrenees than to Paris. But in a figurative sense it lies close to the heart of *la France profonde*. It straddles the Tarn, which drains west into the Atlantic, yet its position on the edge of the Cévennes gives it an Alpine flavour, and it is not far from the source of the Gard, which tumbles down to the Rhône, connecting it to the Mediterranean. It has oak woods and sun-drenched summers. On one side of town are the remnants of a Roman pottery works whose ceramics have been found all across the Roman Empire, while to the west curves a gleaming modern viaduct designed by the British architect Norman Foster. The word may be Roman, but the bridge is ultra-modern – the tallest in the world.

It combines north and south, in other words, and east and west, and old and new. A Celtic settlement, a Roman hub, and now the setting for a modern French drama.

As a farmer, Bové expresses this landscape in his very person. This is sheep country, and his Roquefort cheese is a natural emanation of its sweet pasture and dark caves. Dismayed by America's refusal to allow imports of this famous cheese (sanctions against French delicacies were imposed when the European Union

---

10 It is often said that only a minority in France resisted, and this may be true: in 1943 some 200,000 French children had German fathers, which – even allowing for the fact that a sizeable number were almost certainly conceived by force – implied some willingness to collaborate.

banned hormone-enriched American beef), Bové reacted to the opening of a McDonald's in Millau in the time-honoured way: he boarded his tractor and smashed up the work in progress.

It was a pointed act of vandalism. He objected to the burger joint on the principle that bad (mass-produced, machine-generated) food was driving out the real thing.

At that time France did not have a name for junk food. Now it did – *mal bouffe*.

When the authorities stepped in, he turned his 'trial' into a fiesta, arriving at court in his tractor with a wheel of Roquefort around his neck. With straggly hair and a bushy moustache, he even *looked* like Asterix – but one who had read Bakunin. When he wasn't being a cheesemaker he described himself as an anarcho-syndicalist agitator.

You can't get more French than that.

His trial attracted a crowd of 15,000 – most of whom regarded him as a resistance hero. When he was sentenced to three months in prison and a fine, neighbouring farmers clubbed together to make the payment. The harshness of the punishment (such stunts usually earned nothing worse than a one-month sentence) turned a one-off protest into a movement – an act of stout resistance against the global food chain.

Bové found himself with a new career. He wrote a forceful book (*Le monde n'est pas un marchandise* – The world is not a market) and campaigned against globalisation, winning high-profile supporters on many continents. Of course he attracted critics. It was pointed out that the world had changed, that the tide of modern tastes could not be stopped. But even if he was only raging against the dying of the light, he seemed to symbolise an important national characteristic. France was still the light or conscience of the world, he suggested – as it had been since that famous day at the Bastille.

Another such figure emerged in the summer of 2018, when Cédric Herrou, an olive grower in the South of France, was first fined, then reprieved, for helping migrants cross the mountains from Italy to France. This was the kind of landscape most people dreamed of as a holiday destination, but the refugees were desperate. They had crossed the Mediterranean from North Africa and trekked through Italy on foot.

On the site of a disused railway station, and on his own land, Herrou provided some basic food and shelter. It won him both friends and enemies.

Was he a people trafficker, flouting the law of the land, or a saint, smuggling the Von Trapps through the Alps? A local court judged him to be the former, found him guilty and fined him €3000. But a court in Nice, moved by the simplicity of his defence ('I am a Frenchman'), ruled in his favour, deeming him a patriot. His actions, it said, were consistent with the great principle of *fraternité* – interpreted by the court as being 'the freedom to help others for humanitarian purposes'. It added that since he had not profited from his actions in any way, he could not be treated as a criminal.

By placing such notions on legal record, the court turned Herrou into a new Bové, a new Asterix, a new Joan, a new Napoleon. It was a soft-power firework, lighting the horizon with the message that France was a land of high ideals. Herrou gained 40,000 followers on Facebook, where he appealed to the language of 1789 by styling himself *'agriculteur, éleveur de poulets, citoyen'*. The signal went around the world: the *New York Times* compared him to the heroes of the 'underground railroad' that had helped slaves flee the southern states to relative safety in the north.

There were copycats, too. A professor of geography at Nice University received a two-month prison sentence (suspended) for driving three injured Eritrean girls to hospital. As before, a higher court ruled that these were not crimes but acts of *fraternité*. No one was taking sides: the court continued to insist that Islamic veils must not be worn in school, since that ran counter to the principle that education was a secular space, and perhaps violated the equally sacred notion of *égalité*.

There was a conundrum here: *égalité* was being protected by suppressing *liberté*. But who said the sending of soft-power signals was simple?

It goes without saying that France is a land of contradictions – so is everywhere else. But in France's case it is especially obvious.

These contradictory forces inform many aspects of French life. It is a land both of *monsieur-madame* formality (it is no coincidence that invitations all over the world require people to RSVP), yet there are few greater bywords for rudeness than a Paris waiter. It has ancient ruins and super-modern high-speed trains. It is legalistic and finickity, yet also shrugging and devil-may-care. It is D'Artagnan – bursting with *élan* – yet also Cyrano de Bergerac: a lovelorn poet racked by self-doubt.

The historic upholder of *liberté*, it was content to act the tyrant in Algeria. The home of *fraternité*, it collaborated with Nazi occupiers. The torch-bearer for *égalité*, it has a super-elite school system (if you do not attend the Ecole Nationale d'Administration you can forget about high office[11]) and brims with nostalgic affection for Napoleonic eagles. Its republican vows hide a yearning to be still, somewhat, a Sun King.

It believes not just in the best of both worlds, but in the best of all possible worlds.[12]

Somehow this rarely seems perfidious. If anything it adds to France's glamour. If it were more eager to please it might offend. As it is, wrapped up in itself, a cat licking its own fur, it has a quality – *hauteur* – the world finds hard to resist.

The cockerel is its perfect symbol: all dash and swank, yet a shrill nuisance. Beneath its chivalrous manners lies the belief that France really is the *nonpareil* – not just of Europe, but the world. As James (later Jan) Morris wrote of Paris in the long-ago of 1963: 'It is the inescapable destiny of this city to be the capital of Europe.'

This was a happy echo of de Gaulle's declaration, in 1959, that it was the destiny of Europe, 'from the Atlantic to the Urals', to decide the fate of the world.

---

11 Created after the Second World War by General de Gaulle, the ENA was designed to produce elite civil servants, and that is what it has done. Valéry Giscard d'Estaing, Jacques Chirac, François Hollande, Lionel Jospin and Emmanuel Macron are all alumni. Roughly a third of most modern French Cabinets attended this one school.

12 Dr Pangloss's famous line in Voltaire's *Candide* ('All is for the best in the best of all possible worlds') had a satirical edge. But sometimes satire can fall away, leaving only the original idea.

7

France: Rayonnement

A s we have seen, governments do not create the national story; they merely have temporary control of its reins. The coronavirus shutdown was a bracing reminder that those reins were exceptionally long: national governments could order entire populations to stay at home. But even this could only scratch the surface of France's unrivalled range of soft-power ingredients. It was a world leader in gastronomy, history, landscape, art, luxury and revolutionary ideas. And it had traditionally been more assertive than most in exploiting this glorious past to promote its future.

One of Emmanuel Macron's first moves on becoming president was to embark on a charm offensive, using France's cultural treasures as gifts. In one frankly medieval gesture he gave China's President Xi Jinping a horse named Vesuvius (a gift almost as traditional as offering the hand of his daughter in marriage), adding the compliment that China was 'older than history'. He then offered to lend the Bayeux Tapestry to England, the losing side in the battle it described.

There was something overbearing in these 'gifts'. What do you give a man who has the Bayeux Tapestry in his present drawer? A commemorative mug? And Macron went further. He revived the dream that the French language might one day lead the world by taking active steps to promote it, in old-fashioned sacramental rhetoric. 'French is the language of reason,' he declared, 'the language of light.'

This was not the way most politicians talked, and it struck a grandiose note. But in 2018 he went to Nigeria as part of a specific soft-power bid to make France great again — not by falling back on old traditions but by reaching out. 'To refuse the French language,' he said, 'is to be blind to the future. If we go about it right, French will be the first language in Africa – and maybe even the world – in the coming decades.'

This was a nod to the fact that there were more French speakers in Africa than in France (the figure given was 700 million – though this may have included those with only a smattering), and looking at Africa's expected population growth, which would produce fresh multitudes. It was a soft-charm offensive.

He tried to allay the fears of those who found this itself an imperious idiom. 'I am of a generation that does not tell Africans what to do,' he told an audience of students in Burkina Faso. But in speaking of his desire to make French the 'number one language in Africa' he could not help reviving colonial memories. Appointing the winner of the *Prix Goncourt* Leila Slimani to help develop the project made little difference. Abdourahman Waberi, a Djibouti-born professor in Washington, called it (in *Le Monde*) 'an outdated vision'. Others took the opportunity to ask how many French universities were teaching African literature and culture in a truly serious way.

Accusations of this sort flew thick and fast.

Undaunted, Macron went to Senegal and announced a new €200 million education scheme, and followed it up with a €65 million fund for African digital start-ups. He unveiled an updated portrait of Marianne, laid on a jingle-jangle military parade for Donald Trump on the Champs Elysées, and marked the 300th anniversary of Peter the Great's visit to France by inviting Vladimir Putin to walk in those tsarist footprints. He made a well-publicised visit to France's cosmopolitan football team as it prepared to go to the World Cup in Russia, and no doubt his advice ('Stay united. Work hard') was the key that helped France win. He led his ministers on an ostentatious march from the Elysée Palace to the British Embassy to express his solidarity with the victims of the terrorist attack in Manchester (a showy move he may have borrowed from *The West Wing*, where Martin Sheen marched through Washington to make a political point).

And he advanced into non-francophone Africa, too, travelling to Nairobi to toast the signing of trade contracts worth €2 billion with

Kenya (motorways and solar power). It was the first visit by a French president to the once-British colony since it became independent in 1963. He was taken for a drive in a Peugeot that was made in Kenya.

Of course there was opportunism in these manoeuvres. As François Heisbourg of the International Institute for Strategic Studies put it, Macron was seizing the chance to occupy the vacuum left by others. 'Germany doesn't have a government, Britain has transformed itself into an object of international commiseration and the United States is being seen more and more as part of the problem, not the solution. So who's left?'

But these were bold moves, and the judges were impressed. The 2017 Portland Soft Power 30 attributed France's strong showing mainly to Macron himself: 'It showed what a new leader with a positive outlook can do for a country's global reputation.' And in 2019 he went one better by leading his nation to the top place once again.

France was *The Economist*'s choice as 'Country of the Year' as well. Under the only possible strap line – '*Le jour de gloire est arrivé*' – the magazine applauded the tone and energy of the ex-banker who had come from nowhere to relight the national torch. Macron was also able to turn Brexit to his advantage by narrating France as a glorious story and making it, after a spell on the sidelines, a *chargé d'affaires* once more.

It won him a giddy following at home and abroad which lasted, in accordance with France's finest revolutionary traditions, roughly until his first tax increase.

His most prominent cultural gesture, however, was the launch of a lavish outpost of the Louvre in Abu Dhabi. Like a missionary spreading the gospel to a desert land, he gave a high-minded speech about the way art could 'fight the discourses of hatred'; but also added that with this initiative France was creating a bright beacon 'that would shine out to the whole world'.

He did not mention that the project had been delayed by talk of 'modern slavery' regarding the museum's migrant construction workers.[1] This was *rayonnement*.

---

1 The United Arab Emirates had an interesting migration story to tell. Only one-tenth of its population (ten million) was Arab. The rest were non-citizens from abroad, most of them working on the region's colossal building projects. One-quarter were Indian; another quarter came from Pakistan, Bangladesh and Iran.

There was criticism at home. 'Museums are not for sale,' went the cry, overlooking the extent to which, if they charged for entry, museums *were* for sale, all the time. But those lambasting France for 'selling its soul' were also drawing attention to evidence that soft power *did* carry genuine weight. France's artistic halo was valued, in this instance, at over a billion dollars: the original contract promised $525 million for the name (on a thirty-year lease) and $750 million for loans and management advice.

Designed by a French architect on an island of reclaimed land, the new museum was a bold declaration of French style in a new setting. 'Do try us, please,' said Macron, revealing a clear understanding of what it stood for. 'Not just our wines and luxuries, but also our culture, and the universal and humanist values refracted through it.'

Observers from America and Britain, used to cruder signals, could only sigh.

Dubai, meanwhile, was suddenly hosting famous art from both Africa and Europe. Surrounded by the sparkling waters of the Gulf, visitors could marvel at the portrait of Napoleon crossing the Alps, an Egyptian mummy or Whistler's mother. This was culture as bridge-building and emancipation. It was also highly profitable: a smart new mannequin in the shop window of a state looking to a future beyond oil.

France scores highly on many other 'objective' measures. As a Brexit bonus it offered bankers and fintech start-ups a new home. Among other inducements, it promised a new, English-language Court of Appeals for Paris. And there were moves to make the French capital more enticing to young entrepreneurs (a French word, if not a French habit). A railway station was converted into a smart 'hub' with space for two thousand new businesses. This being France, it was smothered in art by figures such as Ai Weiwei and Jeff Koons, to make the millennials feel at home.

It worked. When Ernst & Young surveyed 450 international investors in 2018, Paris ranked above London as an 'attractive place to do business' – for the first time since 2004. It was also wooing the foreign students Britain seemed happy to lose. In November 2018 France's Prime Minister announced that France

aimed to lift numbers by simplifying visa access and, in a measure aimed specifically at Asia and Africa, adopting English as
the medium of learning. The fact that fees at French universities
were low by British standards was another part of the package. A
good many of the 100,000 European Union students in the UK
were reported to be tempted, while the 36,000 EU academics
who faced an uncertain future in Britain (including one-fifth
of the staff at Cambridge University[2]) also started to explore
other options.[3]

Paris was open to commercial defectors too. A new state
school, Lucie-Aubrac International School, opened in the business
district at a cost of €253 million, to take advantage of the fact that
so many finance houses (Bank of America, J.P. Morgan, Morgan
Stanley, Crédit Agricole) were revealing plans to move staff out
of London.

France was also taking an impressive lead in global health
governance – in recent years it had tripled its spending on international health (to €500 million per year) and in 2006 introduced
a tax on all flights departing from French airports (to be paid
by French travellers rather than by visitors). The proceeds – €2
billion and rising – were earmarked for the fight against AIDS,
tuberculosis and malaria.

None of these were the main event. France's most important soft-
power card was still the range and richness of its many beauties.
Its extraordinary scenery could provide something for everyone:
sunseekers, skiers, hikers, swimmers, shoppers, students, art historians, gluttons and culture mavens alike. You could see cathedrals
in the morning and lie on beaches in the afternoon, have a dip in
the sea first thing and hole up in an art gallery and a restaurant
afterwards. It had cities and villages, glaciers and lakes, five-star
hotels and campsites, forests, rivers and Alpine mountains. It
had Roman amphitheatres and modern theme parks, medieval

---

2 According to evidence submitted by the university to the Migration Advisory
Committee, 21.7 per cent of its employees were European nationals; 62.6 per cent
were British.

3 The Sorbonne is starting to teach history in English, to attract students from Africa
and Asia; at Sciences Po, more than half the teaching is already in English.

monasteries and tennis camps, golf resorts and yachting marinas. It had everything, in short, a tourist might want.

There was money, it turned out, in geography and history. The Côte d'Azur alone received ten million visits, more than most countries. This advantage was consolidated by the fact that the French themselves holiday at home: their splendid landscape means they do not have to travel to find sunnier (or cooler) climes. The north goes south, while the south heads for the hills, or to an air-conditioned city.

When we ask what soft power means in practice, this – tourism – is the most obvious answer. It is how a country's likeability is transformed into a bankable commodity. The slump triggered by the terrorist attacks of 2016 (in Paris and Nice) proved fleeting: tourism remained a momentous resource. In the second decade of the twenty-first century it was generating roughly €200 billion per year. It was estimated that in 2027 at the prevailing rate of growth it could rake in roughly €240 billion. Paris welcomed thirty million tourists a year, almost as many as Britain. Eleven million went to the Louvre, but even more – fifteen million – headed east to Disneyland.[4] Paris catered for them all.

France's heady range of charms created a supplement known as the Paris Premium – a willingness to pay more for French *je ne sais quoi.*

The 2018 Christmas package at Paris's Hôtel de Crillon, which includes a helicopter trip to Château de Chenonceau on the Loire (the historic home of Catherine de Medici), along with a performance by Opéra de Paris and a Renaissance-themed dinner delivered by Michelin-starred chefs, cost €150,000.

The premium is especially valuable, today, in the Chinese demand for luxury goods: high-end fashion, expensive art and wine. Shares in LVMH, the holding group behind brands like Louis Vuitton and Moët & Chandon, rose by 24 per cent in 2018; Hermès stock by 23 per cent in the same period. Meanwhile, Chinese shoppers were happy to pay through their noses for luggage made by Goyard, the exclusive French boutique (*fondée* 1853, in Paris) which

---

4 As it happened Walt Disney based his original conception on Paris. The fairy-tale castle was inspired by Neuschwanstein in Bavaria, but the park's layout – boulevards around a central hub – was inspired by the Arc de Triomphe.

has held itself aloof from the usual sales routines, restricting itself to a handful of outlets and relying on sheer exclusivity.[5]

Goyard has only a minimal presence in China – the voyage to Paris or London is part of the fun. Retail tourists form a queue (the principle that customers be attended to personally permits only a small number to enter at any one time) before paying £700 or more for a leather clutch bag rendered glamorous by the fact that Picasso, Coco Chanel and Meghan Markle have given it their seal of approval.

China's love affair with Bordeaux has been well documented. In 2000 it bought 400,000 bottles of French wine; last year it took eighty million. And Bordeaux is its favoured *terroir*. A growing number of châteaux in the *appellation* (150 at the last count) are Chinese-owned, a trying subject for connoisseurs who find the new labels – Tibetan Antelope, Imperial Rabbit – insufficiently Gallic. But in China itself a new theme park – Wine City – opened its doors in 2017. With the support of Disneyland, it had as its centrepiece a château that might have been imported from the Loire, and a research institute in the shape of an oak barrel, surrounded by champagne flutes. It contained a warning for traditional wine powers, too, since it was more than a visitor attraction: it had the capacity to produce 450,000 tons of wine in the years to come.

It was a living tribute to France, planted in the eastern slopes of China.

The Paris Premium takes more humdrum forms, too. In 1984 an appetising sandwich bar opened opposite Hampstead underground station in north London. It looked French – it sold fresh baguettes and was called Pret a Manger – but in fact was a British idea, the brainchild of Joseph Hyman, a career executive for Rank Hovis McDougall. It was inspired by the *traiteurs* whose treats he enjoyed on summer holidays. The French identity was crucial, even in an American-style, ready-to-go outlet like this.

It wasn't a success: it closed after a year. But a pair of newcomers, Sinclair Beecham and Julian Metcalfe, bought it and turned it into the giant we know today.[6]

---

5 This was why luxury shops like Hugo Boss and Nespresso were targeted by *gilets jaunes* protestors in 2019. They wanted to hit France where it hurts.

6 Metcalfe went on to found the equally successful 'Japanese' outlet Itsu in 1997.

Would it have succeeded had it been called Ready to Eat? Perhaps . . . *non*.

Marks & Spencer has nineteen branches in Paris, selling brie sandwiches that were assembled in Northampton. Some *boulevard-iers*, grabbing a snack near the Place Vendôme, may feel as though they are getting an authentic taste of Britain. But many more, browsing the shelves of Pret a Manger in London, experience a Gallic shiver.

For now the virus has put a stop to all of that in a way that seems bound to cause an economic calamity. In checking the movement of people, and switching off the flow of tourists, it will prevent the flow of international students too. But no one could doubt that, at some point in the future, the world will once again knock on France's door.

There was some tourism in the world of pilgrims and scholars. But in the age of the Grand Tour, foreign travel was something only the rich could contemplate – most people rarely left the village where they were born. Then in 1833 a young Englishman named Thomas Cook, a carpenter turned missionary in the unremarkable Derbyshire village of Melbourne, joined the fight against gin by taking a vow of temperance and swearing off alcohol for ever. A few years later, in Leicester, he was so impressed by the new Midland Counties Railway that he organiséd a day out for his fellow non-drinkers. They went to an alcohol-free rally in Loughborough (10 miles to the north).

The fee was a shilling a head.[7]

It was such a success that he was soon organising more ambitious trips. In 1845 he took a group to Liverpool; in 1846 he sent a smaller party to Scotland; and in 1851 he arranged for 150,000 people to attend the Great Exhibition in London.

He had created a new industry. His first foreign venture (in 1855) saw him send two groups across the Channel to take a closer look at France and Germany.

---

7 Thomas Cook is commemorated by a statue outside Leicester station – right next to a sign helpfully directing new arrivals to 'tourist information'. Ironically, those early teetotal trips ended up, in Britain at least, giving birth to an industry that offered his countrymen an affordable way of getting drunk in someone else's sunshine.

When his sons took over the family business, temperance took a back seat. By 1890 Thomas Cook & Sons were selling three million tickets a year to the new 'tourists', and most of them didn't mind a refreshing glass or two. The detachable coupons the company provided, which could be exchanged for food, drink and excursions, were the roots of another new mechanism: the traveller's cheque.

The boom in foreign travel since then has been one of the world's most spectacular facts. According to the UN World Tourism Organisation, the number of international visits has grown from 528 million in 2005 to 1.4 billion today, making it a tenth of global GDP – bigger than agriculture and construction combined (two sectors heavily dependent on tourism in any case). Thanks to a boom in tourists from China (only 7 per cent of the population hold passports, but this is estimated to rise to 400 million by 2030), this tide (at least until the coronavirus threatened to weaken it) was predicted to keep growing. In 2017, some 143 million Chinese tourists travelled the world, not far short of the entire populations of Britain and Germany.

The Thomas Cook story ended in 2019, when a flight left Florida for Manchester only to discover, an hour later, that the company was bankrupt. But elsewhere the world is on the move. It is sometimes joked that contrary to received wisdom, travel narrows the mind. That may be true. But in most people's opinion it does not narrow the mind so sharply as *not* travelling: the world is in love with holidays.

In recent times this has come into troubling conflict with concerns about climate change and carbon footprints. Until Covid-19 brought international travel to a standstill, the UN was estimating that one in four new jobs created in the coming decade would be associated with the travel trade.

The soft-power implications were clear: in no other area can a nation's attractiveness be so clearly packaged and sold. It is one of the prime ways in which sheer likeability can be leveraged: sunshine, beauty or heritage can all attract the tourist dollar. It is an industry like any other, with financial repercussions of all kinds.

It is double-edged: in some places an arena of sharp soft-power conflict. In May 2019 the Nepalese mountaineer (and former Gurkha) Nirmal Purja MBE released an extraordinary photograph showing the queue at the summit of Mount Everest: a 200-yard jumble of Gore-Tex climbing gear on the world's highest ridge of snow, a place not long ago thought inaccessible. It became the symbol of a worldwide problem: all of the world's hottest beauty spots were struggling to support the weight of foreign feet. More than seven million people a year were pressing through the Taj Mahal; five thousand a day went to the once-empty strip of sand in Thailand where Leonardo DiCaprio filmed *The Beach*; cruise ships were dropping 800,000 passengers to wander through Dubrovnik's Old City, where only a thousand people lived. The Great Wall of China ... the Acropolis ... the Eiffel Tower ... the Trevi Fountain ... the Sistine Chapel ... Venice ... Prague ... Lucerne ... Athens ... the *Mona Lisa* ... the star locations of the Instagram world are these days worth visiting only at dawn.[8]

Even Japan, for so long isolated, was starting to think twice about the value of all these visitors. In 2003 it received five million tourists and launched the Visit Japan campaign in search of more. By 2020 it was expecting forty million per year, and aiming for sixty million by 2030. In the process, one of its most precious features – the calm and graceful texture of its daily life – was under threat. Officials in Kyoto spoke of 'pollution by tourism', and in 2018 there was a minor diplomatic ruction when a Tokyo cosmetics shop put up a sign saying 'Chinese Not Allowed'. Even before the much more dramatic restrictions imposed by the world's response to the coronavirus outbreak, keep-out signs were being posted against Chinese tourism. When China itself acted to discourage overseas travel in the aftermath of that crisis, the groans of pain from places that depended on Chinese footfall – from Bicester Village in England to the shopping malls of Hong Kong – were ironic indeed.

It has all led, in any event, to the emergence of a new word: 'overtourism'.[9]

In the post-corona world, none of this could be taken for

8 Prague received 2.5 million visitors in 2002, most of them interested in history; in 2018 there were nine million, and their main interest was the cheap booze.

9 A term coined by Joseph Cheer, Claudio Milano and Marina Novelli on the 'Conversation' website.

granted – in the short term, at least. Tourism's value as an export, however, remained immense. France was the world's *most* popular country (with ninety million visitors in 2018) ahead of Spain (eighty-two million) and America (seventy-seven million). But tourism was a crucial export almost everywhere. Britain, a mid-range player, boasted thirty-seven million – the same as Turkey and Germany, ahead of Thailand (thirty-five million) and well behind Italy's fifty-eight million. India welcomed only 15.5 million, while the numbers for China were growing, but unclear. According to Beijing, there were 141 million visits in 2018, but three-quarters of those were from Hong Kong, Taiwan and Macau. Attracting visitors was a strategic ambition as well. In China itself, tourism supported some seventy million jobs.

In striving to advance national stories, the countries of the world were competing vigorously for this tourist traffic, not least through image-boosting publicity campaigns such as *Great Britain*, *The Beach is Just the Beginning* (Antigua and Barbuda), *Kingdom of Wonder* (Cambodia), *Where it All Begins* (Egypt), *Truly Asia* (Malaysia), *Once is Not Enough* (Nepal) ... Such campaigns were, inevitably, corny. None reached far into the cultures they represented. But it fitted with the ethos of globalisation that nations should in this respect act like corporations, pushing logos and catchphrases out into the world.

There were signs, before the virus made such variations seem unimportant, that while tourism in France and Italy was surging, in both the US and UK it was slipping. It was evidence of the way soft power could, even then, yield a clear and tangible dividend: and this was a market in which a weakening national currency could become a useful asset. But no one wanted to be left behind. When Sierra Leone became the world's *least* visited country in 2017, few nations wanted to swap.

Abigail Adams (wife and counsellor to John Adams, one of America's Founding Fathers) once said that 'no one leaves Paris without a feeling of tristesse', and meant it as a compliment. But modern Paris can generate a more troubling emotion. In 1986 a Japanese academic, Professor Hiroaki Ota, noticed an increase in the number of tourists returning from France with acute dejection. Further investigation revealed that the feeling was especially striking among those who had been to Paris.

It was, he felt, a genuine ailment – a mental condition caused by the gap their trip exposed between hope (fantasy) and the real thing. He called it Paris Syndrome. The real-life city simply did not match the Paris of people's dreams. Some of the waiters did *not* look like Gérard Depardieu; the hotel receptionists did *not* resemble Catherine Deneuve; and the cobbled alleys of Notre Dame were alive not with dashing musketeers and ballet dancers but with hordes of tourists very much like themselves.

It was enough to make anyone feel let down.

Paris Syndrome may be the first soft-power illness; indeed, it is older than soft power itself. As the world's premier destination, France finds itself in the *avant garde* once again. But these tourist adventures are still a dynamic expression of human curiosity. Tourists act like bees, collecting cultural effects from one place and dropping them in another, acquiring new tastes far from home and taking them back to share with their friends. In the process they read guidebooks and cook books, visit museums and pore over maps. They may go away with suntans and hangovers, but they take impressions and anecdotes home as well. They are how the world meets and mingles.

As the Maori artist Lisa Reihana said in 2016, with reference to her award-winning video installation describing Captain Cook's arrival in Polynesia: 'Once people have encountered each other, history is changed for ever.'

Cultural effects are not immortal. There used to be something indelibly French about the buildings that lined the Grand Union Canal in west London: the whole area was named White City in their honour. It had been built for the Franco-British Exhibition of 1908, an event that attracted eight million visitors, and the Entente Cordiale – the treaty that obliged Britain to help France when Germany invaded in 1914 – was signed there. The buildings were demolished in 1958 to create BBC Television Centre. The name remained, but the memories evaporated. No one walking that way today feels themselves to be in a French *quartier*, or anything like it.

France, like Britain, has scattered pieces of itself all over the world. New Orleans was a French settlement that gave rise to an architectural style – French Colonial.[10] Parts of Ho Chi Minh City still carry echoes of French Saigon, as do cities in the Caribbean and north-west Africa (such as Algiers and Dakar); Quebec is the French-speaking capital of a French-speaking province in Canada, with a skyline dominated by the enormous Château Frontenac Hotel and a parliament building that looks as though it has been carefully extracted from the Rue de Rivoli, while Pondicherry (now Puducherry), a French colonial city on India's east coast (until 1954) still offers boules and baguettes in the 'old town'.

But soft power clings on in less emphatic ways. In 2018 the Pacific island of New Caledonia (named by Captain Cook when he sailed by in 1774 because it reminded him of Scotland) rejected the offer of independence in favour of remaining French. As Nouvelle-Calédonie it became a colonial possession in 1853, and a penal colony ten years later: more than 20,000 French malefactors were shipped there. In 1864 nickel was found, and Nouvelle-Calédonie still controls a quarter of the world's supply.

A lengthy campaign for independence culminated in the 2018 referendum. But even though many indigenous Kanak voters winced to hear their island again referred to as 'southern France' (General de Gaulle had told them *Vous êtes un morceau de la France, vous êtes la France australe*'), a majority chose to remain French.

The fact that the island received an annual subsidy of $1.3 billion was a factor. But Frenchness mattered too. Only 27 per cent of the population saw itself as 'European' – not enough to swing the vote. But this was an island that, though 12,000 miles from Paris, ate croissants for breakfast, played pétanque in tree-shaded squares, and drove Renaults and Citroëns to the Hypermarché . . . on the right-hand side of the road.

---

10 It was formally twinned with the original Orléans, where Joan of Arc died, in 2017.

It was the third referendum since 1987, and anti-colonial campaigners continued to agitate for independence. But the electorate kept voting to stay.

Soft power, it seems, really can decide the fate of nations.

8

Southern Europe: Sweet Reason

In June 2019 seven people drowned when an inflatable boat capsized in the Aegean near the Greek island of Samos. In normal times it would have been a major event, but when it happened it was only the latest disaster in a long-running saga that no longer rated much attention in the news. One day it was fifteen dead ... another, twenty-two ... another, thirty-four. In recent years hundreds had perished in these waters; thousands more had been rescued. More than four thousand were housed in refugee tents on a disused army base on a hill above the town. The local population (33,000) was doing its best – when Nicolas Niarchos visited for the *New Yorker* he found a generous group of women who had been feeding eight hundred people for eight months, unpaid. But the island's resources – and patience – were being tested to the limit.

Samos wanted Greece to share the burden; Greece was trying to persuade the rest of Europe to help. As the wrangle rumbled inconclusively on, the refugees themselves were trapped in a beautiful place, in terrible conditions.

The only thing they knew for sure that no one wanted them.

It was a daunting test of Europe's resilience and confidence, and it was unfolding in a resonant spot, because two celebrated philosophers had grown up in these same green hills: Pythagoras and Epicurus. They represented many of the qualities that had made European civilisation so rich and powerful. How would the intellectual tradition they had helped build react to this heart-rending new challenge?

Samos was by no means the only island feeling the pressure. There were 15,000 people stuck in holding pens elsewhere, waiting for Europe to find a response. 'The isles of Greece, the isles of Greece ... Where grew the arts of war and peace.' That was Byron's tribute. The Aegean had since become a magnet for modern tourists, and now found itself cast as a twenty-first-century Ellis Island. In contrast to the welcome offered to Romantic poets and sunseekers, the refugees were greeted in a different way.

Camp Moria, for instance, a refugee settlement on the otherwise heavenly island of Lesbos, was no one's idea of a resort. Designed for three thousand inmates, it was home to five thousand – sometimes as many as eight thousand. Families of five were housed in tents made for two. There was one toilet per seventy people, and the shower was a hosepipe by a refuse dump: icy in winter, rancid in summer. Sewage trickled through the rubbish.

Aid workers and refugees alike described it as 'hell on earth'. This Afghan farmer had arrived with his wife and three children after their house was destroyed by the Taliban; that woman had escaped from an Isis rape prison; that lost boy had seen his parents die in the crossing and was all alone. The misery was immeasurable.

Some of the stories were made up or exaggerated; most of them weren't.

It was common for refugees to be held in this limbo for a year while Europe wrung its hands over what to do. Which is not to say there was an easy 'solution'. The number of people pouring into Europe outweighed the number that could easily be received; the exploitative trafficking of refugees was becoming a nasty but thriving business; politicians were nervous of sending an encouraging signal to the next boat.[1] When Germany's Angela Merkel admitted a million, no one copied her.

And there were contradictory intentions behind places like

---

[1] 'Africa is sitting with its bags packed,' wrote Dr Asfa-Wossen Asserate, an Ethiopian-born academic based in Frankfurt. No ordinary refugee – he was the Cambridge-educated grandson of Haile Selassie – his 2018 book *African Exodus: Migration and the Future of Europe* described a continent of more than a billion inhabitants, tens of millions of whom were impatient to move.

Camp Moria. They were operated by hard-working, well-meaning idealists, but they also hinted at a 'hostile environment' designed to deter all but the most desperate. On one level they said that Europe was a humanitarian refuge; on another, that it was an exclusive club.

This was a confusing soft-power signal. In 2015, the peak year, more than 850,000 crossed the Aegean in this way. A thousand perished in the attempt, which stemmed the flow somewhat, as did the EU's deal with Turkey (six billion euros, plus visa-free travel for Turks, in effect allowing Turks – rather than the refugees they were being paid to detain on Europe's behalf – to come to Europe). In 2016 only 173,000 attempted the voyage; in 2017 that fell to 30,000; and fewer still came in 2018. But in the first half of 2019 nearly 40,000 came, and as the numbers rose, so too did the death toll.

The UN warned that the Mediterranean might soon be 'a sea of blood'.

Each day brought a horrifying addition to the catalogue of sad stories. If it wasn't the dreadful image of a drowned boy lying on a Greek beach,[2] it was a truck falling into a river or a ravine. One day it was a boat capsizing (or being capsized – some of the 'accidents' were cynical and deliberate); the next day it was people leaping from an inflatable boat on to a Spanish beach in front of British and German sunbathers.

There were heroic tales, too. A Greek coastguard, Captain Kyriakos Papadopoulos, was christened 'Hero of the Aegean' for rescuing five thousand people from the waters off the Turkish coast. But most of the stories were tragic – and there was no end in sight.

The torrent of bad news had been brewing for years. Since 1993, when there were enough such cases for it to look like a trend, more than 27,000 people had drowned at sea attempting this manoeuvre. Two decades later it had become a full-blown crisis.

It was (and is) one of the saddest horror stories of modern

2 The photograph of Alan Kurdi gripped the world. In February 2019, in a ceremony in Mallorca, the German charity Sea-Eye named a rescue ship after him. It was soon rescuing sixty-five refugees off the coast of Libya and dropping them safely in Malta.

times, and it is hard to see how it can end until the disparities that propel it are tamed – no easy task. As the young Somali-British poet Warsan Shire has put it:

> *No one puts their children in a boat*
> *Unless the water is safer than the land.*

Even those who felt that migration had reached impossible levels ('the boat is full') found it hard to remain sanguine in the face of such stories. Arguments about numbers were one thing; individual predicaments could not be ignored. It was not in fact new: in many ways it echoed the years following the First World War, when more than a million people poured out of Turkey into Greece – Orthodox Christians fleeing the last pangs of Ottoman supremacy in Anatolia. But it felt unprecedented.

Greece's population was just over ten million. If a similar ratio had tried to seek refuge in Britain, it would have numbered some six million. Given the panic that broke out when a few hundred 'Iranians' started crossing the Channel in the winter of 2018, it was not hard to imagine how heated the response would have been.[3]

And there was another route across the water, from lawless Libya to Italy. Boats full of half-drowned refugees were being unloaded in Sicily. Rome, the second pillar of the ancient world, had also become an object of pilgrimage.

There was a common thread here, with frail but important links to soft power. This new exodus of migrants was not nursing hopes of a better life in the *east*. As if with one mind it was heading *west* . . . to Europe. Despite the unspeakable wars and horrors that had riven its life for so many thousands of years, Europe still gave off a bright and seductive light.

A pointed contrast was provided by the number of Syrians granted refugee status in Russia (the power more closely involved in the war they are fleeing than any other).

---

3 Some really were Iranian, lured by the fact that Serbia had recently begun to grant visa-free access. Others merely claimed to be, knowing that if they converted to Christianity on arrival they could not be deported, since they would then have a well-founded fear of facing a death penalty. Necessity truly is the mother of invention.

Clue: it is not a big number. According to Russia's own Federal Migration Service, in the early years of the conflict (2011–15) only 2011 Syrians (of the estimated five million dispersed by the war) had claimed asylum in Russia. The number of those who were granted full refugee status was just two. There simply wasn't a reliable system for processing and accepting them. Europe accepted more than a million, and was widely reproached for its callousness.

The soft-power message was (as so often) ambiguous. Modern Europe, it turned out, had two stories to tell. The first had millennia of philosophical, religious, artistic and commercial endeavour behind it. The second was a nervous qualification that Western values were *not* universal, after all. There were limits, and they had been reached.

An internal wrangle developed over which story should predominate. Humanitarians rushed to help, while populist band-leaders cried, 'Enough!' Both were truly European.

One temporary exhibition in London, about life in the refugee camp at Sangatte, captured the power of this European aura in the words of a Sudanese refugee who was clinging to the underside of a lorry when he was stopped by British police.[4]

'They treated me like a gentleman,' he said. 'They put a torch under the truck and said, "You have to come out from under there, Sir." When they called me "Sir" it made me want to go to England with all my heart.'

In this case, politeness alone was a weapon. But it was not straightforward. Some found it moving that a favourable image of British life could be so easily spread; others found it risky, seeing it as a dangerous invitation for others to follow.

Such dilemmas gave a variegated flavour to the idea that Greece – and Europe – was a generous haven. 'I thought Greece would be one of best places to live,' one refugee inmate told the *New York Times*. 'Now I feel it would have been better to drown.'

It was a tribute to Europe's soft power that so many were will-ing to take such risks to reach it. But in this case the 'ability to

---

4 The exhibition was staged by the Migration Museum Project (the author is a trustee). There was a lethal display of 'deathjackets' – orange safety vests stuffed with paper and designed to sink – along with the bald fact, stencilled on the floor, that 75 per cent of Sangatte's inmates were graduates.

attract' was working rather better than many people wanted. It was attracting . . . migrants. And Europe was not glad to see them.

Few paused to wonder, as coronavirus infiltrated Alpine ski resorts, what kind of damage it might wreak when it found its way into the world's refugee camps. It was hard to foresee a happy outcome, since the virus was sharpening Europe's desire to seal its borders tighter than ever. The pandemic was going to inflict terrible harm not just on Europe's economy, and therefore on its politics – but also on its conscience.

It only added urgency to the question: what *was* Europe, exactly?

In the frosty atmosphere of the Cold War it was tempting to see it as a continent split on East–West lines. The 'iron curtain'[5] had created a chasm between the Allied and the Soviet zone: the East pushed ahead with a severe communist experiment while the West became a garish consumer playground.

A generation on we can see the outline of a much older partition – the gulf between north and south. The Graeco-Roman world did not dominate all of Europe. Glance at any map of Rome's Empire and the outstanding feature is the Rhine–Danube line. Civilisation faltered when it ran into the forested wilderness that stretched north of this natural border. The Dacian campaigns gave Rome control of a bulge across the river – what is now 'Romania'. But the pagan gods in the great Germanic forest region proved as frightening to the Roman mind as their giant axes.

By a quirk of geography the rivers almost touch: the Rhine rushes west out of Lake Constance, heading for Holland, only a day's march away from where the Danube bubbles up in the Black Forest before sliding east to Austria and Hungary.

This line was solid enough to resist the march of Roman culture, and even today one can see why. At Basel, for instance, it is roughly as wide and strong as the Thames at Tower Bridge – yet it is still 400 miles from the sea. It was a major physical barrier, in

---

5 It is usually said that Winston Churchill coined this phrase at Fulton, Missouri, in 1946. He may have. But there were earlier usages. Queen Elizabeth of Belgium spoke in similar terms in 1914 of the awkwardness of her German origins (she was originally Elizabeth of Bavaria): 'Between them and me has fallen a curtain of iron.'

other words, and seemed to divide the continent in two. North
of the river-line the land froze in winter, while the southern zone
was a land of sunlight and vines, blue sky and even bluer sea; the
north was a grey wilderness of marsh and fog.

The demarcation is still apparent: romance languages and sun
to the south, Germanic accents and rain to the north; wine and
oil to the south, beer and butter to the north. Investment managers sometimes urge their clients to avoid countries with plentiful
natural resources, on the grounds that these induce complacency;
and it has long been argued that the cultural difference between
Europe's Catholic south and its Protestant north is primarily a
matter of geography – the harshness of life in the wintry northern forest inspired thrift and the Protestant work ethic, while the
warm *terroir* of the Mediterranean produced a more carefree and
pleasure-seeking mentality.

The marauding Romans made only a token effort to cross
this line. Julius Caesar is thought to have built the first Rhine
crossing (near what is now Koblenz) during his campaign
against the Gauls (according to his own account, in Book VI of
The Gallic Wars, wooden pilings were slammed into the riverbed
in a task that took ten days – not long for such a mighty project).
But he soon regretted it. One look at the fearful tribes on the far
side led him to beat a hasty retreat, pulling down his creation as
he withdrew. That first bridge over the Rhine lasted less than
three weeks.

In AD 105 the Emperor Trajan tried again, this time by bridg-
ing the Danube near the Romanian-Serbian border. It was an
extraordinary construction, more than a thousand metres long,
and was built to last – it survived 150 years. But Rome never
occupied more than a small tongue of land north of the water,
and though that campaign was celebrated with 123 days of fes-
tivities (it gave Rome a gold mine and 100,000 slaves), it turned
out to be a fleeting intrusion into northern Europe, rarely secure:
it had to be defended by a tough line of brand-new man-made
fortifications.

From the mouth of the Rhine to Constantinople, this barrier
(what we might call the Roman Curtain) continued to mark the
limes (or 'limit') of Rome's empire. With Hadrian's Wall as its

northernmost outpost, it was a 4000-mile frontier made of forts, villas, ditches and watchtowers.

The Romans even kept a fleet on Lake Constance, the sheet of water that straddles the border between Switzerland and Germany and feeds the Rhine, just in case.

Europe as a whole does radiate a liberal message as the chief strut of its soft power. If America is (still) the land of opportunity, Europe is, in theory, the land of civility. It is something more than geographical chance that leads today's refugees to land on the coasts where that civilisation was born, in Greece and Italy.

Indeed in one way it is ironic, because Greece has often seemed like Europe's least 'European' nation – with its own alphabet, its own culture, its own religious tradition. Its daily texture (climate, food, music, coffee and so on) had as much in common with what used to be known as 'Asia Minor' as with countries like Holland or Denmark.

It resembled its historic enemy, Turkey, more closely than it did Britain.

Yet it was unmistakably the place where Western culture first took root, and was therefore the flame in the lamp that was attracting this new population.

Which way did it face? Did Greece belong to the West or the East?

In the traditional account, European civilisation was given its character by a burst of originality in Ancient Greece. Supported (as everyone now knows) on a scaffold of slave labour, the insights of Archimedes, Homer, Aristotle, Pericles, Plato, Socrates and the rest laid down the grounds for Western science, myth, architecture, art, war, philosophy, astronomy, medicine, politics, sport and everything else. The very words *politics, democracy, physics, galaxy, music, philosophy* and *theatre* derive from Greek – 'Europe' itself is a Hellenic term. Its intellectual categories – theology, ontology, epistemology, geology, cosmology, psychology – are branches of Greek *logos*.[6]

---

6 Indeed, this is why modern brands have a 'logo'. The letters may differ, but we still rely on Greece for the alphabet (or *alpha beta*). In the beginning was the word.

These origins are so embedded that we barely notice them.
The pampered guests at spa resorts raise few glasses to Thales,
the philosopher who swore that the prime substance of life was
water and lives on as *thalassotherapy*; marathon runners rarely light
candles to the winged goddess of victory: Nike. When we debate
economics, snap a *photograph*, visit an *amphitheatre*, check an *encyclo-
paedia*, feel *hyper* or think *chronologically* (Kronos being the Greek
God of time) we are thinking like Greeks without even realising
it. At the height of Greece's financial crisis it was whispered that
if the rest of the world threw a coin in the hat every time anyone
used any of the above words, Greece would soon be out of the
woods. It was not the worst idea. The funeral oration delivered by
Pericles in tribute to the Athenian war dead extolled its political
nature in terms that still ring down the ages: 'Our constitution is
named a democracy because it is in the hands not of the few but
the many.'

How often have we heard that phrase? The principles of
Pericles, the philosophical achievement of Ancient Greece and
by extension the whole European project ... these have been
claimed by politicians of every ideological stripe, even the most
villainous – as William Blake once said, the public good was the
refuge of the scoundrel.

Because soft power is not only a nation's attempt to make
people like it. It is also the way nations persuade people to *think*
along similar lines. This can leave permanent scars. No one thinks
in ancient Greek or Latin any more, but the legacy of those early
civilisations is still woven into the different accents that make
modern Europe.

The question remains: why Greece? What was it about that
sun-struck blur of sea and rock that sparked the classical spirit of
inquiry? Why *there*, rather than in the Alps, the peaceful dales of
England and France, or the inspiring fjords of Norway?

It has been said that Greece's infertile soil, good for olives and
grapes but not much more, encouraged people to become merchants and traders; and that the sparkling Aegean seascape made
them nautical. The Mediterranean, with its warm climate and
convenient landmarks, stimulated marine expansion, thus fur-
nishing the wealth that supported the idle-rich tradition of science

and scholarship; the quarrels between its city states (Athens and Sparta), meanwhile, gave it both a taste and an aptitude for military action – making the Greeks a people drawn towards exploration, war and empire. They had a powerful urge to build new nests across the bright blue water.

These characteristics are all evident in Homer: the willingness to risk all in pursuit of vengeance (against Troy, for instance), along with the love of home and hearth.

Today we can see a more substantial and obvious reason for Greece's prominence: simple geography. Its proximity to the lavish civilisations south and east inevitably made it the first port of call for these mighty systems of thought and knowledge.

It took time for Europe to understand and acknowledge its debt to the Sumerian, Chinese and Arabic civilisations that preceded it. No one disputes, now, the extent to which learning developed in the civilisations of Africa and Asia. The river basins of the Nile and Mesopotamia were the true cradles of human culture – where numbers began, writing was born, animals were domesticated and farming took root. Greece was Europe's first point of connection with Arabic and Asiatic wisdom: the gateway through which those civilisations trickled. Its own virtues, however telling, were secondary to the insistent fact of its position in the eastern Mediterranean.

What happened in Greece could not have happened anywhere else.

In one way it was fitting that modern Greece became the destination for refugees fleeing the war zones of Afghanistan, Iraq, Syria and North Africa. These were the very routes by which early civilisation had drifted into Europe thousands of years ago. It was the continuation of a very old story indeed.

The stepping stone was Minoan Crete. The Bronze Age remains excavated by the British scholar Sir Arthur Evans (only a century ago) revealed the existence of a local civilisation at least 3000 years old, and also suggested the extent to which ideas flowed from south to north and back again. Egyptian traces (papyrus, ostrich eggs) were found in Crete, but also in Mycenae, the citadel from which Agamemnon had launched his epic war to retrieve Helen of Troy. There was Minoan work, meanwhile, in both Greece and Egypt, and the Minoan form of writing, the so-called Linear B script, resembled Egyptian hieroglyphics more than it did the Greek alphabet.

It made sense geographically that Crete should be the route across the Mediterranean from Egypt to Greece, but it also made sense in literature. The original Greek creation myth – Zeus, disguised as a bull, carried off Europa, mother of King Minos of Crete – had Phoenician origins. Zeus was abducting a princess from what is now Lebanon: a bold allegory of cultural appropriation. The myth is also consonant with the Egyptian story of Isis and Osiris – the latter being a bull; it has even been suggested that the ox and ass present at the birth of Christ may be figurative representations of the two worlds on either side of the sea: Asia and Greece.

One could go on. Cretan bull-worship was dramatised by the fable of the Minotaur, the dreadful beast (half man, half bull) kept by Minos in his labyrinth and fed with Greek boys and girls offered up in tribute. When Evans and his team dug into Knossos, one of their most remarkable finds was a fresco of bull-dancing, a 'sport' in which young gymnasts somersaulted over the horns of a charging bull. No one knows whether it was play or murder. It may have been the basis of the Minotaur legend – or a depiction of it.

The labyrinth was built by Daedalus, and his reward was to be locked in a tower so he could not reveal its secrets. In this way Crete gave Europe another founding myth: the doomed flight of Daedalus and his son Icarus, the ingenuity of the father leading to the death of the child when he soared too close to the sun.

That story lives on as an inscription on the back of a €2 coin.

Ideas do not drift in the air, like pollen; they are carried by people. And since ancient travel was arduous, the wisdom of the oldest civilisations did not reach Europe via the Baltic or the Hebrides. It took the nearest route, across the Mediterranean.

It was always two-way traffic. Understanding that soft power grew fastest when it was fed by many streams, many pioneering Greek thinkers headed south. Alexandria was a Greek colony on the trade routes to Asia. The historian Herodotus went there in the fifth century BC and observed: 'There is no country that possesses so many wonders.' He was part of a train of thought that included Archimedes, Aristotle, Plato and Socrates. All sought (and found) enlightenment on the African shore.

This remains a vexed subject. Some conservative historians see such talk, with its implication that European civilisation had multicultural roots, as a plot to undermine Greek originality. From a different point of view, the folding of African and Asian wisdom into the scientific miracle of Ancient Greece is seen by some not as cultural exchange but as mere colonialism and theft. But it does seem certain, contrary to what even its own myths suggest, that Greek culture was built on the work of others.

Genetic research into mummies suggests an intricate overlap between Egyptian and European DNA. Art historians argue that the sticking-up tails on the monkeys in Cretan murals show that they were inspired by Indian, not African, wildlife, suggesting a previously unsuspected breadth of trade. And the curriculum vitae of those ancient thinkers is telling. Pythagoras, who came from Samos (within sight of Turkey), spent two *decades* studying in Babylon, near modern Baghdad – the land from which today's refugees are running.[7] Thales came from Miletus, also in Turkey, while Parmenides, one of the first to suggest that matter was made of 'atoms', came from another overseas colony: Elea, south of Naples.

All were inspired by worlds not their own. Some of the friction generated by migration, in the ancient world as now, expresses itself as creativity.

And then there is Euclid. The great Greek's mathematical precepts have been so well absorbed by textbooks that they no longer seem to have an author. But Euclid remains the fountainhead of Western geometry, laying down the principles on which the rules governing squares, circles, angles and parallel lines were built. In his hands, geometry was a brand-new system for extracting conclusions from partial knowledge, for using two lines and one angle to calculate a third and fourth. As the exemplar of reasoning

---

7 I myself once experienced the dislocating effect of this brief journey on a boat from Kusadasi to Samos. The scale of the transition from Troy and Ephesus to the home of Achilles made me queasy – unless it was the *raki*, and the surprisingly choppy sea.

rather than magic, he stood for the idea that uncertainty could be conquered by logic alone.

His *Elements* is one of the most widely published books in history – second only to the Bible, it is said. Abraham Lincoln insisted that to be taken seriously as a lawyer a man had to master his Euclid – to know what it means to 'demonstrate' a fact – and kept the great man's axioms in his saddlebag to prove it. He was not the only American to be so influenced. The opening words of the Declaration of Independence – *We hold these truths to be self-evident* – are, in their reverence for first principles, pure Euclid.

And he was ... Euclid of Alexandria. He studied in the great library city at the mouth of the Nile. In the age before paper, when learning lived in scrolls kept in the citadels of established power, students had to travel to read the essential books.

Nor can we think of ancient Alexandria as 'Egyptian', since it was largely Greek. Those who wish (rightly) to emphasise the African roots of Western civilisation must also note that Alexandria was, like Carthage, Ephesus, Marseilles and Syracuse, a colonial outpost. Showing a precocious understanding of soft power, Alexander grasped that civilisation could unite people more lastingly than garrisons, and spread Hellenistic habits – philosophy, science, astronomy, medicine, architecture, theatre and politics – across an empire that ran from the Adriatic to the Himalayas.

Alexander himself was the first 'Pharaoh' of Egypt, and his successors – from Ptolemy to Cleopatra – were also, like the spell-binding libraries and lighthouses they helped found ... Greek.[8]

Far from being a complication, this cosmopolitan make-up was the source of its power. In worshipping many gods, Alexandria could embrace all of the most learned tribes: Egyptians, Greeks, Romans, Africans, Arabs, Jews, Armenians, Syrians and (later) Christians. That was why it was a city of libraries and scholars.

And the mathematical discoveries unearthed there became the basis of modern European science: every time a child is taught about equal and opposite angles, the hypotenuse, the diameter,

---

8 Most productions of Shakespeare's *Antony and Cleopatra* present her as a superb Egyptian pharaoh, when in fact she was a Greek-descended wife and mother – she and Antony had three children, none of whom feature in their parents' tragic story.

or the uses to which a compass can be put, he or she is treading in footprints that go back to the muddled origins of Western civilisation.

It was a book of geometry, based on Euclid's principles, that enthralled Albert Einstein when he came across it at the age of twelve such that he could not put it down.

Einstein was not the only modern intellectual to seize on classical learning. Freud launched the twentieth-century push towards self-exploration by rummaging in the ruins of civilisation and its discontents for his lodestars: *eros* and *thanatos* – not to mention Narcissus and Oedipus. He himself was a keen collector of old artefacts: his ashes, buried in a London crematorium, were placed in one of his Grecian urns.

9

Central Europe: A River Runs Through It

There are few better places to brood on Europe's north–south divide than Switzerland, the zone where the three dominant elements – Italy, Germany and France – collide. At one time a province of Rome (Augsburg, in Bavaria, was named after Augustus, and Switzerland's coins still bear the Roman name Helvetica), it later became a German-French-Italian federation that somehow managed to unite these three warring civilisations in a single peaceful union. All three languages appear on its banknotes, along with a fourth – Romansh, the Latin–German dialect of its eastern canton. The lingua franca of the tourist economy, meanwhile, is English.

Its most obvious soft-power asset is its breathtaking lake-and-mountain scenery, which lures four million visitors a year, summer and winter alike. But Switzerland is also a case study in how a small nation can generate a large store of soft power. It has never invaded anyone. Instead, its expertise in engineering (bridges, tunnels, trains and cableways), luxury goods (watches), gourmet foodstuffs (cheese, chocolate) and services (private banking, medicine and hospitality[1]) and above all its fierce reputation for neutrality have given it an influence out of proportion to its size. In the 2019 Portland Soft Power 30 it came sixth – a tribute to its being 'a beacon of stability' in a fractious and fragmenting world.

---

1 César Ritz, from the Alpine village of Niederwald, is one of many noted Swiss hoteliers. He managed grand houses in Lucerne and Locarno before running London's Savoy (an establishment with its own Alpine echoes) and opening his own hotels in Paris (1898), London (1905) and Madrid (1906). His name became a lifestyle: *ritzy*.

In the corridors of soft power, nothing happening is a positive advantage.

If anything, the dazzling brochure imagery of ski and snow has made it too easy to dismiss Switzerland as a bland mall of cheese and cowbells. Everyone likes to quote Orson Welles's famous observation (as Harry Lime in *The Third Man*) that while thirty violent years in Renaissance Italy produced Michelangelo and Leonardo, half a century of democracy and peace in Switzerland inspired nothing more than ... the cuckoo clock. As it happened, cuckoo clocks were not Swiss; they were born in Bavaria (the Swiss contributed only the chalet-style roof). But the barb stuck fast.

Then there were Switzerland's secretive banking laws, which made it even easier to see this small European state as a cynical friend of ill-gotten wealth. When British ministers referred testily to the 'gnomes of Zurich', depicting them as underground sprites deformed by the dwarfish love of money ... that barb stuck too. It grew conventional to see Switzerland as beautiful, but vacuous; stunning, yet cold.

The geographical fact remains: Switzerland is Europe's physical spine. Those soaring mountains protect the crossing points between north and south, east and west. The Alps are also the source of Europe's great waterways (Rhine, Rhône, Po and Inn-Danube), meaning that one can (if one has a mind to) dip one's toe into the Adriatic, the Black Sea, the North Sea and the Mediterranean in a single day.

As such it has been both the backdrop for some of Europe's most stirring adventures – such as the conquest of the Matterhorn – and much Romantic art: Turner, Byron, Mary Shelley, Wagner and a dozen others were all inspired by this sublime landscape.

It has also been a successful experiment in cosmopolitan politics. The reason why Basel was a central hub of humanist Europe (Erasmus was a founding hero of its university, Switzerland's oldest) becomes clear the moment the visitor leaves the airport, with its three well-signed exits: one to each of the countries it serves.

Fifteen miles to the east lie the remains of Augusta Raurica, a Roman outpost that once held 20,000 people, a last burst of Mediterranean life before the north began.

Switzerland has other features: religious variations, an unusual political system, a proud military mentality (for centuries the 'Switzers' were Europe's most feared mercenaries, and the Vatican is still protected by a Swiss guard), a glowing record in medical research, and a more convoluted history than people imagine – the world's most famously peaceful country has as its symbol an army knife. But its chief glory, and deepest soft-power well, derives from its geographical location. Straddling the crossroads of Europe's various national cultures, forced to pursue peace on all fronts, it is a resounding tribute to the softest power of all – the power of compromise.[2]

It is a profitable mix. Switzerland has long been the natural home for international organisations, from the League of Nations and the Red Cross to FIFA, the Olympic movement and the Bank for International Settlements. The global elite gather in Davos, Montreux and Zug, while humanitarians assemble in Geneva, at the UN or the World Health Organization. This is where Syrians and Iranians meet Americans or Russians (in immaculate five-star hotels). Countless peace treaties have been brokered over cigars and brandy in Lausanne, Locarno and elsewhere. Where else to sign the supreme convention on the treatment of civilians but in Geneva? Being a standard-bearer for togetherness has given this mini-Europe an outsized place in the affairs of the world.

Switzerland can hardly be said to have had a good Second World War, and the echoes of those years – when it provided a safety-deposit box for Nazi-looted gold and art, and agreed to turn Jewish refugees from Hitler away at its border – still reverberate.[3] These are indelible stains on the national reputation. But Switzerland did, despite everything, take nearly 300,000 refugees from Hitler – far more than anyone else. It was to reach

---

2 Switzerland cemented this reputation for compromise in 1937 in the arena of industrial relations, when the so-called *arbeitsfrieden*, a no-strike agreement between companies and unions, signalled something very like the end of class war.

3 Bitterness remains over the alacrity with which it agreed to observe the infamous 'J' stamped on Jewish passports (some are displayed in Swiss museums to this day).

Switzerland that the Von Trapps climbed every mountain in *The Sound of Music*; this is where Steve McQueen was heading in *The Great Escape*. Somehow, escaping to Switzerland still remained a synonym for finding safety.

In recent years there have been other dents in the brand. The collapse of Swissair in 2001 was the death of a globally admired icon, as were the struggles of Union Bank of Switzerland. When twenty-one people died in an underground cave in Interlaken, and eleven more in a fire in the St Gotthard tunnel, the image took an even bigger knock. The mask had slipped – Switzerland was *not* exceptional . . . and not pure, either. It had – had it not? – been one of the last countries on earth to give women the vote, in 1971.

More serious damage was done, perhaps, when, in the autumn of 2019, one of the country's most famous banks, Credit Suisse, was forced to sack its chief executive after he authorised private detectives to spy on a rival. The affair, reported with glee around the world, caused 'severe reputational damage'. Understandably: if you couldn't trust a Swiss banker to keep up appearances, whom on earth could you trust?

In becoming more fallible, however, Switzerland also became a little less aloof, a bit more like everyone else. Its past, like most national pasts, was both heroic and callow; simplicity sat along-side luxury, kindness next door to cruelty. Little was lovelier than the sun on Lake Lucerne, or the veil of mist streaming off the Jungfrau; yet little was drabber than Lausanne on a wet Sunday, or the nosiness of neighbours checking you had not put the rub-bish out on the wrong inch of pavement. It was a stage for manly thrills (the Cresta Run) but also the toytown home of mirthless auditors and hoteliers.

And it could still charge a premium: in the most obvious soft-power manifestation of all, Swissness was an enviable commodity. 'Stick a Swiss flag on something and watch the sales rocket,' wrote *Monocle* magazine. It was true: there were few more persuasive marks of quality than 'Swiss Made' or the Swiss flag.

In one sense Switzerland underperforms as a tourist destina-tion: it is too small, and too expensive, to handle mass-market numbers, and prefers to rest on its image as a premium brand. Tourism revenue has declined from a peak of $53 billion in 2011, to $45 billion today. But tourists are still crucial to Switzerland's income, and today they are coming from further afield. The ski resort of Engelberg, for instance, favoured by Bollywood film units as a stand-in for the Himalayas (better facilities, smarter hotels), is popular with Indian film fans. British skiers are often surprised, in January, to find themselves sharing a télécabine with families from Mumbai, climbing not for the thrill of skiing down again, but in order to relive a Bollywood romance.

And there is a cloud on this horizon. Climate change has shrunk Switzerland's ice by up to half in the century since industrial civilisation made its presence felt. The tourists lured to the Alps are doing harm, but not nearly so much as the change in the earth's temperature. According to the World Centre for Glaciology (in Zurich) the planet as a whole is losing 335 *billion* tons of ice each year. The planes that bring holidaymakers to these snow-capped mountains are actually melting them. The Swiss Alps, with their world-leading ski resorts, face an uncertain future.

In considering the soft power of southern Europe we have omitted one large factor: religion. When Greece's star faded, another rose in Rome, and the story continued. Rome may have made only a minor impact on the Teutonic world north of the Rhine-Danube line, but in France, Spain, Britain and the Alps its soldiers, engineers and storytellers imposed a new approach to daily life. In its first phase this took material form, influencing civic habits, architecture and government; but in time it became a spiritual mentor, too. As Rome entwined itself with Christianity (another mighty gift from the Middle East) the whole of southern Europe acquired a new God.

The legacy of Ancient Rome needs no expounding. The millions of tourists in the Roman Forum are only the most visible expression of its enduring power. When America was planning a new capital, where else could it turn to for architectural inspiration other than Ancient Rome: the government buildings, national monuments and even the railway station were modelled on classical Roman temples.

No wonder, at the height of the Watergate affair in 1973, an

American 'senator' on 'Capitol' Hill could quote Shakespeare's Roman play to express his political dismay:

> *Upon what meat doth this our Caesar feed*
> *That he is grown so great?*

Countless books and films have reminded us of Rome's influence on the way we think as well as the way we act. Britain's roads fell into ruin when Rome withdrew, and they were not renewed until the turnpike movement of the eighteenth century. When we feel romantic we are channelling Rome; the world's most famous lover is ... Romeo (even though the man himself was, like Juliet, from Verona). Even these words (I notice) are typed in a font named Times New Roman.

These ancient echoes, reawakened as they were by the Renaissance (itself ignited by the rediscovery of the ancient world), make modern Italy a formidable tourist destination, with two thousand years of art and history on display. Like France it has magnificent food, wine and scenery – and something else as well: the Vatican. As the spiritual and administrative capital of the Catholic Church, a highly charged shard of Italy enters into the daily routines of millions of people on every continent on earth.

The ancient world had multiple gods; the Roman Church (thanks to the Judaism on which it grew) only one. It may have begun, in Roman Palestine, as a protest against a cold and remote empire, but it soon became synonymous with Europe: Christendom.

Is religion soft power? Not always – not when delivered by the muskets that created Europe's empires. But the collision of classical culture and Judaeo-Christian thought that produced Christian Europe can hardly be underestimated. As Michael Burleigh (in *Earthly Powers*) and Tom Holland (in *Dominion: the Making of the Western Mind*) have shown, nearly all the grounds on which liberal democracy, secular humanism and even political correctness stand – the rule of law, equality, human rights, environmental activism and all else – are its direct descendants.

Political progressives often see themselves as opposed to traditional (or established) religion, indeed superior to it (taking it to be the conservative *ancien régime*). And in some ways the post-Christian world may be *more* Christian than its parent – it no longer burns blasphemers and heretics, or threatens eternal damnation. But nearly all its motivating ideas come from Christianity's central tenets. Love thy enemy ... do unto others as you would have them do unto you ... judge not, lest ye be judged ... turn the other cheek ... blessed are the poor ... The old precepts drive today's human rights industry. Even pop music advances ideals – imagine no possessions, all you need is love – that might once have flowed from the lips of monks and nuns.

The past does not die: modern slogans allude to ancient insights, and centuries of Christian history continue to spread Europe's soft gospel today. The development workers and equality campaigners of modern times may not feel like evangelists, but they are standing on platforms deeply rooted in Europe's religious history.

The fusion between Greek reason and Judaeo-Christian belief triggered a powerful release of energy. But it did not deliver peace. On the contrary, Europe was – and has been ever since – a bonfire of conflicting doctrines. Monastic centres preached war while soldiers marched under the cross. From early times it had a dual nature. Even as the home of enlightened thought it revolved around the Church of Rome – a world-spanning institution based on faith rather than reason, led by an elected primate who was a *de facto* statesman. The Pope's approval could sway the fate of nations.

Rome, the capital of ancient Christendom, became the capital of medieval Europe, too. Its dominion stretched from Madrid to Vienna and from castle to monastery.

The Vatican belongs to the world, yet is unmistakably Roman. As Nigel Baker, Britain's Ambassador to the Holy See until 2016, wrote: 'Its global impact is extensive, its voice respected, and its influence real.'

This was famously demonstrated at the height of the Cuban Missile Crisis, when the Pope was encouraged by America to give a speech in praise of peace. The fact that his words appeared on the front page of *Pravda* the following day was taken by the Cold

War analysts in Washington as a coded message that Moscow *was* willing to talk.

That was textbook soft power. And the fact that the Vatican has the trappings of a modern nation, while standing for a religious idea, makes it an ideal peace broker. When the Pope toured the Holy Land in 2014, he bowed his head at Bethlehem's 26-foot wall, and invited Shimon Peres, Israel's Prime Minister, and Mahmoud Abbas, head of the Palestinian Authority to Rome, to a 'prayer summit'. Four years later the Vatican signed a 'deal' with China in which the latter promised to accept Catholic bishops so long as it had a role in their appointment. Some saw this as doing God's work; others thought it kowtowing – Catholicism with Chinese characteristics. Either way, it was soft power: international relations without missiles.

The reputation of the Vatican has been punctured by revelations about the blind eye it turned to its own victims of sexual abuse. Only 15 per cent of America's eighty-seven million baptised Catholics attend mass; more than one-third do not even admit to being Catholic. In the UK more than one-third say they no longer hold with religion in any form. But even this cannot altogether annul the power of its past. Whatever happens, Italy will forever be the rock on which the Christian Church first built its house.

History is not a stable substance, and in modern times there is a plethora of new ways in which it can be approached. From some angles it is a tale of inevitable progress, a march towards sunlit uplands; from others it is a painful saga of disgraceful episodes which demand atonement and repair. In certain lights it can be both these things. John Steinbeck once wrote: 'History is what we wish it to be' – and in this way it really is a foreign country. But it does not follow that the past cannot be visited; only that we must tread carefully when we do so. Recent years have seen a welcome emergence of alternative or neglected histories – women's history, Black history, working-class history, LGBT history, migrant history, all of which have brought fresh dimensions to any consideration of the past. But sometimes the new approaches have sought not just to amend or add to the received picture, but to supplant it. This has elevated arguments about history (which someone once called the story of things that might not have happened told by people who were not there at the time) into tribal rivalries.

In Europe this fractured nature of the past is especially evident. It is the continent of Shakespeare, Mozart and Leonardo, yet also of the slave trade and the Holocaust. Light and dark are interwoven. Chiaroscuro, the artistic rendering of light and shade on canvas that matured in the Renaissance, giving rise to the tradition of realistic images that was later validated by photography, is in this way Europe's signature style.

Its religious tradition, meanwhile, produced an unusual theological idea: doubt.

Not all faiths embrace the idea that they might have no foundation. It is one of Europe's essential messages, and it contains two contradictory threads.

The reasons why the West 'won' the Cold War have been much examined and remain complicated. But one component (visible from the crumbling roads of East Germany) was the constant glow of the West's lifestyle, evident in the values it broadcast and in the colourful cabaret of its rush hour. This too gave off ambiguous mixed signals: it was appealing and colourful, yet chaotic; free, yet uneasy.

Either way, it was a major display of soft power. And the best efforts of communist regimes in the East could not blot it out. The Russian novelist Aleksandr Solzhenitsyn famously told the world that the West, though only a faint presence behind the Iron Curtain, was whole-heartedly venerated in those years: 'For nearly all of our lives we worshipped the West – note that worshipped; we did not admire it, we worshipped it.'

Its symbols reverberated then – and still do now. The students in Tiananmen Square in 1989 created a model of the Statue of Liberty ('the Goddess of Democracy'), as if to recapture the idealism of Paris two centuries earlier. A few months later, the crowd in Prague's Wenceslas Square marked *their* liberation by chanting 'Hey Jude'. David Bowie's famous concert at the Berlin Wall, when crowds gathered on the eastern side to listen, was not a one-off. The Beatles may have done more to rock the communist boat than the strategies devised to weaken it. Even in remote outposts of the Soviet empire their music was adored. Those jangling guitars sounded like ... freedom.

Of what did it consist, this message? Even in its most modern manifestations, a good part of Europe's lustre still pulses in the recesses of its historical foundations. Greece suckled enlightenment from the Middle East and Asia, infused it in Greek ideas, and created what generations of philosophers would hail as Hellenism – 'sweetness and light', in Matthew Arnold's famous phrase (borrowed from Swift). Greece, he added, represented 'the essential character of human perfection'.

And it was not just the summit but the fountainhead. According to Alfred North Whitehead, Western philosophy could be summed up as little more than 'footnotes to Plato'; and while Aristotle might have been miffed, it was true that classics informed almost everything. Kierkegaard wrote his doctoral thesis on Socrates; Marx wrote *his* on Democritus and Epicurus. The Socratic method – the pursuit of truth through questioning – came to underpin all the West's educational and legal procedures. It is an intellectual reflex – stronger even than a habit – that informs the concept of the interview, of *Question Time* and *Any Questions?*, of questionnaires and Frequently Asked Questions, the whole tradition of scepticism and the spirit of enquiry. As a miniature quest, the humblest question faintly echoes the larger pursuit of truth.[4]

---

4 The Socratic method aimed to place society's cleverest citizens in positions of authority – a strategy later criticised as giving the merely brainy an unfair edge. Why should the 'first-rate mind', rather than the nicest face, the strongest arm or the fastest feet, inherit the earth? What need, in short, for experts?

10

Northern Europe: Germania

In the autumn of 2018 the US National Library of Medicine surveyed six years' worth of news stories and found that 259 people had died taking photographs of themselves in dangerous places – mountains, towers, gorges, bridges, the edges of cliffs. This was probably a low estimate – a fair number of 'accidents' in less dramatic locations may also have been caused by the urge to mark the occasion with a bravura self-portrait.

In one way it was no surprise: the world had grown accustomed to the drip-drip of such news since 2014, when the term 'selfie' first appeared in dictionaries. Now it appeared that look-at-me photography was itself a hazardous sport.

The news survey made it official: selfies were killing more people than sharks.

It would be stretching things to propose that the selfie was a European product – a representative expression of its culture. It is a global habit. But in certain ways it does chime with profound European ideas to do with the individual and inner life.

And one can even see faint outlines of a more specific connection with Europe's northern region. If the ancient civilisations of the Mediterranean lit the lamps of science and reason, then the wilderness above the Rhine, Danube and Alps placed something new – the individual consciousness – at the heart of human meaning. Whether as political or religious protest (the insistence that the King did *not* own everything, the claim that even the Pope was fallible) or as a philosophical idea, the egotistical north sought truth not in the outer world but in ... the self.

First Copernicus, in Polish Prussia, proposed that the earth was not the centre of the universe after all, but one of many satellites circling the sun. Then Martin Luther in Wittenberg argued that man, not their Church, was the centre of theology.[1] And then Freud put interior life under the microscope by promoting self-examination and self-knowledge as the sacred duties of civilised life.

The individual conscience was what counted now. The self replaced the soul.

There was a reason why Protestantism was so called. It was an act of protest against a Roman Church whose priests flogged redemption like travelling salesmen. The Reformation was to some extent a war on corruption, offering private morality in place of institutional authority as the highest arbiter of human conduct. It invited the flock to be its own shepherd, to find its own path.

There may have been a straightforward climatic explanation for this – the soft power of sheer geography asserting itself anew. But Europe's philosophers – especially in its northern provinces – soon picked up on the idea of thinking itself as a form of protest. Wycliffe and Jan Hus in England and Bohemia, Calvin in Geneva, Martin Bucer in Strasbourg, Jacobus Arminius in Holland ... These and many others developed further the idea that life's major truths were no longer 'out there', but within.

Europe remained a continent of two halves – a Protestant north and a Catholic south – but now it had a powerful new engine.

In due course the me-me strand in northern European thought would float across the Atlantic and take root in America too, to take on energetic new life in the world's most ambitious experiment in individualism. Eventually it would emerge in all the modern forms of personal identity and self-expression. It breathed through politics, commerce and private life, toppling monarchies and churches alike. Stendhal's joke that God's only excuse was that he did not exist had a brazen northern accent.

It was one of Europe's underlying soft-power ideas: the individual was king.

---

1 In 1928 the French philosopher Jacques Maritain suggested that Luther had indeed 'discovered the self'.

Soft power needed hard rails on which to run, and northern Europe also provided the mechanical innovation it required. In a bold theological advance, the printing machines of Gutenberg and others were able to place the Bible into the hands of ordinary men and women. The new way of thinking was composed on German presses.

The Reformation was geographically rooted in another way. Had Luther not raised his voice at a time when an emerging class of merchants were greedy for just such a message, well, history might not even remember him. If he had nailed (or pinned, or posted – the story is not quite clear) those ninety-five theses to the church door in Wittenberg a generation earlier than he did, he might have been burned at the stake as a heretic. History seems inevitable only in retrospect.

It is now well known that China had invented paper and ink printing many centuries earlier. But German printing was a step-change, since the Chinese language presented a challenge to movable type, thanks to its need for 100,000 characters. Europe's twenty-six-letter alphabet (derived from Arabic) was much easier to handle.

When we think of Germanic soft power it is tempting to think above all of music – the great tradition of Bach, Beethoven, Brahms, Wagner and of course all the Austrians. But this is the fruit of a grander tree. Germany prided itself on being the land of poets and thinkers (*Dichter und Denker*), and in the centuries that followed the Reformation, it led the journey to the centre of the self. Kant and others explored the gap between 'I and not-I' and concluded that the world did not shape the mind – but was shaped by it.

To the Greek proposition that mystery could be illuminated by reason, he answered that mystery was itself an illusion: a figment of human creativity.

Morality, it followed, was not a set of exterior laws, but an internal prompting.

The philosophical leap was immediately visible in art. Greek statuary had not been realistic – it dealt in idealised deities. The Davids of Donatello and Michelangelo were as much exercises in trigonometry as observed expressions of feeling: few sixteenth-century Florentines looked like these marvellous figures. The Gothic mind, on the other hand, was gnarled: its characters were grimacing, strained, agonised.

But the form that best expressed the new way of thinking was the novel. Renouncing the heroic mode, writers began to trace the stories of ordinary men and women in a new form that was also cradled in Germany, the *Bildungsroman*: the adventures of an individual character from childhood to maturity. Goethe's Wilhelm Meister was the prototype of this new style: his 'apprenticeship' was not the medieval notion of learning his father's craft, but a voyage of self-realisation. He may have joined a theatre group and performed *Hamlet*, but what he was really exploring was himself.

In so doing he and all the other protagonists of the European novel set in motion the train of thought that held life stories to be 'journeys', an idea that wound (as we have seen) all the way to Hollywood, in a complicated migratory journey of its own.

Schlegel said *The Apprenticeship of Wilhelm Meister* was as important as the French Revolution. Schopenhauer thought it one of the few worthwhile books ever written. It was admired by Beethoven and Schubert, and gave rise to a tradition of fiction about growing pains and formative years. This was a new note in literature. The heroes of epic poetry – Achilles, Odysseus, Beowulf – had been experienced figures, neither bemused nor afraid. David Copperfield, Jane Eyre, Emma Bovary, Anna Karenina – characters of this more tentative sort had a startling new way of seeing the world.

The first person became the dominant voice in poetry, too. 'Myself I sing,' sang Walt Whitman, and romantic self-expression became the order of the day. It chimed with individualistic Protestant ideas by seeming artless as well as anti-authority, and also echoed the idiom of demotic speech. Latin had folded the first person into its verbs; German (and by extension English) set it free. It seemed only natural: it was how ordinary people spoke. It was the unaffected grammar of everyone's what-I-did-on-holiday anecdotes and even the form (as Freud noticed) of their dreams.

The individualistic drive for identity took other forms. It was visible in the buoyant industry of self-help and self-reliance (from books on how to succeed to wellness programmes). And it informed the heightened modern sensitivity to mental health. It entered politics as the struggle for national 'self-determination' and also for human and civil rights. It underpinned the idea of private property. And it animated more varieties of exhibitionist popular entertainment than can easily be counted.

It may even be visible in the resurgence of communist thought. On the surface it might seem the opposite of individualism – it proposed to rein back private liberty in favour of the communal good. But in the age of social media even left-wing ideas had as much to do with look-at-me chanting as with old-school collective action.

In a giddy new political coming together, Marx had met Narcissus. In the age of influencers and bloggers, new entrepreneurs emerged, with nothing more to sell than . . . themselves. As Dana Budzyn, the California-based social media analyst said, a person's data trail contained 'the digital narrative of who you are, where you have been, what you have done'. There was an existential question here: who owned (or should own) such data? It was a commercial question, too.

The world acquired another new word: self-monetisation.

The fact that Germany has become a leading player in today's soft-power rankings (it came third in the 2018 Portland 30, after the United Kingdom and France, and top of the 2016 *Monocle* chart) is a tribute to the commitment of its government. Berlin invests 'very significant sums' in a range of institutions and programmes, not just to raise its profile on the world stage but, more specifically, to expunge the demons in its past. In 1945 it was, in most of the world's eyes, a monster. Its historic achievements in theology, literature, philosophy, science, industry and music counted for nothing when Hitler tried to rekindle an even older mythology of warrior knights. A land once associated with gingerbread houses and glass slippers, a fairy-tale kingdom of stranded princesses, dwarves and children lost in forests, became a cruel, bloodthirsty beast.

In fact, Germany took such strenuous steps in the post-war years – first by facing its own crimes with clear eyes, then by repairing its broken cultural connections with the rest of the world – that the clouds lifted with surprising speed.

Today it is widely seen as a generous educator and collaborator.

To have climbed from the basement of world opinion almost to the summit is remarkable – and it has been achieved almost entirely by soft means. If a soft-power magazine needed a model to put on the cover, it would probably be German.

The Goethe-Institut employs three thousand staff worldwide and has a budget of more than €400 million a year. Like the BBC and the British Council, it is independent, lest it be weaponised by the short-term whim of any particular administration. It offers German-language classes, scholarships and a heavy schedule of cultural events, all designed to do something quite unusual: to reconnect Germany with its older, wiser self.

Academic exchange is another important strand. The DAAD programme (German Academic Exchange Service) spends more than €500 million a year helping students old and young, in Germany and overseas – almost half of its awards fund foreign academics. It reminds the world that Germany pioneered modern education: when Wilhelm von Humboldt became Minister of Education in 1809 he swiftly introduced the system (the mix of seminars and laboratories in which students taught themselves, under the supervision of eminent scholars) now used in all the leading universities.

There is also a global broadcasting service, *Deutsche Welle*, which spreads calm, serious, well-funded international news in thirty languages, covering a range of subjects (sustainable agriculture, new automobile technology, behind-the-scenes at the opera) not always thought newsworthy by ratings-conscious media executives in Britain and America. The embassies work diligently with partners on events and debates.

As the British Council has (with some envy) noted, the seriousness of this political commitment can be seen in the funding increases announced in 2018 – €35 million extra for the Goethe-Institut and DAAD; €33 million for *Deutsche Welle*, bringing the latter's annual budget to €373 million – vastly more than the £85

million annual provision for the BBC World Service (a sharp
increase from £34 million in 2015).

However important these are – and they move the needle in
surveys – they pale into insignificance besides the grander gestures
a nation can make. In recent decades Germany has embarked on
two adventures – reunification with the East in 1989, and the
acceptance of a million refugees in 2016 – that have done much to
erase wartime memories. The latter has caused friction: there have
been spots of civic trouble and a corresponding surge in far-right
politics; but as early as 2019 it emerged that one-third of those
refugees were in stable jobs – without provoking unemployment.
That meant that two-thirds were not, which was controversial.
But it was a better and more peaceful result than many feared
when the refugees first arrived. They were lowering the average
age of the workforce, and since many were well educated they
were also raising standards in schools, offices, factories and on
sports pitches. They were the power supply of a burgeoning gig
economy – not a traditional German strength – and they filled a
stark gap in Germany's demographic profile.

The head of Daimler (Dieter Zetsche) went so far as to
declare them 'the basis of the next German economic miracle'.
Comments of that sort were heard around the world.

Germany itself declined to think of this as soft power or even
to give house room to the term – it flinched at any formulation
that included the word *power*. 'Our aim is not to project power
but to build trust,' said Hans-Günter Löffler, head of London's
Consular department. The watchwords here were 'partnership'
and 'cooperation'.

The German word for the building of trust is *Vertrauenschaffen*.
Perhaps that, in German circles, is what soft power should be
known as from now on.

It used to be common to speak of the German economic
miracle – the speed with which it rose from the ashes of the
Second World War to become a manufacturing power. But the
cultural miracle was just as substantial. Those government programmes would have made little headway had not the country as
a whole been changing in the world's eyes. Its supreme position
in engineering (especially automobiles) and the dignified way it

processed its own Nazi past (it was frowned on to wave flags at sports events until the 2006 World Cup) made even its former enemies sigh. And the steadiness it brought to its leadership role in Europe ... that too changed minds.

All nations, as we have seen, try to reconcile warring versions of their past. In post-war Germany's case the task took a singular form: it needed to recover the vast tradition outlined above, and retrieve it from the ruins caused by the Third Reich.

One of the most obvious symbols of its success in this venture is the 'Sleeping Beauty Castle' built by Walt Disney in California in 1955. It went on to become not just the 'Cinderella Castle' in Florida in 1971, but the logo of Walt Disney Pictures and thus one of the recognisable hood ornaments of America itself. It has more than one ancestor (eight were mentioned) but the dominant inspiration was Neuschwanstein, the Wagnerian folly created by mad King Ludwig on a rocky Bavarian mountain not far from Hitler's own clifftop hideaway.

The most energetic formative influence on the American child's imagination adopted as its calling card a medieval fantasy from the German mountains.

Neuschwanstein is Germany's most popular castle, with six thousand visitors on busy days. The Disney version effectively rescued the fairy-tale German culture preserved by the Brothers Grimm, but hidden by war and Holocaust, and painted it in bright colours. In giving America new dreams ('Someday my prince will come ... when you wish upon a star'), Disney was incidentally restoring Germany to ... itself. In the process it was installing a deep connection between the German and the American mentality.

It is said that the forest hunting scene in the minstrels' gallery, with its stags and fawns, may have inspired Bambi. The gallery itself, all gaudy medieval flourishes, resembles the ballroom in *Beauty and the Beast*. Hundreds of millions of children's dreams have been shaped by this fusion of German and American aesthetics.

It was a victory for soft power, too. It could not be tracked or measured – no one watched *Snow White* and felt an unaccountable urge to buy a German car. Soft power is not a sales tool.

But on the barely conscious level of imaginary expectations, a kinship was created. A German medieval fantasy blended with an American notion of storytelling (life as a journey through a magical forest, moments of dread redeemed by happy endings) . . . and seduced the entire world. China and Japan both created replica castles for their own people (the one in China is a luxury hotel).

Anyone who thinks this insubstantial must ask: insubstantial compared to what?

The old ghosts still hover. In 2015 it emerged that Germany's biggest carmaker, Volkswagen, had cheated the diesel emissions testing system by installing software that gave a false reading. It was a full-blown scandal; there were damaging headlines around the world. VW was forced to spend €228 billion on refitting eleven million cars and pay court-imposed fines; the share price sank by a third. Worst of all, it struck at the heart of Germany's greatest strength – its reputation for reliable engineering.

Then it got worse. Four years later the chief executive, Herbert Diess, let slip the phrase *Ebit Macht Frei* (profits shall set you free) – a grim echo of the awful legend that used to adorn the gates of Auschwitz – in a morale-boosting address to management, congratulating his employees for weathering the storm.

It is possible that he was thinking about the catchphrase of a sweet (*Haribo macht kinder froh* – 'Haribo makes children glow') but nastier echoes clamped the company back in the stocks. Columnists reminded their readers that Volkswagen, for all its bragging about sustainable motoring, had been created by Adolf Hitler himself.

Stories of this sort – momentary lapses of taste – directly affected the way the world thought about Germany. And there were similar scandals attaching to Bayer, the chemicals conglomerate, when one of its weedkillers was alleged to have cancerous side-effects (causing some €30 billion to fall off the share price), and Deutsche Bank, whose murky loan book led to a stock market slide. In southern Europe (Greece, Italy and Spain) its imposing position at the head of the continent's financial affairs became controversial: it was charged with profiting handsomely from the weak shared currency, the euro, while taking a hard line with its less prosperous neighbours. The aura of invincibility dimmed a little.

But it didn't take long for the view to clear. Surveys showed that people still had 'great faith' in Volkswagen cars. Embarrassing episodes of this sort might even have *enhanced* the national reputation, softening its forbidding image into something more ordinary – Germany could make a mess of things just like anyone else.

There was a point in this concerning the power of national brands. In the frictionless modern world, where international affairs were to some extent a form of storytelling, countries could now sell ... themselves. As Melissa Aronczyk put it in *Branding the Nation*, their national features could be 'managed and manipulated for the purposes of global visibility'. There was a clear role for government here, but the behaviour of private corporations mattered too. At times like these, governments found themselves not deploying soft power but managing or curating it.

Business had long understood the importance of product branding, lionising emblems such as the Coca-Cola bottle or the Nike 'swoosh'. If marketing was the science of grabbing attention, then branding was the science of holding it. It was soft power weaponised, and it sought rather more than loyalty; it wanted affection, too.

It could boast ancient origins of its own. Branding began in the potteries of early China and Egypt: stonemasons left marks on their work as proof of quality. Artists followed suit, adding signatures to denote authenticity; papermakers and silversmiths did the same with watermarks and hallmarks. Farmers had a new motive in branding cattle: they were establishing ownership as much as quality.

It was the commercialisation of hearts and minds, and in the world of social media and online messaging, it was one of soft power's crucial new formats. In the words of the American designer Walter Landor: 'Products are made in the factory. Brands are created in the mind.'

They could die in the mind, too. Sears, Roebuck ... Woolworths ... Pan Am ... Kodak ... Names of that sort once loomed as large and permanent as nation states.

In Simon Anholt's view, winning friends was more useful than winning arguments, so the best way to impress others was not to brag, but to be modest.

'The more you cooperate, the sharper your competitive edge.'

It was a typical soft-power maxim. Less was more.

Like Switzerland, Scandinavia plays a striking role on the world stage – proof that in the mazy world of soft power small countries can punch above their weight. Sweden has a well-maintained reputation as a paragon of good governance, leading the way in socially progressive politics and human rights. It is a prominent peacekeeper, with a strong presence in conflict resolution and mediation. It is the land of Abba, Volvo and Ikea – friendly, unthreatening and accessible. It has technology companies, an enviable film industry (Ingmar Bergman) and a globally famous work–life balance.

Of course this is a caricature: national brands hide as much as they reveal. Sweden has dark sides, like all countries (the novelist Stieg Larsson could not have contrived his set of international bestsellers without them). But the good-natured image is tenacious. When the world tips its hat to the high-minded Nobel Prizes, it rarely thinks of their origins: Alfred Nobel was the inventor of dynamite and gelignite, and the owner of a lethal armaments company, Bofors.[2] In an unruly world Sweden remains in high demand as an honest broker, an impartial go-between and peace envoy.

Something similar can be said about Norway – there, too, ostentatious pacifism has been turned into a useful commodity. But the other big winner in Scandinavian soft power is Denmark. The Germanic promotion of the inner life inspired in Denmark a related emphasis on the home. In buttressing the belief in private property, the cultivation of individuality had political ramifications: a man's home, as the saying put it, was also his castle. Denmark became the designer of its domestic interior.

In 2016 an innocuous lifestyle manual came from nowhere

---

2 On an unflattering obituary published shortly before his actual death, one French newspaper put the headline: 'The merchant of death is dead.'

to dominate the world's bestseller lists. *The Little Book of Hygge: Danish Secrets of Happy Living* had nothing to do with foreign policy. On the contrary, it was a publishing stunt cooked up in London by Penguin, which divined (correctly) that there might be mileage in how-to books by nicely dressed Scandinavian gurus. Denmark scored highly in happiness surveys, so could claim to be an authority on the subject; more to the point, it could be relied on to look good in the magazine photo-shoots where such concepts incubate.

Danishness was an alluring combination of snow and fire. Somewhere in the West's folk memory lurked a notion of Danes as horn-helmeted Viking axemen,[3] but since then the country had produced theologians and physicists, footballers, fairy tales and interior designers. It had credibility as a counsellor on domestic life.

It was serious yet apple-cheeked – melancholia with ringlets and a cinnamon roll. On the one hand it had Kierkegaard; on the other, 'The Emperor's New Clothes'.

An author was engaged (Meik Wiking of Copenhagen's Happiness Institute) and the rest was soft-power history. Denmark became an emporium of cosy fires, pastel-coloured blankets, candle-scented bathrooms and mugs of hot chocolate on frosty nights. Such was the book's success that it inspired follow-ups: *Hygge: the Danish Art of Happiness*, *Hygge: the Nordic Secrets to a Happy Life*, *The Book of Hygge: the Danish Art of Contentment, Comfort and Connection* and many more. Between them, the books sold millions of copies, and 'hygge' won several 'word of the year' awards – not bad, considering no one knew what it meant, or how to pronounce it.

There was even a parody – *Say Ja to Hygge!* – which poked fun at the genre by having a made-up author ('Dr Magnus Olsensen') hand out silly tips on how to install fairy lighting in trees, how to prepare the perfect porridge-and-nut breakfast, and how long it should take a full-on *hygge* disciple to get dressed (twenty-six hours).

*

3 Some Vikings were Danish; others hailed from Norway or Sweden. The public mind ignored such distinctions: they were all marauding Scandinavians, storming their way south with fire and, of course (as *1066 and All That* pointed out), the sword.

The most significant Danish gift to the world, however, may be its cool, clean-limbed architecture. Minimal yet stylish, smart yet neat, the Danish aesthetic is the default setting not just for homes but also for offices, museums, shops and other public spaces. Most of the bathrooms in most of the world's hotels were born in Denmark.

This aesthetic has been a strong presence in the world ever since Ove Arup left Copenhagen for Britain in 1923. Fifty years later he had a construction company in his name employing 14,000 people in thirty-five countries. Its most famous creation was the Sydney Opera House, with its bravura fan of flying sails, which became the symbol of modern Australia, and whose architect was another Dane: Jorn Utzen.[4]

The Danish aesthetic colonised some surprising settings: St Catherine's College, Oxford, for instance. Built in 1962, it was not one of those sets of medieval quadrangles for which the city was known. A geometric pattern of concrete, glass and rectilinear pools, it did not look like a hall of learning. In place of dreaming spires it had modish sculptures. If anything it resembled a Swiss police station or a lunar freight terminal.

The architect was Arne Jacobsen, and though a relative unknown (his only notable building was the SAS Radisson hotel in Copenhagen) he had won the commission against stiff competition. The library, dining hall, seminar rooms, offices, bedrooms, lodge, squash court – all were rooted in the same uncompromising aesthetic. A pared-down Baltic tone was in the plates, the blinds, the cutlery, even the fish in the ponds.

The college divided opinion. A few sceptics (including some of the academics who lived in it) denounced it as self-indulgent, architecture for architecture's sake, aiming only to look good in magazine spreads. One sneered that the cutlery resembled 'a DIY abortion kit'. But Pevsner anointed it as 'perfect', a brilliant re-enactment of classical ideas, and English Heritage listed it as a Grade One protected treasure.

A year after it opened, the Jacobsen style became famous when

---

4 The UN's World Heritage experts declared it 'one of the indisputable masterpieces of human creativity', so there were loud protests when it was used, in 2018, as an advertising billboard for the Sydney racetrack. Talk about fading in the straight.

Lewis Morley shot his notorious image of the woman at the centre of the Profumo spy scandal, Christine Keeler. Charged to capture the naughtiness of the moment, he invited her to drape herself over one of Jacobsen's swan-neck chairs – the Model 3107, the very chair on which St Catherine's students sat every day. It was one of the images of the 1960s.[5]

And it chimed with other expressions of Danishness. Students could not afford the sleek stereo systems made by Peter Bang and Svend Olufsen, the Danish engineers whose wartime radio factory had been burned down by Nazi sympathisers (they were non-collaborators). But they *had* grown up with Lego, and may also have been aware that something remarkable was taking shape in Sydney Harbour. Suddenly it seemed that no one knew better how to marry ingenuity with simplicity.

When a household-goods operation (Flying Tiger Copenhagen) launched in 1995, it became a 900-store chain. And international audiences suddenly found themselves enthralled by police dramas such as *The Killing*, which teased poetry out of Nordic grey. Scandi Noir lumped Denmark with Sweden, Norway and Finland in a single Baltic vibe. But the genre had roots in a Danish bestseller from the 1980s: *Miss Smilla's Feeling for Snow*, by Peter Hoeg. Ever since Hans Christian Andersen's 'Ugly Duckling' there had been a sense that murky wisdom in cute clothing was a Danish art.

This – perhaps inevitably – was not an accident, but by design. In 1972 Denmark's Film Institute began to offer financial support to international productions (feature films and documentaries) that at first sight had little to do with the national interest. They asked only that the projects engage Danish staff. It was a far-sighted policy. A generation of Danish filmmakers acquired technical skills and storytelling know-how overseas. The result was Scandi Noir: a global success story. *The Bridge* was a hit in a hundred countries, each of which received a little touch of Denmark in the night.

---

5 It later emerged that the chair was a Habitat copy, not an original. The reproduction turned out to be more valuable than the real thing, however. Signed by Keeler (and other models such as Elton John and Dame Edna Everage), it sits in London's Victoria and Albert Museum. Morley's famous photograph is in the National Portrait Gallery.

When Denmark appointed the world's first Ambassador for Technology and Digitisation in September 2017, it confirmed the sense that this was a country that lived close to the cutting edge.[6]

All of this made Danishness a powerful brand. That is why in 1961 a Brooklyn ice-cream maker, Reuben Mattus, looked to Denmark for help with his family's frozen-sugar company. He chose the name 'Häagen-Dazs' (he later said) on the grounds that it *sounded* Danish. It didn't – if anything it sounded Dutch. But he was hoping to honour the role Denmark had played in rescuing Jews from Hitler's Holocaust (a truth, but one that needed qualifying by the fact that Sweden could be reached from Denmark by rowing boat – there was no easier country from which to flee). Either way, he was happy to borrow Denmark's butter-rich aura while he was about it.

The new name successfully nudged his father's company upmarket. The first tubs actually plastered maps of Denmark all over the carton, to suggest old-world charm.

That hint of Danish style went down well across Europe, too. When a German chain ran a study informing customers that the ice cream in those colourful pots was from New York, not Denmark, sales fell by 68 per cent. Häagen-Dazs, meanwhile, cheekily sued a rival New York confectioner for calling itself 'Frusen Gladje', on the grounds that this amounted to a theft of its own (fictitious) Scandinavian-dairy theme.

The case was lost. But it was a sign that in modern commerce soft signals could be just as valuable as the tough old staples of taste, convenience and value for money.

Another pair of New Yorkers were at that time pouring even more vanilla-caramel-fudge chunks into their ice cream, in line with a similar marketing strategy. Ben and Jerry were proving that it was *not* essential to be Danish. On the contrary, by presenting their product as a no-nonsense, all-American treat, they managed both to seem 'natural' and to capture a new audience of whole-earth, environmentally friendly ice-cream fans.

---

6 When Japan appointed a Minister of Cybersecurity the following year, it did not have quite the same avant-garde effect. To widespread surprise (and laughter), the new minister celebrated his appointment by admitting that he had never used a computer.

In both cases, image was as important as content.

This is soft power as fiction, and Denmark has profited from it. The sugary treats known as Danish pastries are not in fact Danish, for instance: in Denmark they are called *wienerbrod*, after their true country of origin – Austria. A nineteenth-century strike by Denmark's bakers led to an influx of Austrian chefs whose sticky delicacies hit all the right spots; migrants to America took the recipes with them, and one, L. C. Kitteng, was hired for the wedding of Woodrow Wilson in 1915. His confections became known as 'Danish' pastries; in truth, they were so delicious few cared what they were called.

There are further knots. In a new bakery chain known as Ole & Steen, a single bite of Danish pastry contains more calories than can easily be counted. It was only natural that, in 2018, *The Great British Bake Off* should have a 'Danish Week'. Yet the Danes themselves (according to *hygge*) seem slim and light-footed, with the glow of cross-country skiers. And the land of the sweet bun was also (in 2010, 2011, 2012 and 2014) home to the world's most refined restaurant – a wild one-off based on foraged ingredients.

So it was not noteworthy when the 2018 Ryder Cup – the only sports event in which Europe competes as a team – was captained by a Dane (Thomas Bjorn). There was more to *hygge*, it seemed, than candles. Danish-descended actors such as Scarlett Johansson and Viggo Mortensen were lighting up cinema screens, while Danish-owned ships (Maersk is the world's biggest line) were coasting into the world's ports. None sported woollen scarves printed with snowflake or reindeer patterns.

Stereotypes were fun. But (to generalise) generalisations are *never* true.

Welcome to the soft world.

In January 1417, a hundred years before Luther gave Europe a new way of thinking about God, an Italian book-hunter named Poggio Bracciolini was riffling through old volumes in a monastery library somewhere in Germany (usually thought to be Fulda, near Frankfurt – but it may have been Alsace, or even St Gallen in Switzerland, which Bracciolini visited the previous year) when he came upon something extraordinary.

It was an ancient Greek poem that dealt with the laws of nature in a bewilderingly modern way – it imagined the world as being composed of whirring atoms, forming and reforming themselves in a perpetual commotion, an ever-changing flux. In one way this was terrifying; in another way it told people that they were ... free.

The book was *De Rerum Natura* by Lucretius, and its discovery sparked the burst of mind and soul searching that later became known as the Renaissance. A thousand years of Christian light had, ironically, plunged Europe into an extended 'dark' age. The re-emergence of the intellectual flowering that was Ancient Greece was a rebirth of ancient ideas to their rightful place in the crown of human thought.

This story has been expertly narrated by Stephen Greenblatt in *The Swerve: How the Renaissance Began* (2011). In his hands it was a creation myth: the rediscovery of the classical text resembled Michelangelo's depiction of Adam in the Sistine Chapel (a work contemporaneous with Luther's proclamations).[7] It heralded an uprising against 'the constraints that centuries had constructed around curiosity, desire, individuality, sustained attention to the material world, the claims of the body ... '

It sparked a revolution in science, philosophy and theology as well as art.

The two early currents of European civilisation touch in this story (which, we notice, really *was* a journey). The 'reason' of Ancient Greece (fed by North Africa and Asia Minor) merged with the 'faith' flowing out of Judaeo-Christian Rome. The fact that *De Rerum Natura* was unearthed in a hidden corner of Germania links it to the third great force: the violent energy rising in the lands north of the Rhine-Danube line.

It would thus seem to be a defining soft-power achievement – a walk in the woods and a quiet moment in a library changed the way a continent thought about existence.

It also inspired conflict: a religious war between Catholic and Protestant Europe whose aftershocks judder to this today (what is

---

7 It was not a coincidence that Luther emerged exactly when St Peter's Church in Rome was being built. The Reformation was a tax as well as a theological protest.

Brexit but another break with Rome, half a millennium after the first one?). Soft power is not always soft-hearted.

But it is adaptable, and can root itself in the peace that follows war. That is what happened after 1945, when European culture resolved to close the gap between its endlessly warring factions by subsuming them in a joint project: the European Union. As part of this never-again peace process, the EU was unusual in that soft power was its *only* weapon. It carried economic clout – it could deploy sanctions (and in time would – against Iran, North Korea, Russia and Venezuela). And in theory it had a military strategy, a military doctrine, even a military budget. But these were always deployed in the service of peacekeeping. It sent watchdog missions to Macedonia, Bosnia, Congo, Georgia, Indonesia, Palestine, Sudan, Ukraine and twenty other countries, but direct intervention remained the province of member states. It was 'an economic giant, a political dwarf and a military midget' – in other words: a soft power.

In some eyes this made it a mild presence on the world stage. Without real muscle to back it up, its soft assets were hypothetical. But in other ways it was a dizzy success. As the world's largest economic and political market it commanded attention on every continent, while as an experiment in shared sovereignty it set the pace in human rights and environmental standards, brokering deals in both fields while creating a template for trade that was being imitated everywhere else in the world.

This soft influence became known in diplomatic circles as 'the Brussels effect' and it was a distinctive new force in the world. Politically it had more clout than any one member state could command on its own – as Emmanuel Macron once put it, 'France cannot win against Google and Facebook, but Europe can' – and soon it was becoming the world's largest aid donor too. Its educational programmes (such as the Erasmus scheme for student exchange) bound the continent in an ever-closer union, sponsoring nine million trips abroad and playing midwife (students being students) to something like a million Erasmus babies.[8]

---

8 It is an inspiring initiative, so it is depressing to discover that its name, though of course a reference to the Dutch humanist, was also intended to denote: **Eu**R**opean** **A**ction **S**cheme for the **M**obility of **U**niversity **S**tudents.

Many of these students explored Europe on holiday, too, through Interrail, the agency set up in 1972 to mark the fiftieth anniversary of the *Union Internationale des Chemins de Fer*. This was a concerted attempt to standardise Europe's railways after the First World War, and involved rail gauges, paperwork, customs routines and passenger rights. Europe stitched itself together with railway lines. Travellers gasped when they looked up at departure boards and saw the destinations that lay within their reach: Athens, Madrid, Bordeaux, Prague, St Petersburg, Vienna, Warsaw and all points north.

After the fall of the Berlin Wall in 1989 the EU helped a dozen communist tyrannies transform themselves into democracies[9] without ever breathing a word about naval power or air supremacy. Its only weapon was the appeal of its lifestyle, values and culture. It twisted no arms. It was not magic. Much could be achieved by haggling.

The newly emerging nations all queued up to join.

Since it began as a pact between France and Germany to banish the chance of war, the EU was usually seen as a northern European invention. But Italy was a founder member, and the original Common Market was formed in the Treaty of Rome (in 1957). At a stroke, it united the two great European worlds, South and North. It was not a perfect union – it was a youthful work in progress – but the world soon learned to see Europe in a distinct and remarkable new light. For centuries it had been a byword for war – there were battlefields round every corner. Now it broadcast and stood for a very different principle: cooperation.

'Just think of the millions around the world,' wrote Fraser Cameron, Director of the EU-Asia Centre, 'who watch European soccer, drive European cars, wear European fashion and visit Europe for their holidays.' He could have added that they also eat European food, read European books, speak European languages, use European banks, sing European songs and pray in European churches. The number of people who look to the

---

9 Bulgaria, Croatia, Czech Republic, East Germany, Estonia, Hungary, Latvia, Lithuania, Poland, Romania, Slovakia and Slovenia.

Vatican for religious leadership is matched by the similar number of Protestants around the world. Whether they are Anglican, Baptist, Lutheran or 'other', there is an old and deep European component in their lives.

The European Union had twenty-seven members, but was more than the sum of its constituent parts. It added an additional dimension of its own to each of them.

This was why, in 2012, it was awarded the Nobel Peace Prize. The bringing of peace to a war-blasted continent was an achievement in itself. It could even be said that the intellectual basis of citizenship – at first a Greek idea based on blood, then a Roman notion based on law, and finally a feudal principle based on land (place of birth) – was a European idea. The upheavals that created its principles echoed far and wide.

The way the award was received made it clear that it was not yet a harmonious union. Germany's *Bild*, a mass-market tabloid, cheered the announcement with a bright front page: *27 countries, 23 languages, 67 years of peace.* But Britain's *Sun* took a very different view: *EU have got to be joking!* The *Daily Telegraph* agreed, remarking that the Nobel panel was performing 'a service not to diplomacy, but to comedy'. The British public had been drip-fed mistrust of the EU for a long time, to an extent that would precipitate a new sort of upheaval only four years later.

If the EU was an imposing ship in calm weather, in the storms of recent years it began to look like a leaky tub. It was unable to prevent conflict in the Balkans, and soon trouble flared in other nearby regions: the Middle East, North Africa and Ukraine. In the years after the Second World War the whole continent had been on the move, as displaced peoples made their way home, or sought a new one somewhere else. But the twenty-first-century exodus across the Mediterranean tested the resilience of Europe's moral foundations, and its agonised response to this and other crises – in Darfur, Eritrea, Libya, Rwanda, Syria and Yemen – took some gloss off its reputation.

The well-documented failings of the euro, meanwhile, a technocratic dream that appeared to have outstripped what was feasible (the idea that two economies as different as Germany and Greece could share a currency and an interest rate was sorely tested) dented Europe's image as a place of sound management. The world's business schools knew that it was no longer the cradle of innovation: the life-changing leaps in computing and communications were hatching elsewhere. The bitterness of its political mood swings also blurred its image. The rise of nationalist movements made the entire continent look divided, unsure, and perhaps less free than it seemed.

Modern Europe had a tattered look. The soft-power consequences, at a time when Africa, China, India and Russia were all rising to their full height, were obvious.

The result was most visible in Turkey. In the late 1990s, when it sounded out the possibility of EU membership, great strides were being made in democracy, media freedom, the law and human rights; there were even signs of a more open attitude to sensitive historical topics: Cyprus, Armenia and the Kurds. When membership of the EU was pushed off the table, all went into reverse. The government pivoted towards Russia; lawyers and journalists were sent to prison; old animosities flared up again.

The European Union was designed to forestall urges of this sort: it was an attempt to make sure that the awful events in its past could never recur. In the most obvious way it was succeeding – seven decades without a major conflagration was impressive, by European standards. Brexit might even have been a salutary warning to the European Union, though in asserting its sovereign identity Britain finally managed to achieve what four hundred years of statecraft had avoided by uniting the entire continent against it.

Only two generations previously that continent had regarded Britain as a saviour.

The European Union is not Europe. But even as a political contrivance it manages to borrow the prestige of the various nations it serves. Through the adventures in their past they have remade large parts of the world in their own image. North America speaks English; South America thinks in Spanish and Portuguese; India, Africa and Asia communicate in languages not their own. There are a thousand pieces of Italy or Germany in odd corners of the world.[10] Europe has sent its people – and itself – everywhere.

The global prominence it could once take for granted is now disputed. South Korean pop, Iranian film, Japanese music, Latin American writers, African artists ... The world has unearthed new competitors. But Europe still plays a substantial role. As the world continues to question the old colonial assumptions, 'Eurocentric' has become a pejorative term, evidence of an old-fashioned or blinkered mind. But nothing can change the fact that the world really was shaped in European moulds.

Even prehistory has a European flavour: the Devonian period recalls an English county; the Jurassic evokes a French mountain ridge; Neanderthal man hailed from the German valley above the Rhine, a few miles from Düsseldorf – the place where his fossilised remains were found some 40,000 years after he died in that spot.[11]

Most of the soft-power rankings do not treat the EU as a distinct entity. In the one that does (the 2018 Elcano Global Presence Report) it comes ... top.

---

10 The town of Bariloche in the Argentine Andes, for instance, is a Bavarian-style settlement in the foothills of high mountains, where, it is said, Dr Mengele once took and failed his driving test.

11 In a perfect scientific coincidence, the valley was named Neander after a German pastor who once lived there, and whose name literally meant (in Greek): new man.

11

The Gulf: The Shock of the Old

In the spring of 2015 a young man walked into the ruins of Nimrud, a buried city that had once been a wonder of ancient Assyria, and rammed a pneumatic drill into a historic sculpture. It had the body of a lion, the legs of a bull and the wings of an eagle, and it had survived three thousand years of strife – whole empires had risen and fallen beneath its regal, impassive gaze. But it was about to be vanquished for good. A couple of clattering thrusts with a modern drill was enough to knock its head off.

The noise in the background was not just the roar of the bulldozers demolishing other pieces of this precious heritage: it was the sound of the past screaming.

'They are erasing our history,' the archaeologist Lamia al-Gailani told the BBC. UNESCO called it a war crime, and many others agreed. 'It is a crime against Assyria, a crime against Iraq, and against humanity,' said the historian Tom Holland.

In the midst of so many attacks on human beings it seemed almost tasteless to dwell on the destruction of mere stones; no one liked feeling as outraged by an assault on sculpture as by the execution of hostages. But the razing of Nimrud struck a nerve by escalating the uproar into a message that nothing (except itself) was sacred. And it was not random: it was conducted with obvious and deliberate relish.

Only a week earlier, ISIS[1] had released footage of its faithful

---

[1] Western commentators were not sure whether to call the vandals ISIS (Islamic State in Iraq and al-Sham), Daesh (the Arabic name) or Islamic State. On the whole they shunned the latter, as giving the group too much prestige, and some (such as Barack Obama) also declined to call it 'Islamic' to avoid slurring an immense religion. But headline-writers favour the pithy, so the first was the name that stuck.

followers clubbing other statues to death in Mosul's museum of antiquities, praising Allah as they demolished these 'false idols'. It may not have been as ideological (or idealistic) as it looked: Nimrud was enthusiastically looted before disciples moved in with their drills, and some of those pieces were soon for sale. But it was certainly political: irreplaceable treasures were being seized or destroyed as an act of overt strategy.

Of course, this was not the first time that religious purity had been the enemy of artistic expression. In 1515 the Ottoman Sultan introduced the death penalty for printing (in part to protect his industrious scribes, in part to retain control over divine scripture). And in modern times it was certainly not a one-off. In 2001 the Taliban had destroyed the sixth-century Buddhas of Bamiyan, in their cliff in Afghanistan. Cultural artefacts were enemies to be toppled: sticks of dynamite were planted into timeless treasures, bringing them down in clouds of smoke and rubble.

A few months after the crushing of Nimrud, the Roman treasures of Palmyra were also attacked. A 2000-year-old arch was reduced to pebbles; a 15-ton lion (discovered by a Polish archaeologist as recently as 1977) was blasted beyond repair. It was, the destroyers claimed, a holy obligation. The fact that the original Caliphate had been a diverse swirl of peoples and beliefs was not enough to restrain this fiery new force.

If it was pre-Islamic, it had to perish.

In the event, some scruple prevented the foot soldiers of ISIS from demolishing Palmyra – when it was liberated (by Russian troops) the site was not so entirely flattened as was feared. Perhaps there is something in the stones that cries out against such vandalism – 150 years earlier, the British archaeologists who excavated this site knew better than to touch the burial mound of the prophet Jonah, a place of pilgrimage and prayer for Christians and Muslims alike. It would have been sacrilege.

ISIS was not so delicate. In July 2014 its zealots blew Jonah into the sky.

There was a message in this madness: ISIS wanted to light a fire that would attract new enthusiasts to its cause. To some extent it worked: as many as 40,000 people travelled to the new 'Caliphate' in order to restore the old religious order. And it did have enough credibility to scare most of the world. The pledge to create a united Islamic realm of 650 million people in thirty-six countries suggested that there might indeed be a connective tissue, that the *umma* (or community) really could be held by one 'golden thread'. But many more fled, and the West's strategists were reassured by the thought that the Islamic world never had been united. It was hard to envisage how a union involving lands as various as Libya and Indonesia *could* be forged into a single religious entity. If anything, they thought, it was the last despairing cry of a failing religion, as ageing clerics battled to turn back the ever-rising tide of modern life.

When it came to the destruction of art, the world could hardly plead innocence. The very first 'iconoclasts' were eighth-century Christians opposed to divine images on religious grounds. The Puritans of Reformation England had stolen Catholic treasure; Mao's China did all it could to destroy such heritage (and erased Tibet's, too).

Yet it was still a shock to discover that people wanted to turn the clock back so far. It drove a wedge into the space between ancient and modern, rendering the former invisible. It didn't matter how often people spoke about 'Islamophobia'; or how often international leaders denounced such destruction as 'cowardly'; the grim fact was that these extremist acts of destruction succeeded in both of their aims: they obscured the past, and terrorised the present. The world was so gripped by the awful imagery of modern zealotry that it could barely see the glories of the ancient world at all.

More than half a dozen great empires have sprung from the war-torn lands around what we now call 'The Gulf'. The first group – in Sumeria, Assyria, Babylon, Egypt and Persia, to the west and then the east of the region's great river basins – were the birthplaces of civilisation, home to the earliest discoveries in letters and numbers; but the two that followed were Islamic. The first Mohammedan Empire formed in Mecca in the seventh century AD and became a Caliphate (or series of caliphates) that ran from the Atlantic to India, creating a cosmopolitan web of cities that made up the greatest empire the world had seen. In medieval times a new power rose in Anatolya, which, after capturing Constantinople in 1453, became the Ottoman Empire (named after its founder, Osman). It held sway in Greece, the Balkans, Bulgaria and the Gulf.

When William Hawkins sailed from London to India in 1602, and was ushered in to meet the Great Mogul Jahangir, the two men spoke in Turkish. In those far-off Ottoman days, it was the only way an easterner and a westerner could communicate.

The Empire of Islam has thus been, historically, the only substantial rival to the Christian West, a fact that has inspired several alarmist works (most notably Samuel Huntington's *The Clash of Civilisations*), which warned of an approaching showdown between the two. Huntington's larger point was that the next world conflict would be over beliefs and identities rather than material resources, and this was questionable – when one looked at the rising tension over water, it seemed more likely that conflict would be triggered by a dam.[2] But arguments of this sort hit a popular nerve, even though the internal quarrels of Christendom had been far more violent than anything the Islamic world could offer. The wars between Protestant and Catholic Europe, the deadly colonial rampages and the death toll provoked by the protracted 'clashes' between monarchy, democracy, capitalism and communism had no parallel anywhere.

The heritage possessed by all these empires – both pre- and post-Islamic – is a deep reservoir of religious and cultural soft power. The so-called 'Seven Wonders' of the Muslim world – the Alhambra Palace in Granada, and the fabled mosques of Djenné (Mali), Isfahan, Istanbul, Jerusalem, Lahore and Mecca – are every bit as spectacular as the wonders put forward to represent the rest of the world: Chichen Itza in Mexico, the Colosseum in Rome, the Great Wall of China, the Taj Mahal, Machu Picchu (Peru) and Petra (Jordan). Early Islamic culture created extraordinary cities from Baghdad to Timbuktu and from Alexandria to Lahore. And its innovations became part of European life. Muslim architects took the stone portals of Greece and Rome

---

2 One such project, in southern Turkey, close to the source of the Tigris, threatened not just to obliterate a so-called 'cradle of civilisation' – the valley where agriculture began – but also to deprive northern Syria of its most important watercourse.

and turned them first into light self-supporting mechanisms the shape of an upended horseshoe – the 'arch that never sleeps' – and then (inspired by Indian temples) into the pointed arch admired by European crusader knights (in the mosque in Jerusalem, for instance) and taken up in France, Germany and England as a staple of Gothic design.

Until recently this trove of antique learning had a profound effect on outsiders. That first great encounter with Europe – the Crusades – was, of course, a disaster. But when, more than 500 years later, modern Europeans began to push their commercial noses into the Islamic world, their sensitive side (not always visible) was again entranced.

By places such as Nimrud, for example.

Not far from Nineveh (some 30 kilometres to the north, on the outskirts of Mosul in northern Iraq), Nimrud was an extraordinary mass of castles, palaces and temples in what once had been the heart of the Assyrian Empire. Its many parks and menageries (it was held to be the site of the vanished Hanging Gardens of Babylon) were stocked with flora and fauna, and watered by streams, canals and even an aqueduct.

It was also the capital of a warlike dynasty whose pitiless exploits (enemies were flayed alive and had their tongues cut out) were recorded in vivid friezes. Assyria was far from gentle: it understood siege engines and military strategy, and its cruelties knew few bounds. The lion hunts depicted on the walls were allegorical examples of the way the King was obliged to beat down the always-ferocious impulses of his many foes. One carving showed him nibbling on sweetmeats in his pleasure grounds while the severed head of a defeated opponent swung from a nearby palm tree.

Yet it was a literary culture too – one of the first in history. This was where the earliest form of alphabetical writing (cuneiform, in which letters were pressed into clay using the wedge-shaped tip of a reed or quill) developed, and it was a trade hub – timber from the forests of Lebanon, dates and grapes from Arabia, tin and textiles, silver and gold. Trade agreements were written down on small clay tablets, sometimes even wrapped in miniature clay boxes like ancient envelopes.

Three hundred years of crushing power, in which the Assyrian Empire reached from the Mediterranean to the Gulf, came to an end when Nineveh and Nimrud were sacked by rampaging Persians and Babylonians. A succession of natural disasters (floods and earthquakes) then obliterated this once-lordly vision from human sight.

It remained in hiding from the consciousness of the world until the middle of the nineteenth century, when agents from France and Britain began to compete for commercial sway over the area. Rumours about buried cities abounded, and explorers began to dig. The breakthrough was achieved by a pair of amateur archaeologists, one of whom, Austen Henry Layard, was a British imperial adventurer. After trying Aleppo and Damascus, he arrived in Mosul in 1845 and sniffed a great cultural secret: a high earth mound across the river from Mosul that looked ripe for digging. He swiftly recruited a local nineteen-year-old named Hormuzd Rassam, the son of an archdeacon in the Chaldean Catholic Church, to help with the excavations.[3]

They made a colourful team. Layard was in touch with all the right people in London, while Rassam knew how to haggle in the local market and impress the sheikhs. It was his job to rustle up workmen, supplies and transport.

Their personalities began to blur and blend. Layard, the son of well-born doctors and bankers, had been schooled in England, France and Switzerland, yet favoured Eastern robes; Rassam, meanwhile, dressed like a London stockbroker, in collar and tie. No doubt as many people accused him of having ideas above his station as accused Layard of the opposite (the man's gone native, don't you know) but in Rassam's case it was not a pose: in time he would convert to Protestantism and go to Oxford.[4]

To a modern sensibility the seizing of masterpieces by imperial explorers must seem like simple pilfering, even if they were buried and forgotten by those who lived on top of them. Layard had no such anxieties. And together the pair struck something

---

3 There were many Christians in this part of the world at this time, just as there were many Jews (when Gertrude Bell arrived in Baghdad a few years later she estimated that it was approximately one-third Jewish).

4 'I'd rather be a chimney sweeper in England than a Pasha in Turkey,' he wrote.

rarer than gold: an entire buried city full of clay tablets, with the original cuneiform writing still miraculously legible. With the help of the British Consul-General in Baghdad, Sir Henry Rawlinson (an East India Company hand and a renowned scholar of Persian scripts), some 22,000 pieces were shipped back to London for closer examination.

When he published his findings in a book, *The Monuments of Nineveh: From Drawings Made on the Spot,* in 1849, it was a sensation. London had Assyria fever.

Few knew how to decipher the ancient code, but a young apprentice in the British Museum's store room, George Smith, set himself the task of cracking it. After a Dickensian boyhood – at fourteen he had been apprenticed to a firm of printers and engravers – he fell in love with antiquities and took to loitering in the museum in his spare hours. By the time he was twenty he had, through trial, error and patient study, a good working knowledge of cuneiform, and was taken on by the museum to process the shipments arriving from Layard's excavations. One day he was transcribing a tablet and realised he was reading nothing less than the original of Noah's Ark.

'My eye caught the statement about the ship resting on the mountains of Nizir,' he said later, 'followed by the account of the sending forth of the dove.' The tempest raged for six days and six nights before the waters began to recede.

It was clearly the same story: the wickedness of mankind, the flood, the ship, the animals, the raven ... yet it had been written a thousand or so years before the Bible.

There could be no doubt. Christianity's holy book was not original. It had drawn on legends that had been in circulation in Mesopotamia for centuries.

The story Smith found on this tablet, pieced together with other pieces of this mazy jigsaw, was the world's earliest known fragment of literature: *The Epic of Gilgamesh.* It related (a thousand years before Homer) the grand adventure of an ancient hero (Gilgamesh) who undertook a pilgrimage into the woods to slay a forest demon.

When Smith (a noted figure in this new if small field) presented his findings at the Society for Biblical Archaeology in December

1872, the foundations of Western thought were given a vigorous shake. The very next morning the *New York Times* reported on its front page the news that Noah's Ark might be no more than a myth.

And if Noah was a myth, what about the rest? Was the Bible *all* fiction?

No one needed to frame these questions aloud: they filled the air like tolling bells.

In Britain the *Daily Telegraph*, recognising the importance of the find, gave Smith a thousand pounds to return to Mosul and continue his researches. But the area did not agree with him and four years later he died of dysentery, in Aleppo, at the age of thirty-six. But by then his fame was assured. The Prime Minister, William Gladstone, attended the meeting where the findings were announced. Some present had not read Darwin's great work, *The Origin of Species*, published thirteen years earlier, but they knew the gist, and could see that this was another hammer blow to Christianity as they knew it.

Darwin had suggested that the Bible's creation story was not credible; now George Smith was discovering that it was not even the word of God. When the infant Moses escaped disaster by being placed in a reed basket and cast adrift on a river, he was only doing what Gilgamesh had done a thousand years earlier.

Literature, it appeared, was older than religion.

Many other long-standing assumptions about the primacy of Western civilisation also lay in tatters. Agriculture, astronomy, engineering (aqueducts!), architecture, science ... All these things had clearly flourished in Assyria at a time when north Europeans were living in mud huts, dressing in animal skins and foraging in the woods.

At a stroke – or rather, in a barrage of reed-made strokes – the extent of the West's cultural dependence on the Middle East was revealed in unmistakable relief. The German poet Rilke hailed Gilgamesh as perhaps humankind's first great grapple with the drama of mortality, and declared it 'stupendous', which meant that the West could not even claim the epic genre as its own. Just as Greek science had been nursed by Asian and African influences – owing its eminence chiefly to its fortunate location in the eastern Mediterranean – now it seemed that narrative literature was an import as well. Gilgamesh was two parts immortal, one part mortal, so his adventure was actually more than human drama – it brooded on the relations between gods and men.

Not that he was a saint. As a young man Gilgamesh was cruel ('No son is left with his father . . . his lust leaves no virgin to her lover'). But (centuries before Achilles – or Christ) he represented the divine in human form. 'Whoever is tallest among men cannot reach the heavens,' he cried, acknowledging the limits of mortal life. Humans were fated only to struggle – for 'he who leaves the fight unfinished is not at peace'.

There was more. Gilgamesh's quest led him to face the 'intolerable light . . . whose grace and beauty were greater than the beauty of this world'. Before his adventure he was urged to prepare himself by eating bread and wine (one being the 'staff of life', the other 'the custom of the land'). The very heartbeat of Christianity seemed to pulse through this pre-Christian story. The Word of God could never be the same again.

By the standards of modern archaeology Layard and Rassam were careless: their clumsy diggings spoiled as much treasure as they found. And they did not hesitate to send their finest trophies back to Britain. The grandest were the lamassu (great stone lion-bull figurines); two of these 30-ton monsters were hauled out of the mound, sailed downriver, shipped to London and dragged up the steps into the British Museum.

There are several soft-power lessons in this story.

One is that the past is hard to kill. History, as we have seen, is one of soft power's most important ingredients, and while culture can lie dormant for centuries – in Nineveh's case, for three thousand years – it does not lose its power to stun the world. On the contrary, the passing of time gives it wings. The Assyrian remnants in the British Museum and the Louvre have been astonishing visitors for a century and a half, re-ordering the world's sense of the region, its history – and of European civilisation, too. And it should be noted, if we are tempted to see them as Layard's Marbles – ill-gotten treasures that should be returned – that if Victorian archaeologists had *not* sent them to London (and Paris, and New York) they might not exist today.

The second lesson is that when the past is reawakened it does not always bring glad tidings. Sometimes it flares to life enraged and seeking vengeance. The holy age of martyrs conjured up by today's Caliphate is aggressive and uncompromising, making it difficult to oppose with nothing sharper than a rival story. But part of the challenge for the West, in war-ravaged modern times, is to confront the ISIS version of history with a different narrative. In answering fire with fire it may be laying down its own best weapon. The way to fight fire is not, after all, with flames . . . but with water.

As so often, the past is neither stable nor settled, but pitted with disputes over what history teaches. In the Islamic world, with modernisation squared up against tradition, this is especially acute. So far as soft power is concerned, it reminds us that it is not by definition a soothing balm: sometimes it inflames more violent emotions.

The third lesson is the now-familiar paradox that soft power, far from being a polite alternative to hard power, is often its direct consequence. Empires rarely generate affection, but the footprints they leave, the traces they plant in people's minds, endure. It is not as if ancient Assyria were a placid retreat. It might not have been quite as terrifying as its murals suggest (captured heads on spikes or hanging from palm trees), but life within its walls was bloodthirsty and ferocious. Byron was not joking when he wrote (of the capture of Jerusalem): 'The Assyrian came down like the wolf on the fold / And his cohorts were gleaming in purple and gold.'

According to Jonah, in the Bible, its capitals would surely be punished by God for their wickedness, while the prophet Nahum looked on and cried: 'Woe to the city of blood, the city of lies, full of plunder . . . Who has not felt your endless cruelty?'

In the New Testament this thought emerged as a general moral: 'All who take the sword,' wrote Matthew, 'will perish by the sword.'

This is not an iron law. But the power residing in museums today was born in battles long ago. The largest soft-power reserves are held by nations that subjugated others.

The fourth lesson qualifies this to some extent, because the most ruthless empires (as a rule: Rome was not gentle) leave least behind them when they fall. The intrusions of Germany, Soviet Russia and Japan planted little of themselves in the lands they overran, and the Islamist Caliphate certainly destroyed much more than it created.

The final lesson is the most troubling, because the attacks on the statues of Nineveh and Nimrud, and indeed the whole awful pageant of modern Islamic terrorism, show clearly that soft power is not by definition a force for good. To the extent that soft power is a weapon, it can be used both for good and ill. And nothing could have eclipsed the marvellous cultural story that has its beginnings in the Arabic and Islamic world as successfully as the murder spree conducted by small groups in its name. To some extent it has been state-sponsored or, in indirect ways, state-financed. But on the whole it has been beyond the power of governments to restrain this demon.

To this extent terrorists are soft freelance potentates, doing as they please. And while it might seem that converting planes into bombs, indoctrinating youngsters into suicide missions or taking drills to art are the opposite of soft, these are exercises in diplomacy: publicity stunts. The men who bulldozed Nineveh would not have been feted by the world's press had they submitted think-pieces to cultural magazines. In the age of global communications, only the crudest acts could make people sit up.

The same can be said for all terrorist attacks. From 9/11 to the Madrid bombings, from Bali and Nairobi to the hail of bullets in Paris, from the trucks and cars on Westminster Bridge and Nice's Promenade des Anglais to the raids on German Christmas markets, from the murder spree at the Boston marathon to the bomb at Manchester Arena ... these are all press conferences.

And in one sense they are misrepresentative. In global terms, most victims of Islamic terrorism (as many as 90 per cent, according to some estimates) are themselves Muslim. This is in part because the majority of the attacks take place in Islamic lands; but it also indicates that killing people is not the primary aim: attracting attention is. Ever since the French Revolution, terror has been used as an instrument of intimidation – in the anarchic uproars of the 1890s it was known as 'Propaganda of the Deed'. And the fear it spreads plays havoc with the public's sense of proportion. In the UK, for example, the keenest threat appears to come from Islamic extremism, yet of the ten worst terrorist attacks since 1970, only four have been from this quarter – the rest were all Irish. And they are not such an ever-present danger as the headlines make them seem. Since 2006, six Britons per year (on average) have been murdered by Islamic terrorists, a dreadful yet small number. A UK citizen is eight times more likely to be struck by lightning than to be the victim of such assaults.

The willingness of the world's media to attend these press conferences is a crucial element in this drama. Swarming to the scene of the crime as if it were an inexplicable incident, rather than an event staged for its own consumption, the media can be relied on to play their part in the tragic cycle. It is hard to envisage a way of restraining this – bad news is a valuable commodity, and suppressing news does not come naturally to news outlets, especially when it pulses uncontrollably through social media. But terror asks a difficult question of the world's news editors, one they are not anxious to explore. If they did not attend such events, would they even happen? If there were no cameras to record the unbelievable sight of passenger jets flying into skyscrapers, would there be any reason for them to do so?

Terrorism's most effective ally, it has been said, is information technology. Videos on social media spread the word in milliseconds. Most people are horrified; a few cheer; all are affected. The filming of the attack on two mosques in Christchurch, New Zealand, in 2019 (which presented the murder of forty-nine people as a livecam spectacle) was an ominous sign of how fruitful the alliance had become.

Terror raises another troubling spectre, so far as government officials are concerned, by conducting this dramatic public conversation outside the usual formal channels. It seeks a response in unusual corners of society, and sometimes succeeds.

In the autumn of 2010, for instance, a Florida pastor named Terry Jones decided to provoke his own little clash of civilisations when he proposed to mark the anniversary of 9/11 by burning a copy of the Koran. The reaction was quick and inevitable. The news flashed around the globe at the speed of data, heating heads and inflaming hearts from Casablanca to Kabul. Half a dozen *fatwas* rained down on Jones's neck.

He went ahead anyway, accusing the Koran of 'crimes against humanity'. He did not seem to flinch when his stunt led to fierce reprisals (and in Afghanistan, deaths).

President Obama did his best to dampen the fire, calling it 'completely contrary to our values as Americans', but Jones responded by burning an effigy of *him* as well, before standing as a presidential candidate in the 2012 election (he didn't win).

Two years later he inspired further headlines by supporting a propaganda film called *The Innocence of Islam*. In portraying the Prophet Muhammad as a bloodthirsty sexual pervert, the film earnestly sought to provoke an outcry, and that is what it did. US embassies in Egypt, India, Libya, Pakistan, Sudan, Tunisia and Yemen were attacked; the Stars and Stripes was burned. Half a million people took to the streets in Beirut, leading staff at the embassy to shred documents in case things got out of hand.

There was even a riot in Athens. Norway, Sweden, Switzerland and scores of other countries . . . even the most ostensibly genteel nations felt the tremor of a major upheaval.

It was the kind of affray that in another era could have been fuelled only by politics – opposition to the war in Vietnam, say. But this whole tumult (which claimed over fifty lives) was sparked by a film made by a single anonymous crank in California who turned out to be a petrol pump attendant on parole for bank fraud. His name was Mark Basseley Youssef, and he was an Egyptian-born Christian. That controversial film, it turned out, did not even exist – all Youssef had done was post a spurious trailer.

By the time any of this was known, it was too late. The harm had long been done.

Superpowers learned how to guard military secrets long ago. But how are they to protect themselves in a digital realm where one loose hothead can spread so much venom? This is a new and slippery challenge. The people who took to the streets in Jakarta and Paris were very willing to take one furious evangelist and a single angry video as if this were the authentic voice of America itself. In so highly charged a climate any country reluctant to suppress its nastiest internal critics (that is, any liberal democracy) found itself being judged by its most loutish outbursts.

We should be careful not to read too much into the posturing of this or that pastor or misfit – or to suggest that people should *not* be outraged by the idea of flying planes into skyscrapers. But by ignoring military-imperialist America and attacking a merely symbolic target, the zealots of 9/11 were in fact attacking beacon-of-liberty America – and open-door America. There was much more to it than knocking over a prized asset and poking Goliath in the eye – by igniting a burst of ill-feeling against all foreigners, the plot detonated a bomb in the heart of the American dream, too.

So while the use of airliners as bombs was hard, its purpose was soft. And it worked. The land of 'Bring Me Your Poor' became the land of 'Build that Wall'.

This may be the most disquieting thing of all about terrorism: political leaders like to insist, atrocity after atrocity, that it can 'never be allowed to prevail', but in truth it is, in the short term at least, very effective. The killing sprees of angry white supremacists in America and Europe pursue much the same logic. Aside from the direct inconvenience such attacks impose – fresh layers of security at airports, closer urban surveillance and so on – the underlying motive is to manufacture fear; to create friction in distant societies and poison the atmosphere of trust between peoples.

Free news reporting has been a great liberal idea. It is not easy to accept that it may also be Western civilisation's Achilles heel.

Joseph Nye himself acknowledged this shift in 2006, conceding that soft power could be used to further bad intentions as well as good ones. 'It is not necessarily better to twist minds than to twist arms,' he wrote. 'If I want to steal your money I can threaten you with a gun, or I can swindle you with a get-rich-quick scheme in which you invest, or I can persuade you to hand over your estate as part of a spiritual journey. The third way is through soft power ... but the result is still theft.'

*

Looked at another way, the soft-power messaging of modern Islamic terrorism has backfired. In seeking to draw attention to the many wrongs done to Islam, its most significant achievement may turn out to be the damage it has done to Islam's image in the eyes of the rest of the world. Thousands of years of civilised achievement have been obscured behind the blood-tinged clouds of its modern anger.

On this front there are signs, however, that soft power's more genteel side – its staying power – has not been entirely eclipsed. The Islamist attempt to erase history by clubbing artefacts to death was vicious, but little could have put its cause in a worse light. In tearing down the infidel past, the thugs only drew attention to the glories of that past. When Donald Trump let slip, in the uproar of early 2020, that he was willing to attack Iran's cultural sites, the world reacted in horror – these were not the baubles of today's Islamic Republic, but ancient relics of world civilisation.

Moreover, today's guardians of culture are quicker to respond than once they were; it is harder to obliterate a city now than it was when Nimrud was buried by mud and neglect. It used to take years for bad news of that sort to register with the world outside. Yet only weeks after the destruction of the lamassu in Nimrud, a seventeen-year-old American, Nenous Thabit, was making clay copies of the destroyed sculptures, while in London a colourful model of the winged bull, made of 10,000 date syrup cans, was placed on the 'fourth plinth' in Trafalgar Square, in the shade of Nelson's Column, alongside the assorted Yodas and Darth Vaders that distract overseas visitors strolling along the concourse in front of the National Gallery.

There was an international project, meanwhile, to recreate the seven thousand artefacts looted from the National Museum in Baghdad (troops were quicker to protect oil depots than heritage). And in a strong soft-power initiative the British Museum (acknowledging its own special place in this story) created a programme to train Iraqi conservationists to rescue or replace the objects they have lost. According to Jonathan Tubb, Director of this Iraq Scheme, as much as 60 per cent of ancient Nineveh was wrecked by the Islamist destroyers, and 80 per cent of Nimrud – two great miracles of ancient civilisation.

However harrowing it has been ('these are people who have seen their cultural heritage disappear before their eyes'), modern museum directors are responding. As Rana Bashar Saleh, from Iraq's State Board of Antiquities and Heritage, said, all is not lost. 'When the Museum returns, Mosul will return.' In 2019 a pair of brand-new lamassu were sent to Mosul having been recreated in marble by a British and Spanish creative agency using 3-D scanners to make duplicates of the murdered originals.

An exhibition of Anglo-Saxon treasures at the British Library in London that same year featured a ninth-century gold coin bearing the name OFFA REX – a Latin term for a Welsh king – and also bearing a motto in Arabic: *Muhammad Rasul Allah.* Here was further evidence of the fact that multiculturalism was not some whim of modern social science, but a time-honoured force. The contemporary confrontation between Western interference in the world's oil states and Islam (the West repeatedly supported nationalist politicians, guaranteeing the enmity of Islamic purists) made it easy to forget that the Middle East was for centuries a nirvana of hanging gardens, palaces of scholarship hundreds of years ahead of their time, refined artists and thinkers as well as redoubtable soldiers and visionary storytellers.

12

The Gulf: Beyond Petroleum

Terrorism is not the only thing that has eclipsed the soft spell that might otherwise be radiated by the Gulf's ancient civilisations. That has also been pushed aside by a more encompassing modern force: money. In the second half of the twentieth century the region became synonymous with oil wealth so fast the world was caught off guard. And in one sense this too was attributable to soft power. Just as the walls of Jericho were felled not by siege engines but by trumpets, so the oil-dependent world was shaken not by missiles but by meetings and speeches – by words.

In the summer of 1959 the most profound convulsion of modern times began when a Venezuelan minister named Juan Pablo Perez Alfonso, who had spent a decade hiding abroad in America and Mexico, flew to Cairo to meet Sheikh Abdullah al-Tariki, the son of a camel-caravan operator and the first Oil Minister appointed by King Saud of Saudi Arabia. In the lobby of the Cairo Hilton, amid crowds of people consulting guides to the Pyramids and brochures about Nile river trips, the two men hammered out a 'gentlemen's agreement' by which they would maximise the opportunity they had been given – by geology, by God or by Allah – in the form of oil reserves.

A year later, when Alfonso was invited to fly from Caracas to Baghdad to discuss the matter further, along with counterparts from Iran, Iraq and Kuwait, he could only smile in triumph. For years he had been preaching the message that the world's oil producers should form a united front to face down Western companies and insist on a higher price for their product. Now it seemed that the day of reckoning was at hand.

It was a momentous development, but things did not change overnight. A year passed, then a decade. And then, in 1970, a few days before Christmas, Iran's Oil Minister, Shamshid Amouzegar, dropped in on the offices of the global oil authority in London and delivered a polite warning. 'In pleasant enough fashion,' reported the *New York Times*, 'he announced that the Organisation of Petroleum Exporting Countries would shortly announce demands for huge increases in tax and royalty payments. If refused, he said, the countries might shut off their oil . . .'

The world's oil companies (the so-called 'Seven Sisters') shivered. That word *huge* . . . what might it mean? The price was at this time $3.50 per barrel – and falling, thanks to the famous 'glut'. The idea of an upwards spike was worrying: what if it doubled? In a short space of time America and Europe had become entirely dependent on oil: their ships, planes, trains, cars and homes could not run without it.

Their worst fears turned out to be naively optimistic. The agreement signed on 14 February 1971 (nicknamed the St Valentine's Day Massacre by more than one commentator) recommended a tax increase amounting to some 50 cents a barrel – not an earth-shaking sum in itself. But it set a cataclysmic precedent: the business titans of America and Britain, used to regarding the oil producers as mere camel drivers from the silent sands of Araby, suddenly found themselves, quite literally, over a barrel.

From now on the price of oil would be determined not by what oil consumers were willing to pay, but by what oil producers were willing to accept. The world turned.

It was said that the new cartel was infringing the divine law of free markets. But in quite an obvious way this was an *assertion* of free-market ideas: the producers were simply exploring what price the market would bear, and it turned out to be willing to pay much more than anyone dreamed – the infringement of market principles lay in the way the price had been suppressed. Very soon it would bear almost anything.

In 1973 OPEC raised the stakes further, responding to the Yom Kippur War over Israel by placing an embargo on oil exports to Israel's most loyal supporters: America, Britain, Canada, Holland and Japan. The price quadrupled.

This was the first 'oil shock'. It coincided with a boom in consumption (as mass ownership of cars spawned out-of-town suburbs and shopping centres) and sent prices roaring. By 1974 a barrel of oil cost $12.50; after the Iranian Revolution in 1979 it tripled again – to $34. Early in 2020 it fell back to $25 after Russia and Saudi Arabia came to blows over proposals to curtail production; and the destruction of economic activity by the coronavirus then threatened to change the world's relationship with oil for ever. In normal times a fall in the oil price might have checked investment in renewable energy, but on this occasion it chimed with an unstoppable worldwide movement to reduce carbon emissions. The oil age looked ... old.

In 1974, however, the Western democracies had no answer. In theory they could have imitated OPEC: banded together, cut back and conserved. But it was impossible for democracies to demand such privations from their electorates – no one would vote for them. America did introduce a national speed limit of 55 mph, which lasted until 1995, but this and other measures made little difference: opposition parties always sided with cheap-fuel campaigns. In 1974 America tried odd-and-even rationing – licence plates ending in odd or even numbers could only refuel on alternate days of the month. One result was a truck-drivers' strike; another was that rich people bought two cars. It had little impact on fuel use, apart from creating queues at petrol stations, and giving citizens an opportunity to harangue their useless politicians on live television.

If anything it was an understatement to call it a mere 'shock'. In just three decades as much as $7 trillion was shunted from developed nations to oil producers. That was nearly $20 billion a day gushing out of America, Europe and Japan and into the coffers of the oil-rich states. George Goodman, writing as 'Adam Smith', asked: 'When else was there such a transfer of wealth? When the Spaniards brought back the gold and silver of Peru? When the British Raj ruled India?'

This was a pendulum that was swinging already. Events in Vietnam, where the world's greatest power was being defeated by a ragtag army of men in bare feet, were changing the world's perception of Western invincibility. But while this was classic financial brinkmanship, it was also, in the way it was achieved by the exchange of ideas between people from different lands, a dramatic exercise in soft power.

There were other 'soft' connections between the leading characters. All of them had studied in America. Of the pair who met in Cairo in 1960, one, Abdullah al-Tariki, studied Petroleum Engineering and Geology at the University of Texas, while the other, Perez Alfonso, fled to Washington after the 1948 military coup in Venezuela, and then sat in the Library of Congress, reading up on US oil and developing the notion of an alliance in which oil producers, not oil consumers, could set the price.

Education and migration, two of the most common drivers of soft power, converged. And the leaders of the 1970 conference in Tehran had similar backgrounds. Shamshid Amouzegar of Iran did his PhD at Cornell; Saadoun Hammadi of Iraq did *his* at the University of Wisconsin; Sheikh Yamani of Saudi Arabia, the group's suave figurehead, went to both New York University *and* Harvard Law School.

The implications were hard to grasp at first. The dizzy mountain of newly minted American dollars, now known as petrodollars, was stashed in Western banks, where it created the liquid capital markets that built the modern world. There were some more distressing consequences. The amazing surge of wealth in the oil fields, meanwhile, encouraged nations such as Iran and Iraq to purchase military machines that in time would be hurled at one another. It also helped finance the spread of Wahhabism – the strict form of Saudi Arabian Islam whose future links to *jihad* could not at that time be guessed at. It has been estimated (by the US State Department) that in the last four decades something in the region of $10 billion has been spent on the furthering of Wahhabist ideas through thousands of mosques, schools and charitable foundations.

On the surface this too is a soft-power enterprise: the spreading of ideas. But those ideas turned out to have dangerous teeth. Sometimes, soft can beget hard.

It may in time turn out that the rising oil price actually generated a reversal of fortune by motivating the West to explore alternative fuels, be they nuclear or hydroelectric, solar or wind.

Ironically, the higher the oil price was pushed, the closer the oil world came to signing its own death warrant. And when science began to measure the consequences of too much carbon in the air, the mood swung against oil again.

The important thing is that all of these commotions were born not in the barrels of guns but in the most fertile of all soft power's hothouses: the meeting of minds. It took infrastructure to create the conditions where that could happen – people needed to learn not just to travel but to aspire, not just to protest but to create. But soft moves like that, it transpired, had extremely hard consequences.

The more recent challenge in this part of the world has been how to convert the clout of hard currency into long-term prestige and allure. In this adventure – we might call it power laundering – the Gulf region is working hard to turn its new-found wealth into a durable path to future prosperity.

The most prominent poster child of this process is Qatar. At the turn of the century this tiny nation (it has a population of 2.6 million, only 300,000 of whom are Qatari-born, but an average per capita income of $136,000 per annum) was in a quandary. Precariously close to the war zone between Iraq and Iran, it had to watch the Arab Spring unsettling regimes while the planet's love affair with oil cooled. In seeking a new place in the world's affections, it used every device in the soft-power toolkit to rebrand itself not as an oil-rich desert monarchy but as a progressive modern hub.

In 1996 it hired 150 staff from the BBC's Arabic Service and set up Al-Jazeera, an innovative news channel in a region previously known for sycophantic journalism all too happy to lavish praise on whichever beloved leader held power at the time. In positioning itself as a new voice it of course earned the mistrust of Washington; but by Middle East standards it was radical and enquiring, featuring news and debates on women's rights and other sensitive topics.

This was 'convening power' – the power of hosting; it was not to be sniffed at.

Bolstered by this new profile, Qatar was able to attract prime sports events, in tennis, golf and motor racing, before targeting the world's favourite game: football. First it sponsored Barcelona and FC Roma; then it won the right to host the 2022 World Cup. There was (and still is) controversy about this – allegations surrounding the bid, grim stories about workers' rights, and, of course, the absurdly hot weather – but the bid swiftly achieved the desired effect of putting Qatar and its capital Doha on the map.

Some critics argued that all of this was speculative – the construction boom in Doha was criticised as a speculative white elephant, since there was no visible demand for it. Its sponsors replied that if it was not built, people could not come. It was a gamble.

And it was only the beginning. In 1997 Qatar launched an airline that became an important global carrier. It also built a campus – Education City – with room for the outposts of eight famous foreign universities. It built museums – it was reported that in the first decade of the twenty-first century the Qatari royal family spent over $1 billion on art. And it poured money into a sovereign wealth fund that bought stakes in famous overseas names (Canary Wharf, Harrods and Heathrow; Deutsche Bank, Porsche and Volkswagen; Gaz de France and France Telecom) and swathes of prime real estate.

The aim was not only to diversify capital and make profitable investments but to establish stake-holding connections in Europe, America and across the Arab world. Until recently it was seen by many in the region as a Western stooge, a proxy US military base content to turn its back on Islamic and Arab culture. That changed markedly in the period following the Arab Spring, when Qatar, as if to show that it had not abandoned its historic ties in the region, supported hard-line Islamist groups such as Hamas in Palestine and Hezbollah in Lebanon.[1] In one light it seemed set on becoming the Switzerland of the Gulf; in another, it appeared to be dreaming of a hard-line Islamist revival. And inevitably there were vague but persistent whispers about 'links' between financial institutions in the region and extremist politics. In a

---

[1] It has been accused (by Israel) of giving $1 billion of financial support to Hamas in the last decade.

world awash with conspiracy theories, it was impossible to quell such rumours.

As a soft-power strategy it was, therefore, a work in progress – two steps forward, one step back. But not for nothing did *The Economist* hail Qatar (in 2011) as 'a pygmy with the punch of a giant'. And the same could be said of Abu Dhabi, Bahrain, Dubai and Kuwait, all of which followed similar paths to the post-oil future – airlines, sport, tourism, education, art galleries, financial services and, in the case of Dubai and Muscat, opera houses. It was said that the building boom in Dubai made it home to a quarter of the world's cranes, and while this was not quite true (urban myths are hard to resist) the pace of development was remarkable. Lavish residences sprang up on reclaimed islands like palm trees in the waters of the Gulf, with man-made beaches of white Arabian sand; its skyscrapers contained shopping malls, aquariums, galleries, restaurant parks, indoor ski slopes, zipwires, rollercoasters and cricket domes. It even emerged that when the world convened in Dubai for the 2020 Expo it would not only be confronted with futuristic exhibits on how to turn deserts into farms, but would eat lettuce grown in vertical containers in a hangar near the airport.

The Louvre in Abu Dhabi, opened in 2017 to a worldwide fanfare in a path-breaking joint venture with France, became at a stroke the largest museum in Arabia. Some estimates put the cost in the region of $2 billion – there were few places in the world that could even contemplate an institution on this bravura scale.[2] In soft-power terms it was an interesting experiment in that (money aside) both sides stood to gain: France from having a fashionable showpiece for its artistic tradition (many of the contents, like the architecture, were French), Abu Dhabi from having so worldly a jewel with which to impress visitors. The Louvre was one component in an ambitious project to open a Maritime Museum, a Guggenheim and a National Museum as well.

All such initiatives were intended to connect the seemingly contradictory demands of ancient and modern Arabia. How

---

2 The Louvre in Abu Dhabi, it turned out, was associated with the 'mystery bidder' that paid $450 million for the newly discovered Leonardo da Vinci painting *Salvator Mundi*.

(armed with the wealth won in the tumultuous twentieth century) could the region rise to the challenges of the twenty-first, embracing the trappings of novelty without abandoning the injunctions of the ancestral past?

This was the classic soft-power quandary. What sort of national story could reconcile the competing claims of old and new, religious tradition and modern life? Across the region, people were taking up arms to defend their version of it. In Tunisia and Egypt zealots attacked holiday resorts, while in 2019 a British-Asian football fan on holiday in the UAE was arrested in Sharjah for wearing a Qatar shirt at an Asia Cup match.

In Saudi Arabia, meanwhile, fledgling attempts at progress encountered setbacks. Prince Mohammed bin Salman announced plans to modernise: the ban on women driving cars was lifted; a non-segregated cinema opened in Riyadh; women were permitted into sports stadiums; the 2020 Spanish Super Cup final between Real and Atletico Madrid (a local derby) was held at the King Abdullah Sports City in Jeddah; an extraordinary new eco-friendly city, Neom, described by officials as 'the world's most ambitious project', was taking shape on the shores of the Red Sea; and there was even a ground-breaking 3-kilometre road race for women (though the runners had to wear full-length clothes and veils even in 30 degree heat). But progress was not easy in a land of such strong traditions: the proposal to introduce twenty-four-hour shopping was halted by the religious necessity for stores to close five times a day for prayers – and it was stories like this that tended to catch the eye of foreign headline-writers.

Many such tales travelled the world's airwaves, playing on people's minds in uneven ways. And when the Saudi journalist Jamal Khashoggi was murdered in Istanbul, the national reputation took a sharp leap backwards. Foreign news outlets pooh-poohed Saudi denials, which indeed turned out to be flimsy. The war on Yemen (which had killed 10,000 people since 2015) also attracted yards of negative commentary. Western institutions in receipt of Saudi funding began to question their links with the Gulf. The world declined even to attend a high-level conference in Riyadh billed as 'Davos in the Desert'.

That is how rapidly a modernising programme can unravel

when the soft-power signals flash out the wrong message. Saudi Arabia has also been under pressure to rethink its longstanding support for Wahhabism, the 'pure' (its detractors would say distorted) brand of Islam that many held responsible for extremist ideology.

News of this sort could only put a brake on the charm offensive. It obliged the West's educational institutions to rethink some of their 'ties' (translation: funding relationships) with the Gulf. Qatari foundations alone donated more than a billion dollars to American universities between 2012 and 2018, while more than 100,000 scholarships were financed by Saudi Arabia. Nearly a quarter of the total donations to US universities in those years came from the oil states around the Persian Gulf.

Concerns over the weight of influence this might be buying led to soul-searching. Harvard ended a fellowship programme; an enquiry into the London School of Economics (whose lecture theatre was named after the founder of the United Arab Emirates) concluded that such relationships did carry 'ethical and reputational risk'.

The relative youth of the states in this region has raised other obstacles. Schools in Saudi Arabia have long taught children that they were Muslims first, Arabs second, and Saudis only third – not surprising in a nation born only in 1932. But while the collective memory of nationhood does not run deep, religious authority has historic weight. This might change: in 2018 it emerged (to the author's glee) that three million copies of Richard Dawkins's atheist sermon *The God Delusion* had been downloaded in Saudi Arabia, suggesting that the thirst for heresy may run deep. But there are no grounds for thinking that religious tradition will surrender without a fight.

Soft power can still be strong enough to overthrow monarchs. When the Ayatollah Khomeini returned from exile in France to Tehran in 1979, on a chartered Air France jumbo jet, he was landing in an imposing country. Iran (once Persia) was a fabled kingdom with the thirteenth largest GDP in the world – oil exports brought in $60 million a day. It was bigger than Britain, Italy, Germany, Greece, Holland and Switzerland combined, and thanks to its oil wealth it had the world's sixth strongest military machine. It had robust foreign currency reserves and a well-educated elite.

It was playing a leading role in world affairs, too: its OPEC negotiator, Shamshid Amouzegar, had been Prime Minister until the previous August.

The nearest thing to a weapon on the Ayatollah's plane was a nail-clipper.

This proved more than enough. Within days he had toppled the Shah.

Of course, his arrival was only the final touch of a long campaign. The Ayatollah had been preaching religious revolution for years. But it had been a war waged with ideas, not bullets; words, not dollars. A simple message, repeated until it echoed from every wall in Iran, expelled a monarch and demolished a military state.

One reason it proved irresistible is that those who might have resisted did not take it seriously. Newspaper editors listened to cassette copies of the Ayatollah's sermons, recorded by the man himself in Paris, heard him style himself 'the Supreme guide of the Islamic Nations, the Smasher of Idols, the One Who Humbles Satan, the Glorious Upholder of the Faith', and were tempted merely to laugh. Those endless ranting denunciations of 'the Jews and the Cross-worshippers' that had infiltrated Iran . . . they sounded rash and implausible – almost like satire.

Yet these were indeed the slogans of the hour. Some onlookers, inspecting it through the prism of previous revolutions, presumed that it was the voice of the downtrodden. But it did not promise a better tomorrow, only death to the Shah and his foreign pals. The only bright future, in this uprising, lay in the afterlife. As Amir Taheri, editor of a Tehran newspaper, put it: 'The Shah had tried to teach the "little people" how to live and had failed. Khomeini set out to teach them how to die, and quickly succeeded.'

The public had been 'softened up' by – of all things – a poem. It appeared in the papers in February 1979, a few days before the Ayatollah's glorious homecoming. When Shelley called poets the 'unacknowledged legislators of mankind' he may not have meant it literally, but on this occasion it was emphatically not a figure of

speech. The poem was by Taha Hejazi, and was called 'The Day
the Imam returns'.

> *The Day the Imam returns*
> *No one will tell lies any more*
> *No one will lock the door of his house;*
> *People will become brothers*
> *Sharing the bread of their joys together*
> *In justice in sincerity.*
> *There will no longer be any queues . . .*[3]

That, it needs hardly be said, is not what happened. When the
Imam did return he went to the holy city of Qom and only then
elaborated on what lay ahead: 'Islam was dead or dying for nearly
fourteen centuries; we have revived it with the blood of our
youth . . . We shall soon liberate Jerusalem and pray there.'

For many Iranians this was an ecstatic moment of national sal-
vation. It might mean death – holy war and martyrdom – but in
the euphoria that seemed a small price to pay. Other things conspired to help the message hit home. Liberals sat on their hands in
the hope that since the Ayatollah was the enemy of *their* enemy,
the Shah, he could not be opposed. Student leaders mistook the
Ayatollah's raging rhetoric for the cry of the left-behind. They
had read their Chomsky and seen photographs of the Shah skiing
in gold-plated Swiss resorts, close to his bulging private bank
accounts. They did not imagine that in overthrowing one tyranny
they might only be welcoming another.

And how dangerous could it be? In the end, how many divisions had the Ayatollah?

For soft power it was a historic triumph in that it not only
toppled a tyrant but stirred a global revolution. The impact
was felt at once in Saudi Arabia when, only months after the
Iranian Revolution, insurgents stormed the Grand Mosque in
Mecca. Fearing a Tehran-style uprising, Saudi Arabia reversed its

---

3 Quoted in *Defying the Iranian Revolution: From a Minister to the Shah to a Leader of
Revolution* by Manouchehr Ganji (Praeger, 2002). The author recalls reading the lines
('by until then an unknown poet') in the newspaper on the morning he left Tehran for
good, and saving them as a keepsake that expressed the national mood.

dalliance with modern ways (it had recently permitted television and was contemplating schools for girls) and nailed its colours to a more conservative model.

There were wider implications. Since the end of the Second World War American policy in the Gulf had been straightforward: it provided a military umbrella for regimes willing to keep the supply of cheap oil flowing. Now, one year of violent discontent, nudged into life by centuries-old religious traditions, Iran ripped up this pact.

It had reached the point where it could ignore subservient arrangements of this sort and go it alone. The message was clear: other oil-rich nations could do the same.

The 1979 Revolution did grievous harm to Iran's soft power in the West, changing it (in the tabloid mind) into an unholy land of mad mullahs and hostage crises. One of the world's great civilisations now seemed to be nothing more than a violent mob. Its glories were as nothing beside the news that it was sending children out into the sands of the Iran-Iraq war as human minesweepers, or that it had introduced public stoning and other crude punishments for offences against religious authority (seventy-five lashes for not wearing the full veil). Its international overtures were not very winning, either. In 1989 it launched the famous *fatwa* against Salman Rushdie for taking the Prophet's name in vain in a novel, while honouring the bomber who killed himself in west London attempting to carry out the death threat – he was given a martyr's memorial in Tehran.

This was not the first such time Iran had damaged its own soft-power arsenal. In 1935, as Europe began the slide towards war, the kingdom of Persia changed its name to Iran. The Persian ambassador in Germany had been inspired by the new ideology of racial purity to press for the change. 'Iran' dated back to the Parthians and was in theory a way to celebrate both its independence and its Aryan national pride.

It was understandable in another way. The Anglo-Persian Oil Company was a brash symbol of Western exploitation (indeed it was to polish its image that in 1954 the company changed its name to BP). As a rebranding exercise, however, the national name change was a failure. More was lost than was gained. People did not stop talking about Persian rugs, Persian literature (Omar Khayyam), Persian cats and the Persian Gulf, while the place itself seemed almost to vanish in a sandstorm.

It may have helped to soothe the sting of recent subjugation. But it was risky to sever the national connection with the civilisation that rattled the gates of Troy, raised the towers of Persepolis and propelled Parsis into India, the empire that starred in the founding epics of Greece and Europe and raised the arches of Isfahan. And it obscured the religious debt the West owed to Persian civilisation. The spiritual leader of ancient Persia, Zoroaster (no one knows exactly when he lived, but it was the sixth or seventh century BC), can claim to have been the creator of the monotheistic concept that supported the subsequent faiths of Judaism, Christianity and Islam. It also developed the related concepts of heaven and hell, good and evil, angels and demons (feeding, in due course, the dark-side cosmology of *Star Wars*). It gave the world both the idea and the word for one of its more important ideas: *paradise*.

Zoroaster appeared in Europe as Sarastro, the master magician in Mozart's *The Magic Flute*, and then as Nietzsche's Zarathustra. He was also ever-present in the orchestral work of the conductor Zubin Mehta and the stage performances of the rock star Farrokh Bulsara (aka Freddie Mercury), a proud Zoroastrian who liked to refer to himself as 'a Persian popinjay'.[4]

In erasing some of these cultural footprints, and their soft-power implications, the name-change may even have diluted the nation's own resistance when religious dictatorship arrived. Tampering with the past can be a dangerous game.

Something similar could be said about Egypt. One of the world's great civilisations, ancient Egypt, fell out of sight behind a succession of military coups and Islamic political gestures. It was not a coincidence that the popular upheaval in Cairo's Tahrir Square took place only yards from the National Museum, one of the capitals of this ancient world – but most of its collection was in storage, awaiting the opening of a superb new 'Grand Egyptian

---

4 Born in Zanzibar and educated at a boarding school near Bombay, Freddie Mercury later seemed more or less a typical Londoner.

Museum' next to the Pyramids of Giza. Tutankhamun exhibitions could still amaze the world (the original 1970s tour was seen by more than ten million; and in 2019 there was a second round-the-world tour), but for the most part it was no longer easy to see Egypt as a nation of profound artists and scholars, thinkers and writers. The face of the footballer Mo Salah appeared on so many billboards that he sometimes seemed to be the only figure that could unite the nation.

Sometimes, when it comes to soft power, you can lose more than you win. This matters even in geopolitics, where the ability to deliver actual power may matter less than the general perception that it is there.

There were other surprising soft-power stories. In 1998, for example, a Turkish-made crime drama, *Deli Yürek*, became an unexpected hit in the international market. It proved popular enough in the Balkans to give a brisk lift to Turkey's popularity in the region – and also to give a palpable nudge to its tourist numbers.

It was the first in a wave of such products. *Binbir Gece*, a modern love story with allusions to *One Thousand and One Nights,* was a hit in eighty countries (most of the former Ottoman lands, including Greece), while the slightly saucy final episode of *Gumus* (*Silver*) was watched by eighty-five million viewers, thanks in part to a *fatwa* issued by the Grand Mufti against any channels ungodly enough to screen it, which enticed millions of new eyeballs to find a way of watching it.

No one could have predicted it, but these stories were perfectly pitched. They were popular in the Arabian peninsula because they were, by the strict religious standards in those lands, somewhat risqué – characters might observe Ramadan, but they also drank alcohol, were sexually daring and rarely (if they were women) wore the veil – they were A-list beauty queens, after all. More distant audiences enjoyed them for the opposite reason: compared to salacious American shows they were sedate – ideal for houses with three generations under one roof. African and South American audiences could identify with epic stories of family honour and broken hearts, rural traditions and city lifestyles.

They were not so easy with gender-war identity crises set in the high-rise metropolises of the West.

Chilean parents began to call their newborn children Ibrahim, Nilufer and Sherazad. One saga about the sixteenth-century Sultan Suleiman the Magnificent struck (like *The Crown*) chords everywhere, attracting a global audience of over 250 million.

Suddenly, Turkey was the second-biggest producer of international television shows after America – indeed Netflix climbed aboard the bandwagon by making its own eighteen-part Turkish drama, *The Protector*, about a shopkeeper who must avenge his father's murder and save the city he loves (Istanbul). The soft-power effects were striking: a boom in Turkish language learning, music, food and other aspects of Turkish culture. In the Arab world the episodes (often up to two hours long) were a revelation.

It didn't take long for the productions to beam more focused messages. The 2018 series *Resurrection: Ertugrul* was specifically a birth-of-the-nation parable, a *Game of Thrones* style adventure about the origins of the Ottoman Empire. As President Erdoğan himself pointed out, it was time that Turkey became the author of its own national myth, not a walk-on character in someone else's story. 'Until the lions start writing their own stories,' he said, 'their hunters will always be the heroes.'

It would be hard to improve on this as a soft-power motto. But Turkey was sending out contrasting messages as well. In the crackdown following the failed military coup of 2016, more than 100,000 public-sector workers – soldiers, judges, academics, police officers, lawyers and teachers – were sacked; some 50,000 were in prison pending trial, accused of having supported a banned Islamic cleric exiled in America.

Government purges of this sort do little to enhance a nation's 'power of attraction'. In the summer of 2017 President Erdoğan denied that Turkey was in the business of imprisoning journalists, telling a visiting BBC interviewer, Zeinab Badawi: 'Just two actual journalists are in jail right now.' But a year later Turkey was again named – for the third year running – the world's most energetic detainer of reporters. The fact that no one was able to offer accurate numbers – some agencies said sixty-eight were imprisoned, others 242 – somehow made the picture still murkier.

In the last decades of the twentieth century Turkey had manoeuvred itself into a powerful position as a West-facing Islamic nation poised, thanks to its geographical location, cultural history and political outlook (a democratic, secular Muslim state), to become a regional superpower – a key American ally and, perhaps one day, a member of the European Union. Since the Arab Spring, however, it pivoted to a different, national-populist stance in a way that undid most of the soft-power proceeds deriving from its earlier identity.

This allows us, perhaps, to formulate something like a political calculus of soft power. In the case of governments concerned with the sending of messages rather than the enhancing of communications, it is mere public relations or propaganda. Only when nations have space to breathe can their true nature be seen by others.

This is the path on which modern Turkey is embarked. The speed with which it took military action against the Kurds in northern Syria, following the withdrawal of American forces in the area, completed the picture. Thanks to its deal with the EU over refugees, Turkey was looking after some four million displaced people in a huge and mostly well-organised refugee system; and this would usually have been more than enough to guarantee it a high place in the world's affections. That has been all but forgotten thanks to the more vivid image of Turkey as a repressive autocracy.

It is important to note that in the Islamic world Turkey's embrace of a more traditional religious culture has been heartily welcomed by those who previously tended to see it as a Western lackey. And when, in 2015, Turkey announced that it would build a grand new mosque (the largest in the Balkans) in Tirana, the capital of Albania, it was proposing itself as a leader of the international Islamic world. In 2018 Erdoğan himself visited Cologne to open a new mosque there – a further signal of its international ambitions. Its cultural mission, the Diyanet, was providing Korans and training Imams in more than forty countries. It was whispered that Turkey was aspiring to join or even replace Iran and Saudi Arabia as the chief patron of global Islam.

Most depictions of soft power did not imagine it as religious, even though most of its secular, humanitarian values had derived from Christian heritage. Turkey, like all the actors in the Middle East, was reminding the world that this was an oversight.

The extent to which government policy can drown out a country's natural soft power can be seen even more starkly in the case of Israel – perhaps the most anomalous soft power of all. It demonstrates the folly of imagining that religion might in soft-power terms be a spent force: as a Jewish state surrounded by Islamic neighbours committed to its destruction, it has long provided evidence that the reverse is true. But it suggests something else as well: how easily soft power can be driven underground.

According to the population tables Israel is the hundredth largest nation in the world. That it generates as many international headlines as most of the rest combined would in some circumstances be considered a publicity triumph. But not many of those headlines are positive. It used to be said that all publicity was good publicity; in international relations, that might not be true.

As a result, Israeli soft power is a latent, underground force.

In theory it ought to be colossal. It occupies an extraordinary physical place in the world – the Holy Land, seed bed of three great faiths and hundreds of sacred sites. It also occupies a unique place in the world's imagination, as the homeland of a people whose history seems to capture the pride and anguish of the whole world.

And there is much more to that history than the Holocaust. As Norman Lebrecht (most recently) and others have shown, Jewishness has played a decisive part in – to mention only the most obvious things – American cinema, theatre and song, critical theory, the Pill and other drugs (LSD, the cure for syphilis), philosophy (Marxism), psychoanalysis, classical music, banking, science (not least the theory of relativity), comedy, law, literature, humanitarian relief and almost every other field of human endeavour. In the years following its emergence it was a beacon of egalitarian zeal: its wholesome kibbutz culture made collective farming seem young and inspiring. And thanks to Yotam Ottolenghi and others its cuisine is widely adored.

It represents both intelligence and industry, turning the

region's only sliver of land without oil into its most advanced economy – according to Ed Husain in *The House of Islam*, while the Arab world registered only a few hundred commercial patents in the United States in the years 1980–2000, Israel posted more than 7000.

All of that has been submerged by the harsher associations connected to the lethal treatment of Palestinians in the West Bank and Gaza. In this light Israel is seen more as an aggressor than as a victim. Indeed, it may be in part thanks to this that the Holocaust is losing its place as history's most horrifying parable of good and evil. Modern egalitarians and idealists prefer to dwell on the slave trade as the ultimate byword of human cruelty. There is not exactly a soft-power tussle in history departments over the gradations of horror in these cases; but there are signs that the latter is slowly supplanting the former as the emblem of evil.

Just as international terrorism has done untold damage to the image of the Islamic world, so Israel's rough-edged occupation of new lands has extinguished what once – and not long ago – was the shocked sympathy of the whole world. Today, not many of those who go on protest marches against Zionist 'aggression' even know how many Palestinian rockets are fired at Israel each day (sixty, in busy periods) – though this is an intrusion few nations on earth could accept without some form of retaliation.

Of course, this is partly because those rockets are so ineffective. Since the year 2000 (according to Israeli numbers) some 7500 civilians have died in this turbulence – and the great majority of them – 6371 – were Palestinian. Over 1300 were *children* – more than the total number of Israeli fatalities in this unhappy period.

No one can pretend that this is an even fight.

The soft-power outcome is unavoidable. The world weeps for Palestine, not Israel.

It knows this. In 2005 it launched a 'Brand Israel' campaign to buff up its image abroad, and lavish advertisements for tourist resorts became a common sight. There are energetic attempts around the world (such as the prominent new memorial planned in the heart of London) to prevent the Holocaust from fading in the memory.

Still, despite all this, and its prowess in food, medical

technology, ancient culture and other fields, Israel performs poorly in the Portland Soft Power ranking (it came twenty-sixth on one occasion, and in 2019 was not in the top thirty at all). Israel itself has often seemed scornful of the concept. In 2017 its Defence Minister, Avigdor Lieberman, told the Munich Security Conference that soft power was itself 'a lack of political determination', and indeed responsible for the problems of the Middle East.

In one respect the soft power deriving from Israel's history has been decisive: the enormity of its anguish continues to command the unswerving backing of the United States. The planting of the new US embassy in Jerusalem in 2017 sent a strong (some said provocative) signal that this was not in doubt, and while the Secretary of State, Rex Tillerson, was at pains to say that it was not a comment on Jerusalem's future status, it was a clear enough expression of American support to be condemned by fourteen out of fifteen members of the UN Security Council (the fifteenth being the USA itself).

It may be unwise to draw a general moral from this unique soft-power predicament. But two contradictory conclusions do tentatively suggest themselves.

One is that Israel's indifference to world opinion suggests that contrary to what soft power's apostles say, it is a minor force when it comes to urgent affairs of national security and statehood. Would Israel swap its hard advantage over the Palestinians – its military and financial superiority – for a friendlier image? Patently not.

The second conclusion, however, confirms that governments do have more power to deploy soft power than they think. In this case, nothing matters more when it comes to Israel's international image than its uncompromising approach to Palestinians both at home and over the border. In normal conditions it could bask in the sympathy of the world, which would be greedy to buy its products, read its authors, stay in its hotels, attend its universities and study its history.

In fact (whatever the rights and wrongs), the opposite is the case. In seeking to show that soft power does not matter, Israel only proves how much it does.

13

Russia: Hard Lessons

When the Berlin Wall fell in 1989 the Western powers could not resist celebrating. 'Socialism has lost, capitalism has won,' wrote the economist Robert Heilbroner in the *New Yorker*, and it did indeed seem that the 'Washington Consensus' now ruled the roost. And with the Cold War won, it felt safe to assume that little more needed doing. In due course, went the song, Russia would become a quasi-European nation, buying German cars, sipping French wine, nibbling Swiss chocolate and taking its holidays in Florence, Rome, the Greek islands and the French Riviera.

A handful of cautious voices tried to break through the sound of popping corks. But few paid attention when, for instance, the discredited ex-President Richard Nixon declared, in 1995: 'The Russians did not lose the Cold War. The Communists did ... We should treat Russia today not as a defeated enemy but as an ally and a friend.'

He went on to warn that if the West failed to rise to the occasion, as seemed likely, then Russia might fall prey to 'a more authoritarian, aggressive nationalism'.

That is more or less what happened. America at that time was content to bail out Argentina or Mexico, but the idea of subsidising Moscow still stuck in the craw. In the absence of a Marshall-style plan to bring the 'defeated enemy' into the fold, Russia sank into disarray. The crash of 1998 saw its currency collapse (the rouble plunged from 6 to the dollar to 21) and after failing to implement the usual IMF policy recommendations (tighten your belt, reform the public sector, pay your debts and wait for things to come round), it chose instead to default on its international debts.

The impact on politics and economics was drastic: it spelt the end for Boris Yeltsin and ushered in the age of Vladimir Putin. But the emotional shock was even greater. Britain had not enjoyed losing an empire and seeing its once-gilded place on the world stage so tarnished – and neither did Russia. A few years earlier it had been one of two world-straddling powers; now it struggled to win bronze at the Olympics.

As the old saying goes: when you win you have a party; when you lose you have a meeting. Russia had a meeting. And soft power was a central part of its revival plan.

The plan had several different strands: the hosting of international sports events, the development of modern media outlets, the exploitation of digital technology and the promotion of Russian history through education and pride in Russia. This last was the riskiest, since it required a top-down approach to storytelling that did not always sit well with intellectual movements. But in general it was the standard soft-power menu.

The first element of the charm offensive was the easiest. Sport helped put Russia back on the world map in 2013, with the World Student Games. The following year the Winter Olympics were held in Sochi; the 2016 ice hockey World Championship took place in Moscow and St Petersburg, and the Russian Grand Prix began to wind through the Olympic park in Sochi. Two years after that, Russia invited the world's football community to gather in its cities for the big one: the 2018 World Cup.

The cumulative effect was substantial. Putin demanded that the country focus on 'how we can derive the maximum benefit for Russia's image'; and made a personal show of supporting Russia's bids. In the event, the unflattering stories broadcast in advance of these various games – to do with human rights, LGBT politics, corruption and chemical doping – were washed away by the deluge of positive noise flowing from the stadiums. Preparations for the World Cup cost more than $11 billion – there were seven new stadiums, dozens of smart hotels and upgraded transport facilities (all proof that soft power was not cheap). But the tournament was a success. The policing was tactful, the atmosphere friendly. Visiting fans (over half a million of them, mostly visiting Russia for the first time) were surprised and impressed, and went home with a changed view of the host country. After dire warnings from their own media, they were amazed to find free train travel, cheerful kickabouts, designer rooms and well-stocked bars. It was nothing like the grim Cold War experience they had been led to expect – a dour realm of unsmiling officials, bugged phones and toxic nerve agents.

When Russia beat Egypt 3–1 in the opening game it sparked a burst of joy in the home audience too. 'Russia,' they sang, 'is once more a player on the world stage.' The head of FIFA, Gianni Infantino, declared as much when he said that Russia was 'an incredibly, incredibly rich country, in terms of culture, in terms of history. And we have discovered it. The world has discovered it.'

This may have been a slight overstatement, but it was true that in recent times the grandeur of Russia's marvellous past had been occluded. Not any more.

The next branch of Russia's soft-power strategy was cultural. At the cold height of its power, the Soviet Union was still, unmistakably, the land of Tolstoy, Dostoevsky, Pushkin, Chekhov, Tchaikovsky, Rachmaninov, Stravinsky and the rest. The fact that its own most admired cultural figures tended to be political dissidents – Pasternak, Solzhenitsyn, Sakharov, Nureyev – was inconvenient. But Moscow was synonymous with gravitas and depth. It was a space power, a nuclear power, a military power, and (thanks to strong state support) a world leader in chess and athletics. It was an artistic, musical and literary giant; and over all that flew the red flag of communist revolution. Even those who hated everything about that violent eruption, and the terrors it led to, could not help being swayed by the idealism and grandeur it suggested. Russia was a place of vast distances, intense suffering and the sublime scent of tragic history.

This image faded after the collapse of the Soviet Union and the rise of its new oligarchs. Russia became the Wild East, a lawless zone of violent and criminal gangs.

In seeking to restore national prestige – in short, to make Russia great again – this cultural hinterland became an asset Putin was eager to recover. In 2017 Red Square gained a spectacular (and expensive) new landscaped garden, Zaryadye Park, a green layout of walks, bridges, open-air theatres and galleries by the river; not far away, the Gulag History Museum (launched in 2015) was a sobering display of Stalin-era horror stories – the whole agonised nightmare of Ivan Denisovich and *Cancer Ward* brought expertly to life. If the park softened the memories of all those prisoners who had been dragged towards the nearby Lubyanka prison, to be tortured by secret police before being shunted to labour camps, the museum did the exact opposite.[1]

In 2018 Putin unveiled a new sculpture of Turgenev in Moscow, commissioned to mark the great writer's two hundredth birthday, and said: 'It is impossible to imagine Russian classical literature without him.' He applauded the fact (once used to damn Turgenev) that the novelist had spent so large a part of his life in Paris and Baden-Baden. Now he could be celebrated as a proud Russian who had never for a moment ceased to espouse the 'true eternal values' of his homeland.

The idea was to reach back into the treasure chest of pre-Soviet Russia, not only for its grandeur but also for its glamour – for the old St Petersburg that glistened in the frost, fabulous in fur and Fabergé, or the Moscow of caviar, champagne and chandeliers. The new Russia, like the old, was a dreamland of galleries and concert halls, sparkling shots of vodka and towering domes looming through falling snow.

Putin's associates followed his lead. Russian philanthropists made eye-watering donations to American projects like Carnegie Hall, the Guggenheim and the Lincoln Center, while also buying art galleries, newspapers and football clubs in Britain.

Russia was expanding in these areas just when the world's leading soft powers were winding down. When Syria's army, with Russia's help, liberated the Roman ruins of Palmyra, the orchestra of St Petersburg's Mariinsky Theatre, under the baton of Valery Gergiev (ex-leader of the London Symphony Orchestra, and conductor of Russia's national anthem at the Winter Olympics closing ceremony), staged a resounding performance of Bach, Prokofiev

---

1 Originally the offices of a Russian insurance company, the Lubyanka was said, at the height or depth of its fame, to be the tallest building in Russia, on the grounds that you could see Siberia (i.e. the Gulag) from its cellars.

and others in the very theatre where ISIS had until recently been shooting hostages in the head. Putin himself appeared in a live televised link to celebrate this Russian-led victory over terrorism.

Russia was striding to the future in the glittering uniform of its classical past.

The third element in the plan was the development of new media enterprises, to take Russia's voice across the world. The most important of these was Russia Today, a state-funded twenty-four-hour news operation launched in 2005 to compete with the BBC, CNN, Al-Jazeera and others. Starting with 300 journalists (seventy overseas), it grew into a major television platform, telling world news from an unorthodox and patriotic angle (lavishing attention on the concert in Palmyra, for instance).

Westerners decried it as an instrument of obvious propaganda – 'fake news' – and it did enjoy finding space for scandals in foreign democracies. Senior roles were found for critics of Western policy such as Julian Assange, Nigel Farage, George Galloway and Alex Salmond.[2] And there was little attempt to hide the fact that its entire *raison d'être* was, as Putin put it in 2013, 'to break the Anglo-Saxon monopoly on information streams'. But its strength lay in the organised way it meshed with the fourth arrow of Russia's soft-power strategy: information technology. RT stories were pushed into the social media labyrinth with energy and determination – so much so that RT's own YouTube channel was the first news outlet to reach a billion viewers.

This was the controversial arena in which Russia soon stood accused of international meddling. A 2019 US Congressional Report found that 150,000 Russian Twitter accounts had actively engaged with Brexit, with Donald Trump, and with politics in France and Germany too. After the Brexit referendum it was reported that over 250 anti-EU stories on Russia Today and Sputnik (a radio platform for 'alternative' news founded in 2014) had been 'shared', on an industrial scale, on Twitter and Facebook.

---

2 Alex Salmond's presence on Russia Today was, according to his opponent Ruth Davidson, 'a shameful stain on his reputation'. The station's claim that Britain was guilty of 'Russophobia' was a transparent 'attempt to poison our public discourse'.

Russia, it maintained, had been 'working to undermine democracy' for two decades.

The stories were legion. This was news calculated neither to entertain nor to inform, but to sow discontent. One day the story might be that US mercenaries were secretly stoking violence in the Ukraine; the next it would highlight an academic-sounding report that the West had toppled Soviet Russia primarily to steal its natural resources.

Its annual list of 'Russophobes' became a badge of honour for those included. In 2019 the list included Theresa May's Conservatives (for claiming that the attack on the Skripals in Salisbury was Russian-led); Rachel Maddow, an MSNBC host; the British historian Anne Applebaum; *The Times* foreign-affairs writer Ed Lucas; Hillary Clinton (of course); *The Daily Beast*, a peppery online news publication (owned by *Newsweek* and launched by Tina Brown), which delivered 'rabid Russophobia posing as journalism'; Bill Browder (the outspoken financier); Michael McFaul (a former US ambassador); and the European Union (for suggesting an utterly spurious equivalence between Hitler and Stalin as comparable death-dealing totalitarians).

Even Justin Trudeau earned a spot – for expressing sympathy with Crimea.

It was, in quite a literal sense, a media war. And one side was fighting rather more enthusiastically than the other. As investment (and confidence) in the BBC dwindled – not least because stories about its failures were given such wide circulation by its rivals on the home front as well as by these shadowy foreign opponents – Peter Horrocks, a former director of the BBC World Service, warned: 'We are being financially outgunned.' As if to prove the point, in the following year the budget of the new radio station Rossiya Segodnya (Voice of Russia) was boosted by 250 per cent.

Horrocks was not advocating that one-sided stories from Russia be countered with equally one-eyed falsehoods. He was placing his faith in an older weapon: the truth.

So far as Russia was concerned this was an all too familiar pattern. No other country was so synonymous with the booming traffic in fake news. The busy disinformation campaign against Hillary Clinton in 2016 and the poison-tipped 'news' that soured

Britain's EU referendum were only the loudest eruptions. A media that preferred clicks to accuracy led to the industrial-scale production of sensational 'news'. Much of it was being manufactured robotically in large-scale 'bot farms', before being spread by Russian-based 'web brigades', set up specifically to spin unsettling stories.

The world began to pay close attention when Russian media made a concerted effort to spread the idea that the 2014 uprising in Ukraine had been part of a NATO plot to destabilise Russia by promoting a closer relationship between Ukraine and Europe. Like all the best tall stories, there was an element of truth here – in the soft-power world, everyone was trying to bring new members into their own sphere of influence. But one investigation found that more than 20,000 Twitter accounts were being used to recycle shock-horror claims along these lines.

Similarly, when the Malaysian passenger plane (MH17) was shot down in July that same year, killing 298 people en route to Kuala Lumpur, Russia's officials and media blamed the attack squarely on *Ukrainian* rebels, until a Dutch investigation found that the plane had been hit by a Russian weapon, launched by a Russian-backed unit.

Russian television, meanwhile, was claiming, among other horrors, that a Ukrainian soldier had crucified a three-year-old boy in front of his own mother.

This was something new – fibs refashioned as weapons. And it didn't matter how unlikely the stories were; the more outlandish the better. Nor was there any need for a precise target: the aim was to spread the virus of alarm to areas where it could evolve on its own. Following the 2017 terrorist attack in central London, for instance, one widely seen image showed a Muslim woman in a veil chatting on her phone as she strolled past the injured victims on Westminster Bridge. Though inconclusive (the woman might have been ringing an ambulance) it was open to the interpretation that Muslims were at best indifferent and at worst cold-hearted. The picture was seized upon by 'troll armies' a thousand miles away and poured across social media.

The Baltic states, finding themselves on the front line of this new threat, struggled to make their anxieties heard by other

European leaders. 'It took time,' said Lithuania's Foreign Minister, 'to convince them that lies are not freedom of speech.' There was a genuine conundrum in this: how could state intervention in the free movement of data be an appropriate way to counter . . . state intervention in the free movement of data?

Russia was driving the world into uncharted waters, and the West's media was a ripe and easy target, ever willing to give sensational news a place in its running order. It took time, for instance, for authorities in Germany to expose as false a 2016 story that a thirteen-year-old girl called 'Lisa' had been raped by immigrants, not least because of their need to tread with sensitivity in a case involving someone so young.

This notoriously false story (it turned out that Lisa had been with a friend on the night she was supposed to have gone 'missing', though she *had* initially claimed to have been abducted and raped) was eagerly publicised by Russia Today's German channel (a channel that made a point of covering anti-Islamic marches in Germany live, no matter how sparsely attended) and was fanned into headlines by Germany's angrier political tribes. Russia's Foreign Minister made two statements expressing anxiety about the failures of German policing, accusing them of sweeping the incident under the carpet out of feeble-spirited political correctness, before the truth emerged.

Some of the fake news was oblique: articles on the dangers of genetically modified food (linking it to autism) or on the futility of the MMR vaccine. But some was well aimed. In the case of Britain's EU referendum, voters whose data trail showed that they cared about migration received stories about the way EU membership threatened their borders; those who cared about fishing were sent tales of evil EU trawler fleets plundering their stocks; those anxious about animal rights were force-fed images of donkeys and dogs being mistreated in barbaric European lands.

One investigation (by the communications firm 89up) found that Russian television and radio featured 260 anti-European articles in the months leading up to Britain's referendum, which were then sent raging through social media like a brush fire.

Some of the messages were pumped out under alluring false identities – surfer girls or supermodels known as 'bikini trolls' – on the crude but safe assumption that such images improved the chances of the stories being clicked on. These scantily clad opinion formers engaged with a wide range of fashionable protest causes, not all of them coherently linked: they wanted to catch audiences interested in subjects such as genetically modified food, the gender pay gap and human rights, before slipping in a word about the wickedness of sanctions against Syria or American meddling in the Middle East. They were strongly against fracking on environmental grounds – no need to mention that fracking was an irritating rival to Russia's gas industry.

The fact that Hillary Clinton was outspoken on this subject – as far back as 2011 she was saying, 'We are engaged in an information war, and we are losing that war' – was one of the reasons she herself was subject to so many demeaning inventions. Britain's Theresa May risked a similar reaction when she said, in 2017, that Russia was using 'state-run media organisations to plant fake stories and Photoshopped images in an attempt to sow discord in the West and undermine our institutions'. The head of Russia's state-owned international news agency, Dmitry Kiselev, responded by telling the audience of his television show that May herself was behind the murder of the Skripals in Salisbury, to distract attention from her hapless Brexit negotiations.

There was more to this than the crafty use of news to influence public opinion. The larger aim was to make voters distrust their own political and media landscape. Even when individual stories were discredited, public faith in the principle of truthful news was destabilised – especially when Trump and others began to use the term 'fake news' to refer not to fabrications but to any mainstream criticism of themselves.

Suddenly, *all* news could be dismissed as 'fake' on the grounds that, well, who could tell any more? One of the major achievements of Western civilisation, centuries in the making – a reliable and free-thinking press – was being rapidly undermined.

All of this has been entertainingly documented by authors such as Misha Glenny (in *McMafia*), Edward Lucas (*The New Cold War*) and Peter Pomerantsev (*This is Not Propaganda*); and by documentaries such as *The World According to Vladimir Putin*, which showed Russian media soberly telling the world how British

children were being given detailed instructions on how to be
gay. In exposing the extent of these ploys, Pomerantsev visited
the famous 'Internet Research Agency' in St Petersburg, was
astounded by its scale (a thousand employees making up stories
as if on an ordinary news desk) and by the brazenness of the tactics involved. Truthful statements were muddled with neo-Nazi
claims to imply that they were equally valid; television reports
suggesting that Ukrainian troops were shelling their own people
led some to believe that their houses had been destroyed by
friends, not enemies; seemingly even-handed campaigns urging
Americans to register their despair by not voting (often with a
joke or a cartoon) were sent to only one half of the electorate.

One employee from a bot farm was quoted in the *Washington
Post* as saying: 'You have to write that white is black and black is
white.' There was, warned Pomerantsev, a 'digital Maginot Line'
in cyberspace. In 2018 Twitter released more than nine million
politically motivated tweets that had begun life in Russian troll
farms. Suspicions were aroused when it was noticed that, far from
being spontaneous comments on the passing parade of news, the
senders of these tweets observed office hours.

It was not quite like the Le Carré era – when *Pravda* and the
KGB pumped out Cold War propaganda by the hundredweight –
though it did draw on that tradition. The point was not to tell lies
but to muddy the waters until *nothing* was quite credible.

It was not an information war, said Pomerantsev, but 'a war on
information'.

In the Cold War the Kremlin's main focus was on its own
citizens. It did attempt to shape world opinion by financing communist parties overseas, youth programmes, writers' unions and
sympathetic publications (Moscow would buy 10,000 copies of
the *Morning Star* every day as a way of subsidising a point of view
that might not, left to the free market in ideas, have been com-
mercially viable[3]). But in the digital world it discovered a way to
agitate in foreign space from the safety of its own desk.

America   and   Britain   launched   inquiries;   Malaysia   and

---

3 The CIA did something similar, supporting the intellectual monthly *Encounter* from
1953 onwards. One early editor, the poet Stephen Spender, resigned in 1967 when the
nature of his backing became known.

Singapore made the passing of fake news a criminal offence. It was like trying to stop a wave with a bucket.

On the surface this partisan approach may not seem so different from that which drives Britain's tabloids or America's alt-right shock jocks. The fact that it is subject to state control, however, means that it is not just one strident note in an otherwise plural landscape, but a well-oiled cog of government policy. That in turn suggests that soft power simply does not mean the same thing in Moscow as it does in Washington. In 2012 Putin helpfully clarified this by announcing that soft power, as he saw it, was 'all about promoting one's interests and policies through persuasion'. This was a pointed retreat from Joseph Nye's much-repeated sense that it was, on the contrary, the art of self-advancement *without* stooping to overt persuasion.

There were other signs that Russia's understanding of soft power (and its attempt to yoke it to the national cause) had more in common with embedded KGB habits than with any modern waffle about the wonders of culture and communication. They became especially clear in the contest for Ukrainian hearts and minds in 2014, when Russia began (in the court of world opinion) to lose that particular soft-power struggle. Ukraine appeared to want to join Western Europe – there were noises that one day it might even be eligible to join both NATO and the European Union. So far as Moscow was concerned, this was too close to home: not enough time had passed for the Russian mindset to see Ukraine as an entirely independent nation. It needed to be brought back into the fold, and if tough measures were required, so be it.

On 23 December 2015 Ukraine suffered a nightmarish shock when hackers broke into the systems of three energy companies, shutting off power to 225,000 people for up to six hours. Some were watching television; others were driving home. Screens dimmed; lights failed; ice began to form on hot water pipes. People had been warning for years that modern life was too dependent on the electronic information systems on which it ran – here was the proof. One major breakdown was enough to cause chaos.

The virus was soon crawling into people's laptops, too, black-mailing nonplussed users with a demand for payment in bitcoin. Many victims had no idea how they might lay their hands on one of those – there weren't any in the jar by the kettle.

This, it seemed, was a serious and concerted cyber-intrusion. And in 2016 and 2017 it happened again. Government offices, banks and newspapers in Ukraine all crashed, this time felled by a virus called 'Petya' – the name of an evil satellite in the James Bond film *GoldenEye*. It was by now widely assumed that Russia was behind the attacks – not least since the disruptions of 2017 were timed to take place on the eve of Ukraine's Constitution Day, and one of its first casualties was the National Bank.

The James Bond allusion was no accident, either, recalling as it did the days of SMERSH and SPECTRE. This was exactly the kind of villain 007 would now be obliged to face: the age of the silver-haired ex-Nazi in expensive clothes, sipping champagne as he stroked his pet hammerhead shark, was over. Modern life was digital. The President of Ukraine, Petro Poroshenko, claimed that there had been more than six thousand such attacks. And it was an orchestrated campaign – not much less than soft war.

Intelligence services did not take long to confirm the conspiracy theory: the US and the UK pinned the blame on Moscow. The assault was estimated to have caused more than a billion dollars' worth of damage, and could have been worse, but in an ugly echo of previous disasters the control system at the new Chernobyl plant briefly failed; and companies further afield – container ports in India, chocolate factories in Australia – were hit too. A hospital in West Virginia, USA, lost its entire network.

In a series of articles for *Wired* magazine (and then a book: *Sandworm: A New Era of Cyberwar*), the American writer Andy Greenberg called it a 'digital blitzkrieg ... a sustained cyber assault unlike any the world has ever seen'. Banks and utilities in Estonia had been hacked as long ago as 2007, but the new generation of cyberstrikes were much more threatening. Water treatment plants ... electric grids ... ports ... transport systems ... dams ... elections ... The infrastructure of modern life seemed at risk. A former CIA Director, Michael Hayden, delivered a bleak warning: 'Somebody just used a new weapon, and this weapon will not be put back in the box.'

The Petya virus was followed by NotPetya, an even more destructive toxin. And a fearful new truth was unleashed on a mostly unsuspecting public. What need to invade a country when you could simply ask highly trained geeks to switch it off?

This was war, as Greenberg put it, on 'the machinery of civilisation'. And it had a distinct Russian accent. Kremlin-backed units were held to have conducted a number of advanced intrusions on foreign journalists, foreign governments and foreign media. America, Britain and the Netherlands collaborated on a major study which revealed that highly sensitive agencies had been cyberattacked: airline crash investigations, chemical weapons inspectors, defence installations, international anti-doping bodies and nuclear power plants. Jens Stoltenberg, NATO's Secretary-General, said the evidence showed 'blatant attempts to undermine international law and institutions'. When the report was released, in 2018, 128 Russian intelligence operatives were expelled, and sanctions against Moscow were stiffened.

Protestors in the Muslim republic of Ingushetia found that their WhatsApp connection – their favoured communications method – froze. Putin, meanwhile, referred to the entire internet as a 'CIA project' designed to foment unrest, blaming it not only for the Arab Spring but also for the Ukrainian uprising. There was ominous talk about suppressing seditious elements like LinkedIn and Google, and the possibility of creating a 'sovereign internet' protected from these poisonous foreign voices.

This was a war of words, not weapons. But it could hardly be called soft. Pundits began to speak about 'sharp power' – soft power with aggressive elbows. It was an apt description of public diplomacy, Russian-style. And a spectre began to haunt Europe, of a new Iron Curtain falling across its free-flowing data. The threat of this was tangible enough to provoke a protest against it in Russia itself in the spring of 2019. Thousands marched against the forthcoming 'digital sovereignty bill', an attempt – for 'security reasons' – to place the whole internet under state control.

Was such a thing possible? Not many were willing to bet against it. A 2018 report by British and Dutch governments

alleged that Russian hackers had broken into information systems
at a US nuclear company, a chemical weapons watchdog, power
suppliers, aviation firms and various government agencies. A
report by British MPs a year later estimated that 1100 cyberattacks
had been dealt with by the National Cyber Security Agency (the
body charged to make the digital economy safe).

The sense that Western democracies were vulnerable and had
been caught on the back foot at first gave fuel to the assumption
that Russia was ignorant of soft power's subtle niceties. Then a
more troubling truth began to be visible in the mist: there *was* a
soft message in this digital assault, and it was a simple one. Russia
was ... *ahead*.

That wasn't all. For those with long memories there were
uncomfortable echoes of OPEC. That jarring episode had
exposed the dependence of the developed world on oil; now that
same world was vulnerable to a similar dependence on data. Half
the world could no longer get through the day without access to
computing power – its business and social life had both migrated
to screens. Could it be happening again?

Yet in some ways Russia was indeed one step behind. In 2019
monitoring stations in Norway detected a spike in radiation
near the Arctic port of Archangel, in northern Russia. Fearing a
second Chernobyl, they sounded the alarm at once, and Sweden
was soon asking Moscow to confirm whether something had
gone wrong. Russian state media admitted that there may have
been a minor explosion at a 'small' nuclear reactor, but insisted
that radiation levels were normal and no one had been harmed.

Two days later it emerged that this was not quite right. Five
people had died. Three days after that, the village of Nyonoksa was
instructed to evacuate the area (an order cancelled the next day).
The bay on which the site stood was closed to shipping for a month,
and residents were advised to avoid eating locally farmed vegetables.

It was a hauntingly familiar pattern. There were reports – nois-
ily circulated by Donald Trump on Twitter – that the incident
involved a new horror-weapon, a nuclear-powered missile, with
the Bond name Skyfall, whose existence had been confirmed a
year earlier by Vladimir Putin himself.

Perhaps those knee-jerk comparisons with Chernobyl were not premature.

The reactor fire in 1986 had killed thousands, laid low crops and livestock across a large area, caused evacuations, and blasted radiation across Belarus. It was – and is – one of the worst nuclear accidents in history. And in the absence of free media or political transparency, the extent of the disaster was squarely denied.

The soft-power repercussions were just as negative. Chernobyl was a triple shock to the Soviet model, making the Kremlin itself look weak on the industrial, the political *and* the moral level. As evasion took precedence over the relief effort, it wasn't only radiation that leaked out of Chernobyl – it was trust in the Soviet system. It did not help the symbolism that the doomed reactor had been named after V. I. Lenin himself.

When the Berlin Wall fell three years later it was widely claimed that Chernobyl had been one of the first reverberations that led to *glasnost*, and brought it down.

Russia had changed since then. Or had it? In the weeks following the release of the TV series *Chernobyl,* the drama was criticised, inside Russia, as blatant Cold War propaganda. HBO was accused of ignoring the heroism of the emergency workers (which it did not – it dwelt on their bravery at length); the venerable newspaper *Argumenty i Fakty* called it 'a caricature and not the truth'; and the Culture Minister, though conceding that it was 'masterfully made', called for a libel action against the writer/producer.

It was true that the filmmakers had taken liberties – in tune with modern ideas about equality, they had invented a plucky female character whose only purpose (a useful one, it turned out) was to show up the mediocrity of all those Soviet middlemen.

But now there were rumours of a new Russian miniseries on the same theme, but this time with a different plot. Instead of being a study in Soviet-era corruption, the accident would be an act of crude sabotage by American secret agents sent to Russia by the CIA. The hero would not be a put-upon scientist or the care-worn wife of an irradiated fireman, but a brave Soviet operative hunting down the infiltrator.

We have argued that soft power is an exercise in national story-telling. It follows that in the post-truth world we will see more myth-peddling of this sort. It is not new, after all. America and Britain have long been making films designed to pull on patriotic heartstrings, be it the anthems sung to the righteous courage of the US Marine Corps or the insatiable bravado of James Bond.[4] Shakespeare's *Henry V* was eagerly deployed as rally-the-nation propaganda by Laurence Olivier, while Winston Churchill's friendship with Alexander Korda helped to inspire a range of tub-thumping, morale-bolstering projects about British courage and defiance. It has long been supposed that his tearjerker about Nelson and his wife, *That Hamilton Woman*, played a major part in persuading America to join the war in Europe.[5]

In this sense (as Ed Lucas argued in 2008) the Cold War never really ended.[6] But in the modern world a more subtle approach may be necessary – in soft-power circles, trying too hard can be as pointless as not trying at all.

The fourth branch of Russia's soft-power strategy concerned Russian history – that vast and harrowing saga of tsars, serfs, wars, revolutions, art, religion and terror.

In 2013 Vladimir Putin, as part of his drive to refresh Russian national pride, sighed at the state of history teaching and called for the creation of a single textbook, written in 'correct and beautiful Russian', that would give modern Russians more glorious version of their past. Michael Gove had attempted something similar in Britain, and engaged senior historians to steer the school curriculum into traditional waters – more on the Battle of Trafalgar, less on multicultural hobbyhorses – but Putin was even more

---

4 This is usually depicted as a nostalgic British fantasy. But the most appealing feature of Bond films to UK audiences was the way they depicted exotic foreign locations. They were a form of armchair travel, with popcorn on the side.

5 In the future we may see more films of this sort: Indian pictures, say, about the jaw-dropping cruelties of British troops during the Indian Mutiny (the First War of Indian Independence); or hair-raising Chinese films about Japanese atrocities in Nanking; or Polish portraits of their treacherous so-called allies in 1940; or French films on the destruction of Caen by Allied bombers; or British films about backward Saxons being routed by rather more civilised Norman conquerors. In one sense this is not so much nationalism as modernism – the telling of stories from a different point of view.

6 In *The New Cold War* (2008). The book, written before cyber intrusion was guessed at, charted the emergence of a new Russian empire that took most of its policy cues from the Soviet-era playbook. This was how he earned the enmity of Russia Today.

forthright. The country needed to unite around a single heroic story. The new book (or set of books) would deliver up the whole pageant, from the wonders of the medieval church and Peter the Great to the heroics of Lenin and the Great Patriotic War. A team of academics and officials was charged to produce it.

Quite a few eyebrows, both inside Russia and outside, were raised when it was added that the textbook should be 'free of ambiguities'. Surely the whole purpose of history was to highlight and *explore* ambiguity, not rub it out. What was being ordered here was a triumphalist, feel-good version of the past.

Two years later, in 2015, the seventieth anniversary of victory in that patriotic war was commemorated in a series of events that made those same observers uneasy, since they involved new monuments to Stalin himself. Russia's parliament passed a law saying that 'lying about history' would henceforth be a crime, and that criticising Soviet conduct in the Second World War might fall into that category. Statues of Stalin duly began to appear in a number of Russian cities – most resonantly of all, in Yalta.

Then, in 2017, one of the founding members of Putin's history textbook project, Olga Vasilyeva, a noted scholar on matters related to the Orthodox Church, was appointed Minister of Education. When one newspaper reported her as saying that this was nothing less than 'a realisation of God's will', it confirmed the suspicion (though she later retracted or qualified the phrase) that Russia was pursuing a 'back to basics' path with respect to its Stalinist past, and was content to overlook its manifest horrors – the state-sponsored famine in Ukraine, the infamous Gulag, the purges and the fearful black shadow of the KGB – in favour of seeing it as a source of national pride. In this account, Stalin and the Red Army needed to be rescued from the taint of American propaganda; they had saved not just Russia but also Europe.

Vasilyeva herself spoke about 'pride in the greatness of our country' and said that she aimed to reinstall a respect for 'our history, traditions and spiritual values'.

Soft power was not usually this top-down, but combined with all the other strands – sports events, the cultural prestige and the strong media presence in the world – it was effective. By 2017 polls were recording that as many as 25 per cent of Russians deemed

Stalin's so-called crimes to have been 'politically justified'. The new official line was that the Man of Iron had saved his people, while Gorbachev was a Western stooge. In 2020 Putin went further when he attended the seventy-fifth anniversary of the liberation of Auschwitz in Jerusalem and presented Soviet Russia as a fellow victim – his claim that 40 per cent of Holocaust deaths were Soviet would have been true only if Soviet-occupied Poland was included in the calculation, a gambit that angered Polish leaders to the extent that they boycotted what should have been a dignified occasion.

The involvement of the Church was an unmistakable sign that things had changed. The Soviet State had eliminated religion in part because it was a competitor – not only the opium of the masses but also (as Marx had famously said), the 'sigh of the oppressed creature' and an organ of bourgeois reaction – and in part (as in the English Reformation) because it was very rich. Nearly 30,000 church buildings were destroyed; some 130,000 priests were arrested. The majority were put to death; others were incarcerated as dissidents or mental defectives.

One mentions such horrors only to emphasise how radical has been the turnaround. In 2012 the Russian Patriarch had praised Putin as a messiah who had 'rectified the crooked path of history', and Putin returned the compliment by giving his blessing to nearly a thousand newly built churches a year – some 25,000 in all. In place of the hammer and sickle, here came the onion dome and the cross. And it was not only the aesthetic ceremonies of Russian Orthodoxy that returned (the candles, the incense, the golden robes), but its social ideas, too. After a century of communism, Russia was being returned both to the priesthood and to 'traditional family values'.

Putin underlined this forcefully in 2013 in a state-of-the-nation address when he hailed the importance of 'traditional values that for thousands of years have remained the basis of civilisation'. In passing he took a swipe at the 'sexless and infertile' values gaining ground in Europe. In countries with a sarcastic media this sort of talk is swiftly satirised – as it was when John Major urged Britain to go 'back to basics'. In the absence of concentrated mockery, it could sound high-minded. It took a while for people to realise that 'traditional' meant 'illiberal'.

The consequences were immediate. When the feminist punk rock project Pussy Riot performed unannounced in public places as a guerrilla tribute to progressive ideas, it was condemned as 'sacrilegious' by the Church and denounced by Putin as having 'undermined the morals of the nation'. Three of the women were convicted of 'hooliganism motivated by religious hatred', and despite keen protests (especially abroad) two spent twenty months in prison.[7] When Pussy Riot attempted to perform during the 2014 Winter Olympics they were spray painted by security guards.

There were other manifestations of this return to 'traditional values'. Homosexuality had been decriminalised in Russia only in 1993; now new laws were passed making it illegal to 'promote' it, and there were amiable-sounding seminars called things like 'Future of the Family'. Laws on domestic violence were weakened in deference to the Church's 'traditional' take on women's rights. In Georgia, it was conceded that orthodox believers had a right to be offended by LGBT relationships.

Lastly, the growing number of Russian-backed assassinations on foreign soil was making even hardened diplomats groan. Following the poisoning of the Skripals in Salisbury there were hard consequences – more than a hundred Russian diplomats were expelled by the UK and its allies – but the soft consequences were even more lasting, especially when it began to seem as though there was a pattern here. As many as thirteen deaths in the UK alone were regarded as suspicious by the authorities, the implication being that Putin's Russia was operating a planned programme of assassinations overseas, eliminating its enemies like characters in an airport thriller.

As the death toll rose, Russian protestations of innocence became ever flimsier, in a way that was extremely damaging to the national brand. It may have been in one sense a noble Russian tradition, recalling the day when Trotsky was murdered with an ice axe in Mexico in 1940, but it meant that Moscow was

---

7 Foreign stars were quick to support Pussy Riot; performers like Björk and Madonna said they would be honoured to appear alongside them. But Pussy Riot was not Band Aid: it did not do ticketed concerts in the capitalist way, but performed obscene songs in Moscow's Cathedral of Christ the Saviour. Some of their overseas fans might have quailed at the thought of doing *that* in Westminster Abbey.

increasingly being seen as an unfriendly power not just in diplomatic circles, but by the public.

The international outrage created first by Russian digital gangsterism, then by its authoritarian appeal to 'traditional values', and then by this growing body count, outweighed the gains made through sporting, cultural and media events. And the fact that it was backed by a militaristic foreign policy made it more threatening still. Its interventions in neighbouring countries – Crimea and Ukraine, but also Chechnya, Georgia, South Ossetia and President Assad's Syria ... These were risky steps. Had Russia not grasped that soft power was the art of persuasion, not bullying?

So the story ran. In Western seminar rooms it appeared that Russia was declining to play by the new rules. It scorned soft power in favour of older methods.

There could be no mistaking the extent to which classically hard imperial principles were governing Russia's military backing for Assad's otherwise friendless regime in Syria, or its support for the foundering government of Venezuela. Across Africa and Latin America it was forming alliances and granting military aid in the time-honoured way. The fact that it was hiring European lobbying firms to represent its interests and polish its image (and connections) only added to the sense that it was acting just like the Soviet Union. When it was revealed that it had loaned more than ten million Euros to France's *Front National* it was confirmation of the fact that it had failed to move with the times, and was still counting on old-school arm-twisting and bribery.

Spotting a hole in the market caused by the retreat of America from the world stage, it was simply marching into it. When Trump pulled American troops out of the Kurdish zone of northern Syria in the autumn of 2019, and Turkey at once attacked it, Putin stepped up. One moment he was shaking hands with Turkey's President Erdoğan over a new 'peace deal', effectively carving up northern Syria, the next he was welcoming forty-three African heads of state in the Sochi Olympic Village for the inaugural Russian African Congress. The air space over the Black Sea filled with private jets as African leaders flew in for a two-day summit on collaboration, most of which involved Russian support for their sovereignty in return for access to their markets. Russia's trade with the continent was growing fast (from $6 billion in 2009 to $20 billion in 2018) but was still only a fraction of the Chinese presence. And it did have history in the region: the flag of Mozambique bore a Russian-made Kalashnikov.

Guests at the Congress were impressed by Putin's stance on Syria – he was clearly ready to stand up for his friends – and also by the impact of Russia's media. 'What TASS is doing to change the narrative about its country is spectacular,' said the head of the Ghana News Agency, reminding the world that storytelling was the order of the day. 'We have a saying in Ghana,' he added, and repeated the same lion-and-hunter proverb that President Erdoğan had cited with respect to Turkish history. It was time for new versions of old stories, and there were plenty of new authors in the room.

Interestingly, the man in charge of Russia's Africa push was a billionaire ally of Putin's, Konstantin Malofeev, who had previously organised a joint World Congress of Families with right-wing American groups, anxious to protect the world from the encroaching evils of abortion, same-sex marriage and LGBT rights. This agenda was playing well in Africa, too, where a number of tradition-minded peoples did not like being lectured on their incorrect or outdated morals by bossy Western powers.

As Washington squared up to China, meanwhile, Putin was fast becoming Beijing's new best friend too. In all these areas, Russia was returning to the world fray.

It was still preoccupied with the same pursuit of raw materials that had disfigured earlier times, launching cutting-edge ice-breakers in pursuit of its energy interests in the Arctic, establishing gas and oil contracts in Africa and Europe, and maintaining a close interest in resources closer to home. In 2018 it orchestrated a pact between the five nations that bordered the Caspian Sea (Azerbaijan, Iran, Kazakhstan, Russia and Turkmenistan) in order to establish the legal status of the mineral rights that lay beneath – it was thought to have natural gas reserves similar to Saudi Arabia's. An arcane detail of geography (was it a sea or a lake?) now had significant ramifications, since seas and lakes were governed by different legal protocols. Russia's success in insisting that it be treated primarily as a 'sea' made the superior length of

its coastline the key consideration, strengthening its already powerful position as the leading provider of Europe's gas (almost 40
per cent of which was supplied by Gazprom).

In theory, all of this should have been profoundly damaging to
its soft-power halo. But a surprising new star, seen before only in
glimpses, now rose in the East. Of all the extraordinary things . . .
it began to seem that in soft-power terms Russia's strategy was
working. Authoritarian government had, in the first decade of the
twenty-first century, engineered an economic miracle — wages
rose by 11 per cent per annum, and unemployment fell by two-
thirds, sparking a consumerist spending spree. A people used to
scrimping and saving found themselves able to enjoy a life of cars,
phones and foreign trips.

This was a major reversal for the West's soft-power scholars. Up
to now soft power had been seen — axiomatically — as a liberal-
minded strategy: not just the politest way to put a foot in someone
else's door but a natural extension of the West's irresistible superiority. Russia was not observing this rule: it stood unashamedly for
authoritarian government, the suppression of dissent, aggressive
foreign relations and the rejection of modish concerns. Yet this
seemingly retrograde approach, it turned out, contained (like
the ever-diminishing figures inside a Russian doll) a bold soft-
power message.

It was easily comprehensible in all the world's languages.
Russian governance was clearer, more decisive, more *effective* than
the broken-down procedures of the West.

A terrible truth began to dawn. Soft power was not by definition a set of kind-hearted ideas that could not fail. Dracula had
soft power too.

Could such a heresy be true? Might soft power be not a message — a mild, non-threatening force for good — but merely a
message system; not so much the Ten Commandments as the
tablet of stone on which they were written? Russia was using all
the accepted soft-power methods — media, culture, education, history and foreign policy — but in the service of a non-democratic
world view. The head of the Council on Foreign Relations and
Defense Policy, Sergei Karaganov, stated as much when he said
it was Russia's intention to be 'leader of the non-liberal world'.

Elsewhere he wrote (in 2015) that Europe's '500-year global dominance' was 'drawing to an end'.

There was more than chastening advice here, to say the least. Modern Russia was a humming motor of soft power not in spite of its authoritarian instincts, but because of them. And this did not show up in surveys, because its strengths were not valued by the conventional mark scheme. In the 2019 Portland Soft Power 30 it came . . . thirtieth.

If this was a soft-power reversal (or a wake-up call) for the West, it was in part self-inflicted. In his original book, Joseph Nye (or his publisher) had defined soft power as 'The Means to Success in World Politics'. This was a subtitle designed to give the book more lustre in the self-help market (making it a how-to guide: 'Geopolitics for Beginners'). But in implying that soft power was a mere gambit or ploy it allowed others to dismiss it as superficial. Russia, for one, took the view that it amounted to little more than national advertising – otherwise known as . . . propaganda.

President Putin made this point bluntly in an interview with the *Financial Times* in 2019, when, on the eve of a G20 summit in Tokyo, he said that 'the so-called liberal idea . . . has outlived its purpose'. In this he had the backing of the Russian Orthodox Church, whose Patriarch, a close ally, had recently asked: 'Are Western standards of human happiness applicable to all countries and cultures?' Putin's Defence Minister, Sergei Ivanov, chimed in by coining a portentous new term: 'eastern democracy'.

It was an upset for soft power's keenest apostles. Columnists rushed to repudiate it as a calumny; charts appeared showing that the world's most developed economies were – *fact* – liberal democracies; political scientists insisted that the free institutions and procedures of the West had to be the defining foundations of economic success.

In theory they were right. But electorates, even in the West, were becoming visibly dissatisfied with such freedoms. Where, they wondered, lay cause and effect? Might liberal democracy, far from being the cause of economic growth, be no more than an accessory, an enjoyable luxury attainable only once prosperity had been achieved?

It so happened that many of the world's fastest-growing (and most stable) economies were *not* liberal. According to the *Financial Times* (in August 2019), only five of the forty-three nations that had enjoyed economic growth of more than 7 per cent in recent years could be called free or progressive. And even these were embroiled in uproars of self-doubt.

This was not so bald a truth as it seemed: it is hard for well-established economies to grow at so high a rate, so the only contestants in this race were non-democracies like China, Singapore and other fast-moving Asian nations. It was a bracing soft-power message to send to emerging nations in Africa and Latin America, however. Just as the 2008 financial crash was denting the assumption that savvy finance professionals were the best people to run a national economy, so it could be argued that *illiberal* leadership might have as much if not more to offer to the modern world than the much-trumpeted values of the West, which were being shouted down from within.

There was support for this in the free-thinking cradles of high finance. The Zambian-born thinker Dambisa Moyo (author of polemics such as *How the West was Lost*, 2011, and *Edge of Chaos*, 2018) was not an outsider – she was an economist from Oxford, Harvard and Goldman Sachs – but she argued: 'Democracy is not a pre-requisite of economic growth ... What poor countries at the lowest level of economic development need is not multi-party democracy but a decisive benevolent dictator.'

A vehement chorus of anti-capitalist voices echoed her words. They surfed on a growing sense that individual freedom (in religious, sexual or political matters) was more precious than material progress, and threatened by it. There was a degree of complacency in this – it smacked of well-fed nations taking prosperity for granted, as a universal 'right'. But hungry populations were more easily seduced by the idea that economic progress mattered more than political liberty; in Africa and Latin America, nation after nation was beginning to look at Russia rather than America as a model.

The richest irony of all was that the advanced world too was now toying openly with the idea that 'strong' government was needed to protect traditional ways. Only a generation earlier Russia had been a byword for communist tyranny – complete with Siberian gulags, secret police surveillance and unswerving party discipline. Now its defence of religious and family values was winning it supporters of a right-wing or nationalist bent. In their eyes, the West had lost its way by abandoning its traditions, opening itself up to immigrants and their strange beliefs. Russia became their unlikely ally in the war against political correctness and transgender toilets.

Europe found itself depicted – ironically, in this context – as 'soft', as having another Weimar wobble. The heady burst of freedom in 1920s Germany had soon degenerated into decadence: everything collapsed, including money – people had to sell their houses for a loaf of bread or a box of eggs. So too the modern West could be portrayed as weak, mired in shallow identity politics and pious grandstanding.

It went down well domestically: Putin's popularity rose to 85 per cent after he 'returned' Crimea to the Russian fold. But nationalist movements across Europe also seemed happy to give their approval. When Hungary's Viktor Orbán and others spoke about the need to defend 'Christian culture' and 'traditional family values', they were falling in with Russia's soft-power message. 'A new world has emerged,' said Marine Le Pen, leader of France's far-right party, after meeting Putin in Moscow (in part to thank him for helping to finance her campaign). 'It's the world of Vladimir Putin . . .'

It was a salutary reminder, in the age of corporate responsibility and stakeholders, that individual leadership mattered. Just as Donald Trump's personal profile altered the way people thought about America, so senior figures were impressed by Putin's tough-guy glamour. In 2011 Jeremy Corbyn, leader of the British Opposition, said that Putin was 'more objective on Libya than most', and indicated during the Skripal affair that there was no reason to think his own national intelligence service more reliable than Russia's. In 2014 Nigel Farage echoed his words when he described Putin as the world leader he most admired, notwithstanding 'the whole Syria thing'.

Most famously of all, Donald Trump made a series of flattering remarks about the Russian President, referring repeatedly to 'Putin's brilliance', giving him 'an A for leadership' and comparing him favourably to Barack Obama: 'At least he's a leader, unlike what we have in this country.' Meeting him only reinforced his high opinion. 'He called me a genius,' he confided. 'We got along great, by the way.'

The corralling of so strange a set of bedfellows into the same admiring club was (aside from what anyone might think about the policy implications) an impressive achievement. It was logical that Europe's left-wing parties (Britain's Labour Party, Germany's Die Linke, Spain's Podemos and Greece's Syriza – and a number of East European movements) might sympathise with Russian communism. But the opposite end of the spectrum, the right-wing nationalist space, was also full of Putin fans. The Rassemblement National in France, Greece's Golden Dawn, Hungary's Jobbik, Italy's Northern League and Germany's AfD were all drawn to the flickering flame of this conservative (nostalgic) cultural mindset.

In a strange historical twist, by blending 'strong leadership' with 'traditional values', the Russian Communist Party was suddenly attractive to America's religious right, which only a generation earlier had growled at the smallest sign that the mad Soviet dog was padding around on its own freedom-loving lawns.

These ideological shifts had tangible foreign policy implications. African and Latin American states were happy to support Russia's actions in Crimea and Ukraine in the United Nations. And the fact that nostalgia and tradition were siren calls in Eastern Europe exposed a fault-line in that part of the world. The former Soviet satellites had joined the European Union to *escape* oversight by foreigners – to regain traditional identities, not dissolve them into a larger unity. The new mood music from Moscow encouraged them to be less cooperative with their new partners in Europe – a win for Russia. There was even a division in reunified Germany, where the east was fertile ground for nationalist elements – the right-wing AfD, largely shunned in the western zone, was winning a quarter of the vote in Brandenburg and Saxony. Voters felt ignored by Berlin – though Angela Merkel herself had grown up in East Germany.

This was all greatly to Russia's advantage and in accordance with its wishes. And it was being wrought not by the Stalinist mailed glove but by all the contrivances of soft messaging too.

By offering 'leadership' at a time when Western democracies were divided, Putin sent a clear signal that 'strong' authoritarian government might even be superior to lily-livered liberal democracy — better at restoring national pride. Those photographs of himself in judo robes, stripped to his waist in the snow, toting a rifle, petting a snow leopard or leaning against a motorbike ... they were doing their job.

This was soft power in its most distilled form: the power of example. Standing up for tradition and national pride was enabling Russia to win hearts and minds overseas more effectively than it ever had in its Soviet heyday. T. S. Eliot's famous criticism of *Animal Farm,* expressed in a letter to Orwell himself (in his view the pigs clearly *were* the most intelligent beasts in the barnyard, and therefore the best qualified to run the place), now summoned up more ghosts than the world wanted to know about.

Soft power too moved in mysterious ways.

14

India: People Power

At half past five in the morning on 16 July 1945, an intense flash illuminated the mountains of the New Mexico desert. According to one observer its glare was 'many times that of the midday sun', and it produced a blast of heat and a shock wave that was felt 100 miles away. A towering cloud rose more than 7 miles into the cold morning sky, where it formed itself into the shape of a giant toadstool.

The site had been chosen because it was the nearest thing to the middle of nowhere – flat, arid, windless and uninhabited apart from reptiles and insects. It was at once a military operation – the observer of the flash was Brigadier-General Thomas Farrell – and a scientific project led by the physicist Robert Oppenheimer.

It had been a top-secret race against time – the military put out a report that an ammunition dump had exploded, fortunately with no casualties – so most saw the explosion as an unqualified success. The watching soldiers and scientists clapped each other on the shoulders. But Oppenheimer walked stiffly away, his mind racing.

'We knew the world would not be the same,' he told an interviewer, knowing better than anyone that this was no ordinary bomb. It brought to his highly educated mind a line from an ancient Hindu text, the *Bhagavad Gita*: 'If the radiance of a thousand suns were to burst at once into the sky, that would be like the splendour of the mighty one.'

He was also reminded of an even more momentous line from the same work: 'Now I am become death, the destroyer of worlds.'

A month after the test, a bomb very much like this one was dropped on Hiroshima.

Oppenheimer knew Sanskrit, so the translation was his own. In the Penguin Classics version, two decades later, this would read: 'I am all-powerful time, which destroys all things.' Oppenheimer's more evocative rendering is the one the world remembers.

But why, at such a moment, should he have thought of Indian scripture?

It may have been in his mind all along. When he gave the project its codename – 'the Trinity Test' – he claimed he was inspired by a John Donne poem about death. But it also echoed the divine proclamation in the *Bhagavad Gita* (Chapter 10, Verse 32): 'I am the beginning and the middle and the end.'

There was more to it than that, perhaps. The bomb was a Promethean endeavour, the stealing of fire from the gods: it is not surprising that it felt right to give it a sublime caption. But in giving the moment an Indian accent Oppenheimer was paying tribute to Indian civilisation as a whole, as being the fount of all wisdom. Given that India had not yet shaken off the oppressions of imperial rule, this was an intriguing twist.

The *Bhagavad Gita* was a sacred work. A 2500-year-old story about the ethics of life and death, a dialogue between the warrior-hero Arjuna and his charioteer-deity Krishna, its imposing truths had torn through the nineteenth century's literary circles in English, French, German and Russian translations. Tolstoy revered it (there is still a statue of him in New Delhi); Thoreau thought it 'stupendous'; and in Britain it was taken up by the Romantic poets, who loved its assertion that God breathed through all creation, not just the Church. Its most enthusiastic disciple, William Blake, produced a painting (listed in an 1809 catalogue, since lost) of the translators at work on this text, and borrowed the transcendental vitality of the *Bhagavad Gita* for his own poetry.

The famous imagery in 'Jerusalem', for example (the musical setting of which is the de facto English national anthem), is usually held to be a reference to Elijah, but just as plausibly evokes Arjuna, who spends the *Bhagavad Gita* in his war chariot, quailing at the thought of the coming battle to decide the fate of the world.

Blake's lines certainly suggest a man girding himself for a
holy war – 'Bring me my Bow of burning gold . . . Bring me my
Chariot of fire' – and while it is true that Elijah too was carried
aloft in a 'chariot of fire', there is no hint in Blake's 'Jerusalem'
that the narrator is seeking to abandon the world by ascending to
the heavens – on the contrary, he is rousing himself to defend it in
battle. Nor are there bows and arrows in Elijah's ascent, whereas
in the *Gita* Arjuna is urged by Krishna, his fiery companion, to
take up not just his 'great bow' but 'the sword of wisdom', too.

Elsewhere Blake made even more explicit use of the *Gita*. It
was here that he hit upon the notion that one might see 'infin-
ity in a grain of sand', and in *The Marriage of Heaven and Hell* he
stated: 'The philosophy of the East taught the first principles
of human perception.' The voice of Indian scripture bubbled
through his verse.

The pantheistic sense of spiritual energy in nature was detectable in Coleridge, Shelley and Wordsworth, too, and also in the
celebrated reflection on the interwoven nature of time at the
opening of T. S. Eliot's *Four Quartets* ('Time present and time
past / Are both perhaps present in time future / And time future
contained in time past . . .'). The ending of *The Waste Land* (the
Sanskrit invocation of peace: 'Shantih shantih shantih') was an
even more explicit salute to the epic's mystical power.

This, we might think, is routine literary cross-pollination – the
most popular book in eighteenth-century Britain, after all, was
Spain's *Don Quixote*. But in this case, given the British occupation
of India, there was a more profound transaction. The colonial
intruder was absorbing not just the raw material of its new land,
but its wisdom, too.

Soft power was stirring life (and death) across continental divides.

In so doing it changed the way India was thought about – in
scholarly circles, at least. In earlier days India had been a byword
for luxury. A Shakespearian character (Mortimer, in *Henry
IV Part I*) could praise someone's generous nature as being 'as
bountiful as the mines of India', echoing a line from Marlowe's
Tamburlaine some years earlier, which depicted India as a trove of
jewels, gold, spices and 'steeds swifter than Pegasus'. Thanks to

works like the *Bhagavad Gita*, India was becoming synonymous with the whole concept of spirituality. In 1893 a Hindu monk named Vivekananda kept an international conference in Chicago 'enraptured' by introducing them to a new idea: *yoga*. Travelling through China and Japan, he had developed theories about the shared basis of religious ideas. America heard them first.

By the time he reached Chicago his theme had revealed itself and his mission was clear: to speak for harmony between all faiths. He settled in New York to spread this gospel, preaching meditation as the path to peace. On the way home to India, in 1897, he gave lectures in Britain, France and Italy, little knowing that this demanding religious message would in these heathen hands emerge as an exercise routine. Vivekananda's teachings made their presence felt in another way when the Beatles' George Harrison was introduced to his teachings by his friend Ravi Shankar. He paid his respects to Indian thought by playing the sitar on 'Norwegian Wood', and based a global hit of his own – 'My Sweet Lord' – on the ideas of the Bengali mystic. For much of the twentieth century India's most vivid cultural contribution to the world (thanks primarily to the example of Gandhi, but also, from a different religious angle, to Mother Teresa) was its infinite holiness. Vivekananda himself preached as much. India, he said, was 'the land where humanity has attained its highest generosity'.

That was the world's prevailing opinion: India was a land of infinite depth, a nirvana of holy books, holy men and holy cows, with silent pools of mystical wisdom where one was everything and everything was one and God was present in the wings of a flea.

In 1974, when India exploded its own nuclear bomb, making it the world's sixth nuclear power, it named it 'the smiling Buddha'.

When India achieved independence in 1947 it began to assert a different idea of itself: free, deep and no longer subservient. But in attempting to keep the world at arm's length in the decades after independence, it paid a heavy price. By 1991 it was broke. Roughly 40 per cent of its population (over 300 million people) lived in extreme poverty; the government did not have enough foreign currency to keep the lights on – and half the country didn't have lights anyway. Inflation was running at 17 per cent, eating up whatever savings people had (very little). And then the Prime Minister, Rajiv Gandhi, was assassinated (along with fourteen others) by a Sri Lankan suicide bomber who turned out to be a seventeen-year-old girl.

It was shock therapy, and India changed. Reform was already in the air, but now the pace increased as industry was opened up to private and foreign investment, taxes were lowered, regulations were pushed to one side and the Bombay stock market was set free. The result was dramatic. Foreign investment jumped from almost nothing to $5 billion per year; annual growth surged from close to zero to 7 per cent and rising; the technology sector took off (from almost nothing). A land that didn't have phones or televisions became one in which hundreds of millions had mobiles and couldn't get enough of the cricket on TV.

The culture moved along with it. A mesmerising land of gurus and monks became a supercharged zone of choked roads, hi-tech warehouses and huge industries. Twenty years after the great liberation, only 12 per cent of India's population was living below the extreme-poverty line and it was making three times as much steel as Britain. It has been one of the world's most remarkable stories, and it still has a long way to run.

In an ironic consequence of British imperialism, the fact that India was to a large extent English-speaking made it well suited to the new global market: call centres and back-office support boomed. American Express, British Airways, General Electric and other corporate giants set up operations in India; two decades later this outsourcing industry was worth $150 billion, employed four million and attracted an annual geyser of foreign currency. Rarely had an industry grown so fast.

There was a price to pay: India became a symbol of juddering inequality, a place where gilded skyscrapers overlooked chronic slums. This was the contrast made famous by the film *Slumdog Millionaire*. Mumbai, in particular, became a gold-rush town of raucous cricket crowds, fast cars, thumping music, gambling scandals and get-rich-quick Bollywood excesses. India as a whole was generating (according to James Crabtree in *The Billionaire Raj*) one new billionaire a month, and the emblem of this extravagance,

Mukesh Ambani, built a twenty-seven-storey palace in Mumbai with a ballroom, a theatre, parking for 168 cars, and 25 tonnes of chandelier. It was said to be the world's second most valuable building after Buckingham Palace.

This was conspicuous consumption on a dazzling scale, in a country that until recently had been famous for not having enough taps.[1]

India, it turned out, never had been slow paced or unworldly; merely held back.

It was not even – as it should have been – a significant tourist destination. Everyone knew that as the world grew richer, and the cost of travel fell, tourism was crucial. And India had a magical landscape and heritage, with tigers and elephants, temples and mountains – and was still, as a land of many faiths, a spiritual capital, home to gurus, sages, yoga and personal self-advancement. It was cheap, too: a newspaper cost a few pence; a dollar would buy a taxi ride; two would buy lunch.

These assets were going almost entirely unexploited.

It had too many disadvantages: it was famously unhygienic – even hardened travellers knew to expect a stomach upset or two – and the level of extreme poverty and begging was not easy for everyone to stomach, either. It appealed to hippy travellers, eager to rough it in search of personal enlightenment for five rupees a day on the beaches of Goa or the houseboats of Kashmir; but it had been slow to create the kind of infrastructure – transport and hotels – the rest of the world now expected.

As a result, in 2002 it welcomed just 2.4 million tourists. Tiny Switzerland attracted four times more than that, while Thailand lured fifteen times as many.

That was why, that year, the Ministry of Tourism launched a concerted promotional campaign to attract visitors. Armed with a $200 million budget, the project sought to connect the travel industry (airlines, hotels, transport and visa procedures) to all the

---

1 Though it was not quite new. The wealth of India's Great Kings was legendary. The Maharaja of Alwar owned seven Rolls-Royces, which he used as rubbish vans; when the Maharani of Cooch Behar went shopping for shoes in Italy, she ordered a hundred pairs at a time, many studded with diamonds; the Maharaja of Gwalior had a solid-silver train set built to carry brandy round the royal dinner table.

vibrant images associated with the subcontinent – the Taj Mahal, spice markets on the Arabian Sea, elephant rides through tiger-haunted jungles, Himalayan lakes. It aimed to promote tourism at home but also to create business opportunities abroad.

A British advertising firm (Ogilvy & Mather) came up with the slogan: 'Incredible India'. Amitabh Kant, Secretary in the Ministry of Tourism, emphasised that it was only partly about infrastructure; more importantly it was about the 'ability to inspire'. It sought to present India as a land of 'mind-boggling depth and intensity'. Its first figurehead was the actor Aamir Khan, who urged his compatriots to roll out the welcome mat on the grounds that 'Guests are like God'. But in 2015 he was replaced as brand ambassador by the Prime Minister himself, Narendra Modi.

Of course, a simple slogan could not encapsulate a national culture – let alone one as broad and varied as India's. Critics did point out that 'Incredible India', a colourful parade of elephants and women in saris gazing at the moon, glossed over the plight of the 'marginalised'. Some even saw it as typically 'orientalist' – the Western tendency to regard Asia as mysteriously 'other'. But this was advertising, not cultural criticism. Others saw it as quite the reverse – orientalism deployed to India's own advantage. India was turning the tables on a foreign cliché.

And it was succeeding. The suggestion that India was a place like nowhere else, a backdrop for life-changing experiences, was a compelling one, and hit home.

Tourist visits surged. By 2017 the number had risen fivefold to top ten million. It still trailed smaller countries (Thailand welcomed thirty-two million), but the potential for further growth remained vast. India was the world's largest democracy; English was widely spoken; it had more UNESCO heritage sites than all but five other countries.

It was a soft power in waiting. In a nice act of re-colonisation, it was even, thanks to the purchasing power of its audience, supplanting England as the home of cricket, too.

The fact that none of this has moved the soft-power needle – India does not score well in global rankings and was not deemed worthy of a place anywhere in the 2019 Portland Soft Power 30 – continues to be down to a number of chronic factors. Although India is the world's largest democracy (in theory a soft-power asset), the world has low levels of trust in its government, not least thanks to world-leading levels of corruption: in 2019 more than half the population admitted to having bribed an official in the last twelve months – an unimpressive outcome given that the government had pledged a crackdown. According to some accounts, only a small fraction of its billion-strong population paid tax, so the basic infrastructure – as anyone stuck in Mumbai's clogged traffic knew all too well – was still rickety.[2] Despite making extraordinary strides economically, India still had 200 million people living below the poverty line, more than any other country. When it emerged that it was also home to all ten of the world's most smog-bound cities (in 2019 Delhi was plunged in a cloud of black smoke), travellers were quick to make their excuses and stay away.

Even the fact that Indian food was loved all around the world was not quite a competitive advantage. It was so ubiquitous, everywhere, that there was no need to go there to enjoy it – if anything, poor public health made it safer to stay at home.[3]

One problem was that the government had not developed the kind of institutions – cultural institutes overseas, a media presence in foreign homes – that would have boosted its image. In this area it was proof of a paradox: the clearest way to appreciate what governments *can* achieve is provided by those that decline or fail to do so. But there was a larger problem. All countries, as we have seen, are jangled by arguments about their past. But in India's case this was especially severe, since its own history had been subjugated by the imperial ambitions of others. Its national heritage was not just buried beneath other versions, but treated as an aspect of someone else's story.

This is not only a matter of British imperialism: the ancient

---

2 Though work *has* finally begun on Mumbai's first underground line: a twenty-seven-station metro that will link the southern tip of the city to the airport in the north.

3 The UK alone had 17,000 'Indian' restaurants in 2019 – a misnomer, since 90 per cent were Bengali – though in the face of competition from other national cuisines (and from a boom in home delivery) they were closing at the rate of two per week.

Hindu civilisation was engulfed first by Mughal invaders, and then – after the ascendancy of the Maratha dynasty – by several European colonists: Portugal and France, as well as Britain. But of course it was the last of these that left the most extreme and recent scars. Britain did not seek to remake India in its own image – exploitation was its purpose rather than nation-building – but its presence in India left an indelible legacy.

In Nirad Chaudhuri's sketch map of India's history, each of its historical phases wove a new strand into the lattice of races, religions, languages, myths and traditions that made up modern India. That indeed is what entranced the British (some of them, at least) when they first stepped ashore: they were astounded to see so many faiths (Hindu, Muslim, Sikh, Buddhist, Jain, Zoroastrian, Jewish and Christian too) co-existing in a peaceful fashion. Europe had never achieved anything of this sort, and could barely imagine it. India was the birthplace not just of Buddha (Siddhartha Gautama was born in Lumbini, now Nepal, in the sixth century BC) but, it seemed, of all religious belief.

The result of so many foreign intrusions, however, was that India's own civilisation lay buried. As Mihir Bose has written: 'For a country claiming a history of five thousand years, there exist no known histories left to us by Indians for three-quarters of this period ... Even the name India was invented by foreign invaders.'[4]

Classical historians (Herodotus, Pliny, Plutarch, Ptolemy) depicted it as a jungle. Herodotus wrote that 'all the Indian tribes I have mentioned copulate in the open like cattle', and spent their days collecting gold from the desert while fighting off huge marauding ants – 'somewhat less than dogs, but bigger than foxes'. These surreal beasts were utterly ruthless: 'nothing in the world can touch these ants for speed'.

A similar pattern persisted down the ages. The most famous account of Indian independence, *Freedom at Midnight*, was written by a French–American double act and based on the not always

---

4 In *Histories of Nations* (edited by Peter Furtado). Bose added that this suppression of Indian history was what makes it so fraught a topic today. In 2003 a passing remark in an otherwise serious work about a Maratha king ignited an uproar that led to civic violence. The book had to be withdrawn.

reliable testimony of a German–British royal: Lord Mountbatten.[5] An American reporter, William Shirer, wrote the most widely read account of Mahatma Gandhi's heroic campaign. Another prominent survey, *India: A Million Mutinies Now*, was by the Trinidadian Nobel laureate V. S. Naipaul.

The novels of E. M. Forster, Ruth Prawer Jhabvala and J. G. Farrell saw India through Western eyes, as the setting rather than the subject of their adventures; and a range of foreign historians and reporters – William Dalrymple, Patrick French, Robyn Meredith, Mark Tully and many others – told Indian stories to the wider world.

Much of this writing was fine and sympathetic – but it was foreign sympathy.

The result was that India's culture was occluded. And modern academic approaches – Marxist, capitalist, religious, nationalist – imposed their own ideological slant, using India as a test bed for their theories. Only in recent years have Indian scholars – Irfan Habib, Suketu Mehta, Pankaj Mishra, Sanjeev Sanyal, Romila Thapar, Shashi Tharoor and others – launched a renaissance of interest in their own origins; and even these do not draw the same lessons or interpretations from the national past.

This, it transpired, was an even greater problem. The past was not a stable presence. It could not easily be captured and caged to display any one political point of view.

Three-quarters of a century after the end of British rule it was easy enough to see that imperialism had been an inexcusable imposition. So it was a shock, in 2014, when a YouGov survey found that 59 per cent of Britons actually believed that the nations colonised by Britain were 'better off' for the experience. One-third went so far as to admit that they 'would like it' if they still commanded such an empire.

This eye-opening revelation inspired an impassioned response. In 2017 the historian and politician Shashi Tharoor delivered a speech to the Oxford Union (later a book: *Inglorious Empire*) that left his

---

5 This account inspired the 2017 film *Viceroy's House*, an Anglo-Indian production; but in India the Hindi version was released as *Partition: 1947*.

audience in no doubt as to the extent of the damage the British had wrought. Using figures made famous by the (British) economist Angus Maddison in 2007, he insisted that India accounted for a quarter of global exports in 1500, and only 2 per cent when Britain withdrew – an extraordinary decline, and one which had been imposed with great deliberation, wholly to Britain's advantage.

Two per cent of the 1947 global economy may have been worth as much as 25 per cent of its 1747 equivalent, but there was no hiding the imbalance. Having ruled India for two centuries Britain left it with a plantation economy (tea, jute and cotton) and a broken manufacturing base. Its textile industry had been squeezed to enlarge the market for British cloth.[6] It had a literacy rate of 16 per cent and a life expectancy of twenty-seven years.

Much the same could be said about the hideous slums of Bradford or Preston, of course – Dickensian England was squalid, too – but this was not a proud record.

Naturally there were those who argued that to blame all present ills on colonial oppression was to be as stuck in the past as the reddest-faced imperialist – after seventy years of independence some of India's problems were of its own making. But the underlying truth could scarcely be ignored. British colonial rule was not benign.

Tharoor gave especially short shrift to the idea that the British had somehow 'given' India railways – as if they were gifts from a generous benefactor. In truth, the tracks had been laid by Indian workers who died in their tens of thousands to promote British commercial interests. As for the idea that India could not have built them without Britain: 'Many countries have built railways without having been colonised in order to do so.' Japan, for one, had created a world-class network despite having been deprived of the blessings of British imperial rule.[7]

---

6 Though one must be wary, in saying that 'the British' wreaked this destruction, of suggesting that it was a plot engineered by the national character. Profit-hungry merchants made their money importing cheap Indian cloth, while Lancashire's textile workers demanded high tariffs on Indian imports to protect their own looms.

7 As legacies go, this one is ambiguous. In the three years running from 2015 to 2017, as many as 50,000 people were killed by Indian trains – more than 15,000 per annum. In 2017 alone more than three thousand commuters in the Mumbai area lost their lives – 654 of them falling from overcrowded carriages. These are astounding numbers, even in the context of a railway network that carries eight *billion* passengers per year.

Nor did Tharoor accept 'government' as a British legacy. The Indian Civil Service, as the first Indian Prime Minister, Jawaharlal Nehru, had pointed out, was neither Indian nor civil, nor was it a service. Anyone tempted to think India 'undeveloped' until the arrival of the British had only to glance at the Taj Mahal – a refined masterpiece completed in 1652, when the English were pursuing their own bloody and extremely *un*civil war.

It was, in Tharoor's view, a 'deplorable form of amnesia' to neglect such facts.

He was right, of course. But history rarely conforms to tidy interpretations, and it did not quite follow, from his eloquent denunciations, that Indian history could be rendered clear and purposeful merely by subtracting the British imposition. In truth, the story was complicated from beginning to end. That YouGov survey may have been not so much a measure of what 'the country' thought as an indictment of British education (similar studies were finding that half of British youngsters believed Churchill to have led the nation through the *First* World War). A vague nostalgia for empire was part of a swirl of nationalist emotions stirred by recent politics, a swipe against the idea that Britain was no longer 'Great'. But it was not the general view.

There were other ambiguities. As Jon Wilson explained, in *India Conquered: Britain's Raj and the Chaos of Empire*, Britain's grip had not been absolute or vicelike: 'The idea of strong, effective, consistent British power in India was … a delusion.' Perhaps a third of the country was ruled by princes and maharajas who retained their independence – at least in theory – even during the Raj. Britain brought the outward ceremonies of bureaucratic efficiency – ledgers, timetables, seating plans – but the subcontinent was much too big for a small occupying force to control: in 1890 a continent of 250 million was administered by a mere six thousand sunburnt officials.

Nor could it quite be said that Britain had despoiled a peaceful arcadia. 'No greater indictment of the failures of British rule in India can be found than the tragic manner of its ending,' wrote Tharoor – and this felt true: the horrors of Partition were indeed overwhelming (half a million killed, thirteen million displaced and religious hatred given fresh and enduring life). But in 1930, as the American historian Will Durant stressed in *The Case for India* (1930) – a book that denounced British rule – this was not new: the Muslim conquest of India had been 'the bloodiest story in history'. And Nirad Chaudhuri, in *The Autobiography of an Unknown Indian* (1951), rejected the nationalist argument that sectarian hatred was new. 'Heaven preserve me from the dishonesty, so general among Indians, of attributing this conflict to British rule.'

He and his friends, he recalled, had held the 'mustard seed' of religious animosity in their hands as children, and 'planted it diligently'. To the extent that Britain thought about it at all, it preferred Muslims to Hindus, on monotheistic grounds – though, of course, religious niceties were outgunned by racial emotions – by dislike of 'natives'.

Chaudhuri was so enthusiastic an Anglophile that in some quarters he was regarded as a near-traitor. England, he said, recalling his childhood, was 'like the sky above our head ... always speaking to us in a friendly language'. He was not blind, though, to the fact that the English were also 'the greatest robbers and plunderers that ever disfigured the face of the earth'. While he sought (like Gandhi) to 'hear no hatred' for Britain, he did regard its presence in India as 'satanic'. He thus embodied the tortured feelings – in themselves a form of disfigurement – created by empire.

None of that is to say that Britain's imperial meddling was in any sense justified; only that it was flecked with so many ironies and contradictions that it was hard to turn it into a crisp soft-power message. When India did gain freedom in 1947, its leaders took the unusual step of inviting the departing Viceroy, Lord Mountbatten, to remain for a year as Governor-General – not the usual way to shake off the oppressor. Two years later, when Rajendra Prasad became President of the Republic, he called it 'the consummation and fulfilment of the historic tradition and democratic ideals of British rule' – words that suggested an incomplete resentment of the departing power.

The sad truth is that if Britain had never set foot in India, the latter would probably have been colonised by someone else – by Holland, Portugal, Russia or (most likely) France – just as it had, in the past, been colonised by the Mughal empire. It is always tempting, looking back, to assume that for India the alternative to being conquered was *not* being conquered; but this might not have been the real or relevant question.

That is speculative, but there is another awful sense in which India might have been fortunate. However cruel the Raj, elsewhere, in Africa, the Americas and Australasia, Europeans were even more ruthless, pursuing murderous campaigns to exterminate existing peoples. Despite many horrors, in Bengal and elsewhere, the British made no such concerted attempt in India. Indeed, such was their condescension that they rarely mixed at all. In the early period of East India Company rule, they made themselves conceitedly at home (one in three of the Company's officials left their worldly goods to an Indian woman); but at the height of the Raj they grew ever more remote. Safe in their compounds and bungalows, they never lived half so splendidly as the native nabobs and princes; but they avoided Indians as far as possible, except as servants. Inflamed by the imperial delusion, they saw India as a benighted realm of barbarous savages crying out for the leadership of enlightened souls from Eton, Oxford and the Guards. Charles Grant, chairman of the East India Company, declared that the 'inhabitants' were 'sunk in darkness, vice and misery'. They were, he concluded, 'a race of men lamentably degenerate and base'. It was up to Britain, they believed, to bring light to this hellish limbo.

It cannot be said, however, that Britain deployed the full might of imperial rule to suppress India's voice in the world. On the contrary, even at this early stage of its presence in the subcontinent there were mixed feelings.[8] Within the folds of an exploitative experiment lay a desire not to squash Indian culture, but to learn from it.

Most forms of colonial condescension were insufferable – bossy memsahibs may have done as much harm to the British brand as the worst army officer. But some members of the occupying force were enraptured by everything they saw. The seeds of the cultural

---

8 In 1833 Thomas Macaulay addressed Parliament and predicted that 'in some future age', India would demand and create European-style educational institutions of its own. 'Whether such a day will ever come I know not,' he said. 'But never will I attempt to avert or retard it. It will be the proudest day in English history.'

power that led Robert Oppenheimer to quote the *Bhagavad Gita* at the dawn of the nuclear age were planted as far back as the summer of 1770, when a Somerset-born printer named Charles Wilkins sailed to Calcutta as a 'typographer'.

An adept linguist, he was soon proficient in Persian, Bengali and Hindustani. Charged to produce a Bengali grammar (a tremendous novelty in itself), he went one step further and designed the world's first Bengali typeface, enabling him to produce history's first mechanically printed Bengali book and send it into the wider world.

That alone was enough to earn him the sobriquet: the Caxton of India.

More important, it earned him the respect of Calcutta's holy men, or 'pundits'. They consented to teach him Sanskrit, the sacred language reserved for the priesthood, and soon he became the leading (and for a while the only) British person to master it. When he died, in 1836, the obituary in the *Asiatic Journal* would remember this above all, calling him 'the first adventurer on this literary ocean . . . a sort of Columbus'.

It was an achievement notable enough to attract the support of Warren Hastings, the initial Governor-General of Bengal (which then constituted British India). As an imperial potentate, it is not hard to paint him as a villainous colonial exploiter; and he was impeached for corruption in London court proceedings that ran for seven years. But he was found not guilty, and it may well have been that he was laid low by enemies who deemed him not corrupt *enough*. And he had another side. 'I love India a little more than my own country,' he said, and was captivated by Indian civilisation, launching a range of scholarly projects in Hindu and Bengali culture.

He had an ulterior motive – he hoped that such work would 'diffuse a generosity of sentiment' towards the British, and thus reinforce 'the permanency of the settlement'. In this he was, one might say, an early apostle of soft power. But his cultural interest was genuine, and he did a great deal to expose India's obscured past to the wider world, inspired by the hope (he later wrote) that its art and literature 'will survive when the British dominion in India shall long have ceased to exist, and when the forces which it once wielded of wealth and power are lost to remembrance'.

It was one of the unusual features of British rule that some of its most devoted servants anticipated and looked forward to its dissolution.

One of the first beneficiaries of the Governor-General's enthusiasm was Charles Wilkins. Hastings sent him to Benares (now Varanasi) to study at the feet of India's wisest men. It was a significant move: Benares (according to legend founded by the god Shiva) was the holy cradle of Hinduism, and only a day's walk away was Sarnath, the place where Gautama Buddha delivered his first sermon. This was not a coincidence: it stood on the Ganges at a junction of ancient trade routes. The same geography made Benares the hub of the Raj railway and a central node of modern India's roads. It was a place of pilgrimage, learning ... and trade.

When Wilkins went there Britain had just lost the American colony, and the idea of ruling India was not uppermost in anyone's mind, least of all his. The East India Company was a commercial enterprise, not an instrument of national power. But it was more than a disinterested heritage project: it was a flexing of imperial muscle.

The result was spectacular. In collaboration with his teacher, Kasinatha Bhattacharyya (an East-West partnership similar to that between Austen Henry Layard and Hormuzd Rassam in Nineveh), Wilkins produced that rarest of things: a book that changed the world. The first English translation of the *Bhagavad Gita* was completed in 1784.

A religious epic that dated back two thousand years – and which the world knew nothing about – was about to find an audience outside India.

Wilkins submitted it to Hastings in 1784, and the Governor-General, recognising its significance, forwarded it to Nathaniel Smith, chairman of the East India Company. It was, he told him, 'a performance of great originality, of a sublimity of conception, of reasoning and diction, almost unequalled ... among all the known religions of mankind'. When the book appeared a year later, published by the East India Company in London, this tribute was included as an introductory letter.

It was a mind-altering surprise. In most British minds India was a backward land with a muddle of strange 'gods'. Now it appeared that it was an erudite culture going back thousands of years. More than that, the book had a romantic sensibility that could hardly be dismissed as 'pagan'. On the one hand it was strangely modern: in wondering about the origins of life – 'Who can tell us whence and how arose this universe?' – it chimed with Darwinian science, suggesting that religion itself was a human invention ('the Gods are later than its beginning').[9] It also advanced the overtly religious idea that there was only one God: 'the Spirit Supreme ... the God of Eternity who pervading all sustains all'.

Could ancient India really have perceived this truth, not yet visible in Europe?

There could hardly be a more vivid sign of the complicated tangle of motives even in so seemingly one-dimensional a story as imperial rule. In one sense India's ancient culture was obliterated by Britain; in another it was liberated by it, and sent out across the world.

The fact that Sanskrit literature had until then been a secret, protected by a Sanskrit priesthood, meant that Wilkins's *Bhagavad Gita* caused a global stir. With its divine messages of love, light and self-abnegation, it was an astonishing precursor to the New Testament: 'Be free from vain hopes and selfish thoughts, and with inner peace fight thou thy fight ... He is the light of all lights which shines beyond all darkness ... There are two natures in this world. The one is of heaven; the other of hell ... A man attains perfection when his work is worship of God, from whom all things come and who is in all ... Now I can say "Thy will be done."'

The message swept Europe. In 1802 a British scholar in Paris taught Sanskrit to the German critic Friedrich von Schlegel, who translated the *Bhagavad Gita* into German while his brother put it into Latin. Suddenly, India was transmitting the extraordinary suggestion that the most sacred tenets of the Christian Bible were not entirely original – and were not, therefore, the word of God. Far from being under the heel and on the

---

9 The suggestion that God did *not* create the world obliged Christian theologians, even those who admired the *Gita* as literature, to denounce it.

receiving end of British culture, India was emitting its own light to the world.

That is why it made sense for the first nuclear bomb, the bang that launched modern times, to be ushered in by an ancient Indian mantra. The blinding glare in front of Oppenheimer's eyes was hardly brighter than the flash in his mind.

The discovery of Sanskrit opened up a new way of thinking about all languages, and Wilkins was not a lone explorer. Two years before the publication of the *Bhagavad Gita*, in 1783, another Englishman, William Jones, arrived in Calcutta as a Supreme Court judge. He too was a remarkable scholar (he had translated Persian history and grammar books, and was master of more than twenty languages). Before long he had founded the Asiatic Society of Bengal, a serious and influential body.

Now, inspired afresh, he learned Sanskrit too, and in 1786 published the shocking (at that time) theory that Sanskrit, Greek and Latin might have a common root, with Persian as a related tongue. Sanskrit, he said, was 'more perfect than the Greek, more copious than the Latin, and more exquisitely refined than either'.

This was the concept of Indo-European languages, and it was born right here in the cultural collider of imperial conquest.[10] Even the most racially minded imperialist had to see India in a new light, as a relative, not a rival. Similar revelations in Assyria, as we have seen, supported the equally uncomfortable conclusion (to Victorian Britain) that there may have been highly advanced civilisations long before Europe's.

As H. G. Wells put it, referring to the sixth century BC in *A Short History of the World*: 'From Athens to the Pacific the human mind was astir.'

This was not much less than a soft-power earthquake, and the fact that it was ignited by the encounter between different cultures reminds us that to depict the imperial story as merely one of rapacious greed is, while not untrue, an over-simplification.

Modern scholarship has explained that Jones was not quite the

---

10 One of the more unexpected consequences of this was the prominence of the swastika – a Sanskrit word for a Hindu symbol – in the later history of Europe.

pioneer this story makes him seem. He had predecessors; and he made mistakes. But to accuse him in retrospect of foolishness (he tried to include Chinese and Peruvian in his linguistic family tree) does not detract from the impact he made at the time. He was a Fellow of the Royal Society and a member of Samuel Johnson's circle alongside Burke, Garrick and Adam Smith. He worked with Benjamin Franklin. His linguistic insights changed the way Europe (its scholarly tip, at any rate) thought about India and the world.

There were further knots in the tale. Back in Britain, Charles Wilkins attended the decade-long trial of Warren Hastings and spoke up on the old governor's behalf, as did his Indian collaborator, Kasinatha — indeed, the Sanskrit scholar was the first signatory on a petition that proclaimed Hastings to be a 'chief of science'. Hastings was sufficiently grateful to secure for Wilkins, in 1801, a handsome position as librarian of the East India Company — the agent of India's downfall but also the publisher of the English *Bhagavad Gita*. Four years later, when the Company founded a school in Hertfordshire designed to educate suitable Empire men, Wilkins took the library to the school and stayed there for thirty years. He was knighted in 1833.

It was no ordinary school. The East India Company was, as one of its own directors remarked, 'an empire within an empire', and this was its nursery. Students learned Hindi, Sanskrit and Persian alongside classics, philosophy, mathematics and cricket. Under its new name — Haileybury — it produced a first sea lord, a field marshal, four air chief marshals, seven generals, three admirals and seventeen holders of the Victoria Cross. In due course it would also be Rudyard Kipling's alma mater.

Its founder was Charles Grant, author of the disgraceful remarks cited earlier; but in hiring Wilkins as its librarian it was giving itself an India-loving accent as well. In a further footnote, it was also the alma mater of Clement Attlee, the Labour Prime Minister who drove through the nationalisation of key industries (coal, iron, power and rail), played midwife to the NHS, and appointed Lord Mountbatten to end British rule in India.

Britain's departure from India was as inglorious as much of

its occupation. Gandhi's extraordinary campaigns had laid the foundations of India's freedom; the naval mutiny of 1946 tipped the balance; India was becoming ungovernable; and Britain's moral authority was a spent force. It sought only to disengage as fast as it could. 'Keep India united if you can,' Attlee told Mountbatten. 'If not, save something from the wreck. In any case, get Britain out.'[11]

But it was an obliging soft-power parable. The man who drew down the flag on British rule in India went to the very school that had been founded to govern it.

Attlee is still cherished by Haileybury as 'perhaps its finest son'. When Indira Gandhi called him the 'non-imperial face' of Britain, it was a reminder, if nothing else, that it did have more than one side.

Once again we see how intertwined the transactions of the past can be, and how individual motivations can cut across or blur the procedures of government. And there is another soft truth here: civilisations can lie dormant. Even in India, where British rule was blatantly oppressive, culture could be liberated. In ancient times Indian civilisation had crossed oceans: the greatest Hindu temple in the world was in Cambodia, at Angkor Wat. But only now did the *Bhagavad Gita* reveal itself in the West. In lighting its path, Britain was sowing the seeds of its own demise – and knew it. As Warren Hastings said of the book: 'It will survive when the British dominion of India shall have long ceased to exist.' It was evident to him, even at this early stage of Britain's occupation, that its dominion would prove to be transient.

It is well known that the English language absorbed a new vocabulary from India – bandana, bungalow, Blighty, chutney, dungaree, juggernaut, khaki, pyjamas, sandals, thug and veranda. But Britain also took away, from the earliest days of the imperial intrusion, the larger idea of India as a spiritual civilisation. Those twentieth-century hippies who sought enlightenment in an Indian beach hut, that delicate tradition of yoga and meditation ... all was sparked into life by one hard-working printer

---

11 Mountbatten has often been accused of acting recklessly in beating so hasty a retreat. In the light of what happened (the horrors of Partition) that is inevitable, and may be just. But he did not act alone. Everyone knew that the game was up.

from Somerset, frowning in Calcutta over an old book in a little-known language.

Soft power is made of a thousand such interactions.

In 2017 the Chhatrapati Shivaji Maharaj Vastu Sangrahalaya in Mumbai (formerly the Prince of Wales Museum) hosted a very successful exhibition – in collaboration with the British Museum and the National Museum of Delhi – called 'India and the World'. It used 230 objects to tell nine evocative stories about India's relationship with elsewhere. Its theme was 'shared beginnings'. Objects ranging from Buddhist heads to Gandhi's spinning wheel dramatised the way religion, trade and culture criss-crossed the world. A marble discus thrower from the British Museum (a Roman copy of the Greek) could be compared to Indian sculpture from the same period.

It was a bold illustration of the museum's director's belief in museums as stages on which to 'explore the past, while standing in the present, and brooding on the future'. Sabyasachi Mukherjee was himself a creation of soft power: a youthful apprenticeship at London's Victoria and Albert Museum helped build the partnerships that would later enable him to mount exhibitions of this outward-looking sort.

A decade earlier he had used those same connections to present an exhibition of photographs from the V&A's collection ('Indian Life and Landscape'). The images arrived and were being unloaded on the very day (26 November 2008) that gunmen landed half a mile away and shot their way through the Taj Mahal hotel. Two very different visions of India clashed in the hot skies over Mumbai that day.

That same year, Mukherjee's museum was renamed to wipe away its links to the imperial past, and he struck his own blow for shared history by famously marching out to stop workers from toppling the statue of the Prince of Wales in the museum's front garden, on the grounds that eradicating the past (however much one might one resent it) was not the best way to address the future.

One more wrinkle. In 2012, in a museum storage room, a bronze bust of Gandhi was found wrapped in plastic. Research revealed that it was by a British artist, Clare Sheridan – an unfamiliar name. Mukherjee found that she was Winston Churchill's cousin; the bust had been bought by the Maharaja of Darbhanga, donated to the CSMVS in 1940, and displayed between a statue of Venus and a bust of Napoleon.

The past is painful, and fragmented, but it belongs to everyone.

From a soft-power point of view the problem with shared histories, however (which is also the reason they matter), lies precisely in their convoluted nature, and the fact that they can so easily be seen and interpreted in such radically different ways. India's past is too rich and complicated to be reduced to a simple parable or lesson about identity: the Battle of Plassey, for instance – the clash in which Robert Clive's redcoats defeated the army of Mughal India on a riverside field north of Calcutta – occupies a high place in the annals of British war. Clive's victory, it was said, made Britain the master of Calcutta, Bengal and the subcontinent – and sealed India's fate.

Children's history books tended to show it as a heaving struggle involving elephants and muskets, and since everything about India involves vast numbers, it was usually assumed that the British casualty list must have been shattering.

Not so.

How many redcoats died? Eighteen.

It was more than a skirmish. Clive's army numbered some three thousand (only 950 of whom were British), while the opposing force, led by the Nawab Siraj-ud-Daulah, had more than 50,000. But the Nawab lost five hundred in the first cannonade, and lost heart too. In truth, the battle had been decided before the first shot was fired: Robert Clive (a twenty-five-year-old colonel at the time) had 'persuaded' half of the Nawab's army to defect.

In Britain it has gone down as an epic triumph against great odds; in India it is a typical example of British treachery.

One event: two stories. Such is soft history.

Nor was it quite, or only, part of the tussle between Britain and India. It was a ripple of a distant conflict: the Seven Years' War. The Nawab favoured the French; indeed it was French artillery that failed in the battle, making it such a one-sided affair. The technical difference (British guns could fire several shots per minute, while Indian muskets could fire only once every fifteen minutes) took care of the rest.

How different might the world have been had the French artillery worked that day.

Despite repeated attempts to denounce history as bunk, the scandalous province of 'dead white males', a one-eyed story told by the winners, an unknowable 'other country', or a nightmare from which we are trying to awake, it remains a topic of keen contemporary concern. One can quibble with sweeping definitions – some of those dead white males were awkward revolutionaries, and history is not always a story told by the winners (America did not win the Vietnam War; Jews can hardly be said to have 'won' the Holocaust). But maxims of this sort catch the imagination. All over the world, people and governments look to the past – sometimes the distant past – to mobilise public emotion and illuminate the circumstances of today.

Maintaining or curating this past is easier said than done, however – in part because there are arguments over what it means, and in part because it is usually seen through the prism of modern politics and economics. Modern India is attempting to reconcile the conflicting demands of old and new by clarifying its own swirling past down to a cleansed tale of Hindu supremacy. The re-election of Narendra Modi in 2019 implied that India was turning its back on its old identity as a spiritual land of many faiths in favour of a more assertive, Hindu-first culture. Both the tone and the policies of the new government sought to rally the people behind the banner of Hindu civilisation. And in the closing weeks of 2019 Delhi erupted in riots following a new Citizenship Act that restricted the rights of Muslim immigrants, and appeared to be part of a wider attempt to insist on an exclusively Hindu vision of India.

Not for the first time, the search for a new national character involved a tense rummage through ancient times. But it raised more questions than answers. Could a nation that contained nearly 200 million Muslims, only a fraction fewer than Pakistan, really proclaim itself an irreducibly Hindu state? Not everyone thought so.

The idea of India as a Hindu civilisation that could be revived as policy was formed in 1923 as 'Hindutva', and took a violent turn when Gandhi was assassinated by its disciples on the grounds that he urged tolerance between faiths. Now it was shaking the reins again. Kapil Komireddi, in *Malevolent Republic*, was one of many to object: 'The very narrative of the republic ... has been rewritten.'

There was a wider point. Clarified history can produce only cartoons – which tend to trigger resentment in the excluded. It is history not so much recovered as invented, going against the grain of its most useful lesson, which is that the past is invariably a tangle of contradictory forces that only begin to make sense long after the event. R. H. Tawney famously referred to the convictions of one age as being the challenges of the one that followed.

Anyone can run a morality meter over previous historical periods; the harder truth – that some of history's saints were villains, and some of its villains saints – is not the stuff of national slogans. And this is what makes India unfocused when it comes to soft power. It may not be feasible to marry two such different identities: ancient Hindu mythology and the high-speed modern rush.

It does have one extraordinary soft-power asset, however. India's most important resource may be the simplest of them all ... its people.

In the colonial period India's population was shuffled abroad in vast numbers (up to two million) as indentured labour to the British dominions in Africa, the Caribbean and the Pacific. It was not slavery, exactly, but it was only one rung above it. Return tickets were not part of the arrangement, so the project transformed large regions of the world, planting Indian habits, tastes and priorities in almost every nation.

In more recent times Indian citizens have migrated of their own accord – to America, Asia and Europe, and of course back to the one-time mother country. Something in the region of eighteen million Indian citizens now live overseas – a dispersed nation not much smaller than the population of Australia. Non-Resident Indians are an influential community of ambitious people: artists, lawyers, bankers, scientists, shopkeepers, teachers, doctors, cooks and every other occupation one could name. Thanks to the fact that there are four thousand management schools in India, the world is full of Indian-born chief executives, but an even more potent network has been the population of Indians educated overseas. Some of these eager students have returned to create new ventures in the land of their birth; others have pioneered innovation abroad. They have been especially important in technology: as Michael Lewis put it, noticing the Indian contribution to the intensity of Silicon Valley in *The New New Thing*, the future of the world smelled an awful lot like . . . curry.

As its students pour through the world's universities, India's enormous population is driving new industries as well as old ones. The UN estimates that by 2030 it will have not just the world's largest population, but also – since a third of it is under fourteen – the world's largest *working* population. It has a mighty nation-in-exile to call on. In the era of globalisation this is a gold-plated resource. And since a large segment of this population will speak English, India will be even better placed to play a key role in the future of the world.

There is a sociological term for this: the 'demographic dividend'.[12]

In common (or soft) parlance it is what we might call . . . people power.

---

12 In 2017 Bollywood produced nearly two thousand films, selling 3.6 billion tickets – more even than the 2.6 billion sold by America. Since the majority were not in English, the global impact was not as great as it might have been – but this is still a powerful resource.

15

Africa: Below the Line

It may seem an indecent or Eurocentric presumption to give so small a space, in a survey of this sort, to the world below the Equator. But the standard surveys confirm that soft power is indeed a northern-hemisphere quality. No African nation has ever appeared in the Portland Soft Power 30, and when Nigeria came twenty-fifth in the 2019 *Monocle* ranking it was the continent's first representative in that list. Brazil and Argentina climbed into the Portland reckoning the previous year, but in twenty-ninth and thirtieth place – the last available spots. The fact that the white Commonwealth nations Australia and New Zealand earn higher places (ninth and seventeenth, respectively) confirms the feeling that soft power may be not just a European invention but a European commodity.

This is clearly artificial. As has often been pointed out (and just as often overlooked), Africa, Australia, Latin America and South-East Asia make up a far bigger proportion of the earth's surface than traditional maps suggest, thanks to projections that shrink land south of the tropics. Greenland, for instance, usually appears to be immense, yet at two million square miles it is smaller than both Algeria and the Democratic Republic of Congo.

Something like 2.5 billion people live below the Equator, a third of the global total, but until now they have not been held to generate anything like a similar proportion of soft power. It may be that the things soft power values happen to be the things in which developed nations tend to be richer than the lands they once colonised. It tells us too that the ability to exert influence is a game played with distilled history – history that obscures as much as it reveals. The southern continents have been more acted on than acting: the impositions of Europe and Arabia blocked indigenous voices and dreams to an extent that only now can the latter be heard. And even now they speak in voices not entirely their own, infused with foreign languages, foreign religions (Islam and Christianity) and all the attendant cultural assumptions.

This may be Africa's most important soft-power angle: it can be (and to a large extent is) the place where an immense historical reckoning is being played out.

The extent of the oppression can hardly be exaggerated. When Bismarck, Chancellor of the newly united Germany, invited the world's statesmen to Berlin in 1884 to discuss Africa's future, it was by no means the beginning of the carve-up: Britain had long since occupied large parts of Africa, and France, Germany, Belgium, Holland, Italy and Portugal encroached as well. This brazen 'scramble for Africa' – the tussle for control of land, trade routes, markets and raw materials – flowed from what Jan Morris called (thinking of Britain) 'a frenzy of greed, ambition and do-goodism'.

It was high noon for the 'sphere of influence' – indeed it was at this conference that the term was born. But up to this point the process had been ramshackle; the purpose of the meeting was to divide the cake in an organised and manageable way.[1]

No African (it goes without saying) was consulted or involved in this matter.

It was a hideous project. As many as twenty or forty million Africans (the fact that the number is unknowable is a prominent aspect of the horror) were seized, shackled, tormented and sold as slaves. Nor does it excuse anyone that this was a story with no heroes. All the ancient civilisations – Sumeria, Babylon, Persia, Greece, India, Rome, Egypt – practised slavery, as did Africa itself. When Europe first ventured there it was astounded to

---

1 If the first 'great game' was a tussle for influence in Central Asia, and the second was the Cold War, when nuclear powers sought to gain the high ground across the developing world, we might call modern soft-power initiatives the third such scramble. And now there is a fourth: the race for mineral rights in the Arctic. Tragically, the melting of the polar ice is exposing it to precisely the sort of exploitation – drilling for energy – that will further hasten its own disappearance.

find regions (in Sudan, Ghana and Mali) where up to a third of the population was enslaved. In other parts (Cameroon, Congo and Sierra Leone) it was more like half. The earliest Portuguese traders found that fifteen humans could be bought for a single horse – a heart-stopping bargain. More important, they knew where the gold was.

Arab merchants had long been carting Africans across the Sahara from Timbuktu and out of Indian Ocean ports by the million. And Africa had also enslaved *itself* – the snatching of people was part of everyday life in climates where it was natural to want others to do manual labour, given that no one would do it who had a choice.

Europe wrote an evil new page in this evil old story by shipping millions of these men and women across the Atlantic to the plantations of the New World.

The result was a continent deforested of Africa's greatest resource: its people.

We have said that migrating people are one of soft power's most important engines – but that scarcely holds when those people are chained and scattered against their will. The Africans who were transported to the Caribbean and North America were able, in due course, to give the world new musical genres (from reggae and calypso to blues and jazz) but in most spheres of cultural life they were silenced. Only in recent times – and the painful process of decolonisation and renewal is still in its relatively early stage – was Africa able to contemplate playing its true role in the soft-power world.

It holds some impressive cards.

First, it stands alone as the place where human life evolved: Africa was the cradle of all human life, giving rise even to the 'civilisations' that would later fall on it with such devoted greed. In the winter of 2019 research was published claiming (perhaps ambitiously) that the site of this cradle was a specific wetland south of the Zambezi River in Botswana, some 200,000 years ago. The analysis, published in the magazine *Nature*, merged DNA evidence with archaeological and fossil remains, and was greeted with caution by geneticists. But even if it was wrong, it was not wildly wrong – few disputed its broad conclusion. Whether in the Rift Valley or further south, this is where human beings first appeared.

When ancient climate change created new green land, *Homo sapiens* wandered north and south, sparking a migratory pattern that persists to this day.

It is hard to imagine a greater source of soft power: Africa is the world's parent.

The second card is related to the first, because Africa is not only the world's first human home – it is also the *last* great wilderness, home to lion and elephant, giraffe, crocodile and leopard. The fact that its extreme climate makes it vulnerable to the world's most dangerous animals and insects (the tsetse fly and the mosquito) has also made it unfriendly to the raising of both crops and livestock herds.

In a nice historical twist, in modern times that has become a competitive advantage, since Africa, as precious habitat for some of the world's most endangered species (the black rhino, the painted dog, the mountain gorilla), no longer seeks to offer itself as a mere safari for wealthy overseas hunters – it is also a capital of conservation, with a very particular tourist industry. About a third of the thirty million annual tourist visits to Africa are prompted by a desire to see this wildlife first-hand, and a healthy chunk of the remainder (most of which is business travel) also includes an early-morning drive in search of cheetahs or wildebeest with a pair of binoculars and a camera.

The third aspect of Africa's new soft power lies in its people. Freed at last from the grip of foreign empires, and liberated by modern technology to pursue new initiatives in health, communications, finance and agriculture, the population of the continent is regaining its balance. Today it stands at 1.2 billion, and is still racked by war (in Cameroon, the Congo, Eritrea, Rwanda, Sudan and elsewhere: a study published in *The Lancet* in 2018 estimated that up to five million children had died as a direct consequence of the continent's many conflicts in the previous two decades). Africa's population may even double in the next half century (according to some projections), releasing a torrent of new energy and new demand on the world. And while projections of this sort are fallible (especially with new viruses on the loose), this growth is more likely to be restrained by a lower birth rate than by disease. Africa, after all, is used to worse hazards: the Ebola virus, a much more ferocious enemy, claimed fewer than 12,000 lives – horrifying, but not graph-changing.

It is estimated that half the world's fastest-growing economies will soon be African, and that momentum is being given fresh energy by one of migration's most obvious (yet least trumpeted) benefits: as the economies of Africa liberalise, so its émigré population can return and start new businesses in the land of its birth. From Nigeria to Ethiopia, Africans were returning from America and Europe and setting up new ventures: a restaurant, a clothing factory, a travel agency, an events-management company or a solar-powered internet café. These might be traditional or futuristic, large or tiny, but taken together they represented a significant shift in the way the continent could imagine itself. It is still home to the world's largest concentration of people living in extreme poverty, but these green shoots are signs that this need no longer be Africa's default setting.

Who was it who said that history repeats itself? In truth, it hardly ever does. But there was a second phase of the scramble for Africa during the Cold War, when East and West competed for influence and advantage across the continent. And recent decades have seen a third such 'great game', this time led by vigorous new players.

It happened fast. In 2000, the year when China joined the World Trade Organization, America was by far the leading exporter of goods to Africa, followed by France (thanks to its historic presence). In those days, China was as near to invisible as made no difference. Just twenty years later it was the dominant export player in all but two countries, the Central African Republic and Zimbabwe. In the first fifteen years of the century it loaned nearly $100 billion to the region, overtaking America as the leading investor. Most of this was in infrastructure, and it carried a clear soft-power message: unlike the greedy imperialists that blighted your past, *we are here to help.* By 2018 China had built 30,000 kilometres of road, 2000 kilometres of railway, 85 million tonnes per year of port capacity, 10 million tonnes per day of clean water supply and 30,000 kilometres of power lines. There were projects in places that had never felt the heat of a boom: a $10 billion port near Dar es Salaam, a railway in Ethiopia, economic zones in Nigeria and Rwanda. Overnight, it seemed, Africa had a new strand in its commercial make-up.

It was home to 10,000 Chinese-owned businesses, with perhaps a million Chinese workers on site. Political delegations were looking at new projects and partnerships everywhere. Investment grew from $16 billion in 2011 to $43 billion in 2017. And when President Xi visited Senegal in September 2018 he went one better, announcing $60 billion of fresh resources, most of it provided by two Chinese development banks. In recent years, in Senegal alone, China had built sports stadiums, a wrestling arena, a museum and several roads. Now came this clear statement of renewed support.

The new railway from Addis Ababa to Djibouti turned a three-day road trip into a twelve-hour train ride. The port in Tanzania is set fair to become the busiest in East Africa when it opens in 2022, and news coming out of Beijing, concerning a new 370-mph supertrain that flew on a cushion of air, excited investors still further as they imagined one of *those* racing from the Cape to Cairo. The construction of 'a second Suez' – a $7.5 billion project to cut a new 72-kilometre shipping line alongside the existing canal, which promised to give Egypt a new link to the wider world – was unusual in not being funded by foreign investment, but much of the continent's new infrastructure was supported by Chinese finance; goods were already rattling through brand-new airports in Djibouti; and a $3 billion railway was speeding business travel between Nairobi and Mombasa.

It was not only the physical infrastructure – mobile technology was arriving, too. This was less visible: it was not obvious to everyone that the 'Tecno' logo that appeared on billboards from Mali to Kenya was promoting a Shenzhen-based mobile phone manufacturer named Transsion, which sold a hundred million handsets across Africa in 2018. But this was just as radical an intervention. China was giving the continent a technological brain transplant. Western corporations like Apple and Facebook were transforming African lives too, but on the whole Western governments concentrated on traditional sectors: aid and famine relief. It was China that led the way in wireless communications. It was no surprise when Jack Ma, founder of Alibaba (the spectacular Chinese e-commerce giant founded in 1999 and already worth more than $350 billion), launched a million-dollar prize for internet entrepreneurs, on a *Dragons' Den* style television contest in Ghana. African online retail felt like a thoroughly Chinese idea. The winner was a Nigerian medical delivery company, and Ma told the TV audience that entrepreneurs in Africa today were like himself two decades earlier – 'no background, no money, no technology'. He was living proof of what could be achieved.

In a colonial-era twist, it even began to look as though China might turn Africa into what it had once been itself – a low-cost workshop. When Transsion opened two facilities in Ethiopia it had all the makings of a familiar industrial story: Irene Yuan Sun was not alone in calling Africa the next 'global manufacturing powerhouse'.

The technological initiative brought a new dimension to what until then had been a traditional exercise of soft power: the cultivation of connections to ensure preferential access to raw materials. In the nineteenth-century 'scramble' the prize was diamonds and gold; now it was copper for electronic circuits, and lithium and cobalt for batteries.[2]

Nowhere was the mineral rush more fervent than in the cobalt-rich Democratic Republic of Congo (DRC). Cobalt was the key ingredient in rechargeable batteries for laptops, pads, phones and (increasingly) cars – each car required around 10 grams. And the DRC had the good fortune to contain nearly three-quarters of the world's supply of this rare substance.[3] China was quick to sense a strategic opportunity. By the time forward-thinking car companies like Tesla and Volkswagen came knocking, China had

2 By 2019 China was consuming almost half of the world's supply of copper, and as the traditional mines in Chile and Australia began to run dry, so the newly found deposits in the Democratic Republic of Congo became even more prized.

3 Or misfortune. Economists call this the resource curse: the sad truth is that a rich seam of precious commodities does not necessarily bring prosperity, since it attracts corruption and conflict in the seemingly 'lucky' regions where it is discovered.

already planted its foot in the door. In 2007 it signed a cobalt-for-loans deal worth $9 billion with the DRC, and had gone on to develop not just a mining and smelting operation in Africa (including seven of the ten biggest mines in the DRC), but a battery-manufacturing industry in China as well. Since 2012 it has invested a further $8 billion, and presided over the entire supply chain of this now-essential component.

There was one negative soft-power aspect in this story: it was said (by UNICEF) that up to 40,000 children were being exploited by these mining operations, in squalid conditions. But that did not stop the value of cobalt from tripling between 2016 and 2018, from $26,000 per tonne to $90,000. A year later, Bloomberg predicted that the green revolution would boost demand for cobalt by forty-seven times in the coming decade. To no one's surprise, the bonanza was not trickling down to the impoverished families digging bluish ore out of muddy tunnels and washing it in the stream they used for drinking water – for $2 a day. And not many of the eco-warriors in the West who felt they were taking an advanced moral stand by abandoning fossil fuels spared a thought for the suffering (it was reported that more than five million had perished in the war zone that was the DRC) that lay behind their socially responsible new vehicles. As always, the seemingly clear waters of soft power did not run smooth.

The world had grown used to talking about blood diamonds: precious gems that came with a death toll attached; now it had to face the idea of . . . blood batteries.

China was not the only global player looking to establish a foothold in Africa. Vladimir Putin hosted an Africa–Russia summit with a view to entering the fray by offering African leaders military and political cooperation (and advice on media tactics). In 2017 Germany proposed a 'Marshall Plan for Africa', and the EU promised €40 billion. America, India and Russia followed suit. Turkish and Filipino companies were generating power in Ghana, while Turkish Airlines, with flights to at least forty destinations, was becoming the largest aviation operator in the continent.

At the turn of the century Turkey had a dozen foreign offices in Africa; in 2019 it had thirty-nine, and was the second largest contributor of development aid.

The new scramble was producing new players, too.

In two notable areas Africa has become the site of significant soft-power conflict. In the tussle for control of national histories it is the setting for some of the most intense arguments about the repatriation of colonial-era art; and it is also the subject of the related conversation on reparations for the cruelties and injustices of the past.

The first of these arguments was vividly present when, in 2016, an impressive new building was unveiled in Dakar, capital of Senegal. A city until then better known as the finish of the trans-Saharan car rally was now host to an ambitious new cultural institution: the Museum of Black Civilisations.

A sleek modern pantheon, its low rotunda flanked by fountains and flagpoles, it was the culmination of a long-held dream. Shortly after Senegal achieved independence from France, in 1966, its then-president (the poet and philosopher Leopold Sedar Senghor) articulated a vision of just such an enterprise, but for five decades it had proved beyond his country's parched resources. Now, at last, it gleamed in the African sun.

'This moment is historic,' declared Senegal's President Macky Sall.

It was true – and in a distinctive way. In calling it 'part of the continuity of history', he was drawing attention to one of imperialism's increasingly obvious by-products: the way it interrupted and erased a country's past, replacing it with a story not its own. This museum was not a national gallery, nor even a pan-African project. It aimed to showcase African-themed work from all over the world: one of its first exhibitions involved art from Cuba. It was an attempt, in other words, to look *through* the colonial period – rendering it nothing more than a two-hundred-year blip in the longer history of the region, and reaching to the deeper continuities that lay beneath.

It had a problem, however. There was a grave shortage of things to put in it.

One of the launch exhibitions, 'African Civilisations:

Continuous Creation of Humanity', was characterised above all by what it did *not* display. The fact was, nearly all of Senegal's significant treasures were held elsewhere – most of them in France. As many as 50,000 artefacts (according to some estimates) had been hauled away by the nineteenth-century imperial occupier. It might have been even more.

Not all of these occupiers were looters – as we have seen, there were scholarly motives and benign impulses in the mix too. But this was trophy-hunting on an epic scale. Senegal was scraped to the bone. The absence was tangible, and made an eloquent and timely case that purloined treasure should be returned.

It made the new museum something more than just a prestigious new hub in the arts world. It was a major soft-power statement. Until recently it had been possible for Western museums to argue that they were honourable custodians of rare objects. Curators told of artefacts returned to their country of origin only to resurface in auction rooms a few months later,[4] or to suffer damage in tropical hothouses. This was a dated argument. A top-of-the-range building stood ready to have its contents restored. And it wasn't the only one. There were excellent galleries in Nigeria, Congo and South Africa, too. The idea that Africa could not keep art was no longer tenable.

'It is entirely logical that Africans should get back their artworks,' said Abdou Latif Coulibaly, Senegal's Culture Minister; and this was a familiar cry. Just as Greece was continuing to agitate for the return of the 'Elgin' Marbles (to the extent of threatening to include such a demand in the trade negotiations between Britain and the EU), so the once-colonised kingdoms of Africa wanted their artistic heritage back in the place where it was created.

On the surface it seemed a just claim that would only grow in intensity: an enormous trove of art had indeed been hauled away by imperial adventurers. August voices such as the BBC were bandying the term 'looted African treasures' as if the words were hyphenated, as if there were nothing more to be said on the

---

4 Belgium's Royal Museum returned 166 objects to the Congo in the 1970s. Only twenty-four of them, according to its own figures, are still there today.

subject. And in a telling sign of the times, the superhero in the 2018 film *Black Panther* became an art-history vigilante by stealing back an artefact from 'The Museum of Great Britain' with the caustic riposte: 'How do you think your ancestors got these?'

Audiences cheered. It was possible that this blurred the distinction between ancient works with controversial origins and more blatant instances of recent looting, such as the pillaging of work from Iraq's National Museum in the aftermath of the recent war. When crates of the latter were smuggled into Britain from Peshawar (in Pakistan) in 2002, having been plundered from the ruins by ISIS hunter-gatherers, they were seized, restored, catalogued, exhibited and returned. But newspaper headline writers seemed happy to depict any artistic product housed in colonial museums as having been by definition 'looted', thanks to the unequal balance of power involved.

It was also muttered, in some corridors of soft power, that the new museum in Senegal was not quite the high-minded project it appeared to be, but a canny move by China, which contributed $30 million to the building in the knowledge that it would fuel anti-European sentiments of this sort. It was an idealistic gesture, but also a swashbuckling sign of China's growing hold over Africa: some even suggested that Senegal was doing no more than exchanging one form of colonialism for another.

The fact remained: most of Senegal's heritage was in France, and it was impossible to avoid having a conversation about the rights and wrongs of this. In December 2017 France's new president, Emmanuel Macron, went to Ouagadougou, capital of Burkina Faso, and set many curatorial hearts fluttering by announcing that in his view *all* the treasures filched by France should be returned. He was unambiguous: 'I am from a generation of the French people for whom the crimes of European colonialism are undeniable. African heritage can no longer be the prisoner of European museums.'

He then commissioned a report which, when it was published a year later, agreed that Africa had been grievously injured by the imperial 'system of appropriation'. It proposed that 90,000 artefacts housed in French museums should be repatriated.

In London the historian David Olusoga, among others, was

causing a flutter with his suggestion that there be a 'supermarket sweep' of the British Museum – visiting arts ministers from the old dominions would have five minutes to load their trolley with whichever treasures they most prized – an Egyptian mummy here, an Indian carving there, a Grecian marble, an African bronze, a Korean vase ... It was worrying, too, for the new Humboldt Forum in Berlin. Led by Neil MacGregor, once director of the British Museum, it found its existence questioned before it had even opened its doors.

The point was that the past was not dead. On the contrary, it was full of unexploded devices. In the week that Macron's report was published, a visitor to London from Easter Island (a fragment of Chile in the Pacific Ocean) was demanding the return of the celebrated stone head from the Bloomsbury galleries.[5] There were calls from Australia for the return of a shield taken by Captain Cook's colony in Botany Bay. The government of Egypt was demanding that the slab of ancient writing known as the Rosetta Stone, one of the British Museum's iconic possessions, be sent 'home'. And Jesus College Cambridge was coming under fierce pressure (not least from its own students) to restore a bronze cockerel to Benin, one of the now-infamous 'Benin Bronzes' that had been seized following a punitive military raid in 1897.

A government official on the Isle of Man joined the bandwagon by asking that the British Library 'return' *The Chronicles of the Kings of Mann and the Isles*, a little-known work by thirteenth-century monks (the national library, hardly an illogical home for a rare book, had kept it safe since the dissolution of the monasteries).

In theory there was no limit to such demands. When Tristram Hunt became director of London's Victoria and Albert Museum in 2017 he, a seasoned politician, was 'taken aback' by the intensity of the debate. In his case, the treasure in question was a gold crown taken from Ethiopia in 1868. There was no denying its tainted origins: it had been carted off by British troops after they

---

5 'We are just a body,' said Tarita Alarcon Rapu, Governor of Easter Island, on a visit to London. 'You, the British people, have our soul.'

had stormed the Maqdala fortress in Abyssinia. In all they took enough treasure to fill a fifteen-elephant baggage train.

There were counter-arguments, however – as always, attempting to repair the past was no simple matter. First, not everything in Western museums was 'stolen'. Even when allowance was made for the fact that no transaction in imperial times was between free and equal parties, some of the work was collected or acquired by studious archaeologists with honourable motives. And objects had passed through so many hands, for so many years, that it was no longer possible to unscramble the chain of ownership. It could not even be ascertained where they truly 'belonged' – there were often rival claimants, which would lead to more friction rather than less.

Second, some of the objects were not so much snatched as *saved*. When Timbuktu's Ahmed Baba Library was burned by Islamists in 2013, the curators may well have wished that its priceless manuscripts, now ashes, were safe in airtight vaults far away.

Third, and most important: it was noticeable that repatriation appealed above all to nativist politicians seeking to stir patriotic emotions in their own people. The demand that objects be returned tacitly proposed a world in which nations could possess *only* national treasures, that heritage was by definition chained to its country of origin.

Could anything be more narrow than this – a situation in which nations could display only their own products, like so many stalls in a global culture fair? Who wanted a world in which there was no French painting outside France, no Italian art outside Italy, no Greek sculpture outside Greece ... and no African work outside Africa? The world's great museums were arenas of comparison and exchange. In Neil MacGregor's words, galleries such as the British Museum were monuments '*of* the world, *for* the world' – forums for universal learning, not national hood ornaments. They actively resisted the idea that culture 'belonged' to anyone – it belonged to all. At their best, these museums were expressions not of rapacious imperialism but of civic ambition, staffed by men and women who were by no means colonial trophy hunters.

They aspired to tell the story not of one nation, but of the whole planet.

The complications in this area were more than mere niceties. In 2002 the leading museums issued a 'declaration on the importance and value of universal museums', which argued that while it was possible to regret the past, it was not possible to rearrange or redo it, and that objects gathered in earlier times had to be viewed 'in the light of different sensitivities'. Repatriation was 'yesterday's question'. That turned out not to be the case. Arguments in favour of the status quo sounded self-interested – art and culture were 'contested' spaces that could no longer rest their case on tradition. Any hopes that the demands for restoration could be nipped in the bud were too late. The clamour grew noisier every day, and the West increasingly seemed a selfish child crying finders-keepers as it hugged its ill-gotten gains.

There were soft-power dangers here: neither haughtiness nor bitterness were good for national brands, and the controversy itself was altering the works. It was turning them into emblems of political conflict rather than of human history, objects of notoriety rather than creative miracles – mere trophies in a geopolitical tug of war.

It was easy to say that looting art was wrong; but grabbing it back, after so many centuries, was clumsy too. It was hard to see a way through this either/or impasse.

One possible answer suggested itself: 3-D printing. As the famous Cast Courts at London's Victoria and Albert Museum had long proved, it was possible to create lavish galleries by copying masterpieces (in this case ancient columns, medieval gateways and Renaissance sculptures) while leaving the originals where they were – in Rome, Florence or Santiago de Compostela. Could not something similar be done for the African artefacts in foreign hands? The controversial originals could be returned as crowning highlights of national collections, while copies stood in for them on the world's famous stages. Both the originals and the copies could be shared or exchanged, in accordance with a vision that gave the highest priority to the widest possible display of such things, rather than allowing them to be prize exhibits in a dispute about mere ownership.

The West's museums would not be too badly diminished, and who could object if the restored works did become profitable attractions in the lands of their birth – after all, the Louvre and the British Museum earn handsome incomes from the Greek- and Egyptian-themed biros, tea towels and mouse mats. And whatever the West lost in art kudos it might gain, with interest, in the soft arena of international goodwill.

As a soft-power move, in the spirit of collaboration rather than competition, and as a rebuke to the idea that national art should decorate only the land of its birth, Britain might send not just imperial-era artefacts but pieces of its *own* heritage to Africa: medieval stained glass, Anglo-Saxon helmets, Celtic jewels, Tudor portraits, Turner watercolours or Wedgwood teapots.

When soft power fails, the repercussions can be serious. Nations that fight to hang on to ill-gotten gains risk looking small and mean-spirited. And it so happens that only a small portion of what institutions own is actually on display at any one time. A 2016 survey by the art magazine *Quartz* found that the world's leading museums displayed only 10 per cent of what they owned. Washington's National Gallery of Art owned 199 works by Mark Rothko; only a handful were on the walls. New York's Museum of Modern Art had room for only twenty-four of its 1221 Picassos. European and American basements were full of renowned works. Even Tehran was sitting on a fabled collection of modern art that had been suppressed as 'decadent' ever since the fall of the Shah.

For Britain, a solution of this sort would seem especially inviting. It is too soon to say where Brexit will lead: the United Kingdom might be on the brink of renewing itself, or standing on the edge of disintegration. But the angry divisions it has exposed have already wrought a marked change in the way the country is seen by others, so it would seem politic that it make friendly overtures of this sort. Britain has watched with little interest as China has forged new friendships across Africa (when Theresa May went to Kenya in 2018 it was the first such visit by a British Prime Minister for thirty years); and while Britain may no longer be in the business of building ports and railways – it might well be regarded with suspicion if it tried – in a continent where

millions of people speak its language, observe its religious culture
and follow its football teams it is by no means impotent. Nothing
can reverse the horrors of slavery, but to be in the vanguard of
a new approach to history, at a time when it is a matter of such
fervent concern around the world . . . that is a golden soft-power
opportunity. Britain could – in theory – use that history to burnish the connections it will surely need in the future. And it could
do this most simply by sharing . . . itself.

Sharing art is one thing; trying to repair history itself is quite
another. But the campaign to return art has already developed
into a growing demand that financial restitution be made to the
regions and peoples fractured by slavery and empire. In some
hands, this would include major reparations for all colonial mis-
deeds: a deep and difficult new idea.

No one can dispute that the territories occupied by Europe's
colonial powers suffered grievous harm, and have endured tragic
histories; nor can anyone deny that the imperial nations profited
hideously from the slave trade. Converting that into practical
policies, however, is even more treacherous than the argument
over works of art. Almost every nation has ghosts that need exor-
cising, and these are too well known to need listing. It is hard to
calculate how much should be paid . . . by whom . . . to whom . . .
and for what? The guilty and the innocent alike are all long dead.

Could a legal tribunal assess the merits of such ancient crimes?
A venerable Armenian proverb once declared that the future was
easy enough to understand – it was the past that was unfathomable. Emerging nations needed little encouragement to cherish
and assert their histories (on the grounds that they had been
suppressed by others); but it was hard to see how all these old
grievances could be settled. There are too many horrors in the
world's past to expunge. Moreover, turning the past into a mon-
etary dispute might do history itself a profound disservice by
implying that it could ever be a straightforward matter of heroes
and villains, criminals and victims – the truth is almost always
more ambiguous than that. It might even invite the argument that
reparations *already* existed – in the form of foreign aid. In 2016
Europe gave more than $100 billion to the less prosperous world,

a heavy transfer from the former coloniser to the once-colonised. No one would gain if this were to be cynically 'repurposed' as a fine for evils committed in earlier times. Better, perhaps, to concentrate the world's treasure on the evils of modern-day slavery, a daily evil that still ensnares as many as forty million people in horrifying servitude.

There is no escaping the fact that the shadow of European history weighs heavily on the African continent, and will continue to do so far into the future. That is in part why the continent has been open to the influence of China and Russia, powers that had little to do with the first, harrowing 'scramble'. But this may be only a changing of the guard. Africa is being hustled over again.

Today's scramble may have stars more favourably aligned than its nineteenth-century precursor. Overseas corporations pursue profits, as they always have, but do not seek new domains for Queen or Emperor. Modern Africa is at last writing its own future – to an extent not possible in the era when, as Belloc put it: 'Whatever happens, we have got / The Maxim gun, and they have not'. Having been 'left behind' by industrial Europe – never having had a widespread system of telephone landlines, for instance – Africa has been jump-started by mobile technology to take the necessary leaps forward in economics, politics, technology and education on its own.

Its population is set to double by 2050 – a challenge, but also an opportunity, since by international standards it will be young – the median age in modern Africa is only nineteen, a palpable advantage at a time of changing technology, giving it the ability to leapfrog several generations of automation. This is not just a social force – money is now free to move as never before. From Nigeria to Kenya and from Ghana to South Africa, tech hubs are springing to life like grasslands when the rains come – the number of these mushroomed by 50 per cent in 2019 alone.

Africa may soon be able to do what other parts of the world have been able to do for a long time – marry ancient traditions, in this case nature and wildlife, with futuristic new forms of progress. Villages that once lacked a well now have solar panels; people without electricity can trade cryptocurrencies on their phones (some of which feature cameras customised to capture dark skin tones); microfinance initiatives are giving isolated communities a route into modern commerce; an 'Uber of trucks' transport system in Nairobi is speeding the movement of freight, flashing mangoes and cacao beans along Chinese-built highways; the tumbling rivers whose rock-strewn courses once rendered them useless for navigation are now ideal sites for hydroelectric energy, while the blazing tropical sun is also, suddenly, a power plant.

Nigerian farmers are using machine learning to boost productivity. Kenya has elephants, but also a space programme that has the potential, thanks to its position on the Equator, to be extremely significant. In South Africa, radio telescopes penetrate the heavens in clearings where antelope once roamed; there are even new sporting identities being created.[6] There are projects to turn single-use plastic into boats, and irrigation schemes to make the desert bloom.

There are even signs – tentative, of course – of a political renewal. The decades following decolonisation were neither easy nor peaceful – how could they be? But in 2019 there was a glimmer of a different future when a twenty-year negotiation led to the announcement of what might one day be the world's largest free-trade area, binding fifty-four nations, not all of them stable, into a single trillion-dollar bloc. A continent still synonymous with political instability (there have been twenty-seven changes of national leadership since 2015), and constantly war-torn, is at last showing signs of revival: at the end of 2019 eight francophone nations in West Africa agreed to abandon the imperial-era CFA (the Colonies Françaises d'Afrique) as their currency and develop a common replacement, to be called the *eco*. There may even be freedom of movement for the people of the new bloc, and there is potential for the continent to unite around English or French as common languages. Here, however, the grim weight of colonial history casts a shadow once again, creating profound resistance

---

6 When South Africa's rugby captain Siya Kolisi hoisted the World Cup in 2019 and said he hoped to 'inspire every kid' at home he was reminding the global television audience of the soft power of games. When he was born, in 1991, Nelson Mandela had been free for just a year, and apartheid South Africa was still a sporting pariah.

to this unnatural and unAfrican gambit, however useful it might be – and has been in India, for example.

Like all such unions, the African Continental Free Trade Area will be the subject of long arguments between competing national interests (there is friction between Egypt and Ethiopia about the waters of the Upper Nile, for instance) and dogged by other practical questions – such as the constitution of the central (in this case regional) bank. But as President Macron pointed out, welcoming the end of CFA and the launch of the new currency, it was historic. In calling French colonialism 'a profound mistake' he was helping to clear the path towards a new era in African life.

This may arrive sooner than we think. The UN has forecast that intra-African trade will grow by up to 50 per cent not just in the long term, but in the next five years.

The world might one day find itself marching to an African beat.

16

World on Fire: South America and Australasia

M uch that can be said about African soft power can be said about South America as well. It too is home to a besieged and endangered wilderness – the Amazon rainforest – and thus has a special place in the world's heart. Its Inca and Aztec monuments are a more spectacular reminder of ancient times than anything in Africa apart from the Egyptian Pyramids, and, like them, are a powerful tourist asset. But here too the native culture was all but extinguished by brutal European conquest and occupation. In place of the tragic enormity of slavery it offers revolutionary politics: Che Guevara was a poster boy to millions who could not have said which country he came from. And the present texture of its daily life, from the music-and-football carnival of Brazil to the sizzling cuisines of Mexico and Peru, is a fusion.

Modern South America has continued to attach brakes to this soft-power engine, however. Every now and then a girl from Ipanema or a dazzling goal scorer in green and yellow would capture the hearts of the world. But years of military coups, police crackdowns and authoritarian rule (seventeen of twenty Latin American nations in 1977 were dictatorships) gave its political structures a lethal twist. As in Africa, the world's biggest powers – America, China, Russia – competed for influence and access, and when countries such as Brazil became so vividly careless even of their own forest, logging huge tracts without restraint (in 1995 it was reported that an area the size of Belgium was ripped out every year), it was hard for outsiders to applaud.

The gung-ho government of Jair Bolsonaro, with its cavalier attitude to the destruction of the national rainforest (a precious global resource amounting to roughly 40 per cent of the world's tropical wilderness), continued to support a commercial free-for-all even when that forest caught fire. One-fifth of the Amazon jungle had been lost in a single generation of logging, mining and burning – a blatant act of reputational self-harm at a time when world youth was in uproar over environmental damage.

Of course, foreign powers were greedy for the continent's raw materials: Chilean copper, Bolivian lithium, Brazilian iron, Peruvian gold. And the world was no longer content to see the entire continent as being America's 'backyard'. It was the setting for much Cold War tension as the Soviet Union cultivated radical movements and America tried to choke them. Now the emphasis was on business opportunities.

As in Africa, China took the lead. In the first seventeen years of the twenty-first century it invested more than $100 billion in South America, and its banks advanced $140 billion in loans. Argentina had a Chinese-built space station; Ecuador a 4300-camera Chinese-run surveillance system. From nowhere, China was suddenly Brazil's biggest trading partner. Meanwhile, there were more than forty new 'Confucius Institutes' across the continent – an overt attempt to spread China's language and culture. In boiling cities hard by the Equator and freezing harbour fronts in Tierra del Fuego, young South Americans were learning Mandarin, drinking green tea and making paper lanterns.

Such initiatives tended to go unnoticed in the wider world thanks to the impact of one endless news story: narcotics. It fell to South America to feed the West's drug habit (America alone boasted thirty million consumers), and the industry these consumers supported was turning the continent into a war zone for armed gangs. It made for excellent television drama; it was less successful as a formula for soft-power success.

The murder rate appeared in few tourist brochures (in Acapulco drive-by shootings became so normal that diners in restaurants finished their tacos without looking up); but nowhere in the world compared. In one survey, forty-three of the fifty cities with the highest death toll were in Latin America (seventeen in Brazil, twelve in Mexico and five in Venezuela). Between 2000 and 2017 some 2.5 million people were murdered in drug-sponsored violence – almost triple (according to the University of Maryland's Global Terrorism database) the casualty list in Afghanistan, Iraq and Syria combined.

The number of people killed by terrorism in this period – in the whole world – was less than 10 per cent of this: 243,000.

It was, said the head of the Igarapé Institute in Brazil, 'a war in all but name'.

No wonder people steeled themselves to walk north to the United States.

It is one of soft power's least glamorous attributes that it relies on something as mundane as political stability, but though it is not an easy force for governments to create, it does require state protection. As a result, South America's soft-power potential is as yet untapped. It could be a world-shaking force: its mazy innovations in literature (magic realism) and music[1] have brought vibrancy to long-established models; while its landscapes, sport and cultural heritage are awe-inspiring.

There have been glimmers. It was not a coincidence that Christiana Figueres, the United Nations climate change chief who shepherded 195 nations together to sign the Paris Agreement in 2015, was from Costa Rica, because Costa Rica was a world leader in such matters. Thanks in part to a fluke of geography – its volcanic terrain made it perfect for both hydroelectric and geothermal power – and in part to the 1948 decision (taken by her father, José Figueres Ferrer) to disband the army, Costa Rica had emerged as a peaceful and stable country able to draw 98 per cent

---

[1] In 2007 the usually staid audience at London's Albert Hall was invited to sway in the aisles by the Simón Bolívar Youth Orchestra. Wearing the red, yellow and blue of the Venezuelan flag, the musicians twirled their trumpets and rocked the joint to its Victorian foundations. Under the charismatic leadership of Gustavo Dudamel they had proved, with their performance of Shostakovich's Tenth Symphony, that they could be as suited and serious as any Austrian ensemble. But when they threw themselves into *West Side Story* the place came to life, dragging music away from its bowtie-and-ballgown past. 'Was this,' asked the *Daily Telegraph*, 'the greatest Prom of all time?'

of its energy from renewable sources.[2] It was a beacon of relative calm in a violent continent where the cult of the 'strong man' still held sway. Eight members of the Brazilian cabinet were generals; the drug gangs of Mexico had become an ersatz government of their own in the areas they controlled; and more than three million refugees had been forced to flee the old-school autocracy in Venezuela.

But soft power of this sort cannot make the running on its own. Brazil has developed cultural and educational programmes to support its lively television presence overseas, but on the whole South American governments have not created a systematic way of enhancing their brand. This may in any case be putting the cart before the horse; their most important task may simply be to govern. Only then can their citizens create and develop the networks and institutions from which soft power might flow.

Australasia is a different case in that the British colonisation of Australia and New Zealand was so far-reaching as to amount to the wholesale installation of British habits. In New Zealand's case, an entirely new ecosystem was shipped south – until then the islands knew nothing of pigs, cattle, sheep and rabbits, let alone rugby pitches and Anglican churches. Only in recent times has pre-colonial culture won back its place in the national life. In Australia, Aboriginal children were still taken from their parents and placed in orphanages (by Church missions) up to the 1970s.

This meant more than that Australasia's soft power followed the British model; it was effectively a relay or booster station for that model, a beacon of British values in the wilds of a faraway ocean. It broadcast and stood for the English language, English literature, Christianity, democracy, military courage, sport and tourism. The vaunted Aussie lifestyle (work-hard-play-hard, with surfboards and flip-flops) was a sun-dried version of familiar British habits, exported (not to say deported) to the tropics.

Australia has world-famous beaches, great food, a renowned

---

2 Figueres was also a striking example of soft power's cosmopolitan accent: she attended a German school in Costa Rica before continuing her education in America and Britain (the London School of Economics), where she met her (German) husband, a member of the World Bank's sustainable development team.

wine industry and boundless sunshine. Its enviable sunny lifestyle meant that in the austerity years after the Second World War, when the United Kingdom still rationed bacon and butter, the burning question on millions of British lips was: when shall we emigrate to Australia? The idea of making a home down under would become a staple of reality television.

In one field in particular Australia styled itself as more British than Britain itself, becoming – according to its own image-makers, at least – not just an epitome of cricket excellence (England beat Australia at Lord's, the home of cricket, only once – in 1934 – in the entire twentieth century) but now the upholder of its most precious value: fair play. The baton had been passed, in this mythology, in 1932–3, when England's fast bowlers targeted Bradman's Australians by aiming at their heads (with fielders positioned to trap them) and were roundly accused of betraying the game they until then had claimed to love.

That was the famous Bodyline tour, a showcase for some contradictory aspects of Britishness: pride in the idea of fair play, the blunt will to win, and fear of losing to a colonial 'inferior'. The diplomatic storm it caused showed that soft power could have hard effects: a poor show on the pitch could fracture an imperial myth.

In assuming the mantle of cricketing fair play, Australia turned it into the 'line' – the invisible border that divided tough-but-fair from cheating. Along with a general enthusiasm for sport of all kinds, it became part of *Australia's* national character – take no prisoners, but a beer afterwards and no hard feelings, mate.

That was why the 'Sandpapergate' affair of 2017, in which Steve Smith's Australians scrubbed the ball to make it swing, provoked such an outpouring of wounded disbelief. The fact that they had 'crossed the line' was more than a breach of the game's etiquette: it struck at the heart of Australia's self-image. Michael Clarke, the country's ex-captain, said: 'Please tell me this is a bad dream'; the commentator Jim Maxwell added: 'I don't remember ever being so disappointed'; and before anyone knew it the Prime Minister himself, quick to sense the coldness of the public mood, was denouncing his own players. 'We all woke up this morning shocked and bitterly disappointed,' he said, sounding awfully like the 1930s MCC. 'After all, our cricketers are role models, and cricket is synonymous with fair play.'

As one Sydney professor (Catharine Lumby) put it, the sporting idea of 'the fair go', once an English notion, lay close to the core of Australia's sense of itself.

The official inquiry into the scandal was conducted by an independent body called the Ethics Centre, and the think tank looked to draw general lessons for business from cricket's very public disgrace. Similar morals were drawn from a horseracing crime spree in which one well-known trainer (in Ballarat) was banned for using electrical devices to shock his horses into producing an extra turn of foot when needed.

The fact that sport was not trivial could clearly be seen in the way New Zealand rugby had captivated the entire Pacific region. The bravura Maori culture of the All Blacks, open to Samoans and Fijians alike, was extremely alluring, combining the circus-troupe glamour of the Harlem Globetrotters with a ruthless commitment to excellence that made it by far the world's most successful team. A small and modest nation with a population about half that of London (and whose Prime Minister, Jacinda Ardern, had pulled off a soft-power success with her dignified response to the anti-Muslim killing spree in Christchurch, wearing a veil to express her sympathy with the victims) had won three rugby World Cups and was always the team to beat.

In Australia's case, the fraying of its sporting image symbolised a larger change in its global role. Its destiny, as many noticed, was no longer to be a British-style base in the Pacific, but an Asian nation looking to forge new relationships with China and Japan. There were still soft-power opportunities deriving from its traditional place in the hierarchy of such things – it was well-positioned to develop a trusted English-language news operation for the Pacific region.[3] But like a wind turbine swivelling in the breeze, it was at this time embarked on a transition away from its British roots, looking both back to its Aboriginal prehistory and forwards to the modern, Pacific-facing future it had no option but to embrace.

---

3 In theory, at least. In practice, Australian television was keener on sport and reality shows than old-school foreign affairs reporting.

The first symbol of this change was the Sydney Opera House, designed and built by Danish architects and engineers in 1973 after a long and acrimonious struggle about money (it soared over budget). On one level it was an attempt to align Australia with the European avant-garde; on another, the brilliant design, reminiscent of sails or shark fins in a blue bay, gave it Pacific Ocean glamour. Australia could continue to offer its traditional soft-power components: fun, friendliness, sport and so on. Now, through a world-leading opera house, it could be the voice of Europe in the Pacific.

Modern Australia was built on migration (involuntary, at first) from a Britain that had lost its colonies in America and was seeking new space for its unwanted citizens. In more recent times it was shaped by new migrations – the 2016 census revealed that while 1.5 million migrants came from the UK and New Zealand, the same number came from China, India, the Philippines and Vietnam – placing it (like Britain itself) at a cultural crossroads. The surge in new arrivals inflamed anti-immigrant politics, and while on one level this was not a surprising development – no people has ever liked seeing its national identity undergoing rapid change – in every other way it was short-sighted. Since 1973, when Australia abandoned its 'whites-only' immigration policy, its population had doubled – not a straightforward thing for any country to adjust to. But in that same time frame its economy had grown by more than twenty times – it was hard to imagine a more vivid advertisement for the wealth and dynamism that migration (for all its seeming problems) could bring.

In the past it was a nation's emigrants that moulded the way their home country was seen – all across the British Empire, people were left with a strong sense that the British were a people who gave orders while never doing any menial work of any sort themselves. Now, with improved communications enabling people to send instant video portraits of their new home to those they had left behind, that role increasingly fell to immigrants. It followed that the way a country treated its foreign-born needed (whether the government liked it or not) to be a central part of its soft-power strategy.

Australia has taken a significant risk in this area by taking a tough line with respect to immigration, devising new policies to restrict it, and in some cases going so far as to tow boats crammed with asylum-seekers away from the safe haven they are trying to reach. The thought of the arrival of so many people may have been alarming, but the photographs that went around the world, of a fortunate and prosperous country hanging a 'Do Not Disturb' sign on its door, did more serious damage.

It seemed a Canuteish stance for a forward-looking country. A 2017 government white paper declared that a prime foreign policy aim was 'to ensure Australia remains a persuasive force in our region', but in seeking to make itself harder to enter it was sending a signal that contradicted its hard-won image as an open, sunny, happy-go-lucky place to go.

Once again we can see the complicated dance that soft power imposes on both governments and peoples. Governments, while not all-powerful, are still crucial. A few wrong moves, and a substantial pot can be lost. In Australia this became obvious at the end of 2019, when worse-than-usual bush fires destroyed vast areas of forest (an acreage larger than Portugal, it was said). The flames burned homes and farms, darkened skies over Sydney, turned sunsets scarlet, claimed dozens of lives and damaged habitat so badly that the native koala was declared 'functionally extinct' – conservationists were warning that up to a billion animals (and Australia had the world's most unusual wildlife) may have been roasted alive. Front pages around the world featured orange images of kangaroos and koalas panicking in the flames.

At a time when the *zeitgeist* had moved decisively in favour of an energetic approach to climate change it was hard to imagine a more brand-damaging event. The Prime Minister, Scott Morrison, had himself come to power with the backing of the coal industry (a key Australian export) and was a noted climate-change sceptic. But his New Year's message to the nation – 'We live in the most amazing country on earth. There's no better place to raise kids' – suddenly sounded worse than hollow. Australia was indeed a 'lifestyle superpower', but to the rest of the world it had the potential to be something more: a leader on the front line of the sustainable energy revolution.

No one was saying that government policy had 'caused' the fires; only that the fires were as good as a message from the gods – the burning bush. The country's hot, arid interior had the makings of being the world's largest solar panel, and its huge coast the wherewithal to harness the power of three oceans. Yet its government was slow to concede ground to the new climate-sensitive mood. Given that the Great Barrier Reef, a wonder of the oceanic world, was dwindling – almost half had died since 2016 – it might have been more rather than less concerned with such matters. But while the Greta Thunberg effect was powering Sweden to joint first place in the *Monocle* soft-power ranking for 2019, making it a place and a value-system to be reckoned with, Australia was putting itself in a dangerous place in the court of world opinion.

It chimed with Australia's recalcitrant position on immigration, too, because what was migration, in the modern world, but demographic global warming? Humans have been nomadic since time began – wandering the earth in search of better weather, more fertile soil, kinder neighbours, more interesting food or just a quieter life. Now, accelerated by modern technology, the world's people were being swirled in greater numbers, as if swept between areas of high and low atmospheric pressure. Modern climate change may intensify this in a literal rather than metaphorical way. The World Bank predicts that up to 140 million people will be on the move by 2050 – and since 165 million Bangladeshis live on a flood plain, that might be a low estimate. Some Gallup surveys have suggested that as much as 14 per cent of the global population – that is three-quarters of a billion people – would migrate if it could, enough to put the infrastructure and welfare arrangements of the receiving countries under immense pressure.

Africa and Latin America share this opportunity – the climates that once made them unforgiving now had the potential to make them world leaders in the alternative energies the world most needed. Logic suggests that there are not just commercial but soft-power opportunities in regions where the sun shines, the wind blows and the ocean drums against the shore. Continents with a history of wildlife conservation can be global models. Those unrelenting summers, once a curse, might yet prove a boon.

This would be a telling, if ironic, soft-power victory. Having warmed the planet so dangerously, in pursuit of the fossil fuels required to keep it warm, the northern hemisphere might now need the brilliant sunlight of the tropical south to help restore the balance.

17

China: Soft Authority

On the surface, the re-emergence of China is the world's most obvious fact. Since the year 2000 it has, on its own, accounted for 60 per cent of global economic growth, and while this is astonishing – and the world has gasped accordingly – it also carries risks. In the space of just a few decades, the global economy has become more dependent on Chinese industry for parts and components than it honestly cares to admit. A setback or contraction in the Middle Kingdom would leave no one immune.

In the closing weeks of 2019 it seemed like just such a setback was in the stars, as whispers crept out concerning a fearful new virus in the city of Wuhan, in Hubei Province – a city larger even than London, though few Londoners had ever heard of it. As with previous flu eruptions, this one – caused by a coronavirus – appeared to have been the result of unhygienic animal husbandry. This was an ugly blot on China's image, because it was by no means the first time. Recent decades had seen several such outbreaks of avian and swine flu, all of which emerged in similar circumstances.

But this time China reacted with a speed that was half astonishing, half alarming. It sealed off the city of Wuhan with a resolve that (it seemed at the time) was possible only in a police state. Extraordinary images of a new hospital being put together in a matter of days showed both how decisively China could mobilise, and how grave it knew the threat to be. It was not clear whether this was, for Beijing, a Chernobyl moment – a crushing exposé of its political system's cynical refusal to face difficult truths – or the opposite: an opportunity to rise expertly to the challenge and show what it could do. The way the virus was initially handled seemed to speak volumes about China's authoritarian disregard for the truth, but when it became the first country to send medical supplies and advice to Italy, a time when neither the EU nor the US were in a position to help, there was a noticeable shift of mood.

The world held its breath. Stock markets trembled, as the scale of the world's dependence not just on Chinese industry but also on the dominant size of its market became clear.

It was a dramatic twist in an already spectacular story. Since the loosening of communist chains in 1978, when Deng Xiaoping declared his country open to new forms of business, China's growth and modernisation had sent a billion people on a historic journey. It was a hectic national makeover, that transformed an impoverished low-cost manufactory into a world-leading dynamo, with new cities, new wealth, new transport and new ways of life.

The World Bank estimated that 800 million people were lifted out of poverty by this convulsion, a boom that required the building of 130 million new homes. China itself boasted that life expectancy in this period more than doubled, from thirty-five to seventy-seven years.

The balance of power in Asia and the world was redrawn. But until recently it seemed that there was a missing ingredient: soft power. China was admired, even revered – but not loved. America and Europe continued to send more amiable images of themselves overseas. As the last great one-party experiment, it carried the cold whiff of totalitarian control. The world might marvel at its gymnasts, but it groaned at reports that they had been trained since infancy like performing seals. It wanted a piece of that extraordinary growth, but shrank from the way it was being achieved.

China resolved to change all this in 2007 when, at an extremely formal occasion (the 17th National Congress of the Communist Party of China), Premier Hu Jintao admitted that 'the international culture of the West is strong ... we are weak', and announced a 'great rejuvenation' that would 'definitely be accompanied by the thriving of Chinese culture'. He promised to 'enhance culture as part of the soft power of our country' by investing in education, the media (including the internet) and cultural infrastructure.

This declaration of soft war was no sudden policy shift; change was already in the pipeline. The following year's Beijing Olympics, many years in the planning, amply displayed China's newfound power and confidence. Much of the event's success was down to one Xi Jinping, the man in charge of Olympic preparations. Failure might have seen him banished to the political wilderness, despite the fact that he was a Communist Party aristocrat (his father had been a hero of the revolution); but four years later Xi Jinping succeeded Hu Jintao as General Secretary of the Communist Party and China's 'paramount leader'. He soon echoed the words of his predecessor, announcing: 'We should increase Chinese soft power, give a good Chinese narrative, and better communicate China's message to the world.'

Since then (according to David Shambaugh, Professor of Political Science at George Washington University) China has been spending up to $10 billion per annum on soft-power projects and programmes – roughly fifteen times America's budget for such things. It has even been at pains to show that it can throw a party. In 2010 it sponsored a hundred Chinese New Year celebrations around the world; in 2017 it supported two thousand.[1]

As *The Economist* put it: 'China is spending billions to make the world love it.'

This project has the highest backing: it is a national strategy. In 2017, just three days before Donald Trump's inauguration, President Xi made a debut speech at Davos in which he offered (in contrast to 'America First') to be the new pied piper, allowing China's 'underlying values' to offer 'a new option' to the modern world. That world was both impressed and unnerved. Was it really possible that, as the bottom fell out of the market in the American dream, there might be a Chinese dream instead?

The Beijing Olympics sent a clear message to the world – but

---

1 The parade through London's West End was the largest: a massive crowd gathered in Trafalgar Square to watch a cavalcade of dancing lions, dragons and acrobats, with clashing cymbals and drums, street food and all the other traditional trimmings.

what did it say? The rest of the G20 was torn. Until then it had taken China's extraordinary renaissance as a sign that the Middle Kingdom was at last emerging from the iron grip of the past to join the new global order of things. Now it seemed that far from joining this brave new world, China was feeling self-confident enough to follow its own path. Foreign diplomats could only frown as China swept past the off-ramp that led to the global mainstream and prepared to build its own broad highway into the future.

As one Chinese commentator, Chang Ping, put it: 'Before 2008, "connecting with the world" was a catchphrase in China. After 2008, it disappeared from state media. The new message was: now the world should follow us.'

China had for a while been developing the infrastructure needed to communicate the first of those messages to the world. It was attracting new cohorts of foreign students (by 2019, almost half a million a year) – from Africa, in particular – with scholarships and bursaries. When Yann Algan, economics professor at France's Sciences Po, went to Beijing in 2018, he was surprised to find that his audience was two-thirds African. China was training the next generation of African leaders just as America and Britain, for socio-political reasons of their own, were trying to keep them out.

He called it a 'huge soft-power tool'.

The media was given strong support, too. The national news agency, Xinhua, opened forty-odd overseas offices in two years, giving it 162 in all. A few years later, in 2016, the national broadcasting service launched an international wing, China Global Television Network (CGTN), which (like Russia Today) very quickly became a major platform. By 2019 it was beaming China-inflected news in five languages to a billion people in more than 100 countries, with a twenty-four-hour English service (the new bureau was offering three hundred jobs in its shiny West London headquarters). It also opened a radio channel, Voice of China, with the stated objective of telling 'the story of China' while honouring 'the party's theory, line, principles and policies'.

This new presence in the airwaves was matched by Chinese shoes on the ground, as Confucius Institutes popped up all over the world to project Chinese language and culture (much as the British Council, the Goethe-Institut or the Institut Français had been doing for decades). They often worked in partnership with universities, while a network of Confucius Classrooms operated through schools.

China was playing catch-up, but with unprecedented speed. By 2019 there were more than five hundred of these Institutes, in 140 countries. Their purpose, said Xi Jinping himself, was to 'tell the China story well . . . showcase China's role as a builder of world peace'. The name was part of the message: it declared Confucius himself to be no longer *persona non grata*. Under Mao he had been denounced as a feudal-bourgeois enemy of progress. Now, sensing that the world might not welcome a network of 'Mao Institutes', he was rehabilitated as the fount of Chinese wisdom.

Deng Xiaoping had begun this rehabilitation by channelling the gnomic sayings of the ancient sage to communicate his vision of a new China. 'Cross the river by feeling for stones . . . Keep a cool head and disguise your ambition' – oracular sayings of this sort suited a nation that was veering into risky waters: free-market communism, or 'capitalism with Chinese characteristics'. It suggested that, like most nations, China was engaged in a difficult conflict over its own history and identity. The recruitment of Confucius to the cause of modernisation was a declaration that in signing up to the free world's business model China *was* westernising, but also remaining true to its roots.

China had been in this quandary before – whether to open up to foreign influence or remain aloof. Nearly four centuries earlier, in 1582, at a time when a sixteen-year-old student named Galileo was staring at a swinging chandelier and brooding on the oddly similar motions of celestial bodies, an Italian Jesuit named Matteo Ricci made landfall in Macau, the Portuguese settlement (in those days an island) off China's southern coast.

That makes it sound as though he stepped off a pleasure cruise, so we might pause to recall what a voyage that must have been. He sailed out of Lisbon in March 1578 (a decade before the Spanish Armada set sail) and did not reach Goa, Portugal's colony in India, until the following September. That meant eighteen months on a creaking timber vessel, with nothing in the way of creature comforts, as the ship crawled in the wake of Vasco da Gama to the southern cape, from Benin to Mozambique, without maps, charts or modern compasses, and under strange stars, before sweltering up the Indian Ocean. After four years in Goa, then under the sway of the 'Great Mughal' Emperor Akbar, whose grandfather had fallen on India as an Afghan warlord and who presided over a hundred million people from his roost in Delhi, he was asked to join the Jesuit mission in Macao – an invitation that involved another hellish trip through the tropics of Ceylon and Indonesia, before bobbing his way to the unfathomable Ming empire to the north.

Anyone who doubts that China's closed nature and suspicion of outsiders is a communist-era imposition will be reassured by the fact that even in these years China was not remotely open. There was what one fifteenth-century official described as a 'paramount boundary' around the great kingdom – 'Chinese on this side, foreigners on the other'; and ships were permitted to leave Macao only twice a year. So Ricci was cordially 'uninvited'. But his curiosity and grit soon earned him a very different nickname: Li-Ma-teu – or 'wise man from the West'. A natural student, infused with Renaissance curiosity, he was eager to explore this strange new land, and as a man of unusual talent and energy was able to master both the local language and the many intriguing (to him) local customs. A keen student of grammar, he compiled Portuguese-Chinese dictionaries, and became something of a local celebrity.

Though he did not stray from the Catholic path, and remained a missionary, to some extent he went, as the saying goes, native. He wore Chinese robes and let Confucian ethics guide his daily life. Soon he was translating Confucian texts into Latin. To the horror of his fellow Jesuits he found room in Christian doctrine for ancestor worship.

In 1601 he was invited north to Beijing, where he created a Roman church and met the Chinese elite. He was the first European to set foot in the Forbidden City, and repaid the compliment by producing a map of the world with Chinese characters, which incidentally revealed that China may have had a more advanced understanding of the world's geography than anyone suspected – the map included Antarctica, a continent unknown in Europe, and displayed North America in surprising detail.

While this was the first time that Chinese eyes had been able to look upon the world as a European might see it, the opposite was also true. Europe was being given a glimpse of a very different and in many respects superior civilisation.

Ricci was not the first European to encounter China. Monks and merchants had been going back and forth since the days of Marco Polo (in the thirteenth century) but none had shown so determined or scholarly an interest. And when he met China's foremost scientific thinker, Xu Guangqi, his curiosity was reciprocated. Bound by a love of numbers, they became friends. Xu Guangqi was one of 2500 Chinese to be converted to Catholicism by Ricci, and was quick to explore European ways of thinking.

As so often, the exchange or 'act of conversation' between two intrepid people produced something startling and new. Ricci's Portuguese version of the maxims of Confucius introduced European learning to the wisdom that in time would seem so distinctively Chinese; and followed it up by suggesting, in *The True Meaning of the Lord of Heaven*, that Confucianism and Christianity had more than a little in common.

Xu Guangqi returned the compliment by producing (helped by Ricci, in 1607) a translation of – what else? – Euclid's first six books. It is a sign of how ahead of their time they were that the rest of Euclid would not be published in Chinese for another 250 years.[2]

It was not quite the first such translation of a European classic: Aesop's fables had appeared in Chinese in 1593. But it was a major step forward, and a reminder that soft power has always been a two-way affair: a collaboration. One of the first westerners to face east compared notes with the first easterner to face west. After converting Xu Guangqi himself, Ricci went on to introduce thousands of Chinese to Catholicism.

---

2 Echoes of this encounter linger in the Mateus Ricci College in Macau, the Matteo Ricci Reading Room in the Central Library of Taiwan, the Ricci Building in Hong Kong's Kowloon district, and the Ricci Institute at the University of San Francisco.

Chinese mathematics was, of course, an advanced branch of human knowledge in its own right – in some ways far ahead of European understanding. But it was advanced in a different way: those speedy abacus counters had amazing computational skills (one 1592 maths treatise ran to seventeen volumes) but dealt with the subject in a practical rather than a conceptual way, approached through agricultural (how many sacks of rice per hectare), architectural or astronomical problems. Euclid offered something new: mathematics as an abstract play of pure thought, an exercise in logic that operated from universal first principles.[3] In Euclid's universe, divine rules could solve numerical puzzles much as Confucian axioms could solve the mysteries of life. Chinese scholars could manipulate numbers with dazzling speed, but Euclid worked from the general to the particular, deriving solutions from known laws – the proven fact that the internal angles of a triangle added up to 180 degrees, for example.

This insistence on absolute truths made it seem sacred, more than mere arithmetic, and gave it a wider cultural significance, because this Greek and Italian preoccupation with higher truths was also an advertisement for ... Western civilisation. It was an embryonic deployment of soft power at a time when the Opium Wars and all the other treacheries of British traders were not even imagined.

Just as Euclid 'of Alexandria' had been the product of more than one civilisation, so Ricci carried the scientific spirit of Europe into China. The fact that he also put the 'analects' or axioms of Confucius into Portuguese shows the two-way nature of soft power: it also enlarged Europe's sense of the world by revealing that Confucius himself had resembled a Western-style humanist. 'It is man that makes truth great,' he wrote, 'not truth that makes man great.' Erasmus could not have put it better. Another time, even more concisely, he said: 'The measure of man is man.'

This was the central theme of the European Renaissance, yet here it was, alive and fully formed, half a millennium before

---

3 In another instance of the power of cross-fertilisation it was the Chinese abacus, rather than Greek logic, which by enacting calculations in a physical, binary form could be the basis of the modern computer. Charles Babbage's famous 'Difference Engine', a forerunner of the modern laptop, even looks like a giant abacus.

Christ. Just as the discoveries in Assyria and India had shaken Europe's faith in the uniqueness of its own Bible, so China was casting doubt on its own intellectual originality.

It was not surprising that Mao later denounced Confucius as a feudal spirit of small use in a communist utopia – his maxims were too interior and personal to sit well with party control. But banning him had the unintended effect of tacitly acknowledging the force of his words. For his part, Confucius himself grasped the importance of such things: 'He who exercises government by means of his virtue may be compared to the north polar star, which keeps its place and all the stars turn towards it.' What we call soft power is sometimes no more than ancient prudence – in Confucius's words, 'moral influence'.[4] There is not much new about seeking to make a good impression.

China was at this time (though few in Europe knew it) the greatest power in the world – responsible, if anyone had been able to measure such things, for close to a third of the planet's GDP. But it did not have marine instincts. On the contrary, as its Great Wall showed, it was protective of its boundaries. In 1371 an imperial decree actually banned foreign trade – on pain of death. This was the *haijin*, or sea ban, and it led to the physical closure of ports with rocks and stakes. In 1405, when twenty Chinese traders were caught and returned by Japanese pirates, they were boiled alive in a cauldron.

It is conventional to see 1492 as the year Europe began to turn its face to the west rather than the east, and the discovery of new-found land across the Atlantic certainly did kindle the colonial impulse in Britain, Portugal and Spain. But while the rivalrous states of Europe itched to expand, China, secure in itself, feared pollution by others.

This *haijin* may even have been one of the models for the business concept of the 'Chinese wall': an invisible yet clear barrier – a wall with Chinese characteristics.

China's desire for seclusion was sorely tested by the appearance of European traders. The Portuguese, as we have seen, arrived in

---

4 The very concept of politeness was defined by Lord Shaftesbury, in eighteenth-century Britain, as resembling soft power by being 'a dext'rous management of our words and actions, whereby we make other people have better opinion of us . . .'

1557 and were tolerated on the grounds that they could help suppress piracy. Bit by bit, the sea wall came down. But China never aspired to other people's land: it had no need of extra territory. As a result, it never developed even a modest urge to ingratiate itself with others or impress them with its ways, the better to win them over. It preferred merely to exact tribute. The so-called 'Ming treasure voyages' of the fifteenth century saw Admiral Zheng lead a series of fleets to India, Persia and East Africa, bringing back ships laden with gold, silver, copper, spice, precious stones, ivory, coral, feathers, cloths and animal skins. While this resembled the piratical rovings of English sailors on the Spanish Main, the greedy plundering of the Roman legions or the demands for Danegeld required by the Vikings, no missionaries and government officials followed in its footsteps.

Instead of distant colonies across the oceans, medieval China favoured the famous Silk Roads, the land highways on which caravans laden with Chinese goods trekked through Tashkent, Samarkand, Baghdad and Aleppo to Constantinople and Venice. One of the cities on this route, Merv, in Turkmenistan, was a capital of scholarship as well as trade, and a vibrant meeting place of many peoples. Arabs, Christians, Jews and Persians created a marvellous city of half a million people, living in a paradise of orchards and canals, temples and palaces. It was 'the mother of the world'. The mausoleum of one of its sultans had a blue dome visible a day's march away.

It is a sobering instance of soft power's real-world limitations that Merv, with such splendid cultural assets, was obliterated by Genghis Khan's army in the thirteenth century – culture alone was not enough to repel swords. And the channels in which soft power ran, it turned out, were not, even then, conduits for virtue; they also carried violence and plague. In some accounts as few as four hundred people survived the destruction of Merv. But culture lingers even in broken stones, and many centuries later a future Viceroy of India, George Curzon, would walk in these ruins, catch his breath and feel a shiver: 'The spectacle of walls, towers, ramparts and domes, stretching in bewildering confusion to the horizon, reminds us that we are in the centre of bygone greatness.'

Genghis Khan had ended its worldly power, but the spirit of Merv lived on.

Soft power, even when reduced to an enfeebled flicker, is hard to extinguish.

In the world's boldest soft-power move, the fabled old Silk Roads are being rebuilt. China is investing epic sums in new infrastructure – the so-called 'Belt and Road Initiative' – designed to give it a new high place in the global economy.

When Peter Frankopan was writing his panoramic history, *The Silk Roads* (it was published in 2015), he was inviting readers to think about the world from the unusual vantage point of Central Asia. This antique region had been obscured during the Soviet era. Now that China was returning to the forefront of its affairs, it was time to reconsider things from that angle, and see that China was not so much 'emerging' as regaining its former place. China's 'emergence', in other words, was not a new phenomenon but the expression of a relentless geographical fact – a reversion to the norm. Only in recent times – the 'century of humiliation' – had Europe interrupted this destiny. China's resurgence was a return to business as usual. As Frankopan wrote: 'We are seeing the signs of the world's centre of gravity shifting back to where it lay for millennia.' Many others echoed his words.

In one sense it was an exaggeration: China had never sought to conquer the world by occupying territory in the European manner. But it was clearly regaining the prime position in world trade that its size and energy deserved and demanded. One thread of the new Silk Route was even planned to press through the melting Arctic ice and open up the once impassable North East Passage to the Atlantic.

Ironically, in prophesying a Chinese-forged future, Frankopan was almost too prescient, because the full extent of the Belt and Road Initiative only emerged, in a series of announcements, as his book appeared. The BRI was an ambitious attempt to revive both the sea lanes (the road) and the land routes (the belt) that had given China lordship of the ancient world. In one sense it was a 'Chinese Marshall Plan', designed to revive parts of the world neglected by the empires of the West, on the grounds that this served Chinese interests too. Khorgos, for instance, a long-forgotten halt on the old Silk Route near China's border with Kazakhstan, found itself preparing for a humming future as the world's biggest 'dry port' (a rail hub thousands of miles from the sea) through which millions of tons of Chinese exports would soon be passing.

Having told a thousand-year-old story, Frankopan had to write a sequel at once.[5]

In all, some $200 billion would be spent on this new transport system. A rail link would run from eastern China to Madrid, via Moscow and Germany. New ports would create a marine super-highway from Jakarta to London via Kuala Lumpur, Calcutta, Nairobi, Djibouti and Athens. New roads would ferry goods from Xi'an to Rotterdam. A $57 billion 'economic corridor' would link China and Pakistan.

By 2018 more than a hundred countries had signed up to the Belt and Road (twenty-nine in Africa), and most of the proposals were arresting. There was even a digital thread – an undersea fibre-optic cable linking Pakistan to East Africa.

It was more than an idea or a gesture: it was a multi-billion-dollar investment on a scale that made the world gasp. And it was based on a clear understanding of the extent to which prosperity has always followed lines of communication (still visible in the way the strength of the Roman Empire can be traced by its roads, or the British Empire by its nautical lanes and ports). The new supply routes would be the arterial system of a new Chinese world, letting trade flow across the continents, connecting two-thirds of the world's people and paving the way for a new Asian ascendancy.

It was hard to overstate the impact it was already having. Chinese bullet trains were racing through Uzbekistan; African footballers were kicking off in Chinese-built stadiums. As we have seen, Chinese cranes were swinging over container ports from Sri Lanka to West Africa; there were pipelines and land-reclamation projects from Argentina to Thailand, along with new enterprise zones, dams, bridges and ribbon highways. A barbed-wire compound in Dubai protected a new $2.4 billion trading

---

5 *The New Silk Roads*, 2018.

zone that was intended to create a Chinese-controlled economic foothold in the Gulf. Huge tracts of the world were getting an expensive upgrade along these lines.

In return, the Emir of Dubai made a state visit to China in which he pledged more than $3 billion worth of investment in China in the immediate future.

The most important European knot in the belt was the German inland 'port' of Duisburg, where one third of the arriving trains were from China (thirty per week). The economic rationale was simple. The sea voyage to Duisburg took six weeks; the rail journey took less than two. Almost overnight, it seemed, there were a hundred new Chinese businesses in the city; and this was clearly only the beginning.

In January 2017 Britain became a link in the Belt and Road when a train arrived in London hauling forty-four containers of Chinese-made goods that had left China three weeks earlier, before travelling through Central Asia, Europe and the Channel Tunnel. Some of the grit in those containers had been picked up in Zhejiang province. Two years later, in 2019, Italy welcomed Xi Jinping to Rome by suggesting that yes, it would be *delighted* to be a new notch in the Chinese belt. 'We will have new airports,' said the Prime Minister, Giuseppe Conte, and 'new trade corridors'. The economy minister, Giovanni Tria, called it 'a circle of virtuous, satisfying and diffuse growth'.

A few months later, at a Beijing forum in May, Xi Jinping made an unambiguous claim for the undertaking, calling it 'the project of the century' in terms that reeked of that fashionable new perfume: soft power. 'The ancient silk routes embody the spirit of peace and cooperation, openness and inclusiveness, mutual learning and mutual benefit.' At a time when the West was losing faith in – and cutting back on – such things, this was a dramatic statement of intent.

The Belt and Road Initiative was astonishing in another way, in that it inverted the usual soft-power trajectory. As we have seen, Europe and America used military and economic weapons to impose themselves: soft power came afterwards. China was attempting something new, putting soft power in the vanguard of its policy push.

It made diplomats in Berlin and Washington shiver, because . . . *what if it worked?*

As we have seen, China was especially and most prominently active in Africa. Unlike those wicked imperialists of yesteryear, ran the story, China was a benefactor. By 2018 it had helped with renovation projects everywhere . . . the whole continent seemed to have been given a long-overdue upgrade. Politics followed suit: a stream of high-level delegations poured into the continent to look at new 'partnerships', and investment grew from \$16 billion in 2011 to \$43 billion in 2017. When President Xi went to Senegal in the summer of 2018, he knew that China had in short order become Senegal's second most important trading partner, after France.

Africa was grateful. In surveys, 75 per cent of respondents now had a 'favourable' view of China – much higher than the number who liked America. And there was, as we have seen, a stampede of students – 50,000 Africans between 2013 and 2015 – going to China as part of a plan to train 'leaders of the future', and incidentally introduce them to the Chinese way of doing things. Kenya's schools began to teach Mandarin to ten-year-old children, following similar moves in South Africa and Uganda.

China threw enormous resources behind this soft-power push, and extraordinary developments appeared on every corner of China itself in a bid both to attract tourists and to impress the wider world: theme parks, zoos, theatres, concert halls, libraries and universities. There was a new opera house in Guangzhou, a flying-saucer railway station in Beijing, a new Disneyland in Hong Kong, several Legolands, a Madame Tussauds, a Peppa Pig World of Play, and a French-style wine estate. China was certainly giving the appearance of being open to the world. There were aquariums, golf resorts, five-star hotels, casinos, even a Shakespeare-inspired 'Thames Town'.

New residential developments might find themselves resembling France or Italy, with an imitation Eiffel Tower in the middle, or a castle, or an artificial lake and golf courses; or they might feel hi-tech and futuristic. Some of them went bust, and were ghostly forests of brand-new, empty skyscrapers – but the

momentum did not ease. An enormous arts complex, the Valley
XL, was announced at the Venice Biennale in 2018. A miniature
city devoted to culture, it would be designed by top-of-the-range
architects to include museums, exhibition halls, galleries and
stages. It was 60 miles north of Beijing, but on the new high-
speed rail link that was only a twenty-minute hop.

The domestic transport system was given an upgrade, too.
Along with a new railway (in 2007 China did not have a single
high-speed train; now it had a 16,000-mile network), the mileage
of roads was quadrupling. While Britain continued its sluggish
plan for a new rail link between London and Birmingham, taking
twenty-five minutes off a 125-mile journey, China was building,
in 2018 alone, 2000 miles of high-speed track. And while Britain
continued to ponder a third runway at Heathrow, struggling to
balance economic gain with civic and environmental concerns
(two-thirds of Europeans affected by aircraft noise lived in west
London), China was constructing *eight* new airports per year, with
plans for more than two hundred by 2035.

The biggest of these, Beijing Daxing International Airport,
opened in September 2019 with *seven* runways, all served by a
stylish terminal (designed by a British architect, Zaha Hadid) in
the shape of an enormous steel flower or starfish. It hurtled passengers into central Beijing on a purpose-built 250-mph railway.

This was progress on a scale the world struggled to imagine. China's economy continued to roar ahead by 9 per cent
a year, sucking people into employment at a hectic rate. Even
when growth slowed to 6 per cent, that was still the equivalent
of adding an economy the size of Australia's or Spain's every
single year.

There was a difficult soft-power implication here, however,
because the reform programme was being pushed through with
a degree of state control that would not be tolerated in America
or Europe (not least because the consultation process was not
comparable; while British contractors had to worry about bat and
newt habitats on the route of its new high-speed railway, China
could shunt entire populations out of the way). The Three Gorges
Dam, the project to create the world's biggest hydroelectric power
station, had involved the complete inundation of 140 towns and

1600 villages, not to mention the relocation of a million and a quarter people (roughly equivalent to the forced uprooting of Newcastle, Leicester, Stoke, Plymouth *and* Sunderland).

Western politicians could never countenance such high-handedness: nor was it what their business schools would propose. Yet in terms of getting things done it was obviously effective; more, it was the propulsion unit for an economic miracle. It was thus a compelling challenge, in the eyes of the world, to the 'neoliberal' model supposedly ushered in by the so-called 'end of history'. Just as Putin's Russia was offering the world 'strong leadership' and 'traditional values' as an alternative to milksop liberal democracy, so China was giving fuel to the thought that progress on this scale *was* worth a small price in freedom. Much to the chagrin of Western commentators, there were advantages to authoritarian government: the cost in individual liberty might even be outweighed by the ability to create infrastructure and growth.

As Beijing's uncompromising response to the viral panic in Wuhan showed (it was an intervention the rest of the world looked at with disbelief . . . until it found itself having to imitate it), China was confronting the global elite with an existential question: was liberal democracy *really* the best or only way to run a modern society? What – *help* – if it wasn't? In the new war of ideas, the world wondered if 'strong leaders' were not what really counted; even the freest electorates toyed with the idea of voting for something similar.

There was more. When Jack Ma, founder of Alibaba, addressed the World Economic Forum in 2017, he noted that 'the West' had spent $14.2 trillion on war in the last three decades (in 2018 it was estimated to have spent $6 billion on military action in Afghanistan, Iraq and Pakistan alone) and wondered aloud (and to much applause) whether that money could have been used in more constructive ways.

It was a means of drawing attention to the way in which the 'free' world was trapped as tightly in its own habits and conventions as less liberal regimes. And it helped feed a revival of interest in, of all the unlikely figures, Karl Marx. 'Freedom' suddenly lay open to the charge that far from being a humanitarian ideal it was

little more than a rampant kind of deregulation – the freedom to
monopolise and self-enrich.

There were contradictions here. Anyone could envy an economy (like China's) that was creating more than ten million new
jobs every year, but the coercive political system required to push
through such growth was less easy to admire.

It was obvious to the whole world that China was bursting with
new power. But (once again) was it really soft? While Beijing was
doing all the right things – creating institutions to spread culture,
building infrastructure and communications, preaching the gospel
of peace and togetherness – it was doing many of the wrong
things too, most obviously in the way it practised the opposite
of what it preached. In the most important soft battleground of
all – the delicate arena of human rights, freedom of speech, foreign policy ethics and environmental awareness – it was dragging
its heels.

This had been true even in the case of the 2008 Olympics.
On the surface the Games were a success, but there were echoes
enough of the bad old days to raise familiar doubts about leop-
ards and spots: pollution in the Chinese capital was so dismal that
many athletes contemplated a boycott;[6] human rights organisations aired their (well-founded) concerns about Tibet; further
alarms were sounded over the treatment of migrant workers
during the construction of the stadium (there was talk about
the forced relocation of more than a million local people); the
adorable girl who sang 'Ode to the Motherland' at the opening
ceremony turned out to be just a cute stand-in for the real singer;
there were mutters about doping and underage gymnasts.

All went well on the night: the ceremony thrilled the world.
But not everyone was willing to believe that it was more than
centrally planned window-dressing. So while official pronouncements made a loud point of praising China's age-old tradition
of human togetherness (with wise Confucian maxims – 'when

---

6 The Ethiopian marathon runner Haile Gebrselassie opted to run the shorter 10,000
metres instead of his usual event, fearing for his ability to breathe; the Belgian tennis
star Justine Henin pulled out altogether. Shortly before the sailing event, the sea turned
red, thanks to untreated sewage and agro-industrial waste.

we all add wood to the bonfire, we all grow warm') and painting the Belt and Road as a benign mission, there was a growing
murmur of disquiet which held that host nations paid heavily to
be included. No matter how often Xi Jinping insisted that it had
nothing to do with 'outdated geopolitical manoeuvrings', many
saw it not as 'development' but as a modern form of colonial
encroachment – not quite as friendly as it seemed.

The railway that ran through Laos, for instance, was laid by
Chinese contractors and paid for by loans from the Chinese government amounting to $6 billion – half of the nation's GDP. The
costly highway through Montenegro was christened a 'road to
nowhere'. The East Coast Rail Link in Malaysia was so expensive
(projected cost: $20 billion) that the government ordered work to
halt (it dawned on Kuala Lumpur that its east coast was not where
most Malaysians lived: the railway served Chinese interests more
obviously than its own). Cambodia, Nepal, Myanmar and the
Maldives (where a 'China–Maldives Friendship Bridge' connected
the airport to the capital city) . . . all discovered that Chinese generosity came with strings attached. When Beijing offered to help
build Britain's new high-speed railway (a project that had as many
critics as supporters) it was greeted with both interest and alarm.

In that case, the investment looked to be part of a classical 'sphere of influence' campaign. The entire Belt and Road
Initiative, indeed, was beginning to take on worryingly old-
fashioned overtones. In developing trade infrastructure with
tiny nations such as the Maldives and Sri Lanka, for instance
(and also Nepal, where Chinese money was helping to generate
both hydroelectric power and the nation's first railway (from
Kathmandu to China), Beijing was not just offering a friendly
hand: it was stitching a necklace of interests and partnerships
around its heavyweight neighbour, India.

The mood music between China and Italy, too, raised fears
that China was looking to pick off nations individually instead of
dealing with the European Union as a whole, as the bloc wanted:
diplomats were quick to warn that Italy, like Greece, was being
identified by Beijing as Europe's 'soft underbelly'.

It became common to refer to the project as the Belt, Road *and
Debt* Initiative.

This, they said, was how Europe's own empires had behaved, laying railways across Africa and Asia the better to get at their minerals and markets. Djibouti may have won a sizzling new train; it also got a military base, and a debt to China the size of its annual GDP. When the IMF considered a fresh round of loans to Pakistan it felt obliged to stipulate that they could *not* be used simply to repay the growing debt to China, which was approaching $10 billion. And all those ports and railway lines were clearly intended to serve Chinese trade as much as local interests. At Kribi, in Cameroon, and a hundred other places, sparkling new infrastructure was designed to get iron ore, cotton, coffee and cocoa out, and manufactured goods back in, faster than ever.

In the most famous instance of all, Sri Lanka discovered that it had indebted itself in return for an airport that no planes wanted to use, and an empty deepwater port it could not afford: China had taken ownership of the port in a way not designed to soothe nerves. People began to wonder what, since it now owned such major assets, the People's Liberation Army would do to defend them in the event of an emergency.

In another ominous echo (of the way Victorian Britain shipped thousands of Indians to Kenya, South Africa and Uganda), the population of modern Africa was being stirred in hard-to-predict ways. Some Chinese settlers aimed to marry their sons to local women, so that they could transfer land and business interests into the new wives' names and prevent the Chinese government from ever laying claim to their property.

The world had seen this sort of thing before. Malaysia's President Mahathir Mohamad called it 'a new version of colonialism', and sought to renegotiate the terms of his arrangement with China. Hillary Clinton (then Secretary of State) also referred to China as 'new colonisers', and that became almost the received view. General Joseph Dunford, of the US Joint Chiefs of Staff, called it 'an international network of coercion through predatory economics to expand its sphere of influence'. And Matteo Salvini, Italy's nationalist leader, was edgy, suggesting that he would think 'not once but a hundred times' before agreeing to the offer, outlined in an open letter in the *Corriere della Sera*, to upgrade Genoa and Trieste into world-class ports.

In *China's Second Continent: How a Million Migrants are Building a New Empire in Africa*, Howard French, a former Shanghai bureau chief for the *New York Times*, spelled out how a million Chinese workers were living and working (but not mixing) in Africa; and this was one of a number of such accounts. They pointed to riots in Zambian copper mines, evidence of corrupted officials and racist incidents across the continent as signs that all was far from well. There were reports that while of course China would not dream of meddling in the electoral process, if voters did happen to choose the wrong candidate then the stellar investment in their country might dry up.

Some of these critics had ideological axes to grind; China's friends still insisted that its presence in Africa was not an imposition but a free and fair exchange: Beijing was simply trading the technology and investment Africa needed in return for raw materials and energy (oil). But it was no longer a harmonious picture. Africa was China's biggest trading partner, and in many eyes this was an unequal relationship. As the world looked on, China was busily turning African nations into client states.[7]

The world was well used to 'Made in China'. Was this now being edited into a new phrase: 'Made in Africa Under Chinese Ownership'? When China announced plans to spend $80 million on a new headquarters for African Disease Control, it looked at first like a disinterested and humanitarian gesture. When it emerged that the new body would collect and hold health data generated by the five regional disease control centres, set up in the wake of the Ebola outbreak by the United States (at great expense), the world began to frown. Suddenly, it looked like a surveillance tool.

At a time of increasing concern with the environment, China was problematic, too. Up to one-tenth of its land was contaminated; its cities and rivers were choking on smog and effluent; hundreds of millions of its people lacked access to clean water; and it was producing as much polluting plastic as the next ten

---

7 In Mozambique, French found a businessman who admitted that this was China's strategy. 'We had to find backward countries, poor countries that we can lead.'

worst offenders together. A World Bank study of 2007 suggested that there were 600,000 premature deaths a year caused by bad air and water. Similar studies a decade later showed that things were getting worse: there were now more than a million such deaths, along with 20 million tonnes of crops poisoned. China was a byword for avian flu, swine flu and now coronavirus.

China was well aware of the problem and indeed was leading the way in many green policy areas (especially in renewable energy: wind and solar). And its per capita emissions were by no means out of line. But its sheer size, and decades of neglect, made it the world's number-one emitter of carbon dioxide. At a time when the world was trying to abandon coal (and oil) more than a hundred coal-fired power stations were under construction – it was burning almost as much coal as the rest of the world combined. The Yangtze was by far the most plastic-heavy river, discharging more than 300 million tonnes per year into the ocean (double its nearest rival, the Ganges).

Figures like these did little to help China win over the world's climate-change activists; neither did photographs of the Yangtze glowing a lurid blood-red as it flowed through the city of Chongqing (the authorities said it was caused by 'silt').

Worse, they made all Chinese investment in soft-power efforts elsewhere look like a fig leaf for short-term self-interest. Disrespect for the national anthem carried a three-year prison sentence. And there were other fields in which Beijing's actions cut across its rhetoric. The new Confucius Institutes were beginning to seem less like temples for healing and exchange than devices for the spreading of the gospel according to Beijing. They tended to suppress mention of the 1959 invasion of Tibet (and the atrocities connected to that occupation); nor did they refer to the crackdown on student-protestors in Tiananmen Square,[8] the death toll of Chairman Mao's so-called 'Great Leap Forward', the battalions of political prisoners in its jails, or references to Taiwan that did not refer to 'Taiwan, China'.

When Louisa Lim (author of *The People's Republic of Amnesia*,

---

8 In the year following the crackdown, more than 10 per cent of China's newspapers had been shut down, thirty million books had been confiscated and 150 films blacklisted. No one knows how many thousands of people were arrested in the same purge.

2014) tried showing the photograph of 'Tank Man' – the student filmed walking in front of the armoured column sent to put down the protest in Tiananmen Square in 1989 – to students at four universities in Beijing, most had never seen it before. And when an American academic, Rowena Xiaoqing He, taught a course at Princeton that referred to the episode, she was accused by Chinese students of making things up. Mike Pompeo, the US Secretary of State, was accused of 'lunatic ravings' when he referred to the Tiananmen activists as 'heroes'.

This was not making friends and influencing people; it was propaganda, pure and simple – wolfish power in sheepish cloth-ing. And while in some respects Chinese cunning was revered (Western political advisers loved quoting Sun Tzu's *Art of War*, which gave electoral strategising the glamour of a military cam-paign), in most quarters it was feared.[9] Even Donald Trump's angriest opponents were beginning to admit that in standing up to China he was picking a fight that had been too long delayed.

---

9 Though ironically one of Sun Tzu's most famous maxims – 'winning without fight-ing is the highest form of warfare' – is a perfect definition of soft power.

18

China: The Quick March

The first country to blow the whistle on Chinese interference was Australia. Over a million of its citizens were of Chinese extraction, and a similar number came annually as tourists. China was Australia's leading trade partner – a decade ago it had taken 20 per cent of Australia's exports; now it took 40 per cent. As the coming power in the Pacific it had to be treated with all due respect. Yet in August 2019 Australia's Attorney-General announced that after a blizzard of complaints it was setting up a 'task force' to investigate Chinese influence on Australian academic life and politics. A month later the Australian Signals Directorate declared that cyber-hackers with the support of a 'foreign government' had penetrated Australia's parliamentary computer system.

China was at this time picking off Taiwan's few remaining allies in the world one by one. In 2019 both the Solomon Islands and Kiribati announced that they would no longer recognise Taiwan as a sovereign state rather than a piece of 'One China', after a Chinese offer ($730 million, in the case of the Solomons) to include them on the Pacific Belt and Road. In 1968 Taiwan had been recognised by seventy countries; sixty years later that was down to eighteen (though one was America). In Africa, after Burkina Faso cut its ties, Swaziland became Taiwan's only official friend on the continent. Even the World Health Organization was induced not to recognise Taiwan as an independent nation, a move that became embarrassing when it became one of the best-performing countries in the coronavirus pandemic – by following WHO guidelines.

There was evidence of large contributions to Australia's political parties from donors 'connected', as the saying went, to Beijing, but also from ordinary Chinese students, who represented one-third of Australia's undergraduates and who were becoming increasingly vociferous in demanding agreement with the Communist Party line on Taiwan, Tibet and the pro-democracy movement in Hong Kong. Some universities, it was noted (with horror, in liberal quarters), had signed agreements that gave China a voice in 'teaching quality' – everyone knew what that might mean.

When the Chinese consulate-general in Brisbane praised Chinese students for their 'acts of patriotism' in objecting to academic debates that crossed the party line (they tried to drown out pro-democracy protests with loud music), Australia's Minister for Foreign Affairs, Marise Payne, stated that she would be 'particularly concerned' by anything that might undermine free speech and legal protest. It was a stand-off.

There was ominous talk elsewhere about other cyberattacks, ranging from the theft of personal data from universities to raids on sensitive government departments. A Labor Party politician, Sam Dastyari, was forced to resign following allegations that he had urged Australia to 'respect' China's territorial claims in the South China Sea while accepting donations from Chinese business interests. A waspish book called *Silent Invasion: How China is Turning Australia into a Puppet State* was dropped by its publisher amid fears that Beijing would not enjoy its tone.

One Washington think tank christened this 'sharp power'; whatever it was, it could hardly be called soft. It had a very hard edge indeed.

Education was now Australia's fourth largest export; it was host, in 2018, to 150,000 Chinese students (one-tenth of the total enrolment), and despite the controversy this was a lucrative boat no one wanted to rock. But that autumn New South Wales, Australia's most populous state, closed down the Confucius programme in thirteen of its schools, citing 'inappropriate foreign influence'. A few days later, a Chinese-born Australian, Yang Hengjun (an author, blogger and ex-diplomat), was 'arrested' in China and accused of spying. No one could call this a tit-for-tat response: he had been detained since the beginning of the year for being what his 130,000 Twitter followers called a 'democracy peddler'. But it felt like an ominous sign of the times.

In soft-power terms this sort of thing was counter-productive. Xi Jinping could hail China's 'international influence, ability to inspire and power to shape' as often as he pleased, or pledge China's desire for 'cross-cultural exchanges characterised by harmony within diversity, inclusiveness and mutual learning'. He could talk about 'ecosystems based on respect for nature' and claim that China was striving only 'to safeguard world peace'. But these pleasant claims counted for little when China was also willing to be a world leader in political oppression and the crushing of dissent.

In 2017 the winner of the 2010 Nobel Peace Prize, Liu Xiaobo, died in custody while his wife was placed under house arrest. And in 2018 an extraordinary ethnic project in the western Xinjiang province, where up to a million Muslim Uighur people were herded into 're-education' camps, was brought to the attention of the United Nations and made shocking headlines around the world. There were more than ten million Uighur Muslims in China; now it appeared, to a startled world, that they were subject to constant surveillance, obliged to learn Mandarin, renounce their faith and undergo other forms of state indoctrination. There was even horrifying talk that their organs were being harvested to provide the crucial raw materials for the lucrative transplant business in Beijing and Shanghai. News of this sort moved nervousness about China's growth spurt out of diplomatic circles and into the brightly lit aquarium of public opinion.

Anxieties over Gulf funding of British universities were pushed into insignificance by this new source of unease. The number of Chinese students at British universities had doubled in a decade, to 106,000, and the fees (up to £40,000 per annum) were a major part of this sector's income stream, too. But when Leeds University opened a Business Confucius Institute in 2012 (supported by funds from China) it soon learned that it was expected to invite Chinese scholars to lecture on 'history, culture and related topics' that represented the 'Chinese point of view'.

In 2017 the Confucius Institute at University College London produced maps that showed Tibet and Taiwan as part of China without mentioning that this was disputed.

Slowly, as China grew more brazen in its requests (or demands), such stories became daily news. A House of Commons Committee report, 'Defending Democracy in an Age of Autocracy', claimed that vice-chancellors were coming under increasing pressure to conform to Chinese political ideas, and that there were clear threats to academic and personal freedom on British campuses.[1] There was a 'significant threat', it warned, of research and intellectual property rights being breached.

In 2019 several universities gave in to Chinese demands that they take down posters supporting the protesting students of Hong Kong, and there were rumbles of concern at the power of the Chinese student body. The London School of Economics 'put on hold' a joint venture after concerns that it might involve too many compromises.

Lord Patten, the last British Governor of Hong Kong, recalled being asked, when Chancellor of Oxford, to intervene and stop the university Buddhist Society from hosting the Dalai Lama as a speaker (he declined). MI5 and GCHQ formally warned the university sector to put national security interests ahead of their own concerns.

It was a bracing reminder that while China was enjoying the most impressive economic boom in anyone's memory, it was not necessarily freedom's best friend.

News of that sort was also a hindrance when it came to attracting the world's young, one of soft power's target audiences (as the customers of the future). They were not programmed to think warmly of a place where Google and YouTube were censored, where nightclubs and karaoke bars were closed in advance of major state occasions, where activists were tear-gassed and where very little evaded the beady eye of state surveillance. Under the new 'social credit' system, even routine individual behaviour was tracked and punished in frightening new ways. In 2019 it was

---

1 China was buying independent schools as well, in a well-planned series of acquisitions that were greeted at first with enthusiasm, then with nervousness.

reported that more than thirteen million people had been catego-
rised as 'untrustworthy', and could be denied plane or rail tickets
because of blemishes on their online record, such as playing too
many computer games, failing to dispose of litter or failing to pay
a parking fine.

New technology was often sold as a pathway to individual liberty. Not in China.

In advance of the parade in Beijing marking China's seventieth anniversary, polluting factories were given a day off to
clear the air for the great occasion; clouds were burst to drain
the sky of rain; and streets were cleared so that thousands of
soldiers could rehearse their steps. Big Brother, it turned out,
was Chinese. And the stories kept coming. A hotel chain named
Vienna International was ordered to change its name because it
encouraged the 'worship of foreign things'. When the poster for
the new *Star Wars* appeared in 2019, sharp-eyed fans noticed that
black-skinned characters had been shrunk or erased. And in the
trailer for the *Top Gun* sequel the flags of Japan and Taiwan on
Tom Cruise's flying-jacket had been blocked out. People could
smile at news that Winnie the Pooh was banned (because the
chubby-cheeked bear had been compared to President Xi Jinping
by cartoonists), but they did not like learning that films involving
Richard Gere or Brad Pitt (admirers of the Dalai Lama) were
also banned. And reports that the Chinese version of *Bohemian
Rhapsody* had been doctored to remove any suggestion that
Freddie Mercury was homosexual horrified the younger generation overseas.

There were only thirty-four slots a year for non-Chinese films:
only those that conformed to the government-approved principles
were permitted a free run at the world's biggest population. That
is why, when Dreamworks released its animated film *Abominable*
in 2019, it was inspired by what it called 'proactive appeasement'
to include maps showing most of the South China Sea to be
Chinese, not a universally recognised fact.

The FBI director, Christopher Wray, revealed that his agency
was conducting a thousand or more investigations into Chinese
interference in political and commercial fields. Given that Britain
was at this time withdrawing from its established partnerships

in favour of forging new international links, none of this was welcome news.

Messing with student activists was one thing; industrial espionage was quite another. China had a long-held reputation for pirated goods – the fake Rolex and the copied DVD were iconic brands. Nearly two-thirds of the world's counterfeit goods (a market worth $500 billion per year, according to the OECD – as much as 5 per cent of imports into the EU were thought to be fakes) were Chinese-made.[2] Visiting reporters had long grown used to the idea that their laptops might be emptied as they passed through airport security, and the correct soft-power move would have been to put a stop to such things. But the news stories were growing less and less innocuous.

The FBI was reporting a 53 per cent increase in cases of 'economic espionage' (in 2018), most of them involving Chinese nationals; the Department of Justice confirmed that 90 per cent of such cases involved China. Some were almost comical. A Chinese woman was arrested (and later found guilty) at Donald Trump's own Mar-a-Lago golf resort with a suspicious cache of computers, phones and other devices (she claimed to be on a swimming trip, but had no swimsuit). Others were more serious: six agronomists, five of them employees of a Chinese agribusiness firm, were caught stealing cutting-edge corn seeds from a field in Iowa. Lockheed Martin, the US Navy and NASA made similar allegations about hacked documents and designs. China did not consider this theft and was offended by the suggestion – it was merely a Robin Hood style redistribution of what should be common goods. But it did appear that nuclear, defence and energy secrets could no longer consider themselves quite secure.

This was cyber-infiltration, but old-fashioned spying was alive and well too. Germany reported that 10,000 people in important fields had been approached by 'head-hunters', and offered expenses-paid trips to China to talk about their work.

Espionage had been stitched into the reflexes of the state for

---

2 This made it possible for third parties to profit from someone else's soft power (or brand image). In 2018 it was estimated that the fake-goods trade in fashionable Italian names amounted to €35 billion, more than 1 per cent of the national GDP.

decades. In his 2019 book *Chinese Spies*, Roger Faligot suggested that the Guoanbu, Beijing's ministry of security, would become 'as familiar in the twenty-first century as the acronyms MI6, CIA and KGB were in the twentieth'. Chinese police were said to be installing data-monitoring software on people's mobile phones during random checks. It was cracking down on young Marxists for their treasonous ideas about workers' rights. There were estimated to be three-quarters of a million surveillance cameras in Beijing alone.

In one way it was hard to imagine anything less helpful to the Chinese brand. Nor was locking Wikipedia the smartest route to foreign admiration. The director of the Oxford Internet Institute, Professor Philip Howard, called China 'a global disinformation power'. Unlike most previous expanding empires, it did not dream of new territories and overseas domains on which the sun never set; but it was increasingly determined to control what could be said and published about itself, wherever in the world that might be.

In another way (as we saw with Russia) this had the surprising effect of putting soft power itself, to some extent, in a glaring new light. China, it was clear, was in some quarters actively admired for offering tough, uncompromising leadership. Soft power was not, perhaps, axiomatically a force for good, or a tea-towel full of liberal messages. It could be a conduit for ideas of any stripe. Chinese diplomats, growing in confidence, began to joke that they had hit upon a better system even than democracy – which was hardly covering itself in glory these days, in Iraq, Libya and Ukraine.

As time passed, the focal point for this consternation was the technology company Huawei. This represented both sides of the Chinese conundrum by being, on the one hand, one of the most spectacular business stories in a land of many spectacular stories; yet on the other it was one of the most troubling, too.

In 1987 a senior officer in charge of communications for the People's Army, Ren Zhengfei, had formed a manufacturing firm in the then-new city of Shenzhen to make phone switches (the computerised systems that made old-fashioned switchboard operators obsolete). He gave it a patriotic name (Huawei means 'Made in China') and from the beginning understood that it was a strategic national player. 'A nation that does not have its own switching equipment,' he said, 'is like one that lacks its own military.' This view made him highly eligible for government data contracts.

Less than three decades later Huawei became the world's biggest telecom company, and in 2018, when it overtook Apple, the second-largest provider of smartphones too – behind Samsung. Its revenues topped $100 billion, and Ren Zhengfei was sitting on an estimated net worth of $1.7 billion. With the help of those government contracts, Huawei had grown fast enough to be a major global player.

There were few more vivid symbols of China's unbelievable growth. In the three years between 2011 and 2013, China tipped more cement than America had in the entire twentieth century – gleaming cityscapes appeared one after another. Now, a 1980s start-up had become a technology giant, occupying nearly a fifth of the global market.

It was a triumph not just of industrial might but of innovative vim too. The company HQ in Shenzhen was an extravagant campus around a lake, like a European university city, and full of allusions to international scenes. Its 25,000 employees were given an imitation Swiss mountain train and replica pieces of Paris and Venice.

The world was surprised, then worried; then afraid. Germany claimed that malware had been found in Huawei phones that could track and listen to calls; France revealed that Huawei contractors in Ethiopia were hacking state networks; America took the view that this was a quasi-government enterprise that could not be trusted with delicate data. Australia and Britain voiced equally strident concerns. Experts everywhere shook their heads at the thought that Huawei might be involved in fifth-generation mobile technology – super-super-fast broadband, ten times quicker than the existing system – in which Huawei had somehow become the world leader.

The suspicion that it was open to state interference and might build 'back doors' to permit surveillance of overseas clients could not be quelled. Governments began to express doubts about the security implications of using Huawei in sensitive arenas.

It did not make them sleep any easier when Ren Zhengfei pointed out, in 2019, that Huawei would one day become an 'army' strong enough to 'dominate the world'.

Provoked by the alarm bells rung in Australia, Washington began not just to express concern but to act. It required Google to stop providing services to Huawei phones, which meant that Huawei users could no longer access Google, YouTube or Google Maps. This incidentally demonstrated that US firms were answerable to government too, but the liveliest conversation, at the Mobile World Congress in Barcelona in March 2019, concerned the challenge Huawei posed to global cybersecurity.

The firm's Deputy Chairman, Guo Ping, promised in a keynote speech that Huawei 'has not and will never plant back doors'. But Barcelona was not Beijing, and not everyone clapped. Jeremy Fleming, head of Britain's GCHQ, spoke of 'opportunities and threats' in China's technological prowess, and insisted that fears of 'offensive cyber' were well founded. Many agreed. 'No country poses a more severe long-term threat,' said the Director of the FBI. China was clearly planning to become the world's dominant digital power – and was using illegal means to get there.

There may have been more smoke than fire in this, but it was enough to encourage security agencies to speak gravely of 'significant' security risks. British Telecom and Vodafone announced that they were curbing their dealings with Huawei; others agreed to end licensing agreements; Japan stated that procurement would stop; the Czech Republic warned that since Chinese law could compel a national corporation such as Huawei to cooperate with the government, even if it had no intention of doing so, there was a built-in vulnerability which made caution the only prudent policy.

It was no longer easy to say what this meant for China's 'ability to attract'. Under the old rules it was reckless. Would nineteenth-century Britain have permitted China to operate the Royal Navy? Would twentieth-century America have let China run its missile programme? But the demonstration that it was a leader in technology was excellent for the Chinese brand. The fact that it had stolen a march on the West in the digital arena may even have made up for the fact that it was not entirely trusted.

There was a new flashpoint in December 2018, however, when Meng Wanzhou, not only Huawei's Chief Financial Officer but the daughter of its founder, was arrested in Vancouver in what her father called a 'politically motivated' move (she was accused of infringing sanctions against Iran). China responded by arresting a pair of Canadians on espionage charges, and detaining them for a year without access to law-yers (while Meng Wanzhou endured house arrest in a lavish Canadian mansion) and warning that any countries that fol-lowed America (such as Britain, with its three million Huawei phone users) would be putting at risk billions of pounds' worth of Chinese investment.

A couple of years earlier David Cameron had been treating Xi Jinping to fish and chips and a pint of beer at a sixteenth-century pub in Buckinghamshire; now Britain was pulling up the drawbridge. As Jeremy Fleming warned: 'Some of the behaviour we've seen from certain states or criminals is clearly wrong in any circumstance.'

It did not help when it was reported that some Huawei phones could be customised by schools to monitor pupils' habits (a facility many parents might welcome) or that a song in praise of the new smartphone ('Huawei the Beautiful') included a lyric – 'The battery is durable and the appearance is good. The China-made chip is most precious' – not likely to knock 'Bohemian Rhapsody' off the world's playlists. Huawei denied it all, even though the composer, Zheng Lengheng, was a local government consultant.

America announced that it would ban Huawei from the sen-sitive parts of its digital economy, and Australia, Japan and New Zealand followed suit. Many other nations, however, declined to obey America's request, so when Britain, first through Theresa May and then Boris Johnson, intimated that it was in theory con-tent to permit Huawei to help engineer its fifth-generation data network, it was confirmation that while soft power could spread balm, it could also sow discord. Brexit Britain found itself in very uncomfortable waters: adrift from Europe, and facing a difficult choice. Which of the world's two leading powers (America and China) should it upset?

This complication aside, China's haughty attitude in all these areas – censorship, espionage, colonial bargaining, human rights and the environment – had a corrosive effect on the most important soft-power resource of all: trust. The author Jonathan Fenby has referred to China's 'trust deficit', on the grounds that although the awesome scale of the economic miracle was beyond dispute, China now appeared to be building a new 'great wall' around itself, this time made of silence. The fact that it seemed not to care about the poor impression this made only intensified the concern.

There was a similar shift of emphasis in China's dealings with foreign media. It had long been buying space in existing outlets (the *New York Times*, the *Daily Telegraph*) to insert *China Watch*, a paid-for sheet with hard-hitting items such as 'Rise of China Brings Benefits Globally' and 'China, Belgium Ink Deal for Creative Industries'.

There was a bracing change of tone in the pronouncements of the leadership, too. In 2018 President Xi told the National People's Congress: 'We must ride on the mighty east wind ... steer the wheel with full power ... cleave through the waves and sail to victory!' The head of the Hong Kong Stock Exchange, Charles Li, told European reporters – with reference to the projected takeover of the London Stock Exchange – that China was 'no longer willing to change itself to fit in with the rest of the world. The world is now going to have to change itself to fit into China.'

The bid provoked much opposition and was withdrawn. But the sentiment hung in the air after the fact. Anyone flicking through the axioms of Confucius would have struggled to find an ancient endorsement for ideas as uncompromising as these.

Other initiatives confirmed that the clock had been turned back. After decades of permitting freewheeling growth, old-style central control was back in favour.

A 'Little Red App' was created by the Communist Party to 'widen the channel of learning': users had to digest a state-sanctioned list of facts about Mr Xi's life or be publicly shamed (there was a children's version as well: six-year-olds had to recite snippets about 'Grandpa Xi' such as 'Xi Jinping is the helmsman of our country, the guide of his people . . .'). One patriotic video blended Beethoven symphonies with English rap music, folded in some images of war and refugees, and wondered: 'What can we do? China has a solution.' Another featured 'Belt and Road bedtime stories'.

One prominent Chinese newspaper (*The People's Daily*) ran a piece by New Zealand's former Prime Minister, Jenny Shipley, headlined 'We need to learn to listen to China' – which lavished praise on the Belt and Road Initiative ('one of the greatest ideas we've ever heard') but which she claimed to know absolutely nothing about.

China, it seemed, wanted to remake the world in its own image, and control of the internet was only the most blatant manifestation of this. By the time Russia resolved to restrain the worldwide web (in 2014 Putin called it a 'CIA project') it was already too late – though when Russia moved into Crimea one of its first actions was to seize the main internet relay. But China had mistrusted this anarchic forum from the very beginning. It had, it was said, two million people policing the online world, and never allowed independent institutions to develop space that it could not monitor.

Business was business: Starbucks was still planning to open more than three thousand new Chinese cafés in the coming years – at a rate of roughly one per day (until the coronavirus led many of them to close, and ushered in a revision of such ambitions). But for the world's politicians an intimidating new prospect was lumbering into view. The Iron Curtain in Europe had fallen long ago, inspiring something like a great leap forward, but now an equally drastic divide was taking shape in Asia, a 'bamboo' or 'silicon' partition that would slice the world into two spheres, one American (Amazon, Apple and Google), the other Chinese (Alibaba and Huawei).

The spheres would not only see the world in different ways; they would know different things. A digital arms race appeared to be at hand.

*

There was another, even more alarming possibility. It had long been assumed that the supplanting of America by China as the world's leading power was only a matter of time. According to the IMF, the US was responsible for 27 per cent of world output in 1950, but today produced just 16 per cent. In 2021, it predicted, China would be responsible for 20 per cent, America just 15 per cent. This was a turnaround for which the world was ill prepared.

But it is rarely wise to extrapolate present trends into the future on the assumption that nothing new will deflect the predicted course. Unexpected events are, as Nassim Nicholas Taleb has shown, and contrary to what we tend to think, almost inevitable. The cry that a geopolitical sea change was a foregone conclusion was reminiscent of the 1980s fear that Japan was an ogre poised to take over the world; there may even have been a note of racial unease in the idea that the Chinese were coming, as in the 'yellow peril' stories of a hundred years ago, when 'wily' Orientals were believed (by thriller writers, at least) to be stealing inscrutably through the mists and fogs of London's docks.

Not only that: the rise of China was giving rise to a fear, named after the Greek historian Thucydides, that was fast becoming a foreign-relations cliché. The famous 'Thucydides Trap' held that when one dominant power replaced another there was an ever-increasing risk of actual war. The term had been coined by the Harvard political scientist Graham Allison, whose book *Destined for War: Can America and China Escape Thucydides' Trap?* made primary reference to the decline of Athens and the rise of Sparta, but also mentioned the Thirty Years War (Catholic Europe versus Protestant states), the Napoleonic wars (the crowned heads of Europe versus revolutionary values, the First World War (rising Germany meets declining Britain), the US Civil War (industrial north supplants agrarian south) and many other conflicts.

'The past 500 years have seen sixteen cases in which a rising power threatened to displace a ruling one,' wrote Allison (in *Foreign Policy*) in 2017. 'Twelve of these ended in war ... On the historical record, war is more likely than not.'

That was a grim prediction. And in recent years the 'trap' had been much cited in the context of the US and China, and not just because of China's new economic prowess. Its space programme (it sent a man into orbit in 2004, and landed a robot on the lunar surface fifteen years later) sent shivers down the spines of those who remembered the US–Soviet race to the moon.[3] It became the norm to think that the world was entering a new Cold War as the two powers tussled for supremacy. It was no surprise when, on the eve of a state visit to China by Donald Trump in April 2017, primarily to discuss North Korea, the *New York Times* warned: 'Both players in the region have a responsibility to steer away from Thucydides' trap.'

International relations war-gamers worried away at this scenario. That China was increasingly strident in its foreign dealings could hardly be doubted – it was quick to denounce anyone, from Hollywood celebrities to the National Basketball Association, who expressed support for the students in Hong Kong. In the latter case, a single tweet from the General Manager of the Houston Rockets ('Stand with Hong Kong') provoked an outcry that threatened the entire basis of the NBA's $4 billion operation in China, as sponsors and broadcasters cut their ties with the sport.

China might have been expected to ignore such digs – after all, Twitter was banned in China, so its own population would not read these remarks. But now it seemed willing to police foreign public opinion, too. 'No comments challenging national sovereignty,' said a state television announcer, 'fall within the scope of freedom of expression.' China had never seemed interested in other people's lands; but it was increasingly anxious to control what they thought and said. A few even advanced the proposition that if China ever did decide to show the world its new-found military muscle-power, it would do so not by walking into Taiwan (the old theory) but by testing itself in Vietnam – on the grounds that this was the one place in the world where America could not conceivably intervene.[4]

It ought to be soft power's job to placate such tensions, so it was a matter of global importance that China's soft-power push

---

3 As Professor Hayward of the Royal Aeronautical Society remarked, it sent 'signals to their neighbours – a good way of showing soft power, with a little bit of hard'.

4 In July 2019 a Chinese oil survey vessel steamed into waters claimed by Vietnam, which demanded that it leave. It did. But a month later another ship did the same.

straddled an awkward gap between two clashing stories. In one, China was an ancient land of peace and harmony; in the other it was a strapping bully unwilling to brook dissent. On the one hand it was opening up, inspiring a global competition for the 300 million students and tourists China was sending abroad.[5] On the other it was clamping down, revising its past to demonstrate that the modern Communist Party was the perfect outcome of a timeless civilisation, while imposing an intrusive burden of state surveillance on itself.

Western libertarians shuddered when drone-borne cameras were deployed to monitor the lockdown in Hubei Province – it was a clear, quasi-totalitarian infringement of civil liberties. But all measures that might help defeat the virus were welcome now. In the brave new war against corona, even the most extreme approaches could not be opposed.

Still, the contradictions were painful. 'The Chinese people love peace,' President Xi said in Qingdao in 2018, but only hours later he was watching a military pageant involving thirty-two ships – one an aircraft carrier, another a guided-missile destroyer – and twenty-nine aircraft.

That was not the usual way of signalling a devotion to peace.

Even against such a backdrop the charm offensive was still an effective soft gambit. In 2019 Xi symbolised the *entente* between China and Russia by making a photogenic gift to Moscow zoo: two giant pandas, Ru Yi and Ding Ding. 'Over the past six years we have met almost thirty times,' he said. 'Putin is my best friend.'

America and Europe had been slow to see the growing warmth of this relationship. Now their experts had to scratch their heads and come up with a response.

And all the while Thucydides and his trap lurks in the wings, should things take a turn for the worse.

The fact that China prefers progress to freedom is why it performs poorly in surveys (it came twenty-seventh in the 2018 Portland

---

5 In 2018 Chinese nationals overtook even the British as the biggest-spending customers at Harrods, in London, handing over more than £200 million.

Soft 30, behind the Czech Republic, Hungary and Poland, having slid from twenty-fifth in 2017). Given that it wields more economic and military power than all three of these put together, it can be said to be trapped in something of a soft snare – the more forcefully it tries to project its culture abroad, the more it is mistrusted.

In 2018 London's Royal Court dropped a play about life in Tibet, *Pah-La,* when it learned that to go ahead would jeopardise a forthcoming cultural programme. The Man Booker Prize changed the national origin of a long-listed author from 'Taiwan' to 'Taiwan, China', in an all too clear instance of kowtowing. Cambridge University Press agreed to block three hundred articles on touchy subjects from its Chinese journal.

This might also be the reason why China's cultural products – art, film, literature and music – have so far made a relatively weak impact overseas. 'China's creative and cultural outputs have not yet captured the attention and imagination of the world,' wrote Zhang Yiwu, of Peking University, in the Portland report. This is true: China cannot match America or Europe in such fields. As a result, visitors want to see the Great Wall and the Terracotta Army, but lack even the sketchiest sense of the broader cultural horizon. China also lacks the independent youth culture to give support to the sort of pop groups South Korea produces, though there are signs that, like Japan, it is embracing the European classical traditions with vigour. In Mao's China, revolutionary guards would chop pianos to pieces with axes as hated bourgeois enemies of progress; today it is estimated that forty of the fifty million learning piano in the world are Chinese – some of whom will turn out to be virtuoso performers.

The world *is* beginning to watch Chinese films, too. *Raise the Red Lantern* (1991) and *Crouching Tiger, Hidden Dragon* (2000) were award-winning triumphs, and in recent years China has started to colonise the mass-market box office too. In *Wolf Warrior 2* (2017) Chinese marines hurtled to the rescue of doctors stranded in Africa, while *Operation Red Sea* (2018) sent commandoes to rescue six hundred hostages in Yemen, and *The Wandering Earth* (2019) became the second most popular Chinese film of all time by featuring Chinese astronauts saving the planet from the collapse of the sun. But these are outliers.

Anyone who saw these as propaganda, however, had to admit that they were little different from the Hollywood blockbusters aimed at the same multiplex audience. The love affair with Chinese naval forces in *Operation Red Sea* resembled the hot anthems to Marine Corps ferocity in countless Hollywood products. And the growing power of political correctness in the West (a studio that featured a vicious transgender villain would be no-platformed before anyone could say only-joking) allowed China to insist that its system was no more a threat to 'freedom' than 'so-called' democracy.

In an irony infuriating to the Beijing authorities, however, the Chinese artists most likely to be lionised in the Western sphere tended (like the heroes of Russian literature in Soviet times) to be dissidents. Ai Weiwei, China's most famous creative figure, spent four years wowing the world from Berlin before moving to Cambridge. In China he had helped design the famous 'Bird's Nest' stadium that hosted the Beijing Olympics in 2008, but later he denounced it as 'a stage for a political party to advertise its glory to the world'. In expelling him, China may have been removing a thorn from its foot ... but it was harming itself in foreign eyes.[6]

In the upside-down world of soft power, obliging artists to toe the national line is usually counter-productive. As *The Economist* put it: 'China will find it hard to win friends and influence nations so long as it muzzles its best advocates.'

It may be only a question of time, however. The international success of European and American art did not precede imperial ambition but was a consequence of it. In due course, therefore, the world can expect more Chinese novels and films, if only because China will increasingly influence the means of production. And when this time comes, the sheer size of the Chinese box office (it was worth \$12.3 billion in 2020, more than the \$11.9 billion taken in the United States) will itself be a shaping force, determining

---

6 There was a flutter of concern, meanwhile, in the German city of Trier, in 2018, when a 17-foot-tall bronze statue of Karl Marx, unveiled in the town square on his 200th birthday, turned out to have been paid for by the People's Republic of China.

anything from the slant of a character to the names on maps. In the long run, this strategy may work. Taiwan, Tiananmen and Tibet are already known as the three unmentionables, and Chinese-inflected characters (mostly scientists and sages) pop up everywhere, in joint ventures with Chinese producers. Some make the sly point that long-suffering poverty is more saintly than shallow capitalism.

A franchise like *Kung Fu Panda*, meanwhile, would not even exist without the Chinese audience. So the power of that audience is a soft-power resource in itself: its scale may guarantee that Chinese culture spreads around the world. If the fifty million overseas Chinese acted in concert they would be a nation the size of South Korea (or England), a vehicle strong enough to transmit new national ideas across the waves.

The new long march, in other words, may have only just begun.

There will be further twists, because despite all the above, soft power is not always obedient. Of the huge population of students and tourists China has sent abroad, a number are almost certain to enjoy the values of liberal democracy, chafe at the constraints of life at home, and envy the freedoms on offer elsewhere. These explorers may not remain as conformist as their government might wish.

That is often how diasporas work. Many of the nations that send emigrants overseas – like India, Pakistan, the Philippines, Thailand and Eastern Europe – are stimulated not only by remittances from migrant workers but through the ideas and aspirations they encounter. The cultural liberation of Ireland, for instance, can be attributed largely to the global community that shares Irish descent. In 2015, 52 per cent of Irish citizens voted in support of same-sex marriage, an unthinkable result just a generation earlier, when Ireland was governed by devout Catholic tradition – even condoms were banned until 1979. The Papal visit that year drew more than a million people into Dublin's Phoenix Park; in 2018, only 150,000 attended the same event.

In China, too, migration on this scale may prove the most powerful soft engine of all, stirring as it does the infiltration of foreign attitudes. As George Soros has written, arguing in favour

of 'open' societies (and against one-party states backed by surveillance technologies): 'The Chinese people remain our main source
of hope.' He might have added that the West's greatest soft-power
asset is its uncensored internet – however unwelcome some of its
nastier manifestations might be.

At the end of 2019 there was another leakage of bad news from
China, none of it helpful to the brand. Further details about
indoctrination camps in Xinjiang, the suspension of internet
accounts and interference in video games emerged. When the
Turkish-descended German footballer Mesut Özil tweeted his
support for the Uighur, China cancelled live broadcasts of his club
games – for Arsenal – and erased him from Pro Evolution Soccer.
There was also more evidence of facial recognition being used to
enhance surveillance (admittedly, not just in China but overseas
too); various disappearances and the recalling of ambassadors; the
continuing Hong Kong *événements* ... the drip of such news was
incessant. The Bar Council in London issued a statement deplor-
ing China's human rights record, while a young girl opened a
supermarket Christmas card and found a handwritten note from
a prisoner in Shanghai, pleading for help ('We are foreign prisoners ... forced to work against our will. Please help us ...').

It was not tactful, in the light of so many reputation-damaging
stories, for President Xi to refer to the new €600 million port in
Athens, an important notch in the Belt and Road, as 'the dragon's
head'. There was a step-change in the way world opinion saw
China, and in the hall of mirrors created by instant messaging,
this 'authoritarian lurch' (as the *Financial Times* called it) was
visible not just to diplomats but to the public. Suddenly, China
was not so much an amazing work in progress as an Orwellian
experiment.

The cataclysm caused by coronavirus threw this contradictory
nature of the Chinese message into bold relief. Both the vices and
virtues of secretive, authoritarian rule were in play. The absence
of open politics and media had been part of the problem; China's
awesome ability to self-isolate was part of the solution. Joseph
Nye and others had been warning for a while that China would
not supplant the United States in the near future, on the grounds
that untruthful societies did not thrive for long, but the virus

unsettled all such confident thoughts. Even the uproar over Hong Kong's protestors (and the overseas bloggers who supported them) faded from view in favour of more urgent news about testing kits and ventilator systems.

In soft diplomacy, captivating the world is as important as controlling it. Before the virus, China was keener, perhaps, on the second than the first, but the global nature of this crisis gave it the chance to perform much better in these new likeability stakes. When Serbia's President Aleksandar Vučić appealed for assistance not to Europe but to the 'strong-as-steel friendship' that bound his country to China, it was music to Beijing's ears. To Western eyes, the idea of Serbia becoming a pawn in some grand tussle between superpowers stirred terrible memories, but this was the new reality: a global health panic was becoming a major soft-power opportunity. There was a new force in geopolitics – *pandemic diplomacy* – and China was first out of the blocks.

19

Japan: The Art of Cool

T hanks to Adolf Hitler and Jesse Owens, everyone knows where the 1936 Olympic Games were held. But how many can say where the 1940 version would have been staged had war not intervened?

The answer is . . . Tokyo.

After the war, few spared a thought for the would-have-been host nation. The Land of the Rising Sun had behaved with such well-documented cruelty in Korea and Manchuria, not to mention Pearl Harbor, the Philippines, Singapore and Thailand, that no one shed a tear. True, some had marvelled at the reckless bravery that drove Japan to take up arms against the world's three greatest powers – China, Russia and America – at the same time. But by the end of the conflict it was clearly not in the running to host any sort of sports festival ever again.

It did not take long, however, for the privilege to be re-awarded, and as the 1964 Games approached, Tokyo made its preparations. A city that had been roasted to a crisp by the fire-bombing of 1945 became a construction site. Roads, railways, offices, stadiums and apartment blocks sprang from the ashes: the entire city smelled of concrete. There were 20,000 new buildings and a new sewage system – as the war ended, waste was collected by hand and carted out to manure rice paddies.

The authorities cut it fine. Ten days before the Games began, a futuristic new device was launched, to great admiration – the *Shinkansen*, or bullet train. Japan, the world's most ruined country, somehow or other had the world's fastest railway.

It was a colossal national moment. Some 90 per cent of Japan's population watched the opening ceremony on television, and saw their country at last permitted, after years of global purdah, to salute an anthem, wave a flag and cheer on a national hero.

No one could miss the symbolism. The Olympic Village was built on the site of an Imperial Army barracks. Crowds filled the irradiated central plaza in Hiroshima to greet the Olympic flame, held high by a white-clad runner. At the climax of the gala, thousands of bright balloons floated in the air while doves wheeled over the athletes below. In the blue sky above the city, five aircraft, glinting silver in the sunshine, created Olympic rings out of smoke trails. The sun really was rising again.

It was quite a turnaround. Two decades before the term was invented, Japan was using soft power – sport – to change its place in the world. And who could say that sport didn't matter? When the marathon runner Kokichi Tsuburaya appeared in the stadium in second place, only to be pipped to silver by Britain's world record holder, Basil Heatley, he really did die of shame – four years later he left a note apologising for his failure and cut his wrists. The nation could only mourn when its judo champion (Parliament closed for the afternoon to watch him prove that Japanese agility could outwit European muscle) lost the final to a giant Dutchman, dismaying proof that, contrary to the entire ethos of Japan's favourite sport, size did matter after all.

It was left to the women's volleyball team, drawn from a textile factory in Osaka and trained by a military disciplinarian, to win gold for the home nation after beating the Soviet Union in the final. This may have stirred, in the odd aged mind, recollections of the 1905 naval victory over Russia that had announced Japan's arrival on the world scene. But most people had shorter memories, and celebrated the triumph merely as proof that a crushed and defeated empire was at long last recovering its balance.

And it was doing so by embracing novelty. Runners were timed electronically by the engineering firm Seiko; swimmers were tracked on electronic pads in the pool wall; computers tossed out statistics and tables. It later emerged that even the temple bells at the opening ceremony had been amplified by smart IBM processors.

The world's most traditional nation was fast becoming its most futuristic, too.

Innovation took other forms. Four years earlier, highlights of the Rome Games had been distributed (slowly) on tape. The Tokyo highlights were broadcast by satellite (and in *colour,* if you please). The rest of the world, including America, which only two decades earlier had ruled Japan as an occupying power, for the first time saw an Olympic opening ceremony in its own sitting room, live on television. They also saw a nation rebounding with dizzy speed from a historic catastrophe.

By the time of the closing pageant (a crafty rendition of 'Auld Lang Sayonara') Japan seemed like a nation transformed, if not quite healed.

In truth, it was an unveiling. That bullet train was a clue: an economic miracle was at hand. A country that had (astonishingly) lost up to three million people in the course of the war, seen its industrial fabric destroyed, and witnessed both its cities and its imperial dream in tatters, would soon be the envy of the industrialised world.[1] Cars, motorbikes, ships, steel, chemicals, televisions, semiconductors, musical instruments – Japan mastered them all. The Honda Motor Company built its first car in 1963, the year before the Games; soon it was the leading manufacturer of combustion engines in the world's second-biggest economy.

This was no ordinary comeback. The Japanese seemed superhuman – and not a little scary. A land feted for kimonos and cherry blossom (known to gardeners as Japan's 'horticultural mascot') was bursting forth, like Godzilla (also a Japanese creation[2]) as a predatory monster. Novels and films spread alarm about the assault on America's corporate heights. One Tokyo VIP was quoted as saying that in time America would become Japan's farm, and Europe its boutique . . . and this felt more than likely. The Japanese skiers in Switzerland's pricey resorts seemed to find them comically cheap.

---

1 More than two million of Japan's casualties were military; the civilian death toll was also huge. For perspective, Britain suffered a combined loss of some 450,000.

2 Half-gorilla, half-whale, Godzilla was specifically post-nuclear, a mutant monster rising from the irradiated ocean in a 1954 film by Ishiro Honda. In America's version of the story he became Gigantis, but the original name is the one that has stuck.

It felt like a parable. As victorious Britain fell back on procedures that had served it well in the past, defeated Japan had no option but to trust novelty. Like no economy before or since, in the heart of its grief it found something rare: a clean slate.

We can hardly say it did not look back: Japan remained obsessively reverential towards its own traditions. But one of its eyes was fixed on the future, too.

Not surprisingly, it was widely regarded as having discovered the secret of business success, and executives from America trooped there to learn it. Japanese management was all the rage, and seemed to have three pillars: first, lifetime employment – don't waste government money on sacking people; second, set wages according to age – no overpaid whizz-kids; and third, 'enterprise unions' – fair deals for workers, so they would not be at permanent loggerheads with the boss class.

Japan itself put its advance down to strategic planning. 'America looks forward ten minutes,' noted the chairman of Sony, Akio Morita. 'Japan looks forward ten years.'

If the miracle had a symbolic leader, it was probably Morita. The child of a long-established sake and soy brewing family (you can still buy Morita soy sauce), who trained as a physicist and an engineer, he had glimpsed a simple truth in that nuclear flash over Hiroshima: the terrifying technology gap between Japan and the West. In partnership with Masaru Ibuka he founded an electronics company, Sony, and began by making tape recorders. A generation later their new toy, the Walkman, was putting music in people's pockets. Neat and clever, it was an emblem of Japanese ingenuity – it even worked *underwater*. It swept the world, along with Toyota, Nissan, Yamaha, Hitachi, Toshiba, Fujitsu, Nikon, Panasonic and the rest, giving Japan the means to buy lavish slices of Americana: automobile companies, film studios, skyscrapers, golf courses, department stores . . . almost anything it liked.

Pundits were quick to accuse it of 'invading' America all over again. Akio Morita's dry quip – 'If you don't want Japan to buy it . . . don't sell it' – did not deter them. Thriller writers revived the hoary old staple concerning wily Orientals, this time putting them in corporate boardrooms in skyscrapers.

It did not last – trees do not grow to the sky. When the

Tokyo property bubble burst, so too did Japan's economic zest. Admiration curdled into fear; the delegations from America started looking not for the secret but for cautionary advice. The qualities once regarded as central to Japan's renaissance were now blamed for the opposite. No hiring and firing? Strong unions? Payment by seniority? Government intervention? Five minutes at the Harvard Business School was enough to tell a would-be corporate boss that this could only lead to financial and commercial stagnation.

So: after the economic miracle came the economic reality check. Japan entered a long period of sluggish growth. Its now-immense corporations turned out to be less nimble than the competition. The world's new power brokers – Apple, Microsoft, Google, Facebook, Amazon – were mushrooming on the other side of the Pacific.

Somewhere in the background, however, shifting like mist on a marsh, something else was stirring. Thanks to Nintendo, PlayStation and Pokémon, the world's children were seeing Japan in a new light: as a day-glo playground. A nation of uniform salarymen, keen on callisthenics in the company car park, sadistic TV assault courses, kinky sex parlours and weird *sumo* giants, suddenly morphed into something . . . cool!

This coolness had several components. The first was simple colouring-in. Japanese comic strips (or manga) had for some time been winning a following beyond Japan. They were edgier than Western cartoons – violent, sometimes pornographic – and in a visual idiom that did not always translate. But in their cute, wordless way they were a visual Esperanto. They made a jaunty change from the funny pages of Europe and America, and travelled easily: something like a craze developed in the satchels and bedrooms of the outside world Japan had once fought to keep at bay.

In Asia they were a wild hit, especially when, in 2015, China banned a number on the grounds that they were immoral. Hong Kong and Taiwan became hubs of a new cartooning industry, and manga images and characters became ubiquitous – despite Japan's sizeable language barrier – with the rest of the world. America and Britain had been able to dole out their soft products in

English, a globally recognised medium. Disney could flow where it pleased. Japan had no such advantage – yet prevailed.

To some extent manga was itself a hybrid – the US occupation introduced traditional Japanese graphics to Walt Disney storytelling motifs. Soon there were new versions of Western classics – *Hamlet*, say, set in a dystopian future of climate change and civic collapse, or *Romeo and Juliet*, a fight between Yakuza families in Tokyo.

It seemed only natural when *King Lear* was re-imagined as if the old man were the last of the Mohicans, floundering away in a vain bid to save his ancient kingdom.

But it was when manga met Japanese electronics that the fun really started.

First it was Space Invaders and Pac-Man. Then it was Super Mario and Sonic the Hedgehog. Cinema joined the party, enabling a franchise like Pokémon to invade both the world's theatres (half a billion dollars at the box office) and its mobile phones.

Your Name (2016), in which a boy and a girl exchange bodies in a shrewdly pitched gender-twisting plot, took $350 million, while *Howl's Moving Castle* (2004), *Spirited Away* (2001) and *Grave of the Fireflies* (1988) also captured worldwide audiences. Japan had long been giving the world brilliant film and theatre directors – Kurosawa, Ozu, Ninagawa and others. In 2009 the Best Foreign Language Oscar went to *Departures*, a touching tale about, of all things, a mortician. But these were valued by the few, not the many. Animation was suddenly both a cultural speciality and a potent export. Singapore and Jakarta hosted 'anime' festivals, and nearly 400 million PlayStation consoles were snapped up. When the fourth version of this game system was launched, in 2013, sales hit one million on the very first day.

According to the *Nikkei Asian Review*, in 2017 the anime market in China alone was worth $21 billion. An international festival in Hangzhou attracted more than a million attendees, who spent $290 million on merchandise alone. This was a major commercial fact, but its soft-power implications – the extent to which it planted an enthusiasm for Japan in a new generation of young minds, reared on *Astro Boy*, *Doraemon*, *Miss Kobayashi's Dragon Maid* and others – was even more valuable.

The greatest compliment paid to this product line was that it was mimicked in America. *Power Rangers* was (like *Godzilla*) merely a US rendition of a Japanese idea, but the *Teenage Mutant Ninja Turtles* were actually born in the USA, in a 1984 New Hampshire comic book. Soon, all such work was required to have a marked Japanese flavour: even the pictorial style and the music. The galactic knights of *Star Wars* duelled with light sabres that resembled the night sticks wielded by patrolmen on Tokyo's road junctions – and took up samurai poses before saving the universe.

Japan was . . . fashionable. Words like *emoji* ('picture character') and *sudoku* ('number place') became everyday terms. When a Cheltenham clothing stall decided to expand, in 2003, it adopted a bold Japanese graphic style and a distinctly Japanese 'look', named itself Superdry, and snagged the attention of an eager young audience. The Japanese text in its branding was machine-generated and didn't mean anything, but who cared? It was a look that (backed by celebrities, selling their own soft power to the cause) created a global winner. When it listed on the London Stock Exchange in 2010 Superdry was valued at £400 million; a year later it was worth a billion – not a bad return for brushed cotton with faux-Japanese mumbo-jumbo.

Commentators tended to denounce that sort of thing as trivial froth, but it had a hard edge. Ever since the atomic horror of August 1945, Hiroshima had been a global totem for peace. The scorched city rebuilt itself around an unusual feature: pacifism. The city centre became a large, empty forum with a flame, a flag, a sculpture, an arch, a bell, a conference centre, a mound containing the ashes of 70,000 people, a pool, a fountain, a mother-and-child statue and a museum.

The gates displayed the essential word – 'peace' – in forty-seven languages.

The ruined cupola known as the A-bomb dome was left untouched as a ruin, an unholy relic. A magnet for pacifists, in 1996 it became a UNESCO World Heritage Site. A million visitors a year filed through this sober square to be overwhelmed by sadness as they trooped past the exhibits in the memorial. Some frowned at the idea, prominent in the exhibit, that the atom bomb fell without warning on a peace-loving people who were minding their own business when the silver plane glinted in the blue sky overhead – apparently for no reason. And it is true that the museum does little to contextualise the atrocity. It does not mention the eight million people (estimates vary between three and twelve) killed by Japan in its own imperial conquests. The horrors of the atom bomb have tended to trump more routine atrocities, however brutal.

But no one could deny the impact of the exhibits – the melted watch that still told the time the bomb fell, the child's shirt burned on skin. There were many such souvenirs of nuclear violence – not least a model of the city before it was flattened, which looked, perhaps not surprisingly, like the recreations of Pompeii before Vesuvius.

It received a major seal of approval in 1974 when Japan's Prime Minister, Eisaku Satu, won the Nobel Peace Prize for his anti-nuclear stance. He had also, ten years earlier, been the minister in charge of the Tokyo Olympic Games.

He understood well that post-war Japan needed new weapons. As the Latin motto of a Tokyo school put it: *Calamus Gladio Fortior* – the pen is mightier than the sword.

Suddenly, Japan was a standard-bearer for utopian pacifism. The spiritual purity of Zen Buddhism – a hey-dude pose well-suited to druggy students in the West – made for an appealing brand. It is possible that the reverence for Zen was overdone, because not everyone in Japan was a monk or a bonsai craftsman.

This sentiment fed into one of Japan's strongest soft-power suits: its food. In a miracle of changing tastes, a once-feared cuisine became the world's favourite way to eat.

Like a number of the aesthetic elements that seem uniquely Japanese (ink painting, pagodas, kimonos), sushi began in China, roughly when Ancient Greece was enjoying its golden age in the fifth century BC. It began as a way of preserving fish in salt and rice, became a Japanese speciality a thousand years later, and did not sweep the world until it was introduced to America by expatriates in Los Angeles, where it was seized upon by the health-conscious movie crowd as a delicious novelty.

From there it spread to Europe and the rest of the world.

It didn't take long. The first Japanese restaurant in London was the Hiroko, in 1967, and Britain was at first startled. Poisonous pieces of seafood washed in vinegar? Surely not. Fifty years later there were 277 such outlets in London alone.

Some were high-end restaurants boasting Michelin stars and celebrity guests, but the majority were high-street chains. Wagamama, which opened in Bloomsbury in 1992, spawned a hundred sisters in the malls of modern Britain. Prompted by the idea that you could *not* have too much of a good thing, the first sushi conveyor belt appeared at Waterloo in 1994, seating commuters at a runway of brightly lit fishy allsorts, and they loved it – it was like snacking on a reef. New names – Yo! Sushi, Itsu, Wasabi – popped up everywhere; supermarkets stocked sushi on their lunch counters.

When the Bognor Butlin's announced that it too had a sushi bar, the food revolution was complete. There had been Chinese restaurants for fifty years – now there were ramen bars. In smart kitchens all over the country, people began to keep soy and teriyaki sauce beside the ketchup.

The same story repeated itself in the world's food halls. It made sense that in 2013 Japanese cuisine was listed by UNESCO as 'intangible cultural heritage'.

In a 2009 article in *Foreign Policy*, 'Japan's Gross National Cool', Douglas McGray wondered how, with Japan's economy stagnant, the Nikkei crawling from low to low, unemployment high, property prices flat, debt raging and banking moribund, it was nevertheless becoming a 'cultural superpower'. Some of its products were not what most people would call high art – the jingly J-pop music and those cartoon characters – but something odd was happening. As the tide of Japanese corporate power in the world declined (and China's rose), so Japanese culture seemed to be growing ever more desirable – and ever more profitable.

It was a prescient intervention. In the new soft world a nation's prestige could rise even as its material fortunes stagnated. All over the world people wanted their own little piece of Japan, even if it was only a Muji pencil.

Actually, Muji was a case in point. Its name actually meant

'brandless quality', and this turned out to be a bravura joke: brandlessness as a brand! Making a virtue of unshowy simplicity, it was a pace-setting design machine. Since the opening of its first overseas store in London in 1991 it had become a fixture. Just as the national cuisine's idea of pudding was a perfectly sliced orange, so the Muji aesthetic made a virtue of the unadorned – an undecorated pot, a white bowl, a piece of brown paper. This turned out to be in tune with the world's mood. Today, there are more than four hundred Muji stores outside Japan, and the geographical spread makes interesting reading for Eurocentrics, because while there are a dozen in Britain and twelve more in America, there are two hundred in China, forty-two in Taiwan and twenty in South Korea. The wave of affection for Japan in Britain is only a ripple of the one that has swept Asia.

In 2012 a ministry was created to spread the idea of 'Cool Japan' through public-private partnerships that could deepen Japan's footprint in the international market. Money was made available for exhibitions, galleries and other overseas missions.

Traditionally minded Japanese critics saw this as a dumb marketing stunt (like Cool Britannia) – and a slur on Japan's deep artistic tradition. In their view, it was no more than Ministry Men making a spectacle of themselves by pandering to mass taste.

In one sense Japan was contravening what until then had seemed a soft-power law: little was less cool than a government trying to be cool. But this was more than the exception that proved the rule: it was proof that it *was* possible, with care and tact, for governments to act wisely in the soft arena.

Certainly, in this case, the results were anything but laughable. In 2006 there were 24,000 Japanese restaurants outside Japan; ten years later there were 90,000. And it wasn't just teriyaki chicken and salmon rolls; the world also fell for tiny bottles of heavily marketed fermented milk (Yakult), which only had to mention their country of origin ('From Japan to the world') to attract health-conscious consumers everywhere.

It used to be thought that governments could control supply, but not demand. In the soft world this is patently not the case – appetite *can* be stimulated. If not, there would be no such thing as advertising. In 1867 Japan showed the world its art in Paris at the *Exposition Universelle*. The result was a sensational burst of interest in its woodcuts, ceramics and gowns: Degas, Monet, Manet and Van Gogh became fervent fans. The craze soon had a name – *Japonisme* – which nudged Puccini to write *Madame Butterfly*.[3]

Imperial condescension may have obliged Europeans to treat the Japanese as if they were enchanting, rather picturesque, children. Yeats wrote plays inspired by the highly ritualised Noh theatre; everyone who was anyone flocked to the Savoy Theatre to see Gilbert and Sullivan's *The Mikado*; and when a new store, Liberty's, opened in London in 1875, it was full of elegant Japanese fabrics and furnishings.

This was more than a design fad. There was something uncanny about the Japanese approach to life. It struck a chord in countries like France and Britain, where the gaudy trappings of consumer culture were making people dizzy. It abounded with soft colours and graceful patterns, but also with tremors of mortality: flickering lanterns and silken sighs. Those ferocious samurai warriors seemed to be ... dancing. Even their armour was forged with artistry and zeal. Every object they made, from the meekest pot to the most gilded screen, seemed to be an incantation about honour and death. The landscape itself, in early photographs, looked groomed with nail scissors.

This was the first blooming of Japan's cultural aura. It was rich in Zen paradoxes. The way of the warrior was the way of peace. The way up was the way down. Life was short, but also long. Perfection was within everybody's grasp – yet unattainable. Even the pouring of tea was refined into a dignified ceremony. This might have been a caricature of Japanese civilisation, but it proved gripping.

It was all sacrificed, of course, when Japan became a military power in the twentieth century, and brought to the role a cruelty that shocked the wider world. As we have seen, soft power, many centuries in the making, can be squandered in a flash.

But it has returned, and is still visible in Japan's daily life: the

---

3 In much the same way, nearly a quarter of a million went to the Japan Expo in Paris in July 2013. Now, as then, trade fairs spin soft power into sales.

way a bill is presented with two hands and a bow, as if it were a ceremonial sword; the way ticket inspectors on trains wear uniforms and white gloves, like stewards on a royal yacht; the way airport workers *bow* when the bus leaves the terminal; the ineffable care that goes into every mundane task, from preparing a vegetable to running a bath.

This too is being carefully exported, in stylish new cultural centres. Three 'Japan Houses' have opened in Los Angeles, London and Rio de Janeiro: display cases for modern Japanese design with exhibitions and events around shops and a café.

As with Denmark, so with Japan: the design philosophy inspired by this attitude has been embraced both by noted minimalists (John Pawson) and by mass-market chains. Cool restraint has become almost the norm. Often without knowing it, people toy with Japanese taste every time they turn on a tap in their kitchen, put oranges in a bowl or switch off a lamp. Monasticism may be a spent force in Europe, but the affection for simplicity, for the suggestion of depth in humble objects, is kept alive in Japan.

A more contemporary vibe, meanwhile – the garish neon blare of modern Tokyo – has become an equally vivid strand in a lot of cutting-edge art and music.

There are plenty who mourn the eclipse of old Japan – that watercolour world of geisha, calligraphy, tea and miniature trees – but today's zip and flash is now a fixed part of the global lifestyle. A Japanese enterprise, Uniqlo (Unique Clothing Company), took on Superdry by selling Nippon designs that were, in fact, made in China. From Sydney to Stockholm, from Cairo to Christchurch, young people wore its clothes while tucking into ramen, sipping Asahi beer and reading Murakami.

The kitsch nature of some Japanese products made them even *more* cute. Hello Kitty, for instance, a vacuous cat with a white face and a red bow (she has no mouth – she is *all* feeling), bows to few Western conventions. Yet from modest beginnings – in 1974 she was a children's purse – she too grew into a global bestseller. On her fortieth birthday, celebrated with a four-day festival, she was worth $7 billion a year.

She was especially popular in India, along with other figures from anime and manga. One side-effect of the latter was that fans in Mumbai and Delhi gained a glimpse of something they would never otherwise have contemplated: Japanese family life, with its tidy rooms, neat satchels, artfully arranged food and respect for ancestors.

Disney was doing the same for American family values, even if its boisterous boys and eyelash-batting girls came disguised as deer, rabbits, mermaids or mice.

Ironically, part of Hello Kitty's appeal in Japan was that she was English (she may have been non-verbal – she spoke from the heart: how adorable and inclusive! – but her name was Kitty White). She was a child's toy, but also educational; she gave rise to Hello Kitty toasters, Hello Kitty jewellery, Hello Kitty aeroplanes, a Hello Kitty maternity hospital, a hello Kitty bullet train – even (this being Japan) a Hello Kitty vibrator.

In some singular Japanese way, that was all cool, too.

And if the fact that she was English made her a hit in Japan, everywhere else she struck people as utterly Japanese – how could she be anything else? Either way, she was a merchandising gold mine – the cat that got everybody's cream.

The qualities listed above – pacifism, computer games, cartoons, films, design and cuisine – may seem weightless, but they are not negligible. The children who grew up trading Pokémon cards now meet for rice cakes and green tea, and mean to go to Japan as soon as they can afford it. And Japan has proved itself well able to make them feel at home by perfecting foreign tastes and flavours. What worked for cars and musical instruments has also acted on alcoholic spirits. Malt liquor, a drink once thought an extract of pure Caledonian mist, has re-emerged in a new and golden form, thanks to a happy marriage between malt imported from Scotland and clean Japanese water. Japan now makes more whisky than Ireland.

It is often said that the best place in the world to eat French food is in Tokyo, and Japanese whisky, which was born only in the 1920s (as a determined attempt to reproduce its Scottish ancestor), now regularly scores higher than Scotch in international tasting contests.

In a case like that the hard-currency consequences are clear enough. And in several other sectors — tourism and education — the ramifications are evident. In 1977 it was big news that visitor numbers to Japan had topped a million for the first time; forty years later there were twenty-seven million. In the same period the number of foreign students has risen from a mere handful to almost a quarter of a million. Having identified tourism as one global industry it was failing to dominate, Japan has rapidly turned itself into a visitor attraction both for heritage (temples, monasteries, gardens) and for fun. ·

Seventy years ago Japan was feared. Now it is loved. King Kong has become Princess Mononoke, a Japanese Joan of Arc defending 'nature' against the hurtful influence of humankind. But it has grown in confidence too: Madame Butterfly — a frail flower — has been recast as a superhero. The general picture is hard to miss. And through this refashioning of its image, Japan is laying down fresh reserves of the soft-power currency it threw away in its own warlike quest for imperial dominion.

It is an ongoing story, still in its early stages. In an odd twist, Japan is admired more warmly the further one travels from it. Its near neighbours have bitter memories, and wounds that have not healed. But Japan has done a great deal to win over hearts and minds in more distant time zones. Not since the ugly duckling turned into a very fine swan indeed has there been so striking a metamorphosis. So when the earthquake and tsunami of 2011 (the worst in Japan's history) killed 18,000 people, jolted the country five inches closer to the United States and triggered a nuclear panic at Fukushima, it struck at a nation with a new place in the world's affections. A land reviled in war, then feared for its industrial triumphs, inspired worldwide sympathy and affection.

In London's Holland Park, a small plaque in a stone and bamboo garden expresses Japan's thanks for the kindness of its friends in Britain at that devastating time.[4]

---

4 The Japanese Garden at Tatton, in Cheshire, is an even greener slice of botanical soft power. Inspired by the 1910 Anglo-Japanese Exhibition in London's White City, it was created by a team of Japanese gardeners who produced an immaculate collage of Shinto shrines, lanterns and miniature trees, all harmonised with rocks, water, bamboo and moss. One of the workers married a local barmaid and never went home.

20

Japan: the Magic of Everyday Life

M odern Japan seems stable, prosperous and calm. It marries a reverence for tradition with a zest for innovation.[1] It manufactures goods for the whole world and is the second largest contributor to the United Nations, yet remains a land apart, resolutely itself. Its love of tradition has made it slow to embrace gender equality and other principles, but it bows to no one (figuratively speaking) when it comes to courtesy.

It came as a shock, therefore, when a *Japanese* journalist (Kenji Goto) was beheaded by ISIS extremists in Iraq — even though Japan's NHK was a busy broadcaster, often among the first to report such incidents. It was rare for Japan itself to occupy the foreground of such horrors. The world was not used to images of weeping Japanese families mourning their loss (in this case, of a journalist and children's book author who had converted to Christianity). The outburst of international condemnation was tinged with a new emotion: disbelief.

It was a reminder, too, that any consideration of Japanese soft power needs to begin by recognising the extent to which the national recovery from the thunderclap of 1945 — literally a rise from the ashes — has been a 'soft' achievement. Not a bullet has been fired. It has been accomplished, in three generations, by engineering, technology, art, fashion, food ... and manners. Like Germany, Japan has contrived an extraordinary alteration in the way it is seen by others. In both cases, defeat was a spur, as was

---

[1] Sometimes the two go together. One reason why Japan is so keen on robotics, it has been said, is that it would rather have its houses cleaned, beds changed and drinks served by a machine than by a foreigner.

the fact that they were banned from spending on defence. And neither could have revived without the generosity of the United States – never in history have vanquished empires been treated so kindly.

But this is also a remarkable tribute to the far-reaching effects of soft forces, and a lesson in how rapidly national reputations can fluctuate. Again the comparison with Germany is hard to avoid. When Bismarck unified it with his forceful rhetoric of blood and soil, he gave a black eye to its image abroad (until then a child-friendly confection of fairy tales, music, philosophy and sausages). Kaiser Wilhelm gave it a still more monstrous front, before Hitler took it to the depths. Yet it rebounded from pariah status to a high place in the world's affections in exactly the same period and in many of the same ways. Soft power is not bricks and mortar, but it *can* rebuild.

We have said that migration is one of the channels through which soft power runs, and in this respect Japan is weak. Many of its ingrained instincts are opposed to the idea. Famously, it lived in almost complete seclusion during the long Meiji period (the era of the Emperor and his samurai) until Commodore Perry's ships appeared in Tokyo Bay in 1853 to request – or demand – that Japan join the outside world.

There is a reflexive belief that foreigners are a polluting influence, a fear that Japan's unique traditions would be threatened by exposure to the outside world. In some ways it is a well-founded fear. The veins of Japan's soft power – its rare singularity – might indeed be at risk if globalisation were to dilute it. What it gained in dynamism and variety it might lose in stability and social cohesion – an awkward transaction.

No need for a long list of facts and figures. Suffice it to say that at the last count only 2 per cent of Japan's population was born abroad (in the United Kingdom it is 13 per cent). There were eighty mosques and two synagogues; in Britain there are 1800 and 400.

Japan remains a law unto itself. It is common knowledge that its elderly population is not replenishing itself. In 2018 there were 1.3 million deaths and only 921,000 births, leading one university to calculate that at this rate Japan itself would become extinct on 16 August 3766. Since most of its modest number of migrants were from China, Korea and Vietnam, there was more than enough room for growth.

Change will not be easy. But there are signs that it may be on the way. When the essayist Mitsuyo Okada published a book applauding the 'atmosphere of freedom' she found in New York, and urged her own homeland to embrace diversity of this sort, it sold 400,000 copies. Meanwhile, the government was announcing a relaxation of the rules for foreigners, a change to the visa system to boost tourism, and an educational exchange programme to give international graduates a taste of Japan.

There are other clues. In 1964 Niseko was an isolated village in the snowy wastes of Hokkaido. Now it is one of the buzziest ski resorts in the world.

Most of this is down to its unusual – for Japan – openness to outsiders. Its potential for skiing was noticed in 1910 by an Austro-Hungarian colonel, Theodor von Lerch, an emissary from one empire to another who startled the local farmers by sliding down their volcanic slopes. His statue stands on a plinth in the town of Kutchan. But after his death the village lay dormant, hibernating in the snows of the world's disdain.[2]

It was rediscovered at the end of the twentieth century by Australian surfers looking for something to do in winter. But the remote location and freezing temperatures made it hard to turn it into a resort, even when the 1972 Winter Olympics were held in nearby Sapporo. Newspaper photographs of Japan's ski slopes made them look glum: slim tongues of snow with half a million people jostling for elbow room. The go-to places were still the climbing capitals of Europe and the booming North American domains.

It wasn't until the late 1990s that Niseko began to take off. Developers from Tokyo, Hong Kong and Malaysia followed the Australian lead, buying whole mountains and building villages at their feet. It soon became one of the world's fastest-growing ski areas. Was it the Aspen of the East, or Asia's answer to Whistler?

---

2 Von Lerch was one part military adviser (sent to train infantry regiments in the European art of war) and one part spy. Japan's victory over Russia in 1905 had made it a power to be reckoned with, and von Lerch wanted to find out what made it tick.

Either way, it soon attracted a growing legion of fervent devotees from around the world.

Several things conspired to propel it into this elite club.

The first was geographical: the snow that fell on Hokkaido owed its icing-sugar lightness to salt grains picked up over the Sea of Japan. By sucking moisture out of the flakes, these created what may be the world's finest snow: weightless powder that drifts from the sky in a billowing cloud. The ski slopes are low – the peak at Niseko is only 1380 metres, below even the hairdressing salons of St Moritz – but the northerly latitude provides snow in quantities that Europe can only dream of.

The second was sartorial. The weather in Niseko was so freezing that old-school knitwear was not up to the task. Modern thermal fabrics changed the game.

But the third reason may be the most important. Japan's new image as cool created an itch among the world's ski bums, especially at the intrepid and youthful end of the market. Its blizzard-white streets attracted the young. And these were not any old young. They were drawn by the surfer-dude ambience, but Niseko was never a cheap date – it was a long flight from anywhere. So its new fan base was well-heeled. The lift queues trembled with stories about descents through trees or tumbles in the soft, fairy-tale snow, but also contained global-elite references to the goings-on at HSBC, J. P. Morgan, Credit Suisse and Goldman Sachs. Skiing was not exactly a blue-collar pursuit anywhere; but here the ambience was more than usually elite.

This, the eavesdropper soon realises, is where Japan's soft-power strides have carried it. Niseko is too gruelling for today's fat cats (it is not the place to discuss mergers over cigars on sun-drenched terraces), but to tomorrow's global elite it is a snowy wonderland. The children of Davos will love Japan for the rest of their lives.

So while it may be the least Japanese place in Japan – it is built by foreign money, staffed by foreign workers and fuelled by foreign food: the vans in the village sell curry, fish and chips, and pizza; the supermarket has baked beans and Nutella; the mountain cafés serve spaghetti Bolognese – it may typify something new.

Without Tokyo noticing (the tourist office in the main railway station does not have so much as a leaflet about it), Niseko has created a crack through which the outside world can pour. In a sharp bucking of the trend, while Japan's population is falling, Niseko's is rising. Visitor numbers are also bubbling (up by 25 per cent in 2017). It was only natural when Prime Minister Abe invited Australia's Prime Minister Malcolm Turnbull to head north and ski in Niseko one day. As a fragment of Australia planted in foreign soil – *Sydney-sur-neige* – it would have felt like a home from home.

If Sapporo's bid to host the 2026 Winter Olympics succeeds, Niseko will host the Alpine events; it is also in prime position to become a ski mecca for China, which will soon be producing several *hundred* million keen skiers looking for a new challenge.

Japan showed, in the way it hosted the 2019 Rugby World Cup, that it knows how to welcome foreigners. Until the virus intervened it was hoping to do the same in the 2020 Olympic Games. But in some areas it betrays an attitude towards foreigners that sends a less harmonious signal to the world. When Carlos Ghosn, the one-time Chairman of Nissan, fled Japan for Lebanon in 2020, denouncing what he called 'hostage justice' after spending fifty-three days in jail while authorities searched for a 'confession', it shone an uncomfortable light on Japan's judicial procedures. The fact that it is a land of spectacularly low crime means that the police are inexperienced at solving it when it does erupt, and prosecutors rely almost exclusively on confessions rather than proof (almost 90 per cent of cases are decided that way). It was not only foreigners who fell foul of this tendency. A Japanese MP, Tomohiro Ishikawa, had been held for three weeks in 2010 and 'interrogated' for twelve hours a day in search of such a confession, and continued to rail against the system. But this was not the kind of news to make newcomers smile, whether they were tourists or executives.

There are other fault-lines in the Japanese castle, however. Osaka, for instance, has a large and growing population of Chinese and Korean workers and residents. Japan may be developing robotics in part so it does not have to embrace immigration, but in other ways it may be unable to avoid a more cosmopolitan future.

Osaka may even be the venue for the country's first casino.

This may be a mixed blessing, but Japan may at last be in the mood to gamble.

Rien ne va plus.

Sometimes it takes only a moment to undo many decades of patient work. In 2001 Japan's new Prime Minister, Junichiro Koizumi, broke with convention by visiting Tokyo's Yasukuni Shrine to pay his respects to the war dead. It was a risky step, because this monument to Japan's war record was a no-go area for national leaders – even the Emperor Akihito had declined to visit. So it was no great surprise when China's Foreign Minister reacted furiously. 'What would European people think if German leaders were to visit [shrines] related to Hitler and Nazis?'

President Jiang Zemin fired off an angry letter, too. And one South Korean agitator promised to urinate on the shrine every time a Japanese politician spoke well of it, then posted a picture of himself doing just that.

Koizumi ignored all such talk. To call off his visit after that would be to kowtow.

On Boxing Day 2013, Japan's next Prime Minister, Shinzo Abe, marked his second term of office by doing exactly the same thing, and raising exactly the same emotions. Once again, China raged that Japan was aligning itself with war criminals.

A soft initiative – a walk in a museum – became a brittle diplomatic row. This is why political gestures matter. They can keep old grievances alive.

In December 2017 a bronze statue of the so-called 'Comfort Women' – the 200,000 women forced into prostitution to serve the Japanese army on its rampage through Asia in the Second World War – went on display in San Francisco. Japan had several times apologised for this (not its only crime: thousands of Korean men had been used as slave labour, too). In 1965 Japan and Korea signed a historic agreement that involved Japan paying half a million dollars in guilt money; in 1993 it again acknowledged the 'immeasurable pain' it had caused, and in 1998 Japan's Prime Minister repeated his 'deep remorse and heartfelt apology' for past sins. On that occasion South Korea responded by dropping its ban on Japanese films and other imports.

But many saw these as skin-deep gestures rather than a credible renunciation. The ghosts of the past could not be so easily laid to rest. The Mayor of Osaka declared the Californian statue to be an insult, and threatened to sever the 'sister city' tie.

It was an empty threat. But in alerting the world to an issue it may not have noticed otherwise, he was offering proof that while usually touted as a pathway to peace, soft power can, when it tangles with history, also be a zone of conflict.

Even an incurious tourist in the Yasukuni Shrine can see why it is a contentious place for a prime minister to visit. This is Japan's Imperial War Museum, and pride of place goes to a set of exhibits – a train from the Burma–Thailand railway, a kamikaze plane – that would deeply offend war veterans from many lands. It honours the human torpedoes fired by imperial command as if obedient courage were the only issue.

In America, Britain, China, Burma, Cambodia, Korea, Indonesia, Malaysia, Taiwan, the Philippines and Vietnam these are symbols of cruelty, not courage. Some 320,000 died in Japan-occupied Philippines; two million Vietnamese suffered the same fate. A further million died in Indonesia as casualties of Japan's cruel forced-labour projects.

Yet the shrine depicts Japan as a victim of imperialism, not one of its authors.

It will take more than public relations to change this; nothing less than a whole-hearted confrontation with history will do.[3]

In one way it is not Japan's fault. The strategists behind the nuclear attack did have terror in mind – they fully intended that it create shock and awe. Three million leaflets were dropped threatening that unless Japan surrendered the atom bomb would

---

3 And cultural borrowing can be patchy. Japan absorbed European classical music like a sponge and gave it a clear Japanese dimension: the primary schools of Europe were soon echoing to the sound of children learning the violin, using the Suzuki method. But the equally venerable Western art of oil painting, all those high-collared portraits? Not so much.

be used 'again and again'. But it had a longer-term psychological impact too: it invited Japan to think of itself as the subject of an unprovoked attack rather than as a defeated warrior.

This is the emotion that keeps the Yasukuni Shrine alive: it poses as a cenotaph to the innocent. Some 2.5 million soldiers are mourned in its precincts (only a handful of whom were war criminals). But much of the old ill-feeling remains. There are a lot of vexed spirits in this shady square, a stone's throw from the Imperial Palace.[4]

Japan has more than most to gain from reappraisal and rapprochement, thanks to the growing power of modern China, which marked its seventieth birthday in 2019 by parading a new nuclear weapon in Beijing – the Dongfeng-17, a five-times-the-speed-of-sound missile system with a range of 9300 miles that could obliterate ten cities in one blow. It meant that Japan now had a large, well-armed and ambitious rival in the region, one that saw the Pacific as belonging to China's sphere of influence, and with scores to settle regarding various islands in the region. In an even more forceful soft-power gesture, President Xi chose the occasion to inspect the 15,000 marching troops in a Chairman Mao jacket, a sign that he was aligning his country not with the Confucian pleasantries of the 2008 Olympics, but with a more severe and determined ancestry.[5]

Anyone who hoped that China was intending to become part of the international family of nations could only shiver. A simple sartorial choice showed that it sought not to join the twenty-first-century world but to control it. In circumstances of that sort Japan could hardly afford a bad-tempered stand-off with South Korea, its natural ally.

The two are ethnically close; their languages are related and their aesthetic priorities similar. Yet the Japanese occupation

---

4 The director of London's Imperial War Museum once joked that he was saddled with the three most unpopular words in the English language. One would have to wait a long time for a quip of that sort to come out of the Yasukuni Shrine.

5 Fashion is a soft-power statement. The fact that Japanese dignitaries favour British-style morning dress has specific echoes in late nineteenth-century manners, but also suggests the similarity between these two seemingly different nations: both were war-torn former empires, crowded and class-conscious islands shaped by all four seasons.

of Korea still festers. There are too many signs – the Yasukuni Shrine chief among them – that not everyone is ashamed of it.

South Korea, for its part, has been equally reluctant to lay down the cudgels. In 2018 its courts awarded damages against Japanese companies for using forced labour in the war years; and sportswriters attending the Japan-Korea World Cup Finals in 2002 were asked, in Seoul, please to refer to it as the 'Korea-Japan' World Cup. A new generation of South Koreans has been raised to nurse the same old grievances.

Hostility of this sort leaks into trade and finance – Prime Minister Abe has blocked exports needed by South Korea's semi-conductor industry; beer and fashion sales have also suffered. But the greater damage has been to the emotional connection. South Korea feels that its sufferings have been inadequately addressed; Japan feels that its efforts to apologise have been rebuffed. A 2017 satire titled *Let's Apologise to South Korea* (a bestseller in Japan) even poked fun at the topic by urging Japan to apologise for modernising South Korea with railways, education and civil rights.

Japanese schoolbooks are not written by the government, but must be submitted for inspection and must therefore conform with the official line. And old habits die hard. Works that present the comfort women (let alone the Nanking Massacre) in an unkind light have repeatedly failed to pass muster. One 1982 volume was obliged to alter its claim that Japan had 'invaded' China with a statement that it had merely 'advanced'.

Subsequent textbooks have also downplayed Japanese aggression, provoking storms of protest that led to them being little used. Again, the message was received.

It is true that Japan's allure derives from subtler and more ancient sources, from artful paintings of blue irises in golden skies, or pale ink sketches of villages nestling by forested lakes, or scrolls of calligraphy rescued from the marshes of history. But these alone cannot cleanse the slate. For that, something more dramatic is needed.

As we have seen, it is not easy to apologise for the sins of the past. The guilty parties have fled the scene; present incumbents rarely feel inclined to shoulder the blame; lawyers advise caution lest admitting guilt leads to financial demands. But some things can be addressed, if not solved. In December 1970 the West German Chancellor Willy Brandt visited the memorial to the 300,000 or more Polish Jews in the Warsaw Ghetto murdered by Nazi Germany. Laying a wreath on the rain-soaked stone, he stunned the world by falling to his knees and staying there for a minute, head bowed. It was an ostentatious and unequivocal act of penitence, captured by photographers whose pictures flashed on to front pages everywhere.

'I did what people do when words fail them,' he said later – a perfect phrase.

'There are people who can say more with their back than others with a thousand words,' wrote the Dutch novelist Cees Nooteboom.

This was the famous '*Kniefall*', or 'Warsaw Genuflection'. And while some thought that Brandt went too far – a poll in *Der Spiegel* claimed that 48 per cent of West Germans disapproved – it did much to change West Germany's image (and was one of the main reasons why Brandt won the Nobel Peace Prize the following year).

Apologies of this sort are a time-honoured genre. In 1077 the Holy Roman Emperor stood outside a snowy Alpine monastery for three days in an act of grave penitence to the Pope. And in recent years there have been many such declarations. Ronald Reagan apologised for the treatment of Japanese Americans in the Second World War; David Cameron called the Amritsar Massacre 'shameful'; Britain issued a royal expression of 'deep sympathy' to the people of Ireland. The Pope apologised to the indigenous peoples of America for the 'grave sins' of the past, while Canada's Justin Trudeau has addressed several historic injustices (the 1914 refusal to admit a ship full of Indian migrants; the sexual abuse perpetrated in Catholic schools; the mistreatment of lesbian and gay people; and the hanging of Tsilhqot'in leaders in British Columbia in 1864).

Statements like these, while symbolically important, rarely suffice. When Tony Blair expressed 'deep sorrow' for the slave trade it was regarded as mealy-mouthed. And when he repeated it – 'I have said we are sorry and I say it again' – it only underlined

the extent to which apologies of this sort can feel trite ...
even boastful.

Yet they can also be powerful. If a British opinion-former – ideally a cricket captain – were to perform a *'Kniefall'* in Amritsar to atone for the massacre of 1919, when the infamous General Dyer raked an unarmed crowd with machine guns, killing 379, it might do more for Anglo–Indian relations than anything else. It would tell a billion Indians that Britain was not, in fact, in denial about the cruelties of its empire.[6]

There would be columns and letters in newspapers denouncing it as a politically correct gimmick and concluding that the cricketer (a hapless pawn in this fiasco) had been 'badly advised'. But when these subsided, the land beneath would have changed.

The installation of an 'eternal flame' in Tokyo's Yasukuni Shrine might be divisive too, in the short term. But it would allow China and Korea to see Japan in a new light.

Left unattended, historical scars can linger like unexploded bombs. In Japan's case, the memory of its warlike past resurfaces every time one of its fishermen slaughters a whale. In 2019 it was reported that after a thirty-year lull Japan had once again resumed commercial whaling. A fleet of harpoon-ships had bagged more than two hundred of the great mammals, creating new and bloodthirsty imagery calculated to enrage all the world's environmentalists, for whom 'save the whale' had long been a heartfelt motto.

Japan was unbowed. 'My heart is overflowing with happiness,' said the head of its whaling association. It was an important Japanese tradition, an 'ardent wish'.

In the maelstrom of modern media this was a bloodstain on Japan's soft report card. No appeal to tradition could repair the damage. As so often, the best efforts in one branch of the national life had been sabotaged by the best efforts of another.

At the time of writing it was still not certain that the 2020 Olympic Games, now rescheduled to be held in Tokyo a year late,

---

6 Yet when the Archbishop of Canterbury, Justin Welby, did prostrate himself in a gesture of repentance at Amritsar, in 2019, it was not universally admired. Some thought that he went too far; others argued that the spectacle of a man ostentatiously apologising for something he had not done was superficial and unconvincing.

in 2021, would actually be held. But it was clear that if they ever *did* go ahead, Japan would have another extraordinary opportunity to help steer the world away from the brink. Two weeks of athletics and an ebullient exhibition of human biodiversity framed by Japan's exquisite manners, might just rekindle the world's faith in itself. Sport is competitive, but also friendly, so the Games could be a resounding expression of soft power itself: at once rivalrous and in-it-together.

In the changed psychology of the times, it was even possible that the post-corona Games would revive an old-fashioned truth by reminding the world that, while it was good sport to cheer on one's own medal contenders, it didn't matter who won.

That is how the soft world turns.

The generation that grew up after the Second World War was not disposed to admire Japan. It knew people who had been badly treated in its prisoner-of-war camps, and did not sympathise with a nation intent on dominating the corporate heights.

Minds were changed by the drip-drip of many things: the ink-wash landscapes of the fifteenth-century artists and the prints of Hiroshige; the films of Ozu and Kurosawa; the Shakespeare productions of Ninagawa, the expertise in classical music; the novels of Endo, Tanizaki, Murakami and Ishiguro; the calm Japanese gardens (especially that raked courtyard in Kyoto which held fifteen rocks, only fourteen of which were visible from any vantage point – for in life something is always hidden), the clean interior designs, the sublime ceramics and the deep reverence for pure materials – a perfect pebble, a sheet of paper, an immaculate sliver of ginger.

In all these ways Japan suggested that even the most mundane act – presenting a bill, pouring a glass of water, crossing the road – could carry an aesthetic charge. Only in Japan did the act of putting a postcard in an envelope, or laying down cutlery, become a solemn ritual – if a thing was worth doing, the culture seemed to say, it was always worth doing beautifully. And if a cup of tea could be a poem, then so could a sword. Whether Japan's enemies died more peacefully knowing they had been slain by a work of art is of course questionable, but this refined tradition lives on today in Japan's surgical kitchen knives and precision-tooled golf clubs.

Finally, of course, there were Japanese people and their extraordinary manners. Most foreign visitors returned with amazing-but-true stories about the wallet left in a bar and returned to the hotel, the waiter who hurried across the road to return a tip that had obviously been left in error, or the chambermaid who retrieved the wedding ring from the bathroom drain. Rugby fans touring the country in 2019 could only gasp at the local crowds that took the trouble to learn foreign national anthems, in unfamiliar languages, and sing them enthusiastically inside their immaculate stadiums.

Giant Japanese companies could dominate global markets for all they were worth. But nothing was quite so seductive as these simple acts of kindness.

It is unwise to draw deep cultural conclusions from minor incidents; but stories like this produce the simplest soft-power charge of all: they make a country *liked*. In Japan's case it was the icing on a rich cake. It was no surprise that Japan was leading the way in robotics and eco-friendly pilot schemes such as 'vertical farming' – growing salad in city-centre hot houses. Along with its patient stoicism in the face of natural disasters (from Hiroshima to Fukushima) and that beguiling and ceremonious tradition of hospitality, Japan was conquering the soft-power heights.

Epilogue

A Million Points of Light

I spent most of the time writing this book thinking about exactly how much, in practical terms, soft power weighed. It was elusive. But when I reached the end I concluded that the answer had been tapping me on the shoulder all along: it was too ambiguous and broad to be put in the scales in any simple way. It was not something solid that could be possessed or wielded (much to the frustration of governments). It was a process, a culture, a habit: the means to an end rather than the end itself.

In short, it was a game – a new great game.

But as coronavirus gripped the world by the throat, soft power began to appear in a surprising new light. It was not a philosopher, but it did contain a moral, and that moral concerned ... interdependence. The fear of catching the virus was balanced by the equal-and-opposite fear of giving it. Both people and nations had to avoid spreading it – not least because in passing it on they would endanger themselves.

Here, perhaps, lay soft power's true purpose: to connect these opposing impulses – the natural fear of others, and the dependence on them. Soft power was the juice in the space between individuals and nations, creating the conditions in which mutual self-interest – the understanding that for me to win, you should win too – could thrive.

It could be suppressed by hard power (and needed to be, in an emergency) but not for long. Like the virus itself, soft power would find a way to drift across whatever new barriers might appear. As games went, it was a serious one, and visible in all the new manifestations of human interaction that bubbled out of the period: pianists playing from balconies, neighbours applauding in streets, an internet bulging with comedy, music and video diaries, new ways of shopping, studying and eating, and all the thousands of other improvisations with which the world's people diverted themselves and each other.

And it was a game governments could not opt out of, because their rivals were playing it for all they were worth. If anything, its consequences were more far reaching than ever, thanks to the vibrancy of modern communications and media.

It was especially important for Britain, a nation that in theory *liked* games (and which was committed to a new global charm offensive as it pressed ahead with its divorce from Europe), but it was a near-universal concern. All nations were grasping the importance of making a positive impression abroad, whether through culture or policy – pursuing peace rather than war, liberty rather than oppression, or by playing an energetic role in the war on inequality or climate change. Nearly all looked to expand and polish their international profile as fully as they could.

There is no escaping the fact that soft power is a realm of rapid movement and ever-changing rules, as volatile as a stock market, fluctuating this way and that according to the latest pinprick of news. And it remains a field in which governments are not the masters. Alongside every official programme comes the sound of loose cannons misfiring in the wings. In the call-out culture of social media, especially, a single retiree from Wisconsin can set back America's reputation a hundred years simply by shooting an African lion, giving an entire nation the appearance of being a big-game bully.[1] The same goes for the Florentine trickster who charges visitors from Taiwan €25 for ice cream, or bills them €1000 for a plate of spaghetti. When video clips of Thai policemen thumping Chinese tourists went viral, tourist numbers dipped; when young French backpackers went missing in Morocco, holidaymakers cancelled; when Islamist hotheads pulled out knives in London or stormed beaches in Tunisia, Islamophobia gained new strength.

---

1 The black-maned lion known as Cecil, shot in Zimbabwe in 2015, turned out to have been named after Cecil Rhodes himself. His assassination may not have been what the 'Rhodes Must Fall' movement had in mind.

Governments can neither anticipate nor shrug aside chaotic events of this sort. Whether they concern financial market jitters or scary new diseases, bouts of dreadful weather, terrorist uproars or identity-politics whirlwinds, politicians find themselves in the passenger seat time and time again. Who could have foreseen, for instance, that in 2019, in Whaley Bridge, Derbyshire, coachloads of Chinese visitors would descend en masse to take photographs of the burst dam that threatened to flood both the village and the television news? This was something new: disaster tourism.

People groaned. But takings in the local community café more than doubled.

The topsy-turvy rules of soft power produce other ironic consequences. Sometimes, in areas such as culinary soft power, or what Paul Rockower termed *gastrodiplomacy* − the fine art of 'winning hearts and minds through the stomach' − politicians can get behind a trend. English tea and Austrian *viennoiserie* had the backing of empires, but Italian pizza, pasta and gelato conquered the world without state support. Today, however, such things are the subjects of national promotions. Thai food, for instance, was 'discovered' by American troops on holiday from the Vietnam War, and then by European sun-seekers, but it took a ministry project to help turn it into a global brand ambassador.[2] In 2001 a programme was launched to spread the word, and it was the right idea at the right time. Today there are over 15,000 Thai restaurants outside Thailand, each one a ginger-and-lime scented advertisement for the country itself.[3]

Other countries took note. A North Korean chain, Pyongyang, faltered when its staff defected − a propaganda setback. But

---

[2] In 1992 a delegation of British parliamentarians made an official visit to the Channel Islands. One, new to the island, experienced a time-slip feeling that he was back to the England of his youth. It all felt noticeably − how to put it? − monocultural.

'I wonder,' he asked the group's guide, a local civil servant. 'Is there anything one might call cosmopolitan here? Is there, for instance . . . a mosque?'

The young man looked astonished. 'I don't *think* so,' he said. Then he brightened: 'But we *do* have a Thai restaurant.'

[3] The impact on tourism has been striking. In 2002 there were ten million visits to Thailand a year; in 2019 there were more than 35 million, accounting for roughly 10 per cent of national GDP.

Indonesia, Malaysia,[4] Peru ('Cocina Peruana Para El Mundo'), South Korea and Taiwan (with 'Dim Sum Diplomacy') developed similar plans on the grounds that food does not recognise borders and is an appetising sales tool, boosting both interest and visits. For nations with little formal clout, it is a gentle way of inveigling themselves into the lives of others.

Much the same can be said for cinematic soft power: government agencies can orchestrate the desire of fans to see for themselves the locations where their favourite entertainments were filmed – Harry Potter in England, *Lord of the Rings* in New Zealand or *Frozen* in Norway and Austria. Sometimes these footprints are heavy, but they are profitable, and rarely unwelcome.

Yet soft power does carry mixed messages. Britain's royal pageantry melts some hearts but chills others; French food and wine make some purr (*gratin dauphinois* in the Maldives, *Nuits St Georges* in Siberia) and others groan. News that women are now allowed to drive cars in Saudi Arabia, or dine out in public, revealed both how oppressed they were and how fast things were changing. The divers who rescued the lost boys from a flooded cave in Thailand were a good advertisement for the UK (the helping hand) but also a reminder of the imbalance of resources in the modern world.

This is the hardest soft-power lesson of all, and the reason why governments find it a slippery topic. It requires a protected space in which to flourish, yet can bite the hand that feeds it. Sometimes the national brand is a resource that a single individual can exploit – the voice of Greta Thunberg, for instance, echoes far and wide largely because she is Swedish; an Iranian or North Korean teenager saying identical things would probably not colonise the world's media (let alone its social media) to the same extent. But at other times it can be subverted by private initiatives of that sort.

This also explains why, in soft power, smallness can be a virtue: nations like Ireland, Sri Lanka and New Zealand can be more popular than larger neighbours precisely because they are unthreatening. In the hall-of-mirrors that is soft diplomacy,

---

4 An annual 'Malaysia Night' food experience is held every June in London's Trafalgar Square. Some 50,000 people enjoy a brief taste of Penang by dropping in for spicy pulled beef or curried noodles, washed down with rose-flavoured drinks.

punching above one's weight can be a useful skill. Canada, for example, strikes the world as smaller and gentler than the superpower to the south, while retaining the North American allure of boundless opportunity. This, in international politics and trade, is a valuable commodity – a hint of maple syrup and polar bear in the national image.

In this soft world, politicians have to be flexible. At the 2013 G20 summit in St Petersburg, for instance, a Russian official referred to Britain as 'just a small island', provoking David Cameron into a vehement defence of his country: 'Britain may be a small island, but I would challenge anyone to find a country with a prouder history, a bigger heart or greater resilience.' A century earlier, a British Prime Minister would have been more likely to invoke the Crown or the Royal Navy; in the soft modern world, a quiet boast was both effective and more seemly.

Before the week was out his words had been set to 'Land of Hope and Glory' and posted on Twitter – but not all of it was mockery. It illustrated a general truth, too.

Size wasn't everything.

Soft messages of that sort can carry further than the most bracing facts and figures. The economic boom in South Korea – the 'Miracle on the Han River' – has been in most ways as astonishing as the reconstruction of Japan. But it may not have done as much to burnish the national image overseas as the sudden emergence of its music industry: K-Pop diplomacy, 'Seoul Music' or 'the Korean Wave'. In 2012 a chubby 34-year-old named Park Jae Sang (*aka* Psy) tickled the global funny bone with a loopy dance routine, Gangnam Style, which registered three *billion* hits on the world's video booth, YouTube. And in 2017 a South Korean boy band, BTS, became the world's most popular group, with more Twitter followers (16.4 million) than Donald Trump and Justin Bieber *combined*. In their songs they kicked over traces and defied their boring parents; in real life they were workaholic slaves.[5] Their fans, however, were all too willing to follow their idols on smartphones that were also made in Korea, by Samsung.

---

5 'They live as exhausted celibates,' wrote Richard Lloyd Parry in the *Sunday Times*, 6 October 2018, 'more like overworked salarymen than hedonistic rock stars.'

This is how soft power hums its way into the real world's bottom line. It must be nursed, not forced.

It does not come naturally to governments to play this secondary, enabling role: they prefer to 'project' power with flashes and bangs. State-orchestrated pop music, in particular, would appear to be a contradiction in terms: few governments enjoy the subversive thrill of being against ... themselves. But what they *can* do is maintain the structures and facilities that allow such things to flourish.

Will that approach prove sufficient, however – to return to the question with which we began – to prevent the rise of raucous rivalries, and another global conflagration? That may no longer be the question, because soft power has a more immediate purpose: to help bring the world back together after the triple traumas of plague, quarantine and economic mayhem.

This is a task to which it might or might not prove equal. But there are reasons to be optimistic. Soft power is produced by art, education, migration, globalisation, communications, technology and cultural exchange, and since these are very much the dominant forces in modern life, they may indeed be a resource strong enough to put the world back on the road to recovery.

Of course it may be asking too much to assume that governments will act wisely in this area, given the rising temptation to retreat behind national barricades. In 1984 Barbara Tuchman wrote an entertaining account of historical blunders named *The March of Folly*. It narrated the botched handling of the Reformation by the Papacy, the clumsy British response to American independence, and the quagmire of the Vietnam War, and reached a dismaying conclusion: governments had a dangerous tendency to pursue 'policies contrary to their own interests'. Human beings were magnificent in many arenas: science, literature, music, architecture and philosophy. But government was not one of their strengths. It was not in their nature: incompetence was genetic.

Modern climate science would seem to support this argument. *Homo sapiens* has probably been responsible for the death of some 95 per cent of the planet's species. The crooked timber of humanity often fights against its own best impulses.

This was wry observation rather than theory. But it was something that the new science of behavioural economics does much to support. In 2002 Daniel Kahneman won the Nobel Memorial Prize for blending psychology and economics in a way that exposed the persistent weakness of human judgement. Bad decision-making, he argued, was innate, and he offered many amusing proofs: people tended to believe that one factor (attractiveness or athleticism) indicated others (cleverness, trustworthiness) – when in fact there was little correlation; they had faulty memories, sought confirmation for existing leanings and tended to ignore contrary evidence; they favoured the familiar over the unknown, and gave too much weight to self-protection or wishful thinking.

Unbiased thought, he continued, is simply not a human strength. We are by nature erratic and irrational.

Fifteen years later, in 2017, Richard Thaler won *his* Nobel Memorial Prize for proposing a practical application for these insights: his famous 'nudge'. Based on the idea that, as he put it, 'if you want people to do something, make it easy', he helped bring behavioural economics into the environs of soft power. According to this theory, it was a way of delivering international influence without anyone even noticing.[6]

He did not mention it, but he was all but outlining the practical application of soft power.

In the early weeks of the coronavirus crisis it looked as though governments might still be looking to exploit soft power to work not with other nations but against them, in a contest to gain the cultural upper hand by expanding that greedy old monster: the 'sphere of influence'. In this way it might even act against itself, since the advancement of national stories on the global stage might emphasise not what nations had in common (a viral enemy) but what made them different.

That would be sad, but not surprising. The assumption that nations are governed not just by their own interests but by their very nature has deep roots, and will be hard to shift. The famous

---

6 America was slow to back this innovative approach. In Britain, however, David Cameron established a 'Nudge Unit' in the corridors of power, and charged it to find subtle ways to persuade people to pay fines, update records or donate organs.

1927 essay by Ernest Barker (*National Character and the Factors in its Formation*) saw no need even to argue that there was such a thing as 'national character' – the author was content to assume as much. Its composition could be debated; its existence could not. Barker was a distinguished professor at Cambridge, but almost everyone born in 1874 and alive in the 1920s felt much the same way.

A good deal of historical inquiry since then has suggested that national characters are imaginary or imposed, rather than inherent or fixed. And it is salutary to realise how thoroughly a national identity – or the perception of it – can change. Thanks to *The Sound of Music*, modern Austria suggests raindrops on roses and whiskers on kittens, yet at the height of Austro-Hungarian power Palmerston called Austrians 'the greatest brutes that ever called themselves by the undeserved name of civilised men'.

Before the virus marched into the world, it seemed that most nations were rejecting that sort of thinking as modish sophistry, and clinging to tried-and-tested formulae instead. And while soft power can in theory dissolve antagonisms of this sort, it can also inflame them. In a famous experiment narrated by Judith Rich Harris in *The Nurture Assumption*, American school children were divided into two groups – those with blue eyes and those with brown – and taught separately. It didn't take long for blue-vs-brown fights to break out. A minor distinction, not telling in itself, was enough to fuel brawls.

Identity politics pleads for tolerance and acceptance, but by stressing difference it can also sow anger and division. The same might be true in national identity politics. Indeed it is hard to see how national histories, which inevitably emphasise difference, can be less inflammatory than mild variations in eye colour. So while it may seem academic to quibble about the past, we cannot ignore it. It filters into the present day even if we close our minds.[7] That is why governments need to keep their national stories clear of weeds. History is soft power's mother-lode, and it is an unquiet ghost.

That is why, in recent years, many of the world's most heated

---

7 In 2016 it emerged that the UK Labour Party vote correlated exactly with the map of the British coalfield. In 2019 *The Economist* published a map of Germany that showed the electoral heart of the nationalist AFD to mirror the vote for Hitler in 1934.

conflicts have roots in ancient episodes – virus or no virus. Israel and Palestine dispute each other's right to inhabit the same holy plot. All over Africa and the Middle East people dispute the borders etched on maps by long-dead potentates. Trump's America and Brexit Britain look to restore cherished golden ages. Vladimir Putin lavishes praise on the high noon of Tsarist Russia; China seeks to regain its place as the centre of the world; ISIS harbours dreams of a medieval Caliphate. Viktor Orbán stiffens Hungary's resentment of outsiders with horror stories about Ottoman Turkey, while President Erdoğan kindles Turkish resentment over the Greek burning of Smyrna in 1922, and claims that Muslim sailors reached North America three centuries before Columbus.

On it goes. In India the BJP (the world's biggest political party, with 100 million members) looks to archaeology and epic literature to support Hindu supremacy – overturning Nehru's insistence that it was 'entirely misleading to refer to Indian culture as Hindu culture'. Scottish and Catalan nationalism invites citizens to reopen old wounds. French and German 'patriots' revive the slogans of old causes.[8]

In this context, even light-hearted flag-waving can invoke bad memories, and in celebrating independence many annual carnivals reach into the murkiest fogs of time. Switzerland's National Day marks its alliance against the Holy Roman Empire in 1291, while Faroe Islanders raise their glasses to the Battle of Stiklestad in 1030. San Marino celebrates independence day (from Rome, in September 301) – and this makes it only the third oldest country: Japan's National Foundation Day recalls the crowning of the first Emperor in 660 BC, while South Korea celebrates its founding in 2333 BC. In all countries, former glory is the drug of choice.

It means that history, a brimming well of soft power, is anything but dead.

George Santayana famously pointed out that people who do not study history are doomed to repeat it, but to this it might be added, as some cartoonists have done, that people who *do* study history are destined to look on helplessly while everyone

---

8 Scottish nationalism depicts itself as the victim of English oppression rather than the partner in an amazing joint venture (Glasgow was 'the second city of the Empire').

else repeats it. And there is no authorised version, with which everyone can agree. Soft power might seem a peaceful weapon; but it has a dark and dangerous edge, too. It may seem unrealistic to hope that so many historical dragons can be slain by a single white knight, but this might be soft power's true calling: to heal the world by reminding it that it must find a way to work not as one, but together.

Oscar Wilde once said that the only duty we owed history was to rewrite it. But that itself may now need rewriting. If the horsepower of soft politics is the story of the past, then the duty of governments is not to wave it like a banner, but to provide the light, water and vigilance it needs to survive.

The world has long known that power takes different forms: military power, political power, people power, friendly power, flower power and all the other varieties. Not all of these push in the same direction; some oppose others – hence the 'balance of power'. Francis Bacon said that knowledge was power; Gandhi said that 'power based on love' was a thousand times more effective than power based on fear; Lincoln said that anyone could cope with adversity, but only a few could handle power. Everyone knows Lord Acton's maxim that power corrupts, but absolute power corrupts absolutely; and Orwell once anatomised totalitarian power by noticing the way in which it perverted the dance between ends and means – becoming an end in itself. That, he said, was 'pure power', the most dangerous power of all.

Soft power is still young, and feeling its way. But if it can connect these conflicting varieties and thread them into something unified – *shared* power, perhaps – then perhaps its time will truly have come.

Appendix

Soft Power Rankings

The Portland Soft Power 30 is based on a series of weightings that produce an exact number: thus in 2019 France's 82.28 put it ahead of the UK's 79.47. This reversed their placings of the previous year, when they scored 80.55 and 80.14 respectively.

The method is 'scientific' in that it provides consistency, but of course the weightings themselves have a subjective element. The high marks awarded for government policy favours traditional cultural powers over new nations – Canada and the Netherlands both scored strongly on liberal social policies and attitudes.

The *Monocle* ranking, assembled by a supervisory board, is less statistical, giving more weight to news stories, public profile and impression. Hence Sweden's strong showing in 2019, a result driven wholly by the galvanising impact of Greta Thunberg. Sweden could boast 'exemplary governance', progressive social programmes and (as the home of Skype and Spotify) innovative technology, too. But the youthful activism inspired by one young girl gave a global movement an identifiable Swedish streak.

The power of news stories is visible, too, in the slide of Canada, the UK and the US – the first thanks to the cracking of the Justin Trudeau effect in a flurry of embarrassing missteps, the others down to the lowering impact of Brexit and Trump.

Monocle 2019	Portland 2019
1 =Japan; Sweden	1 France
	2 UK
3 Germany	3 Germany
4 France	4 Sweden
5 Canada	5 US
6 New Zealand	6 Switzerland
7 Switzerland	7 Canada
8 UK	8 Japan
9 US	9 Australia
10 Australia	10 Netherlands

Monocle 2018	Portland 2018
1 France	1 UK
2 Germany	2 France
3 Japan	3 Germany
4 Canada	4 US
5 Switzerland	5 Japan
6 UK	6 Canada
7 Sweden	7 Switzerland
8 Australia	8 Sweden
9 US	9 New Zealand
10 Portugal	10 Australia

Select Bibliography

In a sea of arresting recent titles on the subject of international relations and identities, the following stood out.

Acemoglu, Daron and Robinson, James, *Why Nations Fail*, Profile, 2012.

Alexander, Douglas and Kearns, Ian (eds), *Influencing Tomorrow: Future Challenges for British Foreign Policy*, Guardian Books, 2013.

Allison, Graham, *Destined for War: Can America and China Escape Thucydides' Trap?*, Scribe, 2018.

Arendt, Hannah, *The Origins of Totalitarianism*, Schocken, 1951.

Aronczyk, Melissa, *Branding the Nation: the Global Business of National Identity*, OUP, 2013.

Becker, Jasper, *The Chinese*, John Murray, 2000.

Bernstein, William, *A Splendid Exchange: How Trade Shaped the World*, Atlantic, 2008.

Bhutto, Fatima, *New Kings of the World: Dispatches from Bollywood, Dizi and K-Pop*, Columbia Global Reports, 2019.

Bose, Mihir, *From Midnight to Glorious Morning? India since Independence*, Haus, 2017.

Brautigan, Deborah, *The Dragon's Gift: The Real Story of China in Africa*, OUP, 2011.

Brook, Timothy, *Great State: China and the World*, Profile, 2019.

Burleigh, Michael, *The Best of Times, the Worst of Times: A History of Now*, Macmillan, 2017.

Claybourn, Joshua (ed.), *Our American Story: The Search for a Shared National Narrative*, Casemate, 2019.

Clover, Charles, *Black Wind, White Snow: The Rise of Russia's New Nationalism*, Yale, 2016.

Crabtree, James, *The Billionaire Raj*, OneWorld, 2018.

Damluji, Hassan, *The Responsible Globalist: What Citizens of the World can Learn from Nationalism*, Penguin, 2019.

Dartnell, Lewis, *Origins: How the Earth Made Us*, Penguin, 2019.

Davis, Richard A., Wilkins, Kasinatha, 'Hastings and the First English Bhagavad Gita', *International Journal of Hindu Studies*, 2015.

Durant, Will and Ariel, *The Lessons of History*, Simon and Schuster, 1968.

Ellwood, David, *The Shock of America*, OUP, 2014.

Emmott, Bill, *Rivals: How the Power Struggle between China, India and Japan will Shape our Next Decade*, Allen Lane, 2008.

Farrer, James, *The Globalization of Asian Cuisines*, Palgrave Macmillan, 2015.

Fenby, Jonathan, *Will China Dominate the 21st Century?*, Polity, 2014.

Fletcher, Tom, *The Naked Diplomat*, Collins, 2017.

Frankopan, Peter, *The Silk Roads*, Bloomsbury, 2015.

Frankopan, Peter, *The New Silk Roads*, Bloomsbury, 2018.

French, Howard, *China's Second Continent: How a Million Migrants are Building a New Empire in Africa*, Knopf, 2014.

French, Patrick, *India: A Portrait*, Penguin, 2011.

Friedman, Thomas, *The Lexus and the Olive Tree*, Farrar, Strauss, Giroux, 1999.

Friedman, Thomas, *The World is Flat*, Farrar, Strauss, Giroux, 2005.

Fukuyama, Francis, *The End of History and the Last Man*, Free Press, 1992.

Furtado, Peter (ed.), *Histories of Nations*, Thames and Hudson, 2013.

Goldblatt, Daniel, *The Games*, Macmillan, 2016.

Goodwin, Matthew and Eatwell, Roger, *National Populism: The Revolt Against Liberal Democracy*, Pelican, 2018.

Grandin, Greg, *The End of the Myth*, Metropolitan, 2019.

Hamilton, Clive, *Silent Invasion: China's Influence in Australia*, Hardie Grant, 2018.

Hart, Roger, *Imagined Civilisations: China, the West and their First Encounter*, Johns Hopkins, 2013.

Havel, Václav, *The Power of the Powerless* (1979), Penguin, 2018.

Hunter, Janet E., *The Emergence of Modern Japan*, Longman, 1989.

Jacques, Martin, *When China Rules the World: the End of the Western World and the Birth of a New Global Order*, Penguin, 2009.

Kelts, Roland, *Japanamerica*, Palgrave Macmillan, 2006.

Kennedy, Paul, *The Rise and Fall of the Great Powers*, Collins, 2017.

Knightley, Phillip, *Australia: A Biography of a Nation*, Vintage, 2001.

Krastev, Ivan and Holmes, Stephen, *The Light That Failed*, Allen Lane, 2019.

Landes, David, *The Wealth and Poverty of Nations*, Abacus, 1999.

Lee, John, 'India's Edge Over China', Hudson Institute, 2010.

Levitsky, Steven and Ziblatt, Daniel, *How Democracies Die*, Viking, 2018.

Lucas, Edward, *The New Cold War*, Bloomsbury, 2008.

Luce, Edward, *In Spite of the Gods*, Little, Brown, 2006.

Mahbubani, Kishore, *Has the West Lost it?: A Provocation*, Allen Lane, 2018.

McClory, Jonathan, 'The New Persuaders', Institute for Government, 2013.

McGregor, Richard, *Asia's Reckoning: The Struggle for Global Dominance*, Allen Lane, 2017.

McMahon, Dinny, *China's Great Wall of Debt*, Little, Brown, 2018.

Meredith, Robyn, *The Elephant and the Dragon*, Norton, 2007.

Mishra, Pankaj, *From the Ruins of Empire: The Revolt against the West and the Remaking of Asia*, Penguin, 2013.

Moorhouse, Geoffrey, *India Britannica*, Harvill Press, 1983.

Moyo, Dambisa, *How the West was Lost*, Penguin, 2012.

Muller, Jan-Werner, *What is Populism?*, Penguin, 2017.

Naim, Moises, *The End of Power*, Basic, 2013.

Nye, Joseph, *Bound to Lead: The Changing Nature of American Power*, Basic, 1991.

Nye, Joseph, *Soft Power: The Means to Success in World Politics*, Public Affairs, 2004.

Pakenham, Thomas, *The Scramble for Africa*, Abacus, 1992.

Pomerantsev, Peter, *Nothing is True and Everything is Possible: The Secret Heart of the New Russia*, Public Affairs, 2014.

Porter, Michael, *The Competitive Advantage of Nations*, Palgrave Macmillan, 1990.

Potter, Simon J., *Broadcasting Empire: The BBC and the World 1922–70*, OUP, 2012.

Richmond, Yale, *Cultural Exchange and the Cold War*, Penn State, 2003.

Runciman, David, *How Democracy Ends*, Profile, 2018.

Srivastava, Krishan Gopal, *Bhagavad Gita and the English Romantic Movement*, Macmillan India, 2002.

Stonor Saunders, Frances, *The Cultural Cold War: The CIA and the World of Arts and Letters*, New Press, 2001.

Sun, Irene Yuan, *The Next Factory of the World*, Harvard, 2017.

Tagore, Rabindranath, *Nationalism*, Penguin, 2010.

Tharoor, Shashi, *The Elephant, the Tiger, and the Cellphone*, Arcade, 2011.

Tharoor, Shashi, *Inglorious Empire: What the British did to India*, Penguin, 2016.

Thomas, J. E., *Modern Japan, A Social History Since 1868*, Longman, 1986.

Thussu, Daya Kishan, *Communicating India's Soft Power*, Palgrave Macmillan, 2013.

Tuchman, Barbara, *The March of Folly*, Michael Joseph, 1984.

Van Heysen, Marcel, *Putin's Propaganda Machine*, Rowman and Littlefield, 2016.

Von Wolferen, Karel, *The Enigma of Japanese Power*, Macmillan, 1989.

Watson, Peter, *The German Genius*, Simon and Schuster, 2010.

Webb, Alban, *London Calling: Britain, the BBC World Service and the Cold War*, Bloomsbury, 2014.

Wilson, Jon, *India Conquered: Britain's Raj and the Chaos of Empire*, Simon and Schuster, 2016.

Winder, Simon, *Germania*, Picador, 2010.

Womack, Brantly, 'Dancing Alone: a Hard Look at Soft Power', *Asia-Pacific Journal, Japan Focus*, 2005.

Woodhead, Leslie, *How the Beatles Rocked the Kremlin*, Bloomsbury, 2013.

Wright, Patrick, *Iron Curtain: From Stage to Cold War*, OUP, 2007.

Yasushi, Watanabe and McConnell, David, *Soft Power Superpowers*, M E Sharpe, 2008.

Yergin, Daniel, *The Prize: the Epic Quest for Money, Power & Oil*, Simon and Schuster, 2009.

Soft power has become a topic of continuous interest to newspapers and magazines. *The Economist*, the *Financial Times*, the *Guardian*, the *New York Times* and *The Times* were always useful in this respect, as were many essays in *Foreign Affairs*, notably 'The End of French Exceptionalism' by Claude Imbert (1989), 'The Clash of Civilisations' by Samuel Huntington (1993), 'Japan's Gross National Cool' by Douglas McGray (2009), the Chinese Map of Europe (2015), 'The Rise and Fall of Soft Power' by Eric Li (2018) and 'Are the 2020 Tokyo Olympics in Trouble?' by David Roberts and Robert Whiting (2016).

The Portland Soft Power 30 (2015–19) publishes extensive commentary with its annual findings. The British Council has published several reports: 'Influence and Attraction' (2012), 'Building Nations and Connecting Cultures' (2017), and 'Soft Power Superpowers' by Alistair MacDonald (2018). And the House of Lords published its Select Committee hearings as 'Persuasion and Power in the Modern World' (2014).

Acknowledgements

G rateful thanks for allowing me to pick their brains are due to Alexander Chartres, Zaki Cooper, Hermione Davies, Mary Dejevsky, Sir Ciaran Devane, Edward Faulks, Hartwig Fischer, Sir Simon Fraser, Nigel Gardner, Michael Jary, Richard Lambert, Hans-Günter Löffler, Angus Macqueen, Edwin Samuel, Kit Winder and many others. Also to the patient staff at the British Library and the London Library. And to Jonathan McClory for devising the Portland Soft Power 30 and for giving us permission to reprint it.

Particular thanks to David Godwin for his persistent encouragement. And to Richard Beswick and Nithya Rae, who bent to the task with a will some say is out of fashion, and which can only magnify the soft power of the publisher they represent.

Index

Page numbers followed by fn refer to footnotes.